EU Cohesion Policy

This book brings together academics, members of European institutions, and regional and national level policymakers in order to assess the performance and direction of EU Cohesion policy against the background of the most significant reforms to the policy in a generation. Responding to past criticisms of the effectiveness of the policy, the policy changes introduced in 2013 have aligned European Structural and Investment Funds with the Europe 2020 strategy and introduced measures to improve strategic coherence, performance and integrated development.

EU Cohesion Policy: Reassessing performance and direction argues that policy can only be successfully developed and implemented if there is input from both academics and practitioners. The chapters in the book address four important issues: the effectiveness and impact of Cohesion policy at European, national and regional levels; the contribution of Cohesion policy to the Europe 2020 strategy of smart, sustainable and inclusive growth; the importance of quality of government and administrative capacity for the effective management of the Funds; and the inter-relationships between institutions, territory and place-based policies.

The volume will be an invaluable resource to students, academics and policymakers across economics, regional studies, European studies and international relations.

John Bachtler is Professor of European Policy Studies and a Director of the European Policies Research Centre at the University of Strathclyde in Glasgow, UK.

Peter Berkowitz is Head of Unit for Policy Development, Strategic Management and Relations with the Council in the Directorate-General for Regional and Urban Policy in the European Commission, Belgium.

Sally Hardy is Chief Executive Officer at the Regional Studies Association, UK.

Tatjana Muravska is Professor in Regional Economy at the University of Latvia and Director of the Centre for European and Transition Studies, Latvia.

Regions and Cities

Series Editor in Chief
Susan M. Christopherson, *Cornell University, USA*

Editors
Maryann Feldman, *University of Georgia, USA*
Gernot Grabher, *HafenCity University Hamburg, Germany*
Ron Martin, *University of Cambridge, UK*
Kieran P. Donaghy, *Cornell University, USA*

In today's globalised, knowledge-driven and networked world, regions and cities have assumed heightened significance as the interconnected nodes of economic, social and cultural production, and as sites of new modes of economic and territorial governance and policy experimentation. This book series brings together incisive and critically engaged international and interdisciplinary research on this resurgence of regions and cities, and should be of interest to geographers, economists, sociologists, political scientists and cultural scholars, as well as to policymakers involved in regional and urban development.

For more information on the Regional Studies Association visit www.region alstudies.org

There is a **30% discount** available to RSA members on books in the **Regions and Cities** series, and other subject related Taylor and Francis books and e-books including Routledge titles. To order just e-mail Cara.Trevor@tandf.co.uk, or phone on +44 (0) 20 7017 6924 and declare your RSA membership. You can also visit www.routledge.com and use the discount code: **RSA0901**

111 **EU Cohesion Policy**
Reassessing performance and direction
Edited by John Bachtler, Peter Berkowitz, Sally Hardy and Tatjana Muravska

110 **Geography of Innovation**
Edited by Nadine Massard and Corinne Autant-Bernard

109 **Rethinking International Skilled Migration**
Edited by Micheline van Riemsdijk and Qingfang Wang

108 **The EU's New Borderland**
Cross-border relations and regional development
Andrzej Jakubowski, Andrzej Miszczuk, Bogdan Kawałko, Tomasz Komornicki, and Roman Szul

107 **Entrepreneurship in a Regional Context**
Edited by Michael Fritsch and David J. Storey

106 **Governing Smart Specialisation**
Edited by Dimitrios Kyriakou, Manuel Palazuelos Martínez, Inmaculada Periáñez-Forte, and Alessandro Rainoldi

105 **Innovation, Regional Development and the Life Sciences**
Beyond clusters
Kean Birch

104 **Unfolding Cluster Evolution**
Edited by Fiorenza Belussi and Jose Luis Hervás-Olivier

103 **Place-based Economic Development and the New EU Cohesion Policy**
Edited by Philip McCann and Attila Varga

102 **Transformation of Resource Towns and Peripheries**
Political economy perspectives
Edited by Greg Halseth

101 **Approaches to Economic Geography**
Towards a geographical political economy
Ray Hudson

100 **Secondary Cities and Development**
Edited by Lochner Marais, Etienne Nel and Ronnie Donaldson

99 **Technology and the City**
Systems, applications and implications
Tan Yigitcanlar

98 **Smaller Cities in a World of Competitiveness**
Peter Karl Kresl and Daniele Ietri

97 **Code and the City**
Edited by Rob Kitchin and Sung-Yueh Perng

96 **The UK Regional–National Economic Problem**
Geography, globalisation and governance
Philip McCann

95 **Skills and Cities**
Edited by Sako Musterd, Marco Bontje and Jan Rouwendal

94 **Higher Education and the Creative Economy**
Beyond the campus
Edited by Roberta Comunian and Abigail Gilmore

93 **Making Cultural Cities in Asia**
Mobility, assemblage, and the politics of aspirational urbanism
Edited by Jun Wang, Tim Oakes and Yang Yang

92 **Leadership and the City**
Power, strategy and networks in the making of knowledge cities
Markku Sotarauta

91 **Evolutionary Economic Geography**
Theoretical and empirical progress
Edited by Dieter Kogler

90 **Cities in Crisis**
Socio-spatial impacts of the economic crisis in Southern European cities
Edited by Jörg Knieling and Frank Othengrafen

89 **Socio-Economic Segregation in European Capital Cities**
East meets West
Edited by Tiit Tammaru, Szymon Marcińczak, Maarten van Ham, Sako Musterd

88 **People, Places and Policy**
Knowing contemporary Wales through new localities
Edited by Martin Jones, Scott Orford and Victoria Macfarlane

87 **The London Olympics and Urban Development**
The mega-event city
Edited by Gavin Poynter, Valerie Viehoff and Yang Li

86 **Making 21st Century Knowledge Complexes**
Technopoles of the world revisited
Edited by Julie Tian Miao, Paul Benneworth and Nicholas A. Phelps

85 **Soft Spaces in Europe**
Re-negotiating governance, boundaries and borders
Edited by Philip Allmendinger, Graham Haughton, Jörg Knieling and Frank Othengrafen

84 **Regional Worlds: Advancing the Geography of Regions**
Edited by Martin Jones and Anssi Paasi

83 **Place-making and Urban Development**
New challenges for contemporary planning and design
Pier Carlo Palermo and Davide Ponzini

82 **Knowledge, Networks and Policy**
Regional studies in postwar Britain and beyond
James Hopkins

81 **Dynamics of Economic Spaces in the Global Knowledge-based Economy**
Theory and East Asian cases
Sam Ock Park

80 **Urban Competitiveness**
Theory and practice
Daniele Letri and Peter Kresl

79 **Smart Specialisation**
Opportunities and challenges for regional innovation policy
Dominique Foray

78 **The Age of Intelligent Cities**
Smart environments and innovation-for-all strategies
Nicos Komninos

77 **Space and Place in Central and Eastern Europe**
Historical trends and perspectives
Gyula Horváth

76 **Territorial Cohesion in Rural Europe**
The relational turn in rural development
Edited by Andrew Copus and Philomena de Lima

75 **The Global Competitiveness of Regions**
Robert Huggins, Hiro Izushi, Daniel Prokop and Piers Thompson

74 **The Social Dynamics of Innovation Networks**
Edited by Roel Rutten, Paul Benneworth, Dessy Irawati and Frans Boekema

73 **The European Territory**
From historical roots to global challenges
Jacques Robert

72 **Urban Innovation Systems**
What makes them tick?
Willem van Winden, Erik Braun, Alexander Otgaar and Jan-Jelle Witte

71 **Shrinking Cities**
A global perspective
Edited by Harry W. Richardson and Chang Woon Nam

70 **Cities, State and Globalization**
City-regional governance
Tassilo Herrschel

69 **The Creative Class Goes Global**
Edited by Charlotta Mellander, Richard Florida, Bjørn Asheim and Meric Gertler

68 **Entrepreneurial Knowledge, Technology and the Transformation of Regions**
Edited by Charlie Karlsson, Börje Johansson and Roger Stough

67 **The Economic Geography of the IT Industry in the Asia Pacific Region**
Edited by Philip Cooke, Glen Searle and Kevin O'Connor

66 **Working Regions**
Reconnecting innovation and production in the knowledge economy
Jennifer Clark

65 **Europe's Changing Geography**
The impact of inter-regional networks
Edited by Nicola Bellini and Ulrich Hilpert

64 **The Value of Arts and Culture for Regional Development**
A Scandinavian perspective
Edited by Lisbeth Lindeborg and Lars Lindkvist

63 **The University and the City**
John Goddard and Paul Vallance

62 **Re-framing Regional Development**
Evolution, innovation and transition
Edited by Philip Cooke

61 **Networking Regionalised Innovative Labour Markets**
Edited by Ulrich Hilpert and Helen Lawton Smith

60 **Leadership and Change in Sustainable Regional Development**
Edited by Markku Sotarauta, Ina Horlings and Joyce Liddle

59 **Regional Development Agencies: The Next Generation?**
Networking, knowledge and regional policies
Edited by Nicola Bellini, Mike Danson and Henrik Halkier

58 **Community-based Entrepreneurship and Rural Development**
Creating favourable conditions for small businesses in Central Europe
Matthias Fink, Stephan Loidl and Richard Lang

57 **Creative Industries and Innovation in Europe**
Concepts, measures and comparative case studies
Edited by Luciana Lazzeretti

56 **Innovation Governance in an Open Economy**
Shaping regional nodes in a globalized world
Edited by Annika Rickne, Staffan Laestadius and Henry Etzkowitz

55 **Complex Adaptive Innovation Systems**
Relatedness and transversality in the evolving region
Philip Cooke

54 **Creating Knowledge Locations in Cities**
Innovation and integration challenges
Willem van Winden, Luis de Carvalho, Erwin van Tujil, Jeroen van Haaren and Leo van den Berg

53 **Regional Development in Northern Europe**
Peripherality, marginality and border issues
Edited by Mike Danson and Peter De Souza

52 **Promoting Silicon Valleys in Latin America**
Luciano Ciravegna

51 **Industrial Policy Beyond the Crisis**
Regional, national and international perspectives
Edited by David Bailey, Helena Lenihan and Josep-Maria Arauzo-Carod

50 **Just Growth**
Inclusion and prosperity in America's metropolitan regions
Chris Benner and Manuel Pastor

49 **Cultural Political Economy of Small Cities**
Edited by Anne Lorentzen and Bas van Heur

48 **The Recession and Beyond**
Local and regional responses to the downturn
Edited by David Bailey and Caroline Chapain

47 **Beyond Territory**
Edited by Harald Bathelt, Maryann Feldman and Dieter F. Kogler

46 Leadership and Place
Edited by Chris Collinge, John Gibney and Chris Mabey

45 Migration in the 21st Century
Rights, outcomes, and policy
Kim Korinek and Thomas Maloney

44 The Futures of the City Region
Edited by Michael Neuman and Angela Hull

43 The Impacts of Automotive Plant Closures
A tale of two cities
Edited by Andrew Beer and Holli Evans

42 Manufacturing in the New Urban Economy
Willem van Winden, Leo van den Berg, Luis de Carvalho and Erwin van Tuijl

41 Globalizing Regional Development in East Asia
Production networks, clusters, and entrepreneurship
Edited by Henry Wai-chung Yeung

40 China and Europe
The implications of the rise of China as a global economic power for Europe
Edited by Klaus Kunzmann, Willy A Schmid and Martina Koll-Schretzenmayr

39 Business Networks in Clusters and Industrial Districts
The governance of the global value chain
Edited by Fiorenza Belussi and Alessia Sammarra

38 Whither Regional Studies?
Edited by Andy Pike

37 Intelligent Cities and Globalisation of Innovation Networks
Nicos Komninos

36 Devolution, Regionalism and Regional Development
The UK experience
Edited by Jonathan Bradbury

35 Creative Regions
Technology, culture and knowledge entrepreneurship
Edited by Philip Cooke and Dafna Schwartz

34 European Cohesion Policy
Willem Molle

33 Geographies of the New Economy
Critical reflections
Edited by Peter W. Daniels, Andrew Leyshon, Michael J. Bradshaw and Jonathan Beaverstock

32 The Rise of the English Regions?
Edited by Irene Hardill, Paul Benneworth, Mark Baker and Leslie Budd

31 Regional Development in the Knowledge Economy
Edited by Philip Cooke and Andrea Piccaluga

30 Regional Competitiveness
Edited by Ron Martin, Michael Kitson and Peter Tyler

29 **Clusters and Regional Development**
Critical reflections and explorations
Edited by Bjørn Asheim, Philip Cooke and Ron Martin

28 **Regions, Spatial Strategies and Sustainable Development**
David Counsell and Graham Haughton

27 **Sustainable Cities**
Graham Haughton and Colin Hunter

26 **Geographies of Labour Market Inequality**
Edited by Ron Martin and Philip S. Morrison

25 **Regional Innovation Strategies**
The challenge for less-favoured regions
Edited by Kevin Morgan and Claire Nauwelaers

24 **Out of the Ashes?**
The social impact of industrial contraction and regeneration on Britain's mining communities
Chas Critcher, Bella Dicks, David Parry and David Waddington

23 **Restructuring Industry and Territory**
The experience of Europe's regions
Edited by Anna Giunta, Arnoud Lagendijk and Andy Pike

22 **Foreign Direct Investment and the Global Economy**
Corporate and institutional dynamics of global-localisation
Edited by Jeremy Alden and Nicholas F. Phelps

21 **Community Economic Development**
Edited by Graham Haughton

20 **Regional Development Agencies in Europe**
Edited by Charlotte Damborg, Mike Danson and Henrik Halkier

19 **Social Exclusion in European Cities**
Processes, experiences and responses
Edited by Judith Allen, Goran Cars and Ali Madanipour

18 **Metropolitan Planning in Britain**
A comparative study
Edited by Peter Roberts, Kevin Thomas and Gwyndaf Williams

17 **Unemployment and Social Exclusion**
Landscapes of labour inequality and social exclusion
Edited by Sally Hardy, Paul Lawless and Ron Martin

16 **Multinationals and European Integration**
Trade, investment and regional development
Edited by Nicholas A. Phelps

15 **The Coherence of EU Regional Policy**
Contrasting perspectives on the structural funds
Edited by John Bachtler and Ivan Turok

14 New Institutional Spaces
TECs and the remaking of economic governance
Martin Jones, Foreword by Jamie Peck

13 Regional Policy in Europe
S. S. Artobolevskiy

12 Innovation Networks and Learning Regions?
James Simmie

11 British Regionalism and Devolution
The challenges of state reform and European integration
Edited by Jonathan Bradbury and John Mawson

10 Regional Development Strategies
A European perspective
Edited by Jeremy Alden and Philip Boland

9 Union Retreat and the Regions
The shrinking landscape of organised labour
Ron Martin, Peter Sunley and Jane Wills

8 The Regional Dimension of Transformation in Central Europe
Grzegorz Gorzelak

7 The Determinants of Small Firm Growth
An inter-regional study in the United Kingdom 1986–90
Richard Barkham, Graham Gudgin, Mark Hart and Eric Hanvey

6 The Regional Imperative
Regional planning and governance in Britain, Europe and the United States
Urlan A. Wannop

5 An Enlarged Europe
Regions in competition?
Edited by Louis Albrechts, Sally Hardy, Mark Hart and Anastasios Katos

4 Spatial Policy in a Divided Nation
Edited by Richard T. Harrison and Mark Hart

3 Regional Development in the 1990s
The1 British Isles in transition
Edited by Ron Martin and Peter Townroe

2 Retreat from the Regions
Corporate change and the closure of factories
Stephen Fothergill and Nigel Guy

1 Beyond Green Belts
Managing urban growth in the 21st century
Edited by John Herington

EU Cohesion Policy
Reassessing performance and direction

**Edited by John Bachtler,
Peter Berkowitz, Sally Hardy
and Tatjana Muravska**

First published 2017
by Routledge
2 Park Square, Milton Park, Abingdon, Oxon OX14 4RN

and by Routledge
711 Third Avenue, New York, NY 10017

Routledge is an imprint of the Taylor & Francis Group, an informa business

© 2017 selection and editorial matter, John Bachtler, Peter Berkowitz, Sally Hardy and Tatjana Muravska; individual chapters, the contributors

The right of John Bachtler, Peter Berkowitz, Sally Hardy and Tatjana Muravska to be identified as the authors of the editorial material, and of the authors for their individual chapters, has been asserted in accordance with sections 77 and 78 of the Copyright, Designs and Patents Act 1988.

The Open Access version of this book, available at www.tandfebooks.com, has been made available under a Creative Commons Attribution-Non Commercial-No Derivatives 3.0 license.

Trademark notice: Product or corporate names may be trademarks or registered trademarks, and are used only for identification and explanation without intent to infringe.

British Library Cataloguing in Publication Data
A catalogue record for this book is available from the British Library

Library of Congress Cataloging in Publication Data
Names: Bachtler, John, editor. | Berkowitz, Peter, 1959- editor. | Hardy, Sally, editor.
Title: EU cohesion policy : reassessing performance and direction / edited by John Bachtler, Peter Berkowitz, Sally Hardy and Tatjana Muravska.
Description: New York : Routledge, 2017. | Includes bibliographical references and index.
Identifiers: LCCN 2016027955| ISBN 9781138224643 (hardback) | ISBN 9781315401867 (ebook)
Subjects: LCSH: Structural adjustment (Economic policy)—European Union countries. | Regional planning—European Union countries. | European Union countries—Economic integration. | European Union countries—Regional disparities.
Classification: LCC HC240 .E736 2017 | DDC 338.94—dc23
LC record available at https://lccn.loc.gov/2016027955

ISBN: 978-1-138-22464-3 (hbk)
ISBN: 978-1-315-40186-7 (ebk)

Typeset in Times New Roman
by Swales & Willis, Exeter, Devon, UK

Printed and bound by CPI Group (UK) Ltd, Croydon, CR0 4YY

Contents

List of figures	xvi
List of tables	xviii
Notes on contributors	xx

Introduction: reassessing the performance and
direction of EU Cohesion Policy in 2014–20   1
JOHN BACHTLER, PETER BERKOWITZ, SALLY HARDY
AND TATJANA MURAVSKA

PART I
The impact of Cohesion Policy   9

1 The long-term effectiveness of EU Cohesion Policy:
assessing the achievements of the ERDF, 1989–2012   11
JOHN BACHTLER, IAIN BEGG, DAVID CHARLES AND LAURA POLVERARI

2 Different approaches to the analysis of EU Cohesion
Policy: leveraging complementarities for evidence-based
policy learning   21
RICCARDO CRESCENZI AND MARA GIUA

3 Cohesion Policy and regional development   33
GRZEGORZ GORZELAK

4 Econometric assessments of Cohesion Policy growth effects:
how to make them more relevant for policymakers?   55
JERZY PIEŃKOWSKI AND PETER BERKOWITZ

5 Does Cohesion Policy affect regional growth? New evidence
from a semi-parametric approach   69
NICOLA PONTAROLLO

xiv Contents

PART II
The contribution of Cohesion Policy to smart, sustainable and inclusive growth 85

6 An evaluation of the impact of the construction of motorways and expressways in Poland during the period 2004–13 on accessibility and cohesion 87
PIOTR ROSIK, MARCIN STĘPNIAK AND TOMASZ KOMORNICKI

7 Demographic implications of 2007–13 regional and Cohesion Policy actions in Latvia 101
ALEKSANDRS DAHS

8 The policy challenge in smart specialisation: a common approach meets European diversity 115
HENNING KROLL

9 Resilience and involvement: the role of the EU's Structural and Investment Funds in addressing youth unemployment 127
ELIZABETH SANDERSON, PETER WELLS AND IAN WILSON

10 Whatever happened to gender mainstreaming? Lessons for the EU's 2014–20 Structural and Investment Funds 140
LEAZA MCSORLEY AND JIM CAMPBELL

11 The absorption of Structural and Investment Funds and youth unemployment: an empirical test 151
JALE TOSUN, STEFAN SPECKESSER, CARSTEN JENSEN AND JACQUELINE O'REILLY

PART III
The administration and delivery of Cohesion Policy 169

12 Administrative and political embeddedness: how to improve the institutional environments dealing with the management and implementation of EU Structural and Investment Funds? The experience of new member states 171
NECULAI-CRISTIAN SURUBARU

13 Corruption in EU Funds? Europe-wide evidence of the corruption effect of EU-funded public contracting 186
MIHÁLY FAZEKAS AND ISTVÁN JÁNOS TÓTH

14 Efficient implementers and partners: what do we miss in our understanding of how Cohesion Policy administrators work? 206
ANDREY DEMIDOV

15 Funds for the wealthy and the politically loyal? How EU Funds may contribute to increasing regional disparities in East Central Europe 220
GERGŐ MEDVE-BÁLINT

16 The administrative capacity of the sub-national level in implementing Cohesion Policy in Romania: lessons learnt and future recommendations 241
SEPTIMIU-RARES SZABO

PART IV
Institutions, territory and place-based policies **253**

17 Territorial capital and EU Cohesion Policy 255
UGO FRATESI AND GIOVANNI PERUCCA

18 What institutional arrangements exist to ensure coherent EU Cohesion Policy planning and implementation? 271
LIGA BALTIŅA AND TATJANA MURAVSKA

19 Integrated territorial investment: a missed opportunity? 284
IVÁN TOSICS

20 The place-based approach in development policy: a comparative analysis of Polish and EU space 297
JACEK ZAUCHA AND TOMASZ KOMORNICKI

Index 311

Figures

1.1	Total Structural Funds allocations compared to actual expenditure, 1989–2012	16
1.2	Total Structural Funds expenditure per region and theme, 1989–2012	17
3.1	Demand-side and supply-side effects of the absorption of external funds	38
3.2	Expenditure financed by the EU budget, 2004–11, by voivodeship	41
3.3	Per capita distribution of Cohesion Policy funds, 2007–15, by NUTS3 unit	43
3.4	Dynamics of GDP (real terms), 2007–12, by NUTS3 unit	44
3.5	Value of Cohesion Policy projects, 2007–15, by county	45
3.6	Per capita value of Cohesion Policy projects, 2007–15, by county	46
3.7	Dynamics of own revenues and shares in state taxes, 2007–14, by county	47
5.1	Funds by area of intervention	71
5.2	Density of GDP growth per capita and GVA per worker over the 2000–6 period	72
5.3	GDP growth per capita and GVA per worker over the 2000–6 period, by country	73
5.4	Estimation results for Model 1, non-parametric effects	77
5.5	Estimation results for Model 2, non-parametric effects	79
6.1	Polish high-speed road network	90
6.2	Relative changes in the intranational potential accessibility of Polish gminas in the years 2004–13	91
6.3	Share of EU investment in the total change in the intranational potential accessibility of Polish gminas in the years 2004–13	92
6.4	Relative changes in the international potential accessibility of Polish gminas in the years 2004–13	93
6.5	Share of EU investment in the total change in the international potential accessibility of Polish gminas in the years 2004–13	94
6.6	Relative changes in intranational and international accessibility for eight case studies	96
6.7	Relative changes in the intranational potential accessibility of Polish gminas as a result of the implementation of selected investment from EU funds	97

6.8	Relative changes in the international potential accessibility of Polish gminas as a result of the implementation of selected investment from EU funds	98
7.1	Regional demographic trends in Latvia in the years 2009–14	104
7.2	Average EU funds spent per year per capita in municipalities in the years 2009–13	106
9.1	Changes in the self-reported well-being of programme beneficiaries	135
9.2	Self-reported well-being: individual change	136
11.1	Annual youth unemployment rates, 2000–13	152
11.2	Youth unemployment in EU28 member states, 2000–12	153
11.3	Youth unemployment in NUTS2 regions in six selected EU member states, 2013	154
13.1	Bivariate relationship between WGI-Control of Corruption (2013 point estimate) and CRI and the share of single-bidder contracts	194
13.2	Average corruption risks of public procurement suppliers registered abroad, EU26, 2009–14	195
13.3	Single-bidder shares of EU-funded and nationally funded public procurement contracts by country, EU26, 2009–14	199
13.4	CRI difference between EU-funded and nationally funded contracts in the 2009–14 period	200
13.A1	Overview of bias remaining after matching per variable	202
13.A2	Overview of bias remaining after matching per variable	203
17.1	Territorial capital in EU regions: cluster analysis results	261
17.2	Expected allocation of Structural Funds in different types of regions	264
18.1	Interrelation between territorial resources, institutional framework and regional development	273
18.2	Spearman's Rho correlations of GDP per capita, quality of government index, innovation, 2007–13	273
18.3	Most important regional development issues to be addressed at the national, regional and local levels in the 2014–20 planning period	281
20.1	Key elements of the place-based approach	299
20.2	Frequency of usage of different methods of collecting knowledge necessary for the place-based approach by regional (and local) authorities	302
20.3	Local and/or regional authorities' and stakeholders' assessments of the impact of development policies managed at the national and EU level of governance on the socio-economic and territorial development of their territories	304
20.4	Regional respondents' opinions on whether impact of regional policies is analysed by other authorities	305
20.5	Respondents' opinions on what changes would help to remove barriers to a place-based dialogue	307

Tables

1.1	Case study regions	13
3.1	Cohesion Policy funds assigned to new member states, 2007–13	34
3.2	EU funds assigned to Poland, 2007–13	38
3.3	EU funds assigned through Cohesion Policy to Poland, 2007–13, by programme	39
3.4	Correlation between GDP growth in Polish voivodeships and inflow of EU funds, 2004–12	42
3.5	Effects of the absorption of EU funds in the municipality	48
3.6	Changes proposed to the EU programmes	48
4.1	Comparison of models, variables and data used in the econometric studies	57
4.2	Main results and conclusions from the econometric studies	63
5.1	Estimation results of the semi-parametric model	75
6.1	Territorial cohesion (measured by PAD index) in the years 2004–13	95
7.1	Regional investment and policy instruments in Latvia in the years 2009–13	105
7.2	Effects of regional investment/policy instruments on selected demographic indicators in the years 2009–13: linear model results	109
7.3	Effects of regional investment/policy instruments on selected demographic indicators in the years 2009–13: SWR model results	112
8.1	Number of RIS3 priorities as indicated in strategy	119
8.2	Expected and actual changes to policy based on RIS3	119
8.3	Outcome of RIS3 process: novel insights vs. novel routines	120
8.4	Determinants of the overall assessment of RIS3 processes	121
8.5	Outcomes of RIS3 process by member state group	121
11.1	Effect of ESF, ERDF and total Structural Funds absorption on levels of youth unemployment	159
11.A1	Description of the dataset	160
11.A2	Effect of ESF absorption on levels of youth unemployment (H1A)	161
11.A3	Effect of ESF absorption on youth unemployment growth (H1B)	162

11.A4	Effect of ERDF absorption on levels of youth unemployment (H2A)	163
11.A5	Effect of ERDF absorption on youth unemployment growth (H2B)	164
11.A6	Effect of total Structural Funds absorption on levels of youth unemployment (H3A)	165
11.A7	Effect of total Structural Funds absorption on youth unemployment growth (H3B)	166
13.1	Summary of elementary corruption risk indicators	191
13.2	Bivariate Pearson correlation between 'objective' measures of regional corruption and survey-based indicators for NUTS2 regions that awarded at least five contracts in the 2009–14 period	193
13.3	Linear regression explaining relative contract value, EU27, 2009–14	196
13.4	Unmatched and matched comparisons of EU-funded and non-EU-funded contracts' single-bidder share, EU27 totals, 2009–14	197
13.5	Unmatched and matched comparisons of EU-funded and non-EU-funded contracts' CRI, EU27 totals, 2009–14	197
13.A1	Use of EU Funds in the EU27 for markets that awarded at least ten contracts worth above €125,000 in the 2009–14 period	201
13.A2	Summary of balance in the unmatched and the two matched samples	202
15.1	Results of linear multi-level models for Poland	227
15.2	Results of multi-level Tobit models for Hungary	229
15.3	Results of multi-level Tobit models for Hungary	231
15.A1	Descriptive statistics of the Polish variables	236
15.A2	Descriptive statistics of the Hungarian variables	237
17.1	Territorial capital: a taxonomy	257
17.2	Territorial capital in EU regions: data and sources	260
17.3	Territorial capital across clusters of EU regions: mean values of the standardized indicators	262
17.4	Proportion of funds per expenditure axis: analysis of variance among clusters	265
18.1	Factors affecting use of place-based approach in regional development planning in Latvia	279
19.1	Major steps since 2008 to develop the new Cohesion Policy approach to urban areas	285
19.2	Preliminary estimates of ITI funding in selected urban areas	290

Contributors

John Bachtler is Professor of European Policy Studies and a Director of the European Policies Research Centre at the University of Strathclyde in Glasgow. He specialises in comparative international research on regional development policies in Europe, particularly the implementation of EU Cohesion Policy.

Liga Baltiņa is a Senior Researcher and Manager at the Fondazione Giacomo Brodolini where she provides consultancy on EU social and regional development policies. For over five years, she has been part of the research and expert team in the Centre for European and Transition Studies and Jean Monnet Centre of Excellence at the University of Latvia.

Iain Begg is a Professorial Research Fellow in the European Institute at the London School of Economics and a Senior Fellow on the ERSC 'UK in a Changing Europe' initiative. His main research work is on the political economy of European integration and EU economic governance.

Peter Berkowitz is Head of Unit responsible for Policy Development, Strategic Management and Relations with the Council in the Directorate-General for Regional and Urban Policy of the European Commission. He has worked in the areas of regional and urban policy, rural development, CAP reform and EU enlargement.

Jim Campbell is a Reader in Economics at Glasgow Caledonian University. His current research is focused on the impact of European Structural Funds on economic development in Scotland and in particular how changes in the level of funding and the administration of the funds will affect future economic development.

David Charles is a Deputy Head of School and Professor of Innovation and Strategic Management at Lincoln Business School. His research focuses primarily on regional aspects of innovation and innovation policy, and on the regional and community role of universities.

Riccardo Crescenzi is an Associate Professor of Economic Geography at the London School of Economics and a European Research Council (ERC) Grant Holder. He is also affiliated with the Rossi-Doria Centre for Social and

Economic Research at Roma Tre University. His research focuses on regional economic development, innovation, multinational firms, and the analysis and evaluation of EU policies.

Aleksandrs Dahs is a PhD candidate on the Demography Doctoral Study Programme of the University of Latvia. In his academic work, he is focusing on links between regional socio-economic development, Cohesion Policy actions and local demographic processes at various territorial levels.

Andrey Demidov is a Post-Doctoral Research Fellow in the Amsterdam Center for Contemporary European Studies (ACCESS Europe) at the University of Amsterdam. His main research interests cover a wide range of topics related to EU policy implementation (Cohesion Policy) and the involvement of civil society actors in EU policymaking. He has conducted extensive research on the implementation of the Partnership Principle for the Structural Funds in the CEE member states, as well as on changing meanings of partnership as a result of contestation over this requirement.

Mihály Fazekas is a Post-Doctoral Research Fellow at the University of Cambridge and Director of the Government Transparency Institute. His main research area is high-level corruption in public procurement and its consequences for democratic governance and growth.

Ugo Fratesi is Associate Professor of Regional Economics in the Department of Architecture, Built Environment and Construction Engineering at Politecnico di Milano. He is an Editor and the Book Review Editor of the journal *Regional Studies* and a member of the board (formerly the Treasurer) of the Italian Section of the Regional Science Association (AISRe).

Mara Giua is a Post-Doctoral Research Fellow in the Department of Economics and in the Rossi-Doria Centre for Social and Economic Research at Roma Tre University. Her research focuses on regional economics, economic policy analysis and evaluation with special reference to the policies of the EU.

Grzegorz Gorzelak is Professor of Economics and Director of the Centre for European Regional and Local Studies (EUROREG) at the University of Warsaw. He has published (as author and editor) over 50 books (several of them in English) and over 250 articles. He is Editor-in-Chief of a quarterly scientific journal *Studia Regionalne i Lokalne* and the President of the Polish Section of the Regional Studies Association.

Sally Hardy is Chief Executive at the Regional Studies Association. She is leading efforts to globalise the Association in terms of membership and influences and manages the Association's extensive knowledge exchange programme with those working in policy and practice. As well as her interests in regional policy and development, she lectures on issues relating to academic publishing and in particular on achieving impact from research and the relationship between academia and policy.

Carsten Jensen is Professor of Political Science at Aarhus University. He is interested in comparative political economy and has conducted research on the politics of the welfare state and public opinion formation.

Tomasz Komornicki is a Professor and Deputy Director of the Institute of Geography and Spatial Organization at the Polish Academy of Sciences (PAS). He is also affiliated with Maria Curie-Sklodowska University in Lublin. He is a member of the executive body of the Committee for Spatial Economy and Regional Planning at the PAS. His main areas of interest are transport geography, accessibility, international interactions, border studies and spatial planning.

Henning Kroll is a Senior Researcher at the Fraunhofer Institute for System and Innovation Research in Karlsruhe. He has a background in economic geography and economics. Among other things, much of his current research focuses on regional development and regional innovation policy. Apart from publishing on smart specialisation, he has been acting as a consultant on this subject to several regions.

Leaza McSorley is a Lecturer in Economics at Glasgow Caledonian University. Her research focus is on regional economic development and labour market issues.

Gergő Medve-Bálint is a Research Fellow in the Center for Social Sciences at the Hungarian Academy of Sciences and a Visiting Professor in the School of Public Policy at Central European University. He studies the effects of European integration on East Central Europe, with a particular emphasis on the politics of foreign direct investment, development policies, regional development and territorial inequality.

Tatjana Muravska is Professor of Regional Economy at the University of Latvia and Director of the Centre for European and Transition Studies, Programme Director of the European Studies Master's, Chair of the Academic Council of the Doctoral School for European Integration and Baltic Sea Region Studies, Jean Monnet Chair Ad Personam and academic coordinator of the Jean Monnet Centre of Excellence. Her research and publications cover social and economic issues related to EU integration, including implementation of the EU Structural and Cohesion Funds.

Jacqueline O'Reilly is Professor and Director of the Centre for Research on Management and Employment at the University of Brighton Business School. She is the Coordinator of a large-scale EU-funded project entitled 'STYLE: Strategic Transitions for Youth Labour in Europe' (www.style-research.eu).

Giovanni Perucca is a Post-Doctoral Research Fellow in Regional and Urban Economics in the Department of Architecture, Built Environment and Construction Engineering at Politecnico di Milano. His main research interests are in the fields of regional economics, transport economics and health economics.

Jerzy Pieńkowski is an Analyst in the policy development team of the Directorate-General for Regional and Urban Policy of the European Commission. His work focuses on the analysis and development of EU regional policy and the assessment of its impact. He has also worked in the fields of EU economic, energy and environmental policy.

Laura Polverari is a Senior Research Fellow in the European Policies Research Centre at the University of Strathclyde in Glasgow. Her research interests include the design, implementation and evaluation of public policy, EU Cohesion Policy, regional policy in Italy and accountability in policymaking.

Nicola Pontarollo is a Post-Doctoral Researcher in the Department of Economics, Quantitative Methods and Business Strategy (DEMS) at the University of Milan-Bicocca and Adjunct Researcher for the Research Group in Regional Economics (GIER) at the University of Cuenca. His main research interests include regional economic development, Latin-American and European regional policies, migration and spatial econometrics.

Piotr Rosik is an Associate Professor in the Institute of Geography and Spatial Organization at the Polish Academy of Sciences (PAS). He has participated in many Polish and international research projects, including ESPON and INTERREG projects, and is the author of more than 100 publications. His main areas of interest are transport geography and transport policy.

Elizabeth Sanderson is a Research Associate in the Centre for Regional Economic and Social Research (CRESR) at Sheffield Hallam University. She has worked on several research and evaluation projects focusing on welfare reform, housing and youth employment. Her current research looks at youth transitions and youth marginalisation.

Stefan Speckesser is Chief Economist of the Institute for Employment Studies in Brighton and is an empirical economist specialising in evaluation methodology, programme and policy impacts and the returns to education. He has an academic background in applied econometrics and political science.

Marcin Stępniak is a Research Fellow in the Institute of Geography and Spatial Organization at the Polish Academy of Sciences (PAS). He has ten years' experience of research in the fields of geography, transport and GIS. His research covers transport and accessibility issues, urban geography and the application of GIS in spatial analyses.

Neculai-Cristian Surubaru is a PhD candidate at Loughborough University. His main research interests relate to administrative capacity, governance and politicisation. His thesis evaluates the management and implementation of European funds in Central and Eastern Europe, looking at the absorption capacity of Bulgaria and Romania during their first programming period of 2007–13.

Septimiu-Rares Szabo is a PhD candidate at the Bucharest University of Economic Studies and specialises in the field of regional development with a focus on decentralisation and local economic development. He is also a practitioner in the Romanian Government, being involved in the implementation of EU Cohesion Policy in Romania.

Iván Tosics is one of the Principals of the Metropolitan Research Institute (MRI) in Budapest. Since 2011, he has been one of the Thematic Pole Managers (Programme Experts) of the URBACT programme. He is Vice Chair of the European Network of Housing Research (ENHR) and Policy Editor of the journal *Urban Research and Practice*. His research focuses on integrated urban development, urban renewal, metropolitan areas and EU Cohesion Policy issues.

Jale Tosun is Professor of Political Science at Heidelberg University. Her research interests comprise public policy, international political economy, public administration and European integration. She is the Coordinator of a large-scale EU-funded project entitled CUPESSE (www.cupesse.eu).

István János Tóth is Director of Corruption Research Center Budapest and Senior Research Fellow at the Institute of Economics of the Hungarian Academy of Sciences in Budapest. He is also affiliated with the Institute of Sociology and Social Policy at Corvinus University of Budapest. His research focuses on institutional context and measurement of corruption, government tax policies and analysis of tax evasion.

Peter Wells is Professor of Public Policy Analysis and Evaluation in the Centre for Regional Economic and Social Research (CRESR) at Sheffield Hallam University. He has undertaken evaluations of EU and UK programmes in the fields of regional policy, youth employment and social investment. He has led research projects into the role of civil society organisations in the delivery of public policies and into regional, local and community partnership.

Ian Wilson is a Senior Research Fellow in the Centre for Regional Economic and Social Research (CRESR) at Sheffield Hallam University. He has undertaken research and evaluation projects exploring the impact of regional policy, welfare reform, and housing and employment programmes. His work focuses on the importance of individual- and area-based factors.

Jacek Zaucha is an Associate Professor of Economics at the University of Gdańsk and a National Science Centre (NCN) Grant Holder. He is also affiliated with the Maritime Institute in Gdańsk and the Institute for Development in Sopot. His research focuses on regional economic development, spatial development, maritime spatial planning, Baltic Sea Region spatial development and integration, territorial cohesion and EU Cohesion Policy.

Introduction
Reassessing the performance and direction of EU Cohesion Policy in 2014–20

John Bachtler,[1] *Peter Berkowitz, Sally Hardy and Tatjana Muravska*

In 2013, the Cohesion Policy of the European Union (EU) underwent the most significant and substantial set of regulatory changes since the landmark reform of Structural Funds in 1988. The changes were important in establishing a new policy direction for EU Cohesion Policy, one which aligned the objectives of European Structural and Investment Funds (ESIF) to the overall priorities of the EU, as expressed in the Europe 2020 strategy for smart, sustainable and inclusive growth. The new regulations also introduced requirements for more strategic coherence in the planning and implementation of ESIF programmes, as well as greater thematic concentration through targeting of resources – with a particular focus on research and innovation, SME competitiveness, ICT, the low carbon economy, employment and social inclusion. A new performance framework, ex ante conditionalities, and an emphasis on results in the formulation of objectives in programmes sought to reinforce the effectiveness of planned spending. Place-based policymaking was strengthened through the introduction of new integrated territorial delivery mechanisms for ESIF programmes, a strong commitment to the development of smart specialisation strategies and the regulatory obligation to spend a minimum level of funding on sustainable development interventions in urban areas. Lastly, institutional and administrative capacity was recognised as an important precondition for efficient management of the Funds, both before and during implementation. Finally, the policy has been brought into line with the evolving framework of economic governance within the EU.

These changes were driven by evidence and responded to some important criticisms of Cohesion Policy. During the preparatory phase for the 2013 reform, the European Commission sponsored a wide-ranging reassessment of the policy (Barca, 2009), complemented by extensive consultation with Member State policymakers, and the largest-scale programme of evaluation of the policy in its history (Applica *et al.*, 2009). The results showed, *inter alia*, that the effectiveness of the policy was undermined by the fragmentation of spending across too many priorities with a lack of critical mass, and insufficient consideration of the 'logic of intervention', especially as regards the anticipated outcomes of policy choices in the setting of objectives and allocation of resources. Deficiencies in policy frameworks and institutional capacity at national and regional levels were limiting (or even countering) the potential impact of EU funding. The implementation of policy was also characterised by insufficient exploitation of synergies as a result of a lack of coordination across policy fields and organisational boundaries. In many cases, these problems were not new and (in some regions) had constrained effective programme implementation since the early 1990s (Bachtler et al., 2016).

Translating the ambitious objectives of the 2013 reforms into practice has not been easy. There is clearly a significant shift in ESIF allocations in 2014–20, with alignment of funding with Europe 2020 priorities, a greater use of financial instruments and (potentially) more transparent and measurable results associated with performance frameworks. The introduction of ex ante conditionalities has led to a major investment in addressing institutional, legislative and strategic weakness which could undermine the effectiveness of investment. At the same time, the context for the policy is changing, with the crisis undermining the longer-term gains made in national and regional convergence in some Member States and regions. In addition to the problems of low economic growth and high rates of unemployment (especially among young people), new challenges related to migration have emerged (European Commission, 2015).

Challenges for the Cohesion Policy in 2014–20: an academic and policy debate

It is against this background that the Regional Studies Association and the European Commission's Directorate-General for Regional and Urban Policy (DG Regio) organised the conference 'Challenges for the new Cohesion Policy in 2014–20' in February 2015 in Riga, to facilitate an academic and policy debate between the academic community, European institutions and policymakers from national and regional levels in Member States. Hosted by the Latvian Government and University of Latvia, the aims of the Conference were to make policy officials and practitioners aware of research being conducted on Cohesion Policy, and to give academics a better understanding of the concerns and priorities of the policy communities at EU and national levels.

The conference brought together 183 participants from academia and policy for three days of discussions. Some 83 papers were presented in 25 workshops covering a wide range of themes on the design, implementation and performance of Cohesion Policy – past, present and future. They addressed five main sets of questions:[2]

- Economic geography and Cohesion Policy: how are the economic and social challenges for European Structural and Investment Funds changing?
- Institutions and governance: what can Cohesion Policy do to strengthen public administration and effective management of the Funds?
- Performance and results: how can Cohesion Policy resources be used most effectively and efficiently?
- Instruments: what kind of Cohesion Policy interventions make a difference?
- EU economic governance and Cohesion Policy: what are the implications of governance reforms for Cohesion Policy?

Selecting papers from the rich material presented and discussed at the Conference has not been an easy task. The 20 chapters in this volume are intended to provide a representative selection, covering 4 themes: research on the effectiveness and impact of Cohesion Policy; the contribution of Cohesion Policy to smart, sustainable and inclusive growth; the importance of the administration and delivery of Cohesion Policy; and the inter-relationships between institutions, territory and place-based policies.

The impact of Cohesion Policy

The appropriate mix and spatial focus of Cohesion Policy interventions to maximise its impact is a perennial challenge for policymakers and analysts. Chapter 1 begins with a long-term perspective on the effectiveness of Cohesion Policy by *John Bachtler, Iain Begg, David Charles* and *Laura Polverari*. Based on research in 15 regions of the EU15 over the period from 1989 to 2012, and using theory-based evaluation, it is the first longitudinal and comparative analysis of the relevance, effectiveness and utility of the Funds from 1989 to 2012 covering almost four full programme periods. The research concludes that spending through Cohesion Policy has suffered from a lack of conceptual thinking or strategic justification for programmes, objectives that were neither specific nor measurable, and deficiencies across most areas of management to varying degrees. However, there is evidence of improvement over time and the increasing adoption of what is regarded as 'good practice'. The research provides support for key principles of the 2013 reforms of Cohesion Policy, notably with regard to greater concentration of resources, strategic coherence, integrated investment, and (most of all) the role of administrative and institutional capacity as a precondition for effective implementation.

Investigating whether territorial 'conditioning factors' play a role is the subject of Chapter 2. *Maria Giua and Riccardo Crescenzi* critically analyse the existing scholarly and policy literature on the factors conditioning EU Cohesion Policy and its impacts. Their analysis identifies key gaps in the existing evidence and develops an agenda for future research in this field, informing an evidence-based debate on the future of the policy. The Chapter calls for stronger synergies between the analysis of the territorial factors conditioning the policy impacts and counterfactual methods in order to shed new light on what works (and what does not) in the large variety of territorial contexts of the EU.

Most of the authors at the Riga conference agreed on the need for infrastructure development to be accompanied by support for business development and innovation in a coordinated strategic approach. This issue was central to research conducted by *Grzegorz Gorzelak* (Chapter 3) who discusses the territorial impact of Cohesion Policy in Poland during the 2007–13 period. Statistical evidence at NUTS2, NUTS3 and NUTS4 levels demonstrates the growing variation in levels of development among territorial units. A survey of 1,300 municipalities also proves that the EU Funds have had more impact socially, improving living standards and the state of the environment, than on local growth conditions.

The Chapter concludes with policy suggestions for the 2014–20 programming period.

A broader international analysis is undertaken by *Nicola Pontarollo* in Chapter 5, examining the effects of Structural Funds in Objective 1 regions in 2000–06 with a semi-parametric approach that accounts for possible non-linearities. The main findings are that funds for productive environment are positively correlated to GDP growth per capita mainly in lagging regions, while they do not have an effect on productivity. Funds for human capital, despite the low budgets, are strongly positive for both GDP per capita and GVA per worker growth in majority of regions, while Funds for infrastructure are effective in improving productivity growth only above the threshold of one per cent of regional GVA.

Turning to methodological issues, *Jerzy Pieńkowski* and *Peter Berkowitz* (Chapter 4) undertake a wide-ranging review of the relevance of econometric studies addressing the impact of Cohesion Policy funding on economic growth from the policymakers' perspective. The econometric methods used for this purpose have been enriched recently, for instance by using spatial techniques and non-parametric methods. However, some weaknesses remain: not many studies use good-quality data on Cohesion Policy transfers; the parameters of spatial dependence are very simple; and some important policy variables are excluded from the regressions. The conclusions for Cohesion Policy drawn by these studies are not well developed and contradictory, and the Chapter concludes with some suggestions for future research.

The contribution of Cohesion Policy to smart, sustainable and inclusive growth

As noted above, a major change in the policy context for Cohesion Policy is the Union strategy for smart, sustainable and inclusive growth (Europe 2020). For the 2014–20 period, Cohesion Policy has been cast as the budgetary arm of Europe 2020, with the earmarking of resources for investments in key thematic objectives (RTDI, ICT, SME competiveness, low carbon, social inclusion). An important new conditionality related to Europe 2020 is the requirement for countries and regions to put in place smart specialisation strategies (S3) as a framework for targeted support to research and innovation. In Chapter 8, *Henning Kroll* reflects on the implementation of the RIS3 policy agenda. Based on two Europe-wide online surveys, he underlines that the diverse pattern of institutional arrangements among EU regions poses locally specific policy challenges in which governance capacities are at least as important as actual potentials. Specifically, the study finds that Southern European regions tend to profit from the RIS3 agenda while Eastern European regions face difficulties due to their different institutional arrangements. Nevertheless, one merit of RIS3 processes may lie in their impact on exactly those arrangements.

Notwithstanding the importance of innovation, targeted infrastructure development remains important in certain contexts. In Chapter 6, *Piotr Rosik, Marcin Stępniak* and *Tomasz Komornicki* show that investment in high-quality transport

Reassessing performance and direction 5

infrastructure can lead to greater territorial cohesion at different spatial levels. However, they note that in Poland more emphasis has been placed on improving international connectivity compared to national accessibility. In the context of the country's internal cohesion, the increase of Potential Accessibility Dispersion index values and an increased variation in the accessibility of the country's regions have been observed since 2004. Conclusions drawn from experience are important for the most efficient implementation of EU Funds in the 2014–20 programming period.

With respect to other effects, the demographic impact of EU funding is analysed by *Alexander Dahs* in Chapter 7. He examines the regional demographic implications of the Cohesion Policy interventions in Latvia under the 2007–13 Operational Programme and evaluates the significance of these effects in comparison with other forms of regional socio-economic aid and financial investment. The research finds that Cohesion Policy investments had some impact on local demographic change, although the positive effect has been lower than expected by the authorities. The effects of various forms of regional aid may be either localised or spatially distributed, implying opportunities for better planning of future investment.

Youth employment has risen sharply up the EU's political agenda since 2011 in response to substantial rises in youth unemployment rates in a number of Member States as a result of the economic crisis and on-going recession. In Chapter 11, *Jale Tosun, Carsten Jensen, Stefan Speckesser* and *Jacqueline O'Reilly* address the role of Structural Funds in general, and the ESF and ERDF in particular, in helping to overcome youth unemployment. Empirically, they examine the annual absorption behaviour of the EU Member States between 2000 and 2011, finding that the absorption capacity of Member States had a significant effect on youth unemployment.

The need for a strategic and coordinated approach to youth unemployment programmes is emphasised by *Elizabeth Sanderson, Peter Wells and Ian Wilson* (Chapter 9). Their research looks beyond the now well-established repertoire of ESIF interventions set out in the European Commission's call for action on youth unemployment as well as other guidance. Two possible areas for intervention are considered: the involvement of young people in the design and delivery of programmes and the development of young people's personal resilience as a determinant of successful labour market outcomes. Findings draw on the evaluation of a UK youth employment programme, the Big Lottery Fund's Talent Match.

Importantly, there continue to be differences in equal opportunities for women and ethnic minorities. *Leaza McSorley* and *Jim Campbell* (Chapter 10) argue that EU commitments for gender equality were not given sufficient prominence in the regulatory framework for 2014–20 or followed through in the thematic objectives and investment priorities. Based on an evaluation of ESIF commitments to gender mainstreaming in the Scottish Structural Funds Programme 2007–13, they argue that the ESIF have an important role to play in contributing to Europe 2020 targets by tackling the significant variations in female employment rates and delivering greater gender equality within the EU. However, in order to do so, policymakers need to be aware that interventions funded under ESIF are not gender neutral and gender mainstreaming must be implemented more effectively in all Funds, not solely the ESF, in the 2014–20 period.

The administration and delivery of Cohesion Policy

Several of the reforms introduced in the 2013 regulatory framework are intended to strengthen public administration and the effective management of the Funds. Adequate administrative capacity at national, regional and local levels is considered a prerequisite. Research presented at the Riga Conference identified administrative capacity as a key bottleneck that has to be addressed before sustainable high growth levels will materialise. Poor governance reduces economic growth and entrepreneurship and diminishes the impact of Cohesion Policy.

Nicolai-Cristian Surubaru (Chapter 12) argues that the institutional environment in which domestic national managing institutions are embedded plays an equally important role in the development of administrative capacity and can contribute towards developing new ways for improving the effectiveness of Cohesion Policy, particularly in light of its 2013 reform. Political stability is regarded as a key condition for effective Funds' management as well as avoidance of political clientelism.

An important question is whether EU funding can improve the quality of government. Chapter 13 by *István János Tóth and Mihály Fazekas* offers novel evidence on this question by utilising a large-scale public procurement database, the EU's Tenders Electronic Daily, containing the details of more than 2.8 million contracts from the 2009–14 period. It matches and compares EU-funded public procurement contracts with those that were nationally funded in order to obtain an approximation of the causal impact of EU funding on corruption. Results suggest that on average EU Funds increase corruption risks across Europe by 3–20 per cent depending on the corruption risk indicator used. This effect shows a remarkable variability across regions, underlining the importance of recipient institutional framework.

More fundamentally, *Andrey Demidov* questioned whether the application of concepts such as 'weak bureaucracies' or 'low capacities' in Central and Eastern European countries is obscuring a deeper understanding of the complexity of the motivations and actions of Cohesion Policy implementers. Taking the Partnership Principle for the Structural Funds as a case study, Chapter 14 summarises the findings of an interpretive analysis of how national state officials across four CEE member states – Hungary, Slovakia, Poland and Slovenia – implement Cohesion Policy rules and requirements. The analysis demonstrates the complex nature of actors' understandings of partnership, shaped not only by the actors' own interests but also by institutional identities and larger dynamics of relations with the EU institutions, domestic civil society actors and each other.

In Chapter 15, *Gergő Medve-Bálint* employs multi-level linear and Tobit models to test the effects of both regional and local economic and political factors on the territorial distribution of EU Funds in Poland and Hungary in the

2007–13 programming period. The findings suggest that, all else being equal, in both countries some of the wealthiest regions and especially the wealthier localities have benefited more from the Funds than the less wealthy ones. Furthermore, the Chapter reveals that a political bias has also characterised the funding process, in that the political preferences of central governments seem to have influenced the distribution of the Funds. Based on research in Romania, S*eptimiu-Rares Szabo* (Chapter 16) assessed the impact of the sub-national level in implementing Cohesion Policy in 2007–13, while also looking into the implications of these findings for the 2014–20 period. The study emphasised the importance of strengthening the capacity of middle management within government institutions, and including implementing bodies and beneficiaries in administrative capacity-building efforts, especially for decentralised management of ESIF.

Institutions, territory and place-based policies

In focusing on longer-term development challenges and strategies, with a stronger focus on EU-level objectives, there is the question of how to give meaning to place-based policymaking. The research by *Ugo Fratesi* and *Giovanni Perucca* (Chapter 17) shows the need for Cohesion Policy strategies to be place-sensitive with different mixes of interventions appropriate for different types of region. The Chapter undertakes a multidimensional analysis of the relationship between territorial capital and Cohesion Policy using NUTS3-level statistical data for the 2000–06 period. It finds that regions less endowed with territorial capital tend to concentrate Structural Funds' expenditure on basic infrastructure provision, intermediate regions on various types of business support and better endowed regions on the provision of human capital and other soft territorial capital assets.

Several of the reforms introduced in 2013 are intended to strengthen public administration and the effective management of the Funds. *Liga Baltina* and *Tatjana Muravska* (Chapter 18) highlight the effectiveness of the institutional framework as a key element in achieving Cohesion Policy goals. They show that good administrative capacity at national, regional and local levels is an important prerequisite for the use of the place-based approach for regional development planning, as it is linked with the capacity to develop an up-to-date business environment and to provide citizens with the necessary services.

A broader issue for *Iván Tosics* (Chapter 19) is one of unfulfilled expectations. He argues that the potential of these tools to promote integrated urban development is not being sufficiently exploited, with a regulatory framework which is insufficiently prescriptive in challenging national and regional authorities that are unwilling to devolve budgets and responsibilities, as well as capacity constraints at local level.

However, a place-based approach is challenging. *Jacek Zaucha* and *Tomasz Komornicki* (Chapter 20) discuss how the exploitation of territorial capital has been translated into programming documents in the Polish regions, finding that there has been little practical implementation on the ground. Although Poland is regarded as a leader in terms of legal arrangements in support of a territorial integrated approach, it is lagging behind other countries in the behavioural domain.

****

The focus of the Riga Conference was mainly on the challenges and opportunities for implementing Cohesion Policy in the 2014–20 period at a point in time when a new generation of Structural Funds programmes was only just being launched. As the programme period develops, new evidence on how the 2013 reforms are playing out in practice will become available, combined with further research and evaluation of the impact of Cohesion Policy in 2007–13. This will allow further reassessment of the issues discussed in this book as well as a contribution to longer-term thinking on the future of the policy after 2020.

Notes

1 The information and views set out in the chapter are those of the author and do not reflect the official opinion of the European Commission.
2 A list and summary of the Conference papers are available here: http://ec.europa.eu/regional_policy/sources/conferences/challenges-cp-2014/conference_report.pdf. The papers themselves are available on the Conference website at: http://ec.europa.eu/regional_policy/index.cfm/en/conferences/challenges-cp-2014/.

References

Applica, Ismeri Europa and WiiW (2009), *Ex Post Evaluation of Cohesion Policy Programmes 2007–2013, Financed by the European Regional Development Fund (ERDF) and Cohesion Fund (CF), Work Package One: Synthesis Report.*

Bachtler, J., Begg., Charles, D. and Polverari, L. (2016), *EU Cohesion Policy in Practice: What Does It Achieve?* London: Rowman & Littlefield International.

Barca, F. (2009), *An Agenda for a Reformed Cohesion Policy: A Place-based Approach to Meeting European Union Challenges and Expectations.* Independent report prepared at the request of Danuta Hübner, Commissioner for Regional Policy, AC.

European Commission (2015), *Effectiveness and Added Value of Cohesion Policy. Non-paper Assessing the Implementation of the Reform in the Programming for Cohesion Policy 2014–2020.* Brussels: DG Regio.

Part I
The impact of Cohesion Policy

1 The long-term effectiveness of EU Cohesion Policy

Assessing the achievements of the ERDF, 1989–2012

John Bachtler, Iain Begg, David Charles and Laura Polverari

Introduction

One of the major challenges for EU Cohesion Policy is that, after 25 years of implementing the policy, the evidence for its effectiveness is so inconclusive. Academic research and evaluation studies have reached widely differing conclusions on the results of interventions through Structural and Cohesion Funds (Bachtler and Gorzelak, 2007; Polverari and Bachtler, 2014). At the same time, political and public debate on the performance of the policy has increased, most evident in the discussions on the reforms of Cohesion Policy for the 2007–13 and 2014–20 periods and the pressure on EU and national policymakers to improve performance. This give rise to several questions: is it correct that substantial Cohesion Policy resources have been spent without adequate strategic justification? If so, why has this been the case? And will the new reforms make a difference?

The following chapter seeks to answer these questions based on an evaluation of the main achievements of Cohesion Policy programmes and projects over the longer term. Drawing on research undertaken in 15 selected regions of the EU15, it is the first longitudinal and comparative analysis of the implementation of the Funds from 1989 to 2012, covering almost four full programme periods. Specifically, it involved analysis of the relevance, effectiveness and utility of each of the Cohesion Policy programmes implemented in each of the regions. In assessing the achievements of the programmes, the study adopted a 'theory-based evaluation' approach, going beyond the formally stated objectives of programmes to uncover the mechanisms or theories of change underlying the design of programmes, as well as identifying the ways in which objectives were actually operationalised in practice (Bachtler *et al.*, 2013b).[1]

The chapter begins by outlining the context for the research and the methodology. It then discusses the nature of the strategies implemented over the 1989–2012 period, their relevance to the regional development situation of the 15 regions and the expenditure committed over time and to different themes. The chapter then focuses on the assessment of the achievements of the programmes, and their effectiveness and utility, before drawing together the main conclusions to emerge from the study.

Context

Cohesion Policy has been subject to more extensive evaluation at EU, national and sub-national levels than any other area of EU policy. Successive reforms of the Funds since 1988 have progressively increased the obligations on the European Commission (EC) and member state authorities to undertake systematic evaluations of interventions ex ante, during programme implementation and ex post. The EU budgetary debates since the late 1990s have also been conducted against a background of net payer efforts to limit the growth of the EU budget and redirect spending away from Cohesion Policy and the CAP to so-called 'competitiveness policies' such as R&D, pressures that were intensified by the Lisbon Strategy and Europe 2020 (Bachtler *et al.*, 2013a). This has forced the EC to justify the resources and effectiveness of Cohesion Policy to a greater degree, reflected in greater attention being given to the evaluation of the policy and its performance in preparing the reforms for the 2014–20 period and ultimately the new regulatory framework.

A range of methodological approaches have been used to analyse the effectiveness, impact and added value of Cohesion Policy funding – principally macroeconomic models, regression analysis, micro-economic studies and qualitative case studies. While each has strengths and weaknesses, all of the methods involve difficulties associated with the poor availability of regional data on socio-economic indicators and spending, and the problem of comparing outcomes with a counterfactual, and there is little consistency in the findings (Davies, 2014). Overall, therefore, it is not possible to draw definitive conclusions from the studies on the scale of impacts, or on the factors that condition the effectiveness of Cohesion Policy funding across member states and regions.

Methodology

Against this background, the distinctive methodological approach adopted for this study was an experimental 'theory-based evaluation'. Its essence is to assess whether the programmes implemented by the regions achieved what they were designed to do and whether what they achieved dealt with the needs of the region (as identified at the start of the process) (Hart, 2007; Leeuw, 2012). This methodology does not try to establish a direct causal link between the Cohesion Policy interventions and changes in standard macroeconomic variables at the regional level, such as GDP per capita or the unemployment rate. The focus of theory-based evaluation (as interpreted for this study) is on understanding what it was that policymakers sought to change, and how what was done was expected to influence regional development. It addresses the logic behind the policy interventions, whether such logic was appropriate for the specific regional circumstances, and how policy evolved as initial needs were met and new ones had to be confronted.

The objectives of the study were twofold. First, it sought to examine the achievements of all regional programmes and regionally implemented national programmes co-financed by the ERDF and, where applicable, the Cohesion Fund, that have been implemented in the 15 selected regions from 1989 to 2012. Second, it aimed to assess the relevance of programmes and the effectiveness and utility of programme achievements.

The core of the research involved 15 regional case studies conducted in three types of region (see Table 1.1):

1. six regions eligible for Objective 1/Convergence support from 1989–93 to the present;
2. six regions eligible for Objective 1 or 6 support at one time, but with Phasing-in/-out or Regional Competitiveness & Employment (RCE) status in 2007–13;
3. three regions partially or wholly eligible for Objective 2/RCE status from 1989–93 to 2012.

Research was carried out in each of the regions, using a mix of desk research, online and fieldwork interview surveys with a wide range of respondents and consultative workshops. A central thread of the analysis was the use of eight 'thematic axes' (or themes) as a framework for analysing the programmes' achievements:

1. innovation
2. enterprise
3. structural adjustment
4. infrastructure
5. environment
6. labour market
7. social cohesion
8. territorial cohesion.

Table 1.1 Case study regions.

Country	Objective 1/Convergence	Phasing-in/out	Objective 2/RCE
Austria		Burgenland	
Finland		Itä-Suomi	
France		Nord-Pas-de-Calais	Aquitaine
Germany	Sachsen-Anhalt		Nordrhein-Westfalen
Greece	Dytiki Ellada		
Ireland		Ireland	
Italy	Campania	Basilicata	
Portugal	Norte	Algarve	
Spain	Andalucía, Galicia		
UK			North-East England

Regional needs and the relevance of strategies

At the end of the 1980s, each of the 15 case study regions faced particular challenges, reflecting their geographical situation and historical background. The three main types of needs were categorised as:

1 major underdevelopment and indicators of disadvantage ranging from a lack of basic infrastructure and services, to skills deficits, often compounded by peripherality or significant internal disparities (Dytiki Ellada, Campania, Norte, Andalucía, Basilicata, Algarve and Ireland);
2 restructuring in regions facing either transition from a centrally planned economy (Sachsen-Anhalt) or from an economy dominated by large, declining traditional industries (Nordrhein-Westfalen, Nord-Pas-de-Calais and North-East England);
3 agricultural modernisation and economic diversification in predominantly rural or peripheral regions (mainly Aquitaine, Burgenland, Itä-Suomi and Galicia).

All of the case study regions were at a relative disadvantage at the start of the period, having significantly lower levels of development relative to either national or EU averages, but with significant differences within the group. Up to 2008, most regions performed worse than the EU average in GVA growth over the period. Only Ireland demonstrated a clear virtuous cycle of above-average performance for both output productivity and employment. Others saw some growth based on increased employment or improved productivity, but most struggled to outperform the EU average. Since 2008, many of the regions have seen poorer performance as a result of the recession.

The early ERDF programmes of the case study regions had relatively basic, generic strategies, often with limited assessment of needs; they tried to encompass diverse stakeholder interests with objectives and priorities that were open to interpretation. Initially, there was little pressure to change, and many strategies were remarkably stable during the 1990s. However, programming for 2000–6 saw substantial strategic reassessments in several regions and even more so for 2007–13, driven by the Community Strategic Guidelines or changes in eligibility status.

The conceptual basis for programmes was often weak. Throughout the period since 1989, strategies were not underpinned explicitly by theory or development models, but rather by prevailing assumptions of economic development. Nevertheless, the research found that all of the programmes were at least partially relevant to regional needs (in certain periods or for parts of the programmes), and almost half of the programmes were relevant across the whole period from 1989 to 2012. The main thematic trends over time are a greater emphasis on R&D and innovation, more support for entrepreneurship and more sophisticated SME interventions, the mainstreaming of urban regeneration and a specific focus on community development.

In the early periods (1989–93 and 1994–9), programme objectives were generally neither specific nor measurable due to a lack of quantified targets and non-existent or inadequate monitoring systems. The attainability of objectives was also questionable; strategies were mostly overambitious and did not recognise the limited potential contribution of the ERDF programmes in the wider economic and policy contexts. Even if quantified, programme targets often required adjustments during the programme period. However, the vagueness of objectives allowed managing authorities to report 'success' or interpret effectiveness in different ways. Programme objectives were usually not timely, in the sense that the achievement of objectives was likely to take much longer than the programme period – a factor that was not always acknowledged. The 'SMART' character of programme objectives improved over time, but by 2012 they were still some way from being fully achieved, either because of deficiencies in programme design or delays and difficulties with the operationalisation of monitoring systems.

How much was spent? Programme expenditure, 1989–2012

Analysing trends in the expenditure of Structural and Cohesion Funds over time and across regions has traditionally been problematic. Multiple sources, inconsistent reporting and delays in closing programmes and finalising expenditure have presented major challenges for comparative research. It was only in the 2007–13 period that the EC was able to introduce a structured, systematic approach to member states' reporting on the financial progress of programmes. This study, therefore, had to undertake primary research based on a bottom-up classification and aggregation of measure-level expenditure information, undertaken for each of the 15 regions.

Over the period from 1989 to 2012, more than €146 billion of Structural and Cohesion Funds was estimated to have been spent in the 15 regions (see Figure 1.1). The Objective 1/Convergence regions had the largest share, of 68.3 per cent (c.€99.6 billion), with Phasing-in/-out and Objective 2/RCE regions representing a more modest 21.6 per cent (c.€31.5 billion) and 10.1 per cent (c.€14.7 billion) respectively. Across the entire period, allocations exceeded expenditure by c.€14 billion (c.9 per cent of the initial allocation). This figure should however be interpreted with great caution given that, especially for early periods, it was not always possible to reconstruct the non-earmarked regional allocations of the National Operational Programmes (NOPs) and Multiregional Operational Programmes (MOPs) (which overinflated expenditure compared to allocations) and that this sum was negatively affected by the expenditure delays of the 2007–13 programmes. The discrepancy between planned and actual expenditure was the highest in absolute terms in the Objective 1/Convergence regions (c.€10.2 billion). Again, however, the lack of reliable data on allocations for some of the MOPs/NOPs affected the validity of this assessment.

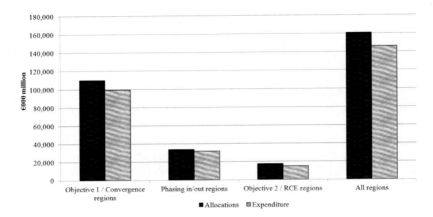

Figure 1.1 Total Structural Funds allocations compared to actual expenditure by regional groups and across all 15 regions, 1989–2012 (€000 million, 2000 values).

Note: Data included are for Regional Operational Programmes (ROPs) and, where applicable, NOPs/MOPs combined. There are some data gaps in relation to the early periods and MOP/NOP expenditure, which could not always be regionalised. Detail can be found in the case study reports at InfoRegio (2015).

The proportion of spend across the eight thematic axes varied among the regions, ranging from a strong emphasis on enterprise support in Burgenland (56 per cent of expenditure from 1989 to 2012) and Itä-Suomi (59 per cent), to a predominance of infrastructure spending in the two Spanish regions (representing 61 per cent of expenditure in Galicia and 49 per cent in Andalucía), in Dytiki Ellada (43 per cent), and in Ireland (37 per cent). Aquitaine and Sachsen-Anhalt showed a concentration of expenditure on two main themes (enterprise and structural adjustment), as did Campania (enterprise and infrastructure), while the remaining regions displayed more mixed expenditure patterns, with no dominant theme (Figure 1.2).

What was achieved? The effectiveness of the programmes

The considerable investments made by the ERDF associated with €146 billion of funding in the 15 case study regions could have been expected to have made significant differences to the development of these regions. The study began its assessment of the effectiveness of this spending by analysing the achievements reported by the regions. However, these data have major problems with reliability, with under- or over-reporting, as well as simple deception, by projects. Consequently, the study also used a range of alternative sources – evaluation studies, academic research and interviews with stakeholders at strategic and operational levels as well as with external experts – in order to make a judgement at programme and measure levels on how effectively programme objectives were achieved.

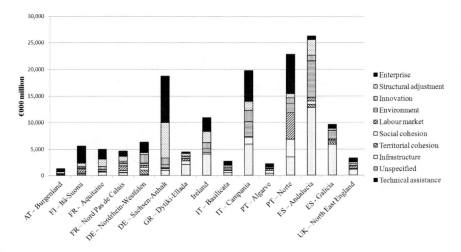

Figure 1.2 Total Structural Funds expenditure per region and theme, 1989–2012 (€000 million, 2000 values).

Note: Data included are for ROPs and, where applicable, NOPs/MOPs combined. There are some data gaps in relation to the early periods and MOP/NOP expenditure, which could not always be regionalised. Detail can be found in the case study reports at InfoRegio (2015).

For most regions and programme periods, the judgement of the research team was that programmes more or less achieved their objectives, although with many caveats. In a few cases, it seemed that the programmes exceeded their objectives, such as in Sachsen-Anhalt (which focused on job creation and significantly exceeded its targets in two of the periods) and Ireland (which also exceeded objectives during the 1990s, but missed its targets in the 2000–6 programme). Several regions had at least one 'bad' period when objectives were not realised, again often due to over-ambitious objectives, and a small group of regions had a poor performance overall.

At a measure level, the variability of judgements on performance increased, with examples of some highly successful measures that considerably exceeded objectives (at least as measured by targets) and others that largely failed to achieve anything. With respect to the main expenditure categories analysed, the following judgements could be made:

- There was a generally positive view of the effectiveness of objectives relating to different forms of *infrastructure* across the regions. Objectives were met, although sometimes only after successive rounds of investment spanning more than one programme period, and infrastructure projects were usually well delivered and had at least some impact on quality of life.
- *Business parks* also had mixed results. Although, floorspace targets were attainable, the jobs that followed were significantly delayed, often beyond the period of assessment of a programme.

- *Structural adjustment activities* and industrial modernisation investments were problematic, often slow to yield results, reflecting the difficulties in changing from established industries to new activities.
- *Tourism* was an important target sector in the regions, and several programmes achieved good effectiveness, with some investments helping to change the external (and internal) perception of the region to enhance its wider attractiveness for investment and mobile people.
- *Innovation* measures also experienced limited short-term effectiveness, but with a (not always justified) expectation of more significant effects in the longer term. Better effectiveness was achieved where innovation measures had a greater emphasis on support for the private sector through knowledge exchange projects and a more sophisticated innovation system.
- Similarly, with *entrepreneurship*, regions reported high effectiveness where they had developed a good systemic approach to supporting entrepreneurship, with a mix of policies including incubators, finance, training and encouragement of a wider entrepreneurial culture.
- *Environmental* measures had mixed results, with good effectiveness for land and water reclamation projects, but limited success with clean technologies until very recently. Most regions had expertise in the restoration of derelict and polluted sites, but few had the capacity to promote clean technologies effectively.
- Experiences were mixed for *social, community and territorial development* actions. Conventional interventions such as urban regeneration schemes were generally effective and met objectives, but some of the softer community measures struggled to achieve targets, in part because of the sheer diversity of activities.

It is notable that those objectives that relied on public-sector intervention appear to have been more readily achieved. Short-term effectiveness appears to be higher for large-scale physical infrastructure, environmental improvements and local business and innovation infrastructure. Objectives dependent on entrepreneurial activity or funding by the private sector had a mixed record; there were common problems in achieving objectives relating to the business start-up rate, innovation and technology transfer, and employment creation. The assessment of achievements also highlighted specific problems with consideration of the additionality of interventions and deadweight.

The utility of Cohesion Policy interventions: did they matter?

'Utility' was defined in the study as the extent to which programmes led to impacts that were in line with 'society's needs and the socio-economic problems to be solved', which could differ from the goals explicitly stated in the programmes or which may have been implicit.

The case studies demonstrated that the ERDF made a significant contribution to regional development; quality of life was better, certainly in the regions that invested massively in basic infrastructure and services (for example, Andalucía). However, in virtually all of the regions, the success in addressing certain needs and problems were only steps on a longer journey of transformation. Most commonly, the regional research found that restructuring was incomplete, and employment creation was insufficient. Also, specific problems remained, such as demographic challenges, low innovation, poverty and organised crime (for example, Campania). Further, changes in regional needs and problems were sometimes territorially uneven. A major concern is that maintaining the capital investment and institutions established with Cohesion Policy support is a challenge for some regions, and that the economic crisis and fiscal constraints are undoing some of gains. Finally, there was evidence that the ERDF played a part in changing the culture and mentality of regions, particularly their internal and external image (for example, Nord-Pas-de-Calais).

Conclusions

This research represents the first attempt to assess the achievements of Cohesion Policy over the long term using a theory-based evaluation methodology, which sought to reconstruct the intervention logic of each programme and assess the achievements of the programme against the original objectives and in relation to the needs of the regions.

The study confirmed several of the problems with Cohesion Policy spending cited at the start of this chapter:

- A lack of conceptual thinking or strategic justification for programmes.
- Programme objectives that were neither specific nor measurable due to a lack of quantified targets and inadequate monitoring.
- Deficiencies across most areas of management to varying degrees.

Progress in addressing these problems has been slow and inconsistent, and some regions experienced a deterioration of implementation quality in the 2007–13 period. Nonetheless, there was evidence of improvement over time and the increasing adoption of what is regarded as 'good practice', for instance in the sophistication of strategies (evidence base, analysis and strategic focus) and programme management (project selection, monitoring and evaluation time).

Reflecting on the implications for 2014–20, the study provided support for key principles of the reformed Cohesion Policy:

- Greater concentration of resources was clearly needed. Especially in the early periods, programmes were characterised by too many projects targeted at local needs; decisions were governed by political interests with insufficient regard to value for money or overall programme effectiveness.
- The research emphasised the need for coherent strategies, integrated approaches to investment and sound project planning to underpin investment choices.

- Many of the problems identified were related to administrative capacity in some form.

Of all of the changes required, perhaps the most important is to encourage and support a more sophisticated approach to long-term strategic analysis, planning and management, drawing on theory and practice in ways that challenge conventional thinking and are rooted in a detailed understanding of the distinctive strengths and weaknesses of individual regions.

Note

1 The study was commissioned by DG Regio, and the full study report and individual reports on each of the 15 case study regions are available on the InfoRegio website (InfoRegio, 2015). However, the opinions expressed in this chapter and any errors are the responsibility of the authors. The study was managed by the authors (John Bachtler, Iain Begg, Laura Polverari and David Charles), with inputs from Riccardo Crescenzi, Ugo Fratesi and Vassilis Monastiriotis; regional research was also undertaken by a team of research associates – full details are provided in the preface of the final report (Bachtler *et al.*, 2013a).

References

Bachtler, J. and Gorzelak, G. (2007), 'Reforming EU Cohesion Policy', *Policy Studies*, 28(4), 309–26.

Bachtler, J., Mendez, C. and Wishlade, F. (2013a), *EU Cohesion Policy and European Integration: The Dynamics of EU Budgetary and Regional Policy Reform*, Aldershot, UK: Ashgate.

Bachtler, J., Begg, I., Charles, D. and Polverari, L. (2013b), *Evaluation of the Main Achievements of Cohesion Policy Programmes and Projects over the Long Term in 15 Selected Regions*, 1989–2012, Final Report to the European Commission, European Policies Research Centre, University of Strathclyde and London School of Economics, available at: http://ec.europa.eu/regional_policy/sources/docgener/evaluation/pdf/eval2007/cohesion_achievements/final_report.pdf (accessed 4 March 2016).

Davies, S. (2014), 'Assessment of effectiveness of Cohesion Policy', in L. Polverari and J. Bachtler (eds), *Balance of Competences Cohesion Review: Literature Review on EU Cohesion Policy*, Final Report to the Department for Business, Innovation and Skills, February, available at: www.gov.uk/government/uploads/system/uploads/attachment_data/file/336227/bis_14_988_BALANCE_OF_COMPETENCES_COHESION_REVIEW_2.pdf (accessed 22 April 2016).

Hart, M. (2007), 'Evaluating EU regional policy', *Policy Studies*, 28(4), 295–308.

InfoRegio (2015), 'Evaluations of the 2007–2013 programming period', available at: http://ec.europa.eu/regional_policy/index.cfm/en/policy/evaluations/ec/2007-2013 (accessed 4 March 2016).

Leeuw, F. L. (2012), 'Linking theory-based evaluation and contribution analysis: three problems and a few solutions', *Evaluation*, 18(3), 348–63.

Polverari, L. and Bachtler, J. (eds) (2014), *Balance of Competences Cohesion Review: Literature Review on EU Cohesion Policy*, Final Report to the Department for Business, Innovation and Skills.

2 Different approaches to the analysis of EU Cohesion Policy
Leveraging complementarities for evidence-based policy learning

Riccardo Crescenzi and Mara Giua

Introduction

In view of the increasingly strategic role and spending capacity of EU Cohesion Policy, its impacts and effects have become a subject of intense academic and policy debate. There is no agreement on the capability of the policy to promote economic growth and convergence among European regions, to reduce the gap between advantaged and disadvantaged areas, "to promote the overall harmonious development" of the EU (Art. 158 Treaty on European Union), to reduce disparities between the development levels of the various regions, and to strengthen their economic, social and territorial cohesion. Depending on the conceptual framework and on some key methodological choices, different studies have reached contradictory conclusions (Mohl and Hagen, 2010). Existing research based on 'traditional' regression methods concludes that the benefits of this policy are fully maximized only in areas with stronger pre-existing socio-economic conditions and/or when benefiting from favorable policy implementation capabilities. Conversely, with a few exceptions (Becker *et al.*, 2013; Crescenzi and Giua, 2015), existing counterfactual analyses have tried to capture the 'net' impact of the policy at the EU level, overlooking the potential heterogeneity across regions that takes center stage in regression analyses.

This chapter reviews and critically analyzes the existing literature on the factors conditioning Cohesion Policy and its impacts in order to develop an agenda for future research in this field and inform an evidence-based debate on the future of this policy. The literature is classified into two key categories:

1 research that has focused on the analysis of the territorial contextual conditions and on the factors conditioning the policy success and failure (*contextualization approaches*);
2 research that has tried to capture the 'net' policy impact by means of counterfactual methods (*identification approaches*).

The discussion of the general methodological challenges to the study of Cohesion Policy and its impacts is followed by the critical review of some key contributions on the contextualization and counterfactual identification of policy impacts.

The conclusion discusses the gaps and possible synergies between these (so far) distinct approaches and presents some ideas for a research agenda in this field.

Common challenges to the analysis of EU Cohesion Policy

Existing empirical studies on Cohesion Policy share a common set of challenges that are linked to the complexity of the policy, its nature, design and practical functioning (Baslé, 2006):

- The policy operates in very different local contexts and targets very heterogeneous economic and social regional contexts. Even if Cohesion Policy has a unified regulatory framework, it must address different national and regional circumstances embedded in a variety of institutional arrangements. Moreover, its operations comprise a multiplicity of measures and a multiplicity of national, regional and local rules and systems (Bachtler and Wren, 2006). The programs consist of a range of interventions (physical and economic infrastructures, business and technological developments, human resources, innovation and environmental improvement) based on a mix of financial instruments for many types of beneficiaries. This multiplicity of targets and contextual conditions is per se a challenge for any evaluation exercise.
- EU financial resources are bound to be an addition to national expenditure; the empirical analysis and the quantitative measurement of this 'additionality' principle remain very complex practical tasks (Bouvet and Dall'Erba, 2010).
- In terms of the timescales involved, policymakers are often called to take decisions on policy changes and reforms well in advance of the availability of long-term evaluations of the status quo; decisions on each programming period are taken well before the previous expenditure cycle is concluded, limiting the opportunities for policy learning. Furthermore, as regards spatial analyses, the policy's mechanisms deploy different spatial levels, making it difficult to identify an 'optimal' spatial unit of analysis for policy analyses.
- The lack of data and the heterogeneous definitions of relevant indicators further complicate the analysis. Both policy and economic performance/ outcome indicators can be measured/proxied by different variables and the choice of these proxies may have important implications for the results of the various analyses (Pastor *et al.*, 2010). In most cases, the policy variables under study are 'payments' or 'commitments' and 'GDP Growth Rate Per Capita' or 'Employment Rate' are used as proxies for economic performance. The choice of the policy variable can, in particular, be a determining factor for the design and final results of empirical analyses. The use of actual policy 'expenditure' data instead of 'commitments', for instance, means having to take account of the duration of the entire procedure leading to the final disbursement of the payments by the Commission. Depending on the administrative capacity of the various countries, this procedure could be very different in length and effectiveness, resulting in higher actual expenditure

in the most administratively efficient countries and regions. Consequently, the use of 'payments' as a policy variable can entail a mechanical correlation between national institutional quality and Cohesion Policy actual expenditure that can bias the analysis of impacts. On the other hand, 'commitments' are fundamentally a proxy for the resources potentially deployed by the policy. For reasons similar to those regarding payments (e.g. countries' differing capacities to fully develop planned projects), committed funds may differ considerably from the funds actually spent on the ground.

- Additional evaluation challenges are directly linked to policy design and implementation. First of all, we should consider that the territorial level adopted for policy targeting and evaluation may not be the most appropriate to identify impacts in their entirety (OECD, 2009). In particular, 'functional areas' are generally deemed a more valid unit of analysis than administrative/statistical regions (Stilianos and Ladias, 2011). However, statistical data are often impossible to collect and re-aggregate for functional spatial units.
- An additional challenge for measuring the impact of the policy is linked to the role of spillovers. For example, funds earmarked to 'Objective 2/more developed regions' generate spillovers in neighboring 'Objective 1/less developed' regions that can consequently benefit from positive externalities deriving from areas more capable of attracting investments. However, these indirect benefits are hard to conceptualize and account for in evaluation exercises (Baslé, 2002). Additional indirect effects may be even more difficult to capture. According to Mairate (2006) and also to Begg (2010), Cohesion Policy:

> [c]annot be judged purely on directly measurable outcomes, but needs to be judged on its contribution to the wider economic development effort and how it improves the strategic use of other policy instruments, with one source of added value being to push member states to follow good practice.
>
> (Begg, 2010: 85)

Different studies have taken different approaches in order to address the challenges discussed above. Some empirical contributions have focused on the characteristics of the socio-economic environment in which the policy is implemented (contextualization), while others have concentrated their attention on the development of appropriate counterfactuals in order to assess policy net impacts (identification).

Regional contextual conditions and Cohesion Policy

Putting Cohesion Policy in context makes it necessary to assess its links to social and economic outcomes by taking full account of the direct and indirect influence of a broad set of territorial factors. There is a consensus in the literature that studies of the relationship between Cohesion Policy and economic performance need to consider a broad set of territorial factors. However, different contributions have focused their attention upon a very heterogeneous set of territorial features. These elements are different and proxied differently. The degree and the nature of the policy contextualization that characterizes each empirical study strictly depend on the corresponding theoretical foundations. In contrast to the analyses based on purely neoclassical frameworks (e.g., Boldrin and Canova, 2001), later studies have explained economic growth as the result of a diverse set of determinants (e.g., research and development, human capital, institutional quality), non-linear processes/relations (e.g., innovation systems/institutional analyses), and the balancing of opposing forces (e.g., dispersion/agglomeration). The analyses developed in all these different conceptual frameworks investigate the impact of the policy within a 'conditioned' version of the convergence model.

From a methodological point of view, overlooking (some of) the elements that influence the relationship between Cohesion Policy and regional economic performance entails *omitted variable* and *reverse causality* biases in the corresponding regression analyses. This bias can emerge because some territorial elements are not considered relevant in a given conceptual framework. However, in some cases, they are simply not observable or unmeasurable. As a result, many analyses make allowance for the existence of an 'unobserved component' specific to each region/territorial unit by adopting a panel data approach.

Panel data approaches make it possible to partially control for (although not directly identify) unobserved time-invariant factors affecting the relation between the policy and the outcome variable. Time-invariant unobserved components of the regional growth process are isolated by exploiting the fact that data for the same observations are repeated over time. Since regional characteristics accounted for by the 'unobserved specific component' are likely to be correlated with other regional aspects included in the model, the Fixed Effect (FE) methodology is generally preferable to the Random Effect methodology (Rodríguez-Pose and Fratesi, 2004; Soukiazis and Antunes, 2006). In order to further disentangle both dependent and independent variables from any additional source of endogeneity, FE panel methods are integrated with different kinds of Instrumental Variable (IV) strategies (e.g. Bouvet, 2005).

Similar specifications have been tested by means of the General Method of Moments in order to remove endogeneity linked to the autoregressive pattern of the variables. The results suggested a 'conditioned' (Ederveen *et al.*, 2002, 2006), limited (Esposti and Bussoletti, 2008) or non-significant (Crescenzi and Rodríguez-Pose, 2012) policy impact. Conversely, by using appropriate IVs for both policy and growth, Beugelsdijk and Eijffinger (2005) concluded that Cohesion Policy has a positive impact on European regional growth.

An additional conditioning factor of the link between Cohesion Policy and economic performance is 'spatial autocorrelation'. The performance of the policy can be influenced by spatial interdependences exhibited by spatial units for both dependent and explanatory variables. In this sense, spatial econometric techniques through the use of spatial filters derived from spatially weighted matrixes can explicitly account for the non-independence of neighboring observations. Both spatial correlations in the residuals and spatial interactions among variables in the form of inter-regional spillovers can be fully accounted for by these methods (Griffith *et al.*, 2003). In these studies, the policy effect is generally non-significant (Mohl and Hagen, 2010). However, some studies identify a stronger performance for Objective 1 funds (Dall'Erba *et al.*, 2007; Bouayad-agha *et al.*, 2010, and a faster convergence for cohesion countries' regions (Ramajo *et al.*, 2008).

Panel data and spatial econometrics techniques make it possible to 'control' for unobserved components shaping the link between the policy and its outcomes. However, controlling for these factors forms only the basis for the contextualization of Cohesion Policy. Various contributions have explicitly included in their analysis, and focused their attention upon, a variety of (time-variant) territorial factors in order to explicitly identify their influence on the policy impacts, while at the same time employing panel data methods to account for unobservable time-invariant factors. In this emerging stream of research, a number of recent studies have looked at:

- *institutional* and *structural* regional factors;
- the interaction between Cohesion Policy and other (EU and national) policies with territorial impacts; and
- local political economy factors.

With respect to the *institutional* factors, the impact of Cohesion Policy is positively influenced by the degree of decentralization in the countries in which it is implemented (Bahr, 2008), as well as by the presence of national-level 'supportive institutions' in terms of inflation controls, trust, openness and the lack of corrupt practices (Ederveen *et al.*, 2006), the degree of openness of the economies (Ederveen *et al.*, 2002) and the national 'institutional quality' in terms of the rule of law, corruption, bureaucracy, expropriation risk and governments' treatment of contracts (De Freitas *et al.*, 2003).

With reference to the regional *structural* factors in the impact of Cohesion Policy, the geographical position of the beneficiary regions with respect to either the geographical 'core' of the EU (Neven and Gouyette, 1995) or national decision-making centers (Soukiazis and Antunes, 2006), plays a key role. The initial conditions of the regions under analysis are also crucial, with a positive effect identified in less developed European regions ('Objective 1' regions and cohesion-country regions) (Bouayad-agha *et al.*, 2010). Furthermore, country-level effects are also relevant; once regions are clustered by country, the positive impact of Cohesion Policy on convergence is not confirmed for Germany, Greece or Spain (Esposti and Bussoletti, 2008).

'Soft' regional innovation factors also influence policy impacts. Policy impacts are more pronounced in European areas with stronger technological absorptive capacity and weaker in the most disadvantaged areas (Cappelen *et al.*, 2003). In addition, Cohesion Policy has sometimes contributed to attracting R&D-intensive industries to regions lacking in the necessary endowment of highly skilled workers (Midelfart-Knarvik and Overman, 2002). Finally, regional innovative capacity and favorable Social Filters (i.e. innovation-prone regional socio-economic environments) are key pre-conditions for transport infrastructure investment under the European Territorial Infrastructural Policies (TEN-T) to produce their expected benefits on local economic development (Crescenzi and Rodríguez-Pose, 2008, 2012).

Cohesion Policy's relations with other EU policies—whether spatially targeted or sectoral policies with spatial impacts (e.g., the Common Agricultural Policy (CAP) or competition policies)—are extremely relevant (OECD, 2009; Duhr et al., 2010) to its impacts on territorial cohesion. EU institutions and researchers continue to stress the joint contribution towards cohesion of all areas of EU policy-making. Particularly important in this regard is the role of EU Rural Development policies; their 'spatially targeted' nature maximizes their synergies with Cohesion Policies (Crescenzi et al., 2015). However, it is increasingly recognized that the CAP's market measures (i.e. the so-called 'First Pillar' of the CAP) also have spatial implications. In particular, they are suspected to have a counter-treatment effect on cohesion (European Commission, 2010). In line with the sector aim of agricultural support, CAP resources can be 'captured' by dynamic, highly specialized, and more productive agricultural actors (Duhr et al., 2010). This feature of First Pillar CAP has a potentially perverse impact in terms of 'distributive equity', favoring the polarization of agricultural income, and excluding less developed areas from its benefits (ESPON, 2004) with negative impacts on regional convergence (Bivand and Brundstad, 2003; Bureau and Mahé, 2008).

The existence of this potential counter-treatment effect on territorial cohesion by the CAP's First Pillar is not, however, unanimously supported by the available evidence. Some studies show that it can be mitigated by rural development measures (Shucksmith et al., 2005). Other research concludes that the CAP does not counteract the impact of Cohesion Policy (Esposti, 2007) and that once regional characteristics are controlled for, its contribution to cohesion is even greater than 'Objective 1' funds (Montresor et al., 2011).

Finally, although their study has received far less attention in the existing literature, Garcia-Milà and McGuire (2001) have shown that national policies operating simultaneously at the local level can be an additional relevant influencing factor.

In order to complete the review of the territorial elements capable of shaping the impacts of Cohesion Policy, political economy factors must also be considered. First, the political situation within a country and a region, and the relations between various layers of governance influence the allocation process of Cohesion Policy funds. Furthermore, the implications of Cohesion Policy in the balance between 'efficiency' and 'equity' differ depending on whether countries have federal or centralized governments (Kemmerling and Bodestein, 2006). Moreover, meta-political objectives concerning the organization of political and administrative power also influence regional investments (Albalate et al., 2010); for example, in Spain the distribution of funding for the development of infrastructure has followed a logic of concentration in favor of core areas rather than redistribution in favor of the most disadvantaged regions.

To conclude, Crescenzi and Giua (2014) have attempted to cross-fertilize these somewhat divergent streams of literature, exploring the link between Cohesion Policy and economic growth in the European regions by comprehensively looking at a large set of territorial characteristics, including the simultaneous influence of other EU policies (i.e., the CAP and Rural Development measures). They conclude that Cohesion Policy has a positive and significant influence on economic growth in all European regions. This impact is stronger in the most socio-economically advanced areas and is maximized when Cohesion Policy expenditure is complemented by Rural Development and CAP funds.

Counterfactual analyses and the 'net' impact of Cohesion Policy

A growing body of research has attempted to identify the 'net' impact of Cohesion Policy. Contributions in this emerging stream of research compare the policy outcome with a counterfactual scenario. In this methodological framework, all contextual conditions—which take center stage in the literature reviewed in the previous paragraph—are simply instrumental to the identification of appropriate policy counterfactuals. In other words, these analyses can 'clean' the measurement of the policy impacts from other possible confounding factors, but this comes at a cost of remaining uninformative on the factors influencing or conditioning the estimated impacts.

This stream of literature leverages the strengths of experimental methods, originally developed for laboratory experiments in which individuals/units are randomly assigned to either a 'treatment' or a 'control' group. In this context, individuals who receive the treatment only differ from individuals who do not receive the treatment (the control group) in respect of the treatment itself. Under these conditions, the effect of the treatment can be estimated reliably (Angrist and Pischke, 2009).

Such a situation (randomized experiments), however, is not easily reproducible in the social sciences in general and in practical policy-making in particular. In this case, the subject of the researcher's interest is not a randomly assigned treatment but natural events (natural experiments) or behavior (non-natural experiments). Under these conditions, the control group is no longer the direct 'counterfactual scenario' of the treatment group, as the two groups could differ not only in respect of the treatment but also in respect of other factors that are neither randomly distributed nor identifiable (e.g., unobservable or unmeasurable factors).

Several statistical methodologies—Regression Discontinuity Design (RDD), Propensity Score Matching (PSM), Differences-In-Difference, Synthetic Control—have been developed in order to adapt randomized controlled trial methods to the non-randomized scenarios that are common in the social sciences. These quasi-experimental methods aim to create an 'as-good-as-random' scenario in non-randomized policy contexts by developing a counterfactual that minimizes the effect of observable confounding or spurious variables (Blundell and Costa Dias, 2009). Given their strengths, quasi-experimental designs are increasingly adopted in different fields of empirical economics. By contrast, so far, they have found more limited application in the empirical literature on Cohesion Policy even if they may represent valuable alternatives to classical regression tools. While the latter are valid for the exploration of the policy environment and contextual conditions, they are unable to assess the policy's exogenous 'net' impact. This criticism is particularly significant for territorial policies, as they are interdependent upon one another within the context in which they work. Experimental methods, by contrast, can overcome the methodological problem of endogeneity deriving from the interdependencies of the policy with respect to the regional context.

PSM methods applied to the identification of the impacts of Cohesion Policy suggest a positive effect on regional economies (Mohl and Hagen, 2010). In the case of Germany, a binary PSM approach identifies higher labor productivity growth in regions funded by Cohesion Policy compared to non-funded regions (Alecke *et al.*, 2013) thanks to the higher treatment intensities in beneficiary regions.

More recently, RDD approaches have leveraged the GDP threshold as a discontinuity for the assignment of the EU regions to 'virtual' treatment and control groups, studying the 'as-good-as-random' scenario of regions with GDP values as close as possible to the assignment threshold value. These studies suggest that European 'Objective 1' regions were able to grow more than other regions (Becker *et al.*, 2010; Pellegrini *et al.*, 2013). Some of these studies have also identified the level of regional GDP per capita growth that maximizes Cohesion Policy funds received by the treated regions and suggested that some regions are receiving too much funding and other regions too little (Becker *et al.*, 2010). Other contributions in this stream of research have leveraged administrative boundaries between 'Objective 1' and 'non-Objective 1' regions in order to develop their counterfactual. Giua (2014) looks at the Italian regions with this method and finds a positive and significant impact of Cohesion Policy on local employment. By following this same 'spatial RDD' approach, Crescenzi and Giua (2015) are able to estimate the causal impact of Cohesion Policy for a larger set of countries while isolating, at the same time, the role of national-level contextual conditions. Separate but fully comparable estimations for various EU countries (Germany, Italy, Spain, and the UK) confirm a generally positive impact of Cohesion Policy on the employment growth of 'Objective 1' regions, showing at the same time that national-level differences are the real key drivers of the policy's success and failure. Other contributions have aimed at estimating a heterogeneous local average treatment effect by showing that 'absorptive capacity' (as measured by the quality of regional institutions and the stock of human capital) is a relevant explanatory factor for differences in policy outcomes across EU regions (Becker *et al.*, 2013).

The strengths of quasi-experimental methods are maximized at the micro level. In this case, the properties of randomized experiments can be fully exploited; an 'as-good-as-random' scenario can be identified on the basis of the distribution of micro rather than macro observable and unobservable elements. However, notwithstanding their advantages, only a few studies have so far used these methodologies to assess the impact of Cohesion Policy measures (some exceptions are Accetturo and de Blasio, 2011; Andini and de Blasio, 2012; and Bondonio and Greenbaum, 2012).

Conclusions

This chapter has critically analyzed the existing literature on the impacts of Cohesion Policy and on the factors conditioning its success and failure. The literature has been classified in terms of its focus either on contextual conditions and conditioning factors (*contextualization*), or on the 'net' impact of the policy estimated by means of counterfactual methods (*identification*).

In analyses focused on policy contextualization, panel data methods and spatial econometrics have been extensively applied in order to capture unobservable components and possibly minimize omitted variable bias. A wide set of structural features of the target regions shape the influence of the policy on regional economic performance. However, the interaction of Cohesion Policy with other EU (and non-EU) policies, as well as with political economy dynamics, is also a crucial factor conditioning impacts. Conversely, the literature focusing on the causal identification of the policy effects has relied on a variety of features of the policy in order to build appropriate counterfactuals and—while often silent on conditioning factors—has identified a generally positive 'net' impact of Cohesion Policy on growth and employment, overcoming the lack of consensus of previous studies based on 'traditional' regression techniques.

The exploration of the existing empirical studies on Cohesion Policy suggests that different methods and approaches should be used in a converging, synergistic, and eclectic fashion in order to provide policymakers with relevant information on a variety of important features of the process of regional development in Europe and on how territorial policies can promote economic and social cohesion.

Therefore, in order to inform a truly evidence-based debate on the future of Cohesion Policy after 2020, an ambitious research agenda in this field should:

- further improve the contextualization of the policy in order to analyze simultaneously the territorial features and the policy structures and arrangements that shape Cohesion Policy's link to economic performance;
- progress with the clear identification of 'net' policy impacts by means of appropriate counterfactual methods at both the regional and micro (firm and individual) levels;
- develop stronger synergies between the analysis of conditioning factors and counterfactual methods in order to shed new light on what works (and what does not) in the large variety of territorial contexts of the EU, overcoming the fundamental limitation of the rigorous (but merely binary) results provided so far by most of the analyses based on counterfactual methods.

A necessary condition for the adoption of the research agenda outlined above by an increasing number of scholars and policy analysts remains the availability of high-quality open-access data on all aspects of Cohesion Policy design and implementation for all EU countries and regions. Many member states and the European Commission are already moving in the right direction, but further progress is urgently needed in this area.

References

Accetturo, A. and de Blasio, G. (2011), "Policies for local development: an evaluation of Italy's 'patti territoriali'", *Regional Science and Urban Economics*, 42(1–2), 15–26.

Albalate, D., Bel, G. and Fageda, X. (2010), "Is it redistribution or centralization? On the determinants of government investment in infrastructure", XREAP Working Paper 2010–15.

Alecke, B., Mitze, T. and Untiedt, G. (2013), "Growth effects of Regional Policy in Germany: results from a spatially augmented multiplicative interaction model", *Annals of Regional Science*, 50(2), 535–54.

Andini, M. and de Blasio, G. (2012), "Local development that money can't buy: Italy's Contratti di Programma", ERSA Conference Papers ersa12p464, European Regional Science Association.

Angrist, J. and Pischke, J. (2009), *Mostly Harmless Econometrics: An Empiricist's Companion*, Princeton: Princeton University Press.

Bachtler, J. and Wren, C. (2006), "Evaluation of European Union Cohesion Policy: research questions and policy challenges", *Regional Studies*, 40(2), 143–53.

Bahr, C. (2008), "How does sub-national autonomy affect the effectiveness of Structural Funds?", *Kyklos*, 61(1), 3–18.

Baslé, M. (2002), "Bonnes gouvernances recherchées et stratégies de connaissance de l'action publique: la place des évaluations", *Revue d'économie publique*, 10(1), 118–22.

Baslé, M. (2006), "Strengths and weaknesses of European Union policy evaluation methods: ex-post evaluation of Objective 2, 1994–99", *Regional Studies*, 40(2), 225–35.

Becker, S. O., Egger, P. H. and von Ehrlich, M. (2010), "Going NUTS: the effect of EU Structural Funds on regional performance", *Journal of Public Economics*, 94(1–2), 578–90.

Becker, S. O., Egger, P. H. and von Ehrlich, M. (2013), "Absorptive capacity and the growth and investment effects of regional transfers: a Regression Discontinuity Design with heterogeneous treatment effects", *American Economic Journal*, 5(4), 29–77.

Begg, I. (2010), "Cohesion or confusion: a policy searching for objectives", *Journal of European Integration*, 32(1), 77–96.

Beugelsdijk, M. and Eijffinger, S. (2005), "The effectiveness of structural policy in the European Union: an empirical analysis for the EU-15 in 1995–2001", *Journal of Common Market Studies*, 43(1), 37–51.

Bivand, R. S. and Brundstad, R. J. (2003), "Regional growth in Western Europe: an empirical exploration of interactions with agriculture and agricultural policy", in Fingleton, B. (ed.), *European Regional Growth*, Berlin/Heidelberg/New York: Springer, pp. 351–73.

Blundell, R. and Costa Dias, M. (2009), "Alternative approaches to evaluation in empirical microeconomics", *Journal of Human Resources*, 44(3), 565–640.

Boldrin, M. and Canova, F. (2001), "Inequality and convergence in Europe's regions: reconsidering European regional policies", *Economic Policy*, 16(32), 205–53.

Bondonio, D. and Greenbaum, R. (2012), "Revitalizing regional economies through enterprise support policies: an impact evaluation of multiple instruments", *European Urban and Regional Studies*, 21(1), 79–103.

Bouayad-agha, S., Turpin, N. and Védrine, L. (2010), "Fostering the potential endogenous development of European regions: a spatial dynamic panel data analysis of the Cohesion Policy on regional convergence over the period 1980–2005", TEPP Working Paper, 2010–17.

Bouvet, F. (2005), "European Union Regional Policy: allocation determinants and effects on regional economic growth", *mimeo*.

Bouvet, F. and Dall'Erba, S. (2010), "European Regional Structural Funds: how large is the influence of politics on the allocation process?", *Journal of Common Market Studies*, 48(3), 501–28.
Bureau, J. C. and Mahé, L. P. (2008), *CAP Reform beyond 2013: An Idea for a Longer View*, Notre Europe, Studies and Research, 64, available at: www.institutdelors.eu/media/etude64-cap-propositions-en_01.pdf?pdf=ok (accessed 22 March 2016).
Cappelen, A., Castellacci, F., Fagerberg, J. and Verspagen, B. (2003), "The impact of EU regional support on growth and convergence in the European Union", *Journal of Common Market Studies*, 41(4), 621–44.
Crescenzi, R. and Giua, M. (2014), "The EU Cohesion Policy in context: regional growth and the influence of agricultural and rural development policies", LSE Europe in Question Discussion Paper Series, 85, December.
Crescenzi, R. and Giua, M. (2015), "How does the net impact of the EU Cohesion Policy differ across countries?", paper presented at the RSA Conference *Challenges for the New Cohesion Policy in 2014–2020: An Academic and Policy Debate*, Riga, February.
Crescenzi, R. and Rodríguez-Pose, A. (2008), "Infrastructure endowment and investment as determinants of regional growth in the European Union", LSE Research Online Documents on Economics 23323, London School of Economics and Political Science, LSE Library.
Crescenzi, R. and Rodríguez-Pose, A. (2012), "Infrastructure and regional growth in the European Union", *Papers in Regional Science*, 91(3), 487–513.
Crescenzi, R., de Filippis, F. and Pierangeli, F. (2015), "In tandem for cohesion? Synergies and conflicts between regional and agricultural policies of the European Union", *Regional Studies*, 49(4), 681–704.
Dall'Erba, S., Guillain, R. and Le Gallo, J. (2007), "Impact of Structural Funds on regional growth: how to reconsider a 7-year-old black-box", The University of Arizona Discussion Papers, GRD 06–07.
De Freitas, M., Pereira, F. and Torres, F. (2003), "Convergence among EU regions, 1990–2001: quality of national institutions and 'Objective 1' status", *Intereconomics*, 38(5), 270–5.
Duhr S., Colomb, C. and Nadin, V. (2010), *European Spatial Planning and Territorial Cooperation*, London: Routledge.
Ederveen, S., de Groot, H. and Nahuis, R. (2006), "Fertile soil for Structural Funds? A panel data analysis of the conditional effectiveness of European Cohesion Policy", *Kyklos*, 59(1), 17–42.
Ederveen, S., Gorter, J., de Mooij, R. and Nahuis, R. (2002), *Funds and Games: The Economics of European Cohesion Policy*, The Hague: CPB Netherlands Bureau for Economic Policy Analysis.
ESPON (2004), *ESPON Project 2.1.3: The Territorial Impact of CAP and Rural Development Policy – Final Report*, August, available at: www.espon.eu/export/sites/default/Documents/Projects/ESPON2006Projects/PolicyImpactProjects/CAPImpact/fr-2.1.3_revised_31-03-05.pdf (accessed 1 February 2016).
Esposti, R. (2007), "Regional growth and policies in the European Union: does the Common Agricultural Policy have a counter-treatment effect?", *American Journal of Agricultural Economics*, 89(1), 116–34.
Esposti, R. and Bussoletti, S. (2008), "Impact of Objective 1 funds on regional growth convergence in the European Union: a panel data approach", *Regional Studies*, 42(2), 159–73.
European Commission (2010), *Europe 2020: A European Strategy for Smart, Sustainable and Inclusive Growth*, Brussels: COM(2010) 2020.

Garcia-Milà, T. and McGuire, T. (2001), "Do interregional transfers improve the economic performance of poor regions? The case of Spain", *International Tax and Public Finance*, 8(3), 281–95.

Giua, M. (2014), "Spatial discontinuity for the impact assessment of the EU Regional Policy: the case of the Italian Objective 1 regions", WP Dipartimento di Economia, Roma Tre University, 197–2014.

Griffith, R., Redding, S. and Van Reenen, J. (2003), "R&D and absorptive capacity: theory and empirical evidence", *Scandinavian Journal of Economics*, 105(1), 99–118.

Kemmerling, A. and Bodestein, T. (2006), "Partisan politics and regional redistribution", *European Union Politics*, 7(3), 373–92.

Mairate, A. (2006), "The added value of European Union Cohesion Policy", *Regional Studies*, 40(2), 167–77.

Midelfart-Knarvik, H., and Overman, H. G. (2002), "Delocation and European integration: is structural spending justified?", *Economic Policy*, 17(35), 322–59.

Mohl, P. and Hagen, T. (2010), "Econometric evaluation of EU Cohesion Policy: a survey", ZEW Discussion Paper, 09-052.

Montresor, E., Pecci, F. and Pontarollo, N. (2011), "Rural development policies at regional level in the enlarged EU: the impact on farm structures", paper prepared for presentation at the 114th EAAE Seminar *Structural Change in Agriculture*, Berlin, 15–16 April 2010.

Neven, D. and Gouyette, C. (1995), "Regional convergence in the European Union", *Journal of Common Market Studies*, 33(1), 47–65.

OECD (2009), *Regions Matter: Economic Recovery, Innovation and Sustainable Growth*, Paris: OECD.

Pastor, J., Pons, E. and Serrano, L. (2010), "Regional inequality in Spain: permanent income versus current income", *The Annals of Regional Science*, 44(1), 121–45.

Pellegrini, G., Busillo, T., Muccigrosso, T., Tarola, O. and Terribile, F. (2013), "Measuring the impact of the European Regional Policy on economic growth: a Regression Discontinuity Design approach", *Papers in Regional Science*, 92(1), 217–33.

Ramajo, J., Marquez, M., Hewings, G. and Salinas, M. (2008), "Spatial heterogeneity and interregional spillovers in the European Union: do cohesion policies encourage convergence across regions?", *European Economic Review*, 52(3), 551–67.

Rodríguez-Pose, A. and Fratesi, U. (2004), "Between development and social policies: the impact of European Structural Funds in 'Objective 1' regions", *Regional Studies*, 38(1), 97–114.

Shucksmith, M., Thomson, K. and Roberts, D. (2005), *The CAP and the Regions: The Territorial Impact of the Common Agricultural Policy*, Wallingford: CABI.

Soukiazis, E. and Antunes, M. (2006), "Two-speed regional convergence in Portugal and the importance of Structural Funds on growth", *Ekonomia*, 9(2), 222–41.

Stilianos, A. and Ladias, C. (2011), "Optimal allocation of investment and regional disparities", *Regional Science Inquiry Journal*, 3(2), 45–59.

3 Cohesion Policy and regional development[1]

Grzegorz Gorzelak

Introduction

The countries of Central and Eastern European (CEECs)[2] became members of the European Union (EU) after a difficult process of post-socialist transformation. It is still debated whether this transformation has been completed. The success of this unprecedented political, social, institutional and economic transformation and restructuring has allowed them to become part of the world's largest common market and to become actors in the development of the EU's manifold policies, to improve standards of living and to open their societies to the outside world.

In spite of unquestionable successes in terms of economic growth, social advancement, and political and institutional reforms, post-socialist transformation and the early years of EU membership did not allow the CEECs to overcome several critical weaknesses in their overall socio-economic and institutional structures. The global financial crisis of 2008–9 hit most of the CEECs especially hard; Poland was the only exception without a single year of recession. It brought starkly into focus the disjuncture between a fast growth in productivity and a rather poor performance in developing innovative capacities to support longer-term sustainable growth and assure the competitive positions of these countries in the future. Also, the processes of territorial development have led to an increase in regional differences, which have not been alleviated by Cohesion Policy whose benefits have been enjoyed by the CEECs.

Macroproportions

Considerable funds have been apportioned to the new member states within the 2007–13 financial perspective (Table 3.1). Out of a total €336.5 billion earmarked for Cohesion Policy in the period 2007–13, over €175.5 billion (more than half) was assigned to the ten new member states from Central and Eastern Europe. Although the spending of these funds continued into 2015 and 2016, to overlap with the next financial perspective of 2014–20, the truly 'rich' perspective of 2007–13 has virtually come to an end. It is an opportune moment, therefore, to look at some of the achievements and shortcomings in the implementation of strategies since the CEECs were granted EU membership, in particular those related to the use of EU funds.

Table 3.1 Cohesion Policy funds assigned to new member states, 2007–13.

Country	Value (€ billions)
Bulgaria	6,674
Czech Republic	26,303
Estonia	3,403
Hungary	24,921
Latvia	6,775
Lithuania	4,530
Poland	65,222
Romania	19,213
Slovakia	4,101
Slovenia	11,361
Total	**172,503**

There are two good reasons for analysing how the EU funds, mainly those available as part of Cohesion Policy, have been used:

1 There are statistics on the financing of specific initiatives under this policy, and data can be found on the pace of development in the territorial units in which such funds have been expended. This will be done for the example of Poland, for which preliminary statistics are available for the period post-2007.[3]
2 The experiences on how these monies have been spent have already been collected on a comparative basis within the new member states.

External assistance and development

The issue of external assistance in development processes, introduced in the literature in connection with the assistance extended to the developing countries, has been the topic of multifaceted research (Bauer, 2000; Pronk, 2004; Moyo, 2009; Ramalingam, 2013). The evaluation of external aid is, on the whole, moderately negative in relation to developing countries, as the majority of studies indicate that it fails to accelerate development (although some studies also provide positive examples). Two topics of discussion on external assistance seem to be of particular interest: the role of endogenous and exogenous factors in development, and the possible directions and effects of such assistance.

Assistance is granted on the assumption that it will serve to create the foundations for accelerated growth. Such aid is intended to help developing countries break out of the vicious circle of poverty and provide a stimulus for growth, which, once put in place, will trigger independent, speedy economic development, thereby enhancing convergence. By definition, assistance should be relatively short term, because offering it on a permanent basis would mean that it has failed to initiate or accelerate growth and has significance predominantly as a social measure. This invites the question as to the conditions for using such assistance for development. It is two-fold:

1 Can every kind of assistance act as a pro-growth stimulus?
2 How should it be used?

Let us start with the latter question, pertaining to the relationship between endogenous and exogenous development factors. I investigated this issue several years ago (Gorzelak, 2004). The essence of that research was that external assistance – just like other exogenous factors, such as increased demand for the raw materials present in a given country or region – can only have a pro-growth significance if endogenous conditions allow it to be used for accelerating the structural change needed to adapt the features of a given territorial socio-economic system to the current (or, even more desirably, future) development mechanisms and the resultant location criteria. Pronk (2004: 14) took a similar view when he wrote: 'Benefits of growth may occur to the poor through trickle-down effects, but often only if additional parallel or subsequent action is taken'. The key to benefiting from such assistance mainly rests with the political and economic elites, as they decide how a series of favourable external factors will be utilised.

This is the very reason why the message of one of the most important books in recent years, *Culture Matters*, is so pertinent (Harrison and Huntington, 2000). For some (Acemoglu and Robinson, 2012), 'culture' is a product of institutions, since institutional change is particularly crucial as it often (mostly in developing countries) poses a serious obstacle to modernisation and primary accumulation of capital (De Soto, 2000; North, 2005). It has also been argued that institutional deficiencies can even lead to negative effects of external assistance in countries with poor institutions (Ederveen *et al.*, 2006).

History offers many instances of the inappropriate use of a 'window of opportunity'. Poland and Spain of the sixteenth and seventeenth centuries can serve as model examples. Both of these countries were offered a historic opportunity which resulted in obstructing their long-term development instead of bolstering it. As Landes (1998: 175) wrote, 'Spain became (or stayed) poor because it had too much money . . . The Spanish . . . indulged their penchant for status, leisure, and enjoyment'. Landes (1998: 173) also wrote that: 'Easy money is bad for you. It represents short-run gain that will be paid for in immediate distortions and later regrets'. By the same token, Poland's dependence on grain exports, which were extremely profitable owing to the 'price revolution' in Europe that followed the Age of Discovery, led to an excessive economic, political and military strengthening of the gentry, the deterioration of the King's power, a return to feudalism, a dependence on agriculture and the underdevelopment of cities and industry – consequently leading to the erasure of Poland from the map of Europe for 123 years (1795–1918). The countries dependent on gas and oil exports are yet another example of economic, technological and social backwardness and instability, with Russia being the most obvious but also the most dangerous recent case (not to mention Venezuela).

Assistance to poorly developed regions, which in the 1970s was expanded by aid to regions losing their traditional economic base (industry, fishing), represented the 'founding principle' of the regional policy so far. However, the list of cases in which such assistance mostly played a social role rather than a pro-development one is quite long. The Mezzogiorno, Appalachia, the former GDR, eastern Poland: these are all among the best-known regional systems that have for centuries remained underdeveloped, despite receiving substantial inward assistance for several decades. Some measures aimed at overcoming the negative consequences of restructuring have been successful, yet also extremely costly.

We know the results of studies looking at the effectiveness of EU's pro-equalising regional policy (for an overview, see Bachtler and Gorzelak, 2007). Although drawn several years ago, the conclusions provided by Boldrin and Canova (2001) are still valid:

- Poorer regions tend to develop faster in periods of economic expansion, and slower during an economic slump.
- Three factors are responsible for a region's low level of income: overall low productivity of the factors of production, low employment figures and a high proportion of agriculture.
- Regional and structural policies mostly serve to promote redistribution goals which arise from the desire to achieve a state of political equilibrium (stability).
- Such policies have little in common with the desire to accelerate economic growth.

The overall conclusion of Boldrin and Canova's report was unequivocal: funds directed to less developed countries and regions mostly play a social rather than a developmental role.

Statistical analyses failed to prove that external funding could result in a lasting and substantial acceleration of development in these countries and regions. Rodríguez-Pose and Fratesi (2004) went a step further, writing that Structural Funds were not able to generate sustainable development of backward regions and that, in the long term, the traditional approach (relying on constructing heavy transport infrastructure, but also for R&D) may even have a negative influence on underdeveloped regions by crippling their competitiveness. This conclusion has been recently confirmed by a study conducted for the new member states by Komornicki (2014). Projects – mostly larger-scale infrastructure projects – initiated in less developed regions were for the most part carried out by external companies as these regions lack the capacity to do so themselves, which in consequence leads to the redirection of the funds to more affluent regions. A similar view is presented by Midelfart-Knarvik and Overman (2002).

As we can see, assistance will not necessarily foster convergence. On the contrary, there are reasons to suggest that it can lead to divergence. This is so because more developed regions tend to use the assistance more effectively than less developed regions owing to their greater endogenous potential. An analysis of the utilisation of the funds transferred to the former GDR can be viewed as proof here (Lenz, 2007).

Preliminary evaluations of the impact that EU funding has made in Poland indicated that these funds contributed to a more significant acceleration of the development of the most developed regions rather than of weaker regions (MRR, 2008; for a more general confirmation of this thesis, see Cappelen *et al.*, 2003; Marzinotto, 2012). This should not be surprising since, as Moretti (2013) argues, accelerated growth requires specific conditions (such as an innovative milieu and a 'thick' labour market, above all) that the backward regions cannot offer and that cannot be created by external funding either.

Furthermore, the possibility of receiving unconditional external assistance (simply because a region is poor) often develops attitudes of 'benefit dependence'. This is a most undesirable scenario which weakens the endogenous potential for growth and contents the local elites, who believe that making the frequently painful structural changes is not necessary because they can 'always' hope for receiving external assistance. In addition, becoming dependent on external assistance can also lead to the suppression of a region's own preferences and development priorities. The majority of the current development strategies of Poland – but also of other new member states (Ferry, 2014) – can be seen as a proof of this. These documents in fact follow the priorities formulated by the European Commission (EC), avoid formulating strategic choices (and a choice is the base for any strategy!) and are created in the most general way possible in order to accommodate any EU-financed programme or project. In general, this is but a mindless repetition of the framework rules adopted by the 'donor', in the conviction that this will secure a steady inflow of funds. There is also a tendency to look for problems that may be resolved using available sources of funding, instead of seeking funds to solve problems that are pertinent for a given territorial system.

It should also be noted that historical considerations are a barrier that is difficult to overcome in a short period (Gorzelak and Jałowiecki, 2002). In Poland, the old borders established in 1815 between the states (Austria, Prussia and Russia) that partitioned Poland are visible even today, not only as disparities in the development level of the entire historic regions, but also as belts of underdeveloped municipalities (or *gminas*) situated along the Prussian (later German) and Russian borders during the period 1815–1918. Contemporarily, it can be observed that those regions of the former GDR that had a more varied socio-economic structure and a relatively higher share of private enterprise reported more robust dynamics after reunification (Kawka, 2007). As we can see, 'easy money' is not always a pro-growth factor. In some cases, it can even work against its recipient. This should serve as a warning for EC officers, member state governments and, in particular, the territorial authorities that are the final beneficiaries of external assistance.

Two factors combine to produce the aggregate effect of the inflow of external funds and their absorption: the demand-side effects and the supply-side effects (they are included, for instance, in the HERMIN model). These are illustrated in the diagrams in Figure 3.1.

The demand-side effect is always positive, although only for a limited period, because the demand-side multipliers are higher than zero but lower than 1. On the other hand, the supply-side effect can be either positive, of zero value or even negative, in an utterly unfavourable situation (its potential changes over time are skipped).

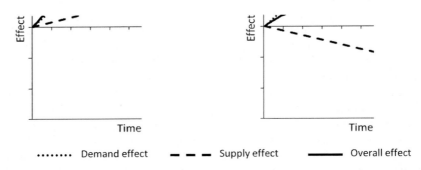

Figure 3.1 Demand-side and supply-side effects of the absorption of external funds.

Therefore, the overall effect, which is the outcome of the inflow of external funds and their use locally, is the sum total of the supply-side and the demand-side effects, the ultimate amount of which depends on how these funds were expended.

In the remainder of the chapter, we will examine to what extent these effects took place in Poland.

The case of Poland

The national level

Table 3.2 shows a summary of the EU funds made available to Poland under Cohesion Policy and Common Agricultural Policy (CAP) in the 2007–13 financial perspective.

The figure of €97 billion represents a gross amount that also includes Poland's contributions to the EU budget estimated at around 25 per cent of the total disbursements. This means that in the 2007–13 period,[4] the net EU funds assigned to Poland totalled around €73 billion. It is also estimated that a large proportion of these funds (50 per cent, or perhaps more or less?) 'goes back' to the net contributor countries, where the headquarters of the companies carrying out construction work in Poland and selling licences, machinery and so forth are located. It is difficult to interpret this 'returned' proportion of the EU funds. Anyhow, these funds are used to finance projects, the results of which will remain in Poland. Moreover,

Table 3.2 EU funds assigned to Poland, 2007–13.

Programme	Allocation (€ billions)	Share of allocation (%)
Cohesion Policy, total	67.9	70.1
Rural Development Programme	13.2	13.6
Sustainable Development of Fisheries Sector and Coastal Fishing Areas	0.7	0.7
Direct payments	15.1	15.6
Total	**96.9**	**100.0**

Cohesion Policy and regional development 39

such companies, when implementing construction contracts such as roads, hire Polish contractors and buy Polish raw materials and other supplies, thereby generating local demand and helping in this way (at least in theory) to enhance the effectiveness of management owing to upgraded infrastructure or technological progress. Given the above, this €70 billion should be reduced by an amount that is hard to specify; to be on the safe side, let us make a conservative assumption of €10 billion, which means an overall net inflow of around €60 billion in the period 2007–13 (and in fact up to 2015).

Is that a lot or not?

Let us compare these figures against other categories. In 2007–13,[5] Poland's aggregate GDP totalled around €2,500 billion, which means that €97 billion represents 3.8 per cent of this amount, although when expressed in net terms this share falls to 2.4 per cent. Taking this into account, the net contribution of EU funds flowing directly into the Polish economy can be estimated at around 2.5 per cent of GDP.

The period 2007–13 saw the inflow of around $104 billion in foreign direct investments (FDIs). In the period 2007–13, Poland invested around $25.4 billion abroad.[6] A comparison of these amounts indicates that the EU funds represent approximately two-thirds of the net value of aggregate inward investment into the Polish economy. It should be noted, however, that the inflow of foreign capital is driven by expected economic gains, to be obtained as a result of creating new jobs, undertaking production or providing services, and as such indisputably fosters development.

Since the EU funds are assumed to stimulate Poland's development, it would be worthwhile comparing them against the aggregate volume of investment. In 2007–13, this totalled around €400 billion. Let us set this figure against the proportion of EU funds that can be regarded as that which is really used to cover the costs of investment projects (to see their structure, see Table 3.3).

Funds expended under the Infrastructure and Environment and Innovative Economy programmes and, to a lesser extent, the Development of Eastern Poland programme and Regional Operational Programmes, are the most investment-oriented of all. Altogether, they total around €57 billion. Unfortunately, there is no information about what proportion of CAP funds is spent on investment and

Table 3.3 EU funds assigned through Cohesion Policy to Poland, 2007–13, by programme.

Programme	Allocation (€ billions)	Share of allocation (%)
Infrastructure and Environment	28.3	41.8
Human Capital	10.0	14.7
Innovative Economy	8.7	12.7
Development of Eastern Poland	2.4	3.5
Technical Assistance	0.5	0.8
European Territorial Cooperation	0.7	1.1
16 Regional Operational Programmes	17.3	25.4
Total	**67.9**	**100.0**

what proportion on consumption. Funds within the Human Capital programme are mostly spent on current matters, seldom on investment. Furthermore, not all of the funds from Cohesion Policy programmes are spent to finance investment goals. Since we are using rough estimates only, with a wide margin of error, we can assume that the value of investment projects financed by the EU funds is not higher than €60 billion (which is probably a seriously overstated figure anyway). This accounts for around 15 per cent of all investment expenditure made in the Polish economy, and around 35–40 per cent of the total outlay in the public sphere.

This is without question quite a sizeable amount if spent on pro-development projects and initiatives – which, as will be shown below, has not quite been the case – and should make a lasting input to the growth of the Polish economy. However, let us first reflect on the role that the external assistance may have in national and regional development.

Territorial data and hypotheses

It would be interesting to see how the potential benefits from the inflow of external funds are distributed across the country. Do demand-side effects prevail nationwide and in individual regions? Are supply-side effects also important? Furthermore, if convergence-based cohesion is to be the order of the day, the less developed regions should receive more funds to accelerate their development. However, as we recall from a short review of the analyses looking at the effectiveness of Cohesion Policy, so far this has not been the usual practice in the EU. Could such a correlation be observed in Poland?

The available data on the territorial distribution of the EU funds are rather fragmentary,[7] for a number of reasons:

- Information on the funds received under the CAP is available only for 16 voivodeships, with no disaggregation at the NUTS3 level, let alone at the county (NUTS4) level.
- The disaggregation of many notable projects (railways, motorways, IT systems servicing institutions operating many field branches, etc.) into smaller territorial systems is difficult, if not at times impossible.
- By the same token, territorial disaggregation of many smaller projects (training, consulting, etc.) is not possible as such services are typically provided in many locations.

As a consequence, we can only use approximate figures which, at the regional level, do not capture the large proportion of the funds that is as yet undisbursed and, at the municipal and county levels, do not include the expenditure on 'big' infrastructure of supralocal significance, training and advisory services, agriculture and rural areas.

One additional difficulty stems from the limited possibility to gauge the categories measuring economic growth or, more broadly, the development of the territorial units. In the case of voivodeships (regions) and NUTS3, such categories include GDP and the labour market situation, although the most recent GDP data for the NUTS2 level (voivodeships) and NUTS3 are available only for 2013 (however, in a different territorial division than for previous years – six new units were created in 2013). For counties (NUTS4), we can only know the value of the sum of their own revenues and shares in the national taxes of such counties and their constituent municipalities, which is a category that closely approximates GDP at the NUTS3 level, but is probably a less handy tool in the case of counties (for which there is no point in assessing the GDP).

The regional level

A full picture of the correlation between the inflow of EU funds (from all of the sources) and the regional GDP dynamics is provided in a study prepared by Misiąg *et al.* (2013). Figure 3.2 shows the breakdown of EU funds by voivodeship for the years 2004–11, in per capita terms.

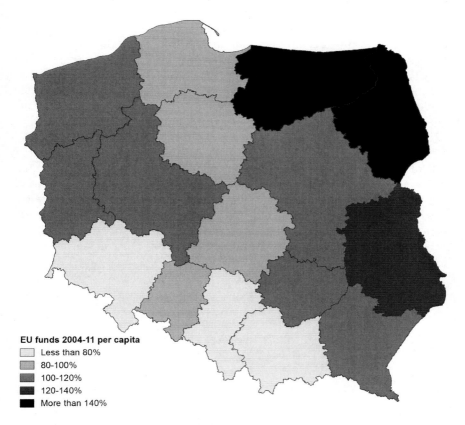

Figure 3.2 Expenditure financed by the EU budget, 2004–11, by voivodeship (per capita, Poland = 100).

Source: Misiąg *et al.* (2013).

The most underdeveloped voivodeships received relatively (per capita) more funds than the better developed ones. However, an analysis of this correlation indicates that despite such an injection of funds, until 2011 these regions were not able to achieve a higher rate of growth than the better developed regions, which in effect led to a further widening of the gap relative to the country's average GDP in per capita terms, and thereby to an increase in the disparities between regions across the country (Table 3.4).

The negative correlation between the volume per capita of the EU funds coming into the voivodeships and the growth dynamics of their GDP prove – as could be expected considering the patterns consistently observable in other countries – that external intervention failed to spur the development of Poland's weakest regions and help them to attain a faster level of growth than the national average. These regions were still growing more slowly than the regions with large cities (and, in some years, some of them even regressed in absolute terms), which was due to the metropolisation of regional development, a process quite comprehensively described in the literature on the subject (Gorzelak and Smętkowski, 2008).

A positive correlation between the rate of growth of the regional GDP and outlays on infrastructure was due to the fact that the better developed regions received a larger part of such funds. This is in line with the hypothesis put forward by Misiąg and his team, which held that development processes are influenced by the absolute value of the incoming funds rather than their value in relation to the size of the population.

The NUTS3 level[8]

Figure 3.3 shows the distribution of a proportion of the funds[9] (with an aggregate value of projects in the order of PLN 363 billion, that is 72 per cent of the value of projects completed in the programmes concerned in the period 2007–15), received from the EU together with the national contribution, in the period 2007–15, by NUTS3 unit. The distribution of the funds earmarked for enterprise support was similar to the average one, while relatively fewer monies for the development of human capital were spent in the south-western regions, and relatively more in the eastern regions. Interestingly, the two most urbanised Polish regions, Warsaw and the Silesian conurbation, received relatively fewer

Table 3.4 Correlation between the rate of GDP growth in Polish voivodeships and the inflow of EU funds, 2004–12.

EU funds per capita	GDP dynamics
Total funds	−0.59
CAP funds	−0.67
Funds for infrastructure from the ERDF and ESF	0.38

Source: Misiąg et al. (2013).

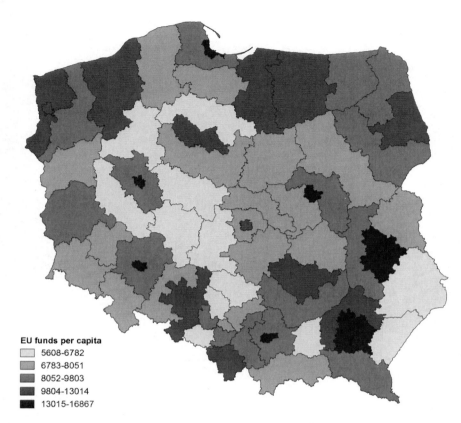

Figure 3.3 Per capita distribution of Cohesion Policy funds, 2007–15, by NUTS3 unit.

funds in per capita terms for the development of transport than less urbanised regions. This stands in contradiction to the recommendations formulated on the basis of analyses of the structure and effectiveness of expenditures in Cohesion Policy in Spain (De la Fuente and Vives, 1995) according to which less developed regions should receive relatively more funds for education, and the better developed ones for infrastructure (i.e. in each case for the sectors whose underdevelopment is a barrier to their growth).

Figure 3.4 presents the dynamics of GDP (real terms) in the period 2007–12, by NUTS3 unit. As in the entire period since the Polish economy regained its capacity for growth (1992), the fastest GDP growth has been observed in the metropolitan cores and their metropolitan regions, while the slowest has taken place in non-metropolitan ones.

In the period 2007–12, the correlation between the per capita expenditures from Cohesion Policy in the NUTS3 units and the rate of growth of GDP in these units was negative but weak (with the correlation coefficient of −0.28); in the

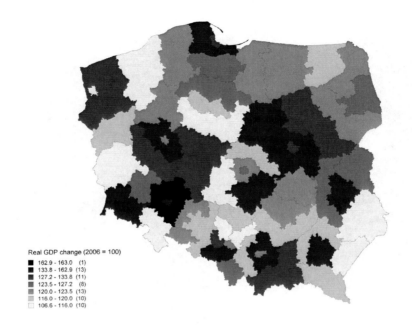

Figure 3.4 Dynamics of GDP (real terms), 2007–12, by NUTS3 unit.

period 2008–12, a period of slower growth due to the global economic crisis, the negative correlation was stronger (equal to a correlation coefficient of −0.35). This proves that up to the middle of the programming period (i.e. with only around one-third of appropriated funds spent as at 2012), the EU funds (excluding the CAP) failed to accelerate growth in the least developed regions sufficiently to drive their rate of growth above the national average, which would help them to close the gap with the better developed regions.

Naturally, we cannot know what the mutual relations between the rates of growth of these spatial units would be had they not received any support; it is quite likely that the disparities would be even wider.

The county level

Some more insight into the spatial processes can be obtained at a still lower level of territorial division of Poland: the county level – NUTS4 (Figures 3.5 and 3.6).

Both the absolute and per capita values were highest in the urban centres; the larger the centre, the higher these values. The per capita expenditures under the programmes financed by the EU (together with national input) in the period 2007–14 are not correlated with the changes in the counties' and municipalities' own revenues (Figure 3.7) or with any changes in the county labour market.

Figure 3.5 Value of Cohesion Policy projects, 2007–15, by county (NUTS4).

Figure 3.7 reveals that in general the counties with urban centres and also those located around them improved their situation at a slower pace than several rural counties located in the central north–south belt and along the eastern border. However, there are also several rural counties that have not achieved a fast positive change. Nevertheless, the correlation coefficient of the initial values of own revenues and share in taxes per capita, aggregated to NUTS4, and the dynamics of this category in the period 2007–14 equals −0.414, which shows a territorial convergence.

Extending the analysis to 2015 could provide more insight into the relationship between territorial growth and inflow of EU funds – but we will have to wait for the statistical data. Moreover, including data on funds transferred within the framework of the CAP – which obviously flow more significantly to the rural areas – could add a new explanation for the relatively fast growth of these areas.

Nevertheless, even these results lead to an observation that, in general, the more developed (urbanised) local units receive relatively more Cohesion Policy funds, and that at the same time these local units noted less improvement in the

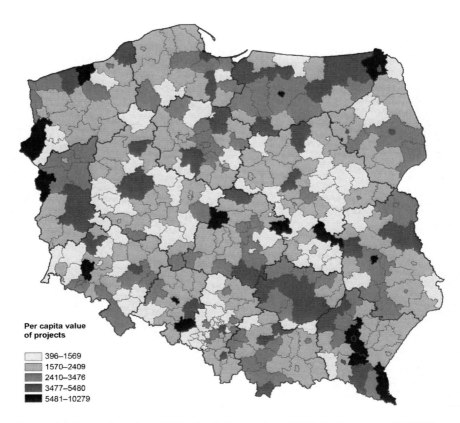

Figure 3.6 Per capita value of Cohesion Policy projects, 2007–15, by county (NUTS4).

financial situation of their local governments. This would suggest that Cohesion Policy has not become a factor of accelerated development at the local level.

Some insight into the possible impact of Cohesion Policy on factors of local development can be brought by examining the structure of this policy intervention in particular types of local units. Principal component analysis revealed that the values of factor scores for the first component (which positively correlated with such variables as the size of locality, value of own revenues per capita, total spending of Cohesion Policy funds and for R&D and culture, and negatively correlated with unemployment rate and spending of Cohesion Policy funds on labour market improvement) were the highest for the metropolitan areas. On the other hand, the second component (correlated with spending of Cohesion Policy funds on labour market improvement and on human capital) assumed the highest values of factor scores in peripheral, mostly rural territories. A hypothesis emerges that this second type of intervention could be a more efficient means of accelerating growth in less developed regions (thus supporting the suggestion made by De la Fuente and Vives (1995)).

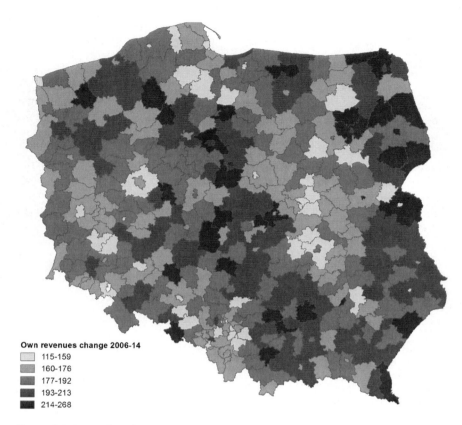

Figure 3.7 Dynamics of own revenues and shares in state taxes, 2007–14, by county (NUTS4).

EU funds as viewed by the municipal governments

In 2013, EUROREG conducted a survey in the municipalities (urban, urban-rural and rural, with a population of up to 50,000) on a number of aspects related to the operation of local governments in Poland. The survey was a follow-up to a similar exercise carried out in the period 1995–7. With the survey having received answers from over half of the municipalities (over 1,300 units), we can conclude that its findings are reliable, offering a comprehensive picture of the operation of local governments and accurately representing their opinions and views.

The survey found that, according to local governments, EU funds have helped to enhance the quality of life and, to an even greater degree, have led to improvements in the condition of the natural environment rather than serving to reinforce various factors driving economic development (Table 3.5).

More than half of the municipalities noted that the EU funds had average or little impact, or none at all, on the economic development of the municipality, enhancing the competitiveness of local businesses, improving the labour market situation or encouraging the inflow of new investors. Quite strikingly, the impact of the EU funds on increasing agricultural output was the least positively evaluated, which points to a predominantly social rather than pro-productive role for the CAP and direct payments.

Prior to the launch of the new financial perspective for 2014–20, local governments had strong and clear views on what they regarded as desirable changes to the way in which EU funds can be used and spent (Table 3.6). One popular proposal was to increase the volume of funds, particularly those earmarked for local infrastructure, and there were no major differences between regions in that regard. At the same time, local governments suggested relaxing procedures in the awarding of funds and also the auditing and reporting requirements. In a similar vein, respondents were in favour of increasing grants for businesses and of direct payments for farmers. According to the majority of municipalities, the budget for training should not be increased, which can be viewed as a negative evaluation of this type of project.

Table 3.5 Effects of the absorption of EU funds in the municipality (n = 1,251).

	Strong and very strong	Average and weak	No effect	Difficult to say
Accelerated economic growth	22.1	51.3	8.4	12.8
New jobs created	11.5	60.1	12.3	9.4
Increased agricultural output	23.8	37.3	19.3	13.1
More competitive businesses	15.7	49.0	11.8	16.6
Inflow of new investors	12.5	48.4	20.9	10.6
Decreased unemployment	7.8	55.5	15.6	13.2
Improved standards of living	44.5	41.0	2.8	7.1
Improved condition of the natural environment	55.9	30.1	4.0	5.0

Note: Since not all of the municipalities listed all of the effects, percentages do not add up to 100.

Table 3.6 Changes proposed to the EU programmes (n = 1,251).

		Percentage of municipalities (%)
Municipalities proposing changes		87.1
Type of change	Increase the volume of funds	81.7
	Loosen the criteria for awarding funds	68.7
	Reduce reporting and control requirements	71.5
	Increase non-returnable grants for enterprises	70.8
	Increase returnable grants for enterprises	63.2
	Increase funds for local infrastructure	83.8
	Reduce funds for training	52.3
	Increase direct payments for farmers	64.5
	Strengthen the LEADER programme	64.9

The opinions expressed by local governments on the effects of EU policies and desirable changes, thanks to which the EU funds would more effectively foster local development, indicate that these policies are currently regarded first and foremost as a simple and easy source of financing for local infrastructure and projects that improve the quality of life and enhance the condition of the national environment, but do not play any significant role in stimulating development. In addition, local governments would like these funds to be easily obtainable and subject to as little control as possible.

Conclusions and policy suggestions

The question of the primacy of one of the two effects, supply-side and demand-side, should be answered in favour of the latter. This conclusion relies mostly on the opinions of the representatives of local governments and on the lack of statistical correlation between the inflow of Cohesion Policy funds and the rate of territorial growth. Some positive impacts of the EU-funded expenditure on territorial convergence (of beta-type, not yet of sigma-type) may be discerned from the fact that the convergence process began around 2010. However, this convergence should not be attributed to the effects of Cohesion Policy alone. It could also be prompted by the transfers made within CAP. The effects of diminishing returns can also be hypothesised, as well as the different efficacies of particular types of intervention in different types of territory. It will be possible to draw more definite conclusions once data covering the entire period of spending the funds during the 2007–13 perspective (i.e. up to 2016) have been obtained.

As the GRINCOH project 'Growth – Innovation – Competitiveness: Fostering Cohesion in Central and Eastern Europe' (GRINCOH, 2015) reveals, the processes visible in Poland can also be observed in other new member states of Central and Eastern Europe. The empirical research conducted in these countries, coupled with statistical analyses made in Poland, may lead to the formulation of several suggestions for Cohesion Policy in the current programming perspective of 2014–20 (GRINCOH, 2015):

1   EU funding needs to be put into perspective. Cohesion Policy brings direct and easily measurable funds which translate into spending and incomes, and results in visible material effects. Not surprisingly, it is widely considered to be the main, if not the only, benefit of EU membership. In public and political discourse, benefits such as political stability and openness, accessibility to the largest market in the world, increased inflow of FDIs and new technologies, openness of labour markets across the entire EU, the exchange of students and researchers and so forth are often, if not usually, missing from the public consciousness. A major effort is required by both the academic and policy communities to put the role of Cohesion Policy into its rightful – important but not unique – place among all of the positive (and sometimes negative) impulses that come from membership of the CEECs in the EU. The alternative is that EU membership is associated exclusively with funding and that

when the budgetary transfers diminish, so does support for the EU (as has occurred in some EU15 countries).
2. The 2014–20 period may be the last phase of significant transfers to the CEECs under Cohesion Policy. It is critical for the CEECs – and for the policy – that the funding is used effectively for sustainable growth and cohesion. The experience of some EU15 countries is that the 'added value' of Structural and Cohesion Funds was highest in the second or third period of funding, once stakeholders were experienced in the management and implementation of the policy and, at the same time, were prepared to use the funds to promote innovation and change in economic development. For the CEECs, the main requirement is to shift away from the focus on absorption (important though this is to meet the decommitment rule) and instead concentrate on investing funds in economically and socially viable projects that have been developed through sound project planning and meet the strategic objectives of the programmes and the needs of the regions. Genuine strategic self-reflection should be strongly encouraged at all levels of governance – national, regional and local – which would create a basis for adapting the EU programmes and projects to the real needs of the recipient subjects.
3. The EU has agreed ambitious goals for Cohesion Policy in the 2014–20 financial perspective, especially in the area of performance and the contribution of the policy to the objectives of the Europe 2020 strategy. Indeed, the volume of funding allocated to the policy in this period is predicated on the policy's ability to deliver. As the current programming phase demonstrates, the EC is demanding that objectives are specified with reference to results, that realistic targets are set, that ex ante conditionalities are in place and that the performance of the programmes is properly monitored. The first review of performance by the Council and Parliament will be in 2017, with a particular focus on Poland and other member states receiving a major share of funding. This reinforces the need for managing authorities and implementing bodies to allocate funding in line with strategic priorities and to demonstrate the results being achieved.

Looking beyond 2020, the EU institutions have already begun to reflect on possible changes. Although an active debate has not yet begun in earnest, the EC will need to present proposals for reform by 2018. For the CEECs, post-2020 funding will almost certainly be smaller and there is a need to consider the following issues:

- **Domestic regional development strategies**: CEECs should actively take forward the recent work undertaken to prepare national development strategies, in particular the desirable strategic goals of social and economic development and the strategies, means and sources of domestic funding for realising those goals. There is a need to bring about a shift in psychological attitude – away from the assumption that the effort of developing the public sphere should be externally financed, and towards an acceptance of the need for a greater share of self-financing – which should already be promoted during the current financial perspective.

- **Development models**: Part of the strategic assessment – and one of the messages of this study – is the need to formulate a new development model. More stress should be put on the creation of innovative economic structures and entities at the expense of funding infrastructure, and also in the R&D sphere. Infrastructure should be created only where and when its underdevelopment is a barrier to economic efficiency and social cohesion, and not where and when it satisfies the ambitions of the national, regional and local elites.
- **Differentiation**: One of the major questions for the reform debate is whether the current multi-level governance approach remains appropriate. Differentiation in the regulatory framework has so far been limited and relies on EC services and member states being willing to adapt the regulatory requirements to the needs of individual countries/regions through negotiation. The question is whether a different model of managing the allocation of resources from the EU is required, with an alternative division of responsibilities and greater scope for differentiation between member states depending on their development needs, challenges and strategies and their administrative capacity. These are particularly pertinent questions for the CEECs, which have tended to resist a differentiated approach in the past.
- **External learning**: The lesson from other research is that openness to ideas, knowledge exchange and a willingness to adapt are key factors in promoting effective regional development strategies. Consequently, more engagement in interregional cooperation should be encouraged in the spheres co-financed by Cohesion Policy, especially in areas such as R&D and innovation creation and dissemination, where networking is critical. For example, the regional innovation strategies that follow the RIS3 pattern should be mutually co-ordinated – at least among the regions of a given country – in order to avoid replication of simple patterns of profiling regional R&D structures (as is already being done, in part, by DG Regio through initiatives such as the Smart Specialisation Platform).
- **More and better evaluation, and its use**: Lastly, evaluation should become more strategic and substantial and less formal. In several countries, Cohesion Policy has introduced evaluation as a part of the entire system of public policies – one of the most positive impacts of CEEC membership of the EU – not least because of the activities of the EC. However, evaluation often becomes an activity that does not translate into action directed towards the improvement of future activities. Moreover, the fragmentation of Cohesion Policy into several Directorates General within the EC (and its separation from another important policy of the EU, the CAP) translates into fragmented evaluation studies conducted in the member states. An integration of evaluation studies is urgently needed as part of wider evaluation strategies, and its implementation would allow for a more comprehensive assessment of EU interventions. It would allow for assessment of the combined/cumulative impact of particular EU policies (Cohesion, Agriculture, Innovation, etc.) on territories of the CEECs and their regions and localities.

Notes

1 This chapter is based on the Final Report of the FP7 project 'Growth – Innovation – Competitiveness: Fostering Cohesion in Central and Eastern Europe' coordinated in 2012–15 by EUROREG (GRINCOH, 2015), and on my paper 'The Cohesion Policy and development: a preliminary assessment' (Gorzelak, 2015).
2 Central and Eastern Europe consists of the ten countries that joined the EU in 2004 (Czech Republic, Estonia, Hungary, Latvia, Lithuania, Poland, Slovakia and Slovenia) and 2007 (Bulgaria and Romania).
3 There are some obstacles to getting a coherent picture for the entire period 2007–15. Firstly, the GDP for NUTS is available only up to 2013; however, in that year a new division was introduced, making comparison with the statistics from earlier years impossible. This has led to comparing the distribution of Cohesion Policy funds with the GDP dynamics in NUTS only for the period 2007–12, although data for Cohesion Policy expenditure in territorial units (NUTS3 and NUTS4) is now available for the entire period 2007–15.
4 As mentioned above, these funds are in fact to be spent during the years 2008–15/2016. In 2007–8, funds from the 2004–6 financial perspective were still being expended, and funds from the 2014–20 financial perspective will be made available in 2014–15, although their amount in the first year will be minimal. Therefore, it is difficult to assess the actual impact for the individual years without specific data from the Ministry of Finance, although it can be assumed that using the figures showing the budgeted inflows in the individual financial perspectives will be sufficient for our purposes.
5 The choice of periods used for comparisons is not a straightforward matter. The funds from the 2007–13 perspective have in fact been spent in the years 2008/9–15/6, while in 2007 and 2008 there was still spending from the 2004–6 perspective. Moreover, the 2014–20 perspective has already released some funds in 2015. Therefore relating the amount of the EU funds spent in the years 2007–13 to the GDP created in this period is one of the possible options, providing only rough approximations in real terms.
6 www.nbp.pl/home.aspx?f=/publikacje/pib/pib.html
7 Although the report *Impact of Poland's EU Membership and Its Cohesion Policy on the Country's Development* issued by the Ministry of Infrastructure and Development in April 2014 (Ministerstwo Infrastruktury i Rozwóju , 2014) did offer a territorial breakdown of the 2004–13 Cohesion Policy funds, these figures are misleading due to the much simplified method whereby the linear (national roads, railways) and national expenditures were broken down into voivodeships, counties and municipalities (and the term 'balanced distribution' is utterly unclear; it should probably be understood as average, i.e. the same for all of the analysed territorial units).
8 The data for the NUTS3 and county levels were collected and computed by Adam Płoszaj and Maciej Smętkowski.
9 The calculations are based on the KSI data (February 2016 version). The 2007–15 financial perspective included the following programmes: OP Human Capital, OP Infrastructure & Environment, OP Innovative Economy, OP Development of Eastern Poland, and 16 regional programmes. Only the projects completed in 2015 were considered. National and supranational projects were excluded: intervention categories: 12, 16, 17, 18, 19, 20, 21, 22, 26, 27, 31, 32, 34, 36, 37, 38, 49, 85, 86 (purchase of rolling stock, TEN-T and TEN-TIC infrastructure, national roads, local and interregional inland waterways, technical assistance); OP HC national projects ascribed to Warsaw were also excluded (IT development in public administration, etc.).

References

Acemoglu, D. and Robinson, J. A. (2012), *Why Nations Fail: The Origins of Power, Prosperity, and Poverty*, New York: Crown Business.

Bachtler, J. and Gorzelak, G. (2007), 'Reforming EU Cohesion Policy: a reappraisal of the performance of the Structural Funds', Policy Studies, 28(4), 309–26.

Bauer, P. (2000), *From Subsistence to Exchange, and Other Essays*, Princeton, NJ: Princeton University Press.

Boldrin, M. and Canova, F. (2001), 'Inequality and convergence in Europe's regions: reconsidering European regional policies', *Economic Policy*, 16(32), 205–53.

Cappelen, A., Castellacci, F., Fagerberg, J. and Verspagen B. (2003), 'The impact of EU regional support ongrowth and convergence in the European Union', *Journal of Common Market Studies*, 41(4), 621–44.

De la Fuente, A. and Vives, X. (1995), 'Infrastructure and education as instruments of regional policy: evidence from Spain', *Economic Policy*, 10(20), 13–51.

De Soto, H. (2000), *The Mystery of Capital: Why Capitalism Triumphs in the West and Fails Everywhere Else*, New York: Basic Books.

Ederveen, S., de Groot, H. L. F. and Nahuis, R. (2006), 'Fertile soil for Structural Funds? A panel data analysis of the conditional effectiveness of European Cohesion Policy', *Kyklos*, 59(1), 17–42.

Ferry, M. (2014), 'Cohesion Policy and its components: past, present and future', GRINCOH FP7 Project, WP8 Summary.

Gorzelak, G. (2004), 'The poverty and wealth of regions: assumptions, hypotheses, examples', in H. Karl and P. Rollet (eds), *Employment and Regional Development Policy: Market Efficiency Versus Policy Intervention*, Hanover, Germany: DATAR-ARL, pp. 101–22.

Gorzelak, G. (2015), 'The Cohesion Policy and development: a preliminary assessment', in A. Kukuła (ed.), *Cohesion Policy and Development of the European Union's Regions in the Perspective of 2020*, Lublin, Poland: Wydawnictwo KUL, pp. 113–31.

Gorzelak, G. and Jałowiecki, B. (2002), 'European boundaries: unity or division of the continent?', *Regional Studies*, 36(4), 409–19.

Gorzelak, G. and Smętkowski, M. (2008), 'Metropolis and its region: new relations in the information economy', *European Planning Studies*, 16(6), 727–43.

GRINCOH (2015), *Final Project Report*, available at: http://grincoh.eu/reports (accessed 31 January 2016).

Harrison, L. E. and Huntington, S. P. (eds) (2000), *Culture Matters: How Values Shape Human Progress*, New York: Basic Books.

Kawka, R. (2007), 'Regional disparities in the GDR: do they still matter?', in S. Lenz (ed.), *Restructuring Eastern Germany (German Annual of Spatial Research and Policy)*, Berlin/Heidelberg/New York: Springer, pp. 41–57.

Komornicki, T. (2014), 'Assessment of infrastructure construction: its role in regional development', GRINCOH FP7 Project, Working Paper, available at: http://grincoh.eu/working-papers (accessed 31 January 2016).

Landes, D. S. (1998), The Wealth and Poverty of Nations: *Why Some Are So Rich and Some So Poor*, New York: W. W. Norton.

Lenz, S. (ed.) (2007), *Restructuring Eastern Germany (German Annual of Spatial Research and Policy)*, Berlin/Heidelberg/New York: Springer.

Marzinotto, B. (2012), 'The growth effects of EU Cohesion Policy: a meta-analysis', Bruegel Working Paper 2012/14.

Midelfart-Knarvik, K. H. and Overman, H. G. (2002), 'Delocation and European integration: is structural spending justified?', *Economic Policy*, 17(35), 322–59.

Ministerstwo Infrastruktury i Rozwóju (2014), *Wpływ członkostwa Polski w Unii Europejskiej i realizowanej polityki spójności na rozwój kraju*, Warsaw: Ministerstwo Infrastruktury i Rozwóju, available at: www.mr.gov.pl/media/3244/Raport_Wplyw_czlonkostwa_ Polski_w_Unii_Europejskiej_i_realizowanej_polityki_spojnosci_na_rozwoj_kraju.pdf (accessed 20 April 2016).

Misiąg, J., Misiąg, W. and Tomalak, M. (2013), *Ocena efektywności wykorzystania pomocy finansowej Unii Europejskiej jako instrumentu polityki spójności społeczno-gospodarczej oraz poprawy warunków życia*, Rzeszów: WSIiZ.

Moretti, E. (2013), *The New Geography of Jobs*, Boston/New York: Mariner Books.

Moyo, D. (2009), *Dead Aid: Why Aid Is Not Working and How There Is a Better Way for Africa*, New York: Farrar, Straus & Giroux.

MRR (2008), *Oddziaływanie funduszy strukturalnych i Funduszu Spójności na gospodarkę Polski w okresie 2004-I połowa 2007*, Warsaw: MRR.

North, D. C. (2005), *Understanding the Process of Economic Change*, Princeton, NJ and Oxford, UK: Princeton University Press.

Pronk, J. P. (2004), 'Aid as a catalyst', in J. P. Pronk (ed.), *Catalysing Development? A Debate on Aid*, Malden/Oxford/Carlton, UK: Blackwell, pp. 1–21.

Ramalingam, B. (2013), *Aid on the Edge of Chaos: Rethinking International Cooperation in a Complex World*, Oxford, UK: Oxford University Press.

Rodríguez-Pose, A. and Fratesi, U. (2004), 'Between development and social policies: the impact of European Structural Funds in "Objective 1" regions', *Regional Studies*, 38(1), 97–114.

4 Econometric assessments of Cohesion Policy growth effects
How to make them more relevant for policymakers?

Jerzy Pieńkowski and Peter Berkowitz

Introduction

EU Cohesion Policy is expected to contribute to two main policy objectives. The first objective, explicitly stipulated in the EC Treaty, is to reduce disparities between the levels of development of the various regions and the backwardness of the least favoured regions. The second objective, increasingly important, is to contribute to economic growth.

The purpose of this chapter is to assess, from the policymakers' perspective, the contribution of a number of key papers that make use of econometric approaches to address the impact of Cohesion Policy on economic growth and convergence. The second section discusses the theoretical framework for regional growth and convergence and the implications for regional policy. The third section gives an overview of the scope and methodology of the reviewed econometric studies and their relevance from a Cohesion Policy perspective. The fourth section analyses the data on Cohesion Policy transfers used as an input into the regressions. The fifth section describes the results of the studies and the relevance of the results for Cohesion Policy. The final section concludes with an assessment of issues that need to be addressed to make future research more relevant for policymakers.

Theoretical framework of regional growth

There is an abundance of economic literature that attempts to explain the main factors of regional growth, their impact on convergence and divergence, and their implications for regional policy.

In the neoclassical growth model, economic integration, market competition and free trade lead to movement of production factors until there is uniform distribution among countries and regions. This leads to economic convergence between territories (Barro, 2012). In the absolute convergence hypothesis, per capita incomes converge towards one steady state for all regions. This implies, in principle, that economic integration promotes convergence and that there is no need for regional policy.

In practice, growth rates and the steady states depend on features specific to each economy, such as production factor endowments, the quality of institutions and various local factors. Regions with similar levels of production factors and other characteristics form 'convergence clubs'. Within their clubs, regions converge towards locally stable steady states, but it is difficult for them to move to another, 'higher' club.

The new economic geography argues that economic integration leads to regional inequality and divergence. With a general reduction of transportation costs, trade openness sends productive factors towards the 'core' regions where returns are higher, at the expense of peripheral areas. High fixed costs, positive externalities and the concentration of skills and research and development (R&D) activities stimulate agglomeration effects (Boldrin and Canova, 2001). The increasing gap between core and peripheral regions is supported by endogenous growth theory and innovation economics. These theories imply that if the goal of the economic policy is to minimise interregional inequalities, less developed and peripheral regions should be supported by regional policies in order to counteract the impact of market forces working towards divergence. However, such interventions will not necessarily be efficient from the point of view of maximising total growth.

Both of these contradictory trends – towards convergence and divergence – can be observed in practice within groups of countries or regions. As regards the EU regions, the recent Cohesion Report of the European Commission (2014) shows a marked tendency towards the reduction of disparities between member states and, at the same time, some regional divergence within member states. The economic crisis interrupted this process of regional convergence.

It is less clear to what extent these trends were the result of Cohesion Policy. Therefore, as described in the following sections, we have sought evidence in the recent econometric studies dealing with the growth effects of Cohesion Policy.

The scope, methodology and relevance of econometric analysis

We have reviewed a number of econometric studies that make use of econometric approaches to address the impact of Cohesion Policy funds on economic growth and convergence (Table 4.1).

In these studies, growth is usually modelled in line with the neoclassical model. The dependent variable is usually GDP growth per capita (or per worker). It is a function of a number of factors including initial GDP level, a variable representing Cohesion Policy and a limited number of other factors. The choice and number of explanatory variables for regression differs widely between studies.

The geographical scope of the regressions is usually very broad; the regressions assess the impact of Cohesion Policy on regional growth in EU15, or in less developed (ex-Objective 1) regions. Only a couple of studies analyse the impacts in particular regions (Le Gallo *et al.*, 2011; Becker *et al.*, 2012b), which reveals heterogeneity in the impact of the funds across regions. As the data for analysis end in 2006, there are hardly any studies concerning new member states.

Only a few studies, such as Midelfart-Knarvik and Overman (2002), use insights from the new economic geography. However, this study assesses the

Table 4.1 Comparison of models, variables and data used in the econometric studies.

Author(s)	Framework	Dependent variable	Main explanatory variables	Spatial dimension?	Cohesion Policy data used
Crescenzi and Giua (2015)	Regression discontinuity design	Variation in employment	Initial employment, dependency ratio	No	Objective 1 eligibility
De Dominicis (2014)	Neoclassical growth model	GDP growth per worker	GDP dispersion, initial GDP, population growth	Spatial Durbin model	Objective 1 eligibility
Fratesi and Perucca (2014)	Barro-like growth model	GDP growth per capita	Initial GDP, regional specialisation, territorial capital, ERDF, CF	Spatial autocorrelation tested	ERDF and CF transfers broken down by categories
Maynou et al. (2014)	Neoclassical convergence model	GDP growth per capita	12 variables including Structural Funds (SF) transfers	Spatio-temporal adjustment	SF transfers at country level
Pellegrini et al. (2013)	Regression discontinuity design	GDP growth per capita	Initial GDP	Results controlled for spatial effects	Objective 1 eligibility
Rodríguez-Pose and Garcilazo (2013)	Neoclassical growth framework	GDP growth per capita	Initial GDP, government quality, SF, infrastructure, education	Population density as proxy	SF and CF payments
Rodríguez-Pose and Novak (2013)	Neoclassical growth framework	GDP growth per capita	Initial GDP, investment, innovation, quality of institutions, SF	Proxy indicator in the regression	SF payments
Tomova et al. (2013)	Empirical model	Socio-economic development indicator (SEDI)	Initial SEDI, public debt and deficit, net foreign liabilities, ESIF	No	ESIF payments at country level
Becker et al. (2012b)	Generalised propensity score estimation	GDP growth per capita	SF transfers	No	ERDF and CF commitments

(continued)

Table 4.1 (continued)

Author(s)	Framework	Dependent variable	Main explanatory variables	Spatial dimension?	Cohesion Policy data used
Becker et al. (2012a)	Regression discontinuity design	GDP growth per capita	Initial GDP, SF, education, government quality	No	ERDF and CF commitments
Le Gallo et al. (2011)	Neoclassical growth framework	GDP growth per capita	Initial GDP, population growth, technical progress, SF transfers	Local spatial lag model	Not clear
Becker et al. (2010)	Regression discontinuity design	GDP growth per capita, employment growth	Employment, population, investment	Results controlled for spillover effects	Objective 1 eligibility
Mohl and Hagen (2010)	Neoclassical growth framework	GDP growth per capita	Initial GDP, investment, population growth, technical progress, SF	Spatial weight matrix	ERDF and CF commitments
Dall'Erba and Le Gallo (2008)	Neoclassical convergence model	GDP growth per capita	Initial GDP, industry share, unemployment, SF	Spatial weight matrix	No details given
Esposti and Bussoletti (2008)	Augmented conditional convergence	GDP growth per worker	Initial GDP, SF, human capital, R&D, infrastructure	No	SF payments per capita
LeSage and Fischer (2008)	Spatial Durbin model	GVA growth per capita	23 variables (but not SF)	Spatial Durbin model	None
Ramajo et al. (2008)	Conditional convergence model	GDP growth per capita	Initial GDP, employment rate, agriculture share	Spatial weight matrix	None
Puigcerver-Peñalver (2007)	Hybrid model	GDP growth per capita	Initial GDP, public and private co-financing, SF	No	ERDF, ESF and EAGGF transfers

Ederveen et al. (2006)	Neoclassical growth framework	GDP growth per capita	Initial GDP, ERDF payments, human capital	No	ERDF payments
Barrios and Strobl (2005)	Semi-parametric regression estimate	GVA growth per capita	Initial GDP	No	None
Rodriguez-Pose and Fratesi (2004)	Neoclassical growth framework	GDP growth per capita	Initial GDP, SF, employment	No	SF commitments (4 categories)
Midelfart-Knarvik and Overman (2002)	Shift-share analysis of industrial reallocation determinants	Change in share of country/region in an industry	Many variables including size of country, market access, SF, national state aid	No	ERDF, ESF and EAGGF expenditures per capita
Boldrin and Canova (2001)	Barro convergence model	Dispersion of GDP per capita and labour productivity	Initial GDP per capita	No	None

impact of Cohesion Policy funds on industrial location and not on economic growth. The neoclassical growth model has, however, been enriched to better accommodate the specific needs of regional growth analysis.

First, spatial econometric methods have been used to capture regional spillover effects. Regional economic growth depends not only on production factors of a given region, but also on the features of neighbouring regions and the spatial connectivity structure of the regions (LeSage and Fischer, 2008). Likewise, Cohesion Policy funds have an impact not only on the economy of the region receiving funds but also on the economies of neighbouring and other regions.

In order to overcome this difficulty, spatial econometric techniques have been developed since the mid 2000s: spatial lag of the dependent variable, spatial lag of explanatory variables, spatial Durbin models, etc. However, fewer than half of the reviewed studies have introduced a spatial dimension into the analysis.

In spite of progress in spatial econometric techniques, they still have one weak point from the perspective of geographers and policymakers: the parameters of spatial dependence are very simple in comparison to the complex trade, capital and people flows actually taking place between regions. In several studies, the same weight in spatial matrixes is given to a certain number of the nearest neighbours of each region, and zero weight to all the other regions. In three studies, other weights were used: the inverses of the squared distance between the centres of regions. Therefore, doubts may arise as to whether such simple weight matrixes give a good indication of interregional spillovers. None of the studies used more complex weightings known from the literature (Abreu *et al.*, 2005).

Second, some progress has been made on improving relevance and addressing the issue of endogeneity of variables used in the regressions.

Distinguishing the impact of Cohesion Policy transfers from the impact of the other factors of economic growth is not easy; catching-up by less developed regions is a natural feature under the neoclassical growth model, independently from the receipt of EU transfers (Becker *et al.*, 2012b). Growth regression results may be biased due to reverse causality; for instance, the allocation criteria for Cohesion Policy transfers are likely to be correlated with the dependent variable, economic growth (Mohl and Hagen, 2010).

There is also a risk that the omitted variables, not included in the equations, may actually better explain growth than the variables included in the equations. The literature stresses that there is a trade-off between the arbitrary selection of a small number of variables which may give rise to omitted variables bias, and the introduction of a large set of variables which may make it difficult to identify important ones (LeSage and Fischer, 2008). In the reviewed studies, the authors usually opted for a limited number of variables, which creates the risk that some important growth factors could have been omitted in the regression. In particular, none of the studies included national policies affecting regional growth (such as labour laws or minimum wage regulations). Other important regional growth factors not included in the regressions are the national redistribution of public funds to poorer regions and the business climate. Only a couple of studies included quality of institutions among the explanatory variables. However, many of the studies applied statistical tools to control for omitted variables and other sources of endogeneity.

The third issue on which progress has been made is the use of new econometric techniques such as regression discontinuity design (RDD), generalised propensity score estimation and other non-parametric methods. RDD has been used in particular to compare growth in less developed (ex-Objective 1) regions receiving more substantial Cohesion Policy support ('treated group') with non-Objective 1 regions receiving much lower or no Cohesion Policy support at all ('control group'). This method shows an important discontinuity of regional GDP growth at the threshold point corresponding to the border between Objective 1 and non-Objective 1 regions (75 per cent of average EU GDP per capita), which clearly shows the impact of Cohesion Policy 'treatment' (Becker *et al.*, 2010; Pellegrini *et al.*, 2013; Crescenzi and Giua, 2015).

In spite of the important progress made over recent years, there remain some weaknesses and unexplained issues in the analysed studies.

One of them is the impact of business cycles, which is not captured in the regression analysis. The econometric analysis covers long periods of time (7–14 years), depending on data availability, and is not related to the economic cycles. The literature shows that the impact of Cohesion Policy and other public investment in boom years is different from the impact in the recession periods. The impacts of business cycles also differ by region; the poorest regions tend to be less affected by business cycles than the more competitive and market-oriented regions (Le Gallo *et al.*, 2011).

Another unexplained issue is the consequence of the neoclassical growth model's assumption of full employment. In reality, many regions receiving Cohesion Policy funds have substantial unemployment rates. The studies do not explain whether this difference between the theory and the reality has an impact on the relevance of the estimations.

There are two further weak points of the econometric studies, which we analyse in the following two sections. First, econometric studies do not always use robust and consistent data series, and second, the implications for Cohesion Policy drawn from the results are not well developed.

Cohesion Policy data used for econometric analysis

The use of good-quality data is crucial for achieving meaningful results from econometric analysis. In this section, we examine in particular what Cohesion Policy funds data have been used in the analysis (see also Table 4.1 above).

There are several datasets for Cohesion Policy transfers that have been used in econometric studies, especially SWECO (2008) for 2000–6 and ESPON (2005) for 1994–9. Data about regional Cohesion Policy transfers for 2007–13 are not available yet, so analysis does not cover the period after 2006.

Some studies have made a significant effort to construct and integrate a broad dataset of Cohesion Policy transfers, even before the SWECO database became available (Rodríguez-Pose and Fratesi, 2004; Esposti and Bussoletti, 2008; Mohl and Hagen, 2010). However, even in these studies, it is not always clear which EU funds are included in the dataset: ERDF and Cohesion Fund only, or also ESF and EAGGF? Some of the other studies do not give details of which data they use for the Cohesion Policy variable.

Although Cohesion Policy payments are the main variable of interest in the examined growth regressions, many of the studies do not use the actual amounts of transfers in the analysis, but instead use dummy variables indicating whether a given region is eligible for Objective 1 transfers or not. This binary indicator is either included in the regressions as one of the explanatory variables, or used to distinguish two datasets ('Objective 1' and 'non-Objective 1' regions) on which separate regressions are run.

Using dummy variables for Structural Funds payments neglects substantial differences in aid intensities between regions. As regional maps in ESPON (2005) and SWECO (2008) show, regional EU transfers intensity varied from below 1 per cent of GDP in some Objective 1 regions to above 10 per cent in others. Higher intensity of transfers is normally expected to have a higher impact on growth, but it has also been argued that there are declining returns of EU transfers when their intensity increases (Becker *et al.*, 2012b).

Only a couple of studies use the data about Structural Funds transfers broken down by categories of expenditure (such as human capital, public infrastructure, business support), although such data are available (Rodríguez-Pose and Fratesi, 2004; Fratesi and Perucca, 2014). Including such data in the regressions is useful to examine the growth impact of different types of expenditure.

Finally, the issue of data availability for regression analysis concerns not only the data on EU funds transfers but also the other variables. For instance, several studies assume that technological progress and depreciation jointly amount to 5 per cent in all EU regions, which means that in practice their differences are not taken into account.

Results of the studies and their implications for Cohesion Policy

The majority of the reviewed econometric studies found a positive, although usually small, impact of Structural Funds on regional growth, especially in less developed regions. This small positive impact was found both by the studies using traditional growth regression analysis and by the studies using a dose-response function (Table 4.2). A small number of studies found no significant impact on regional growth, or even a negative impact. These differences in results may be explained by the different methodologies, variables and datasets used in the regressions, and also by the different time periods covered by the analyses.

The results of these studies lead to conclusions that are relevant for Cohesion Policy. Such conclusions are important for policymakers, who may be less interested in the details of the econometric approach and more in the policy implications.

However, the conclusions drawn from these studies – even from those with similar results to the economic analysis – differ substantially. Several studies conclude that Cohesion Policy is effective and should continue to focus on supporting

Table 4.2 Main results and conclusions from the econometric studies.

Author(s)	Main results of the study	Conclusions for EU Cohesion Policy
Crescenzi and Giua (2015)	Positive impact of Objective 1 interventions in Italy, Spain and UK; negative in Germany.	The results support the role of Cohesion Policy and suggest a stronger 'place-based' dimension.
De Dominicis (2014)	Inequality has a positive impact on GDP growth in less developed regions; no significant impact in the other regions.	The concentration of Structural Funds in a limited number of regions may enhance growth in the early stages of developments.
Fratesi and Perucca (2014)	Cohesion Policy not very effective per se, but more effective in regions more endowed with territorial capital.	Investing Cohesion Policy funds in regions more endowed with territorial capital is more effective.
Maynou et al. (2014)	Significant positive effect of SCF on GDP growth at country level; no significant effects on convergence.	No direct conclusions for Cohesion Policy.
Pellegrini et al. (2013)	Positive effect of Objective 1 interventions on regional growth, but modest impact on convergence.	The growth effects of Cohesion Policy are rather modest.
Rodríguez-Pose and Garcilazo (2013)	High impact of government quality on growth in poorer regions; smaller impact of Cohesion Policy funds.	Cohesion Policy transfers should be accompanied by improving local institutions.
Rodríguez-Pose and Novak (2013)	Positive impact of 2000–6 SF on regional growth, but no impact in 1994–9.	The effectiveness of Cohesion Policy has improved.
Tomova et al. (2013)	Cohesion Policy funds contributed to improving socio-economic development; higher impact when combined with sound economic policies.	Making Cohesion Policy funds conditional on sound economic policies is likely to improve their effectiveness.
Becker et al. (2012b)	Growth effects of Cohesion Policy transfers decrease with increasing transfer intensity.	A part of transfers should be reallocated to regions receiving less funds.
Becker et al. (2012a)	'Objective 1 treatment' has significantly higher growth impact in regions with good human capital and government quality.	Objective 1 transfers should be focused in regions with the best human capital and government quality.
Le Gallo et al. (2011)	Positive impact in some regions, negative in some others. Important spatial spillover effects.	No direct conclusions for Cohesion Policy.
Becker et al. (2010)	Positive effect of 'Objective 1 treatment' on GDP growth.	No direct conclusions for Cohesion Policy.

(continued)

Table 4.2 (continued)

Author(s)	Main results of the study	Conclusions for EU Cohesion Policy
Mohl and Hagen (2010)	Positive but small impact of Cohesion Policy funds in Objective 1; no clear results for Objective 1+2+3.	Objective 1 transfers are effective in promoting growth, but transfers to Objective 2 and 3 regions are not.
Dall'Erba and Le Gallo (2008)	Insignificant SF effect on regional GDP growth.	SF may be insufficient to counterbalance the agglomeration process.
Esposti and Bussoletti (2008)	Limited but positive impact of Objective 1 funds on growth; negative impact in some regions.	No direct conclusions for Cohesion Policy.
LeSage and Fischer (2008)	Spatial dependences are important for regional growth.	No direct conclusions for Cohesion Policy.
Ramajo et al. (2008)	Strong regional convergence, especially in Cohesion countries.	Regional policy has good effects in Cohesion countries.
Puigcerver-Peñalver (2007)	SF had significant impact on growth rates; higher in 1989–93, lower in 1994–9.	SF will not reduce gaps between regions quickly.
Ederveen et al. (2006)	Negative impact of SF on growth; positive only in countries with good institutions.	SF should be directed towards institution-building.
Barrios and Strobl (2005)	Inequalities rising up to a certain level of development, then decreasing.	SF would provide greater welfare if more concentrated in richer regions.
Rodríguez-Pose and Fratesi (2004)	No significant relationship between SF and regional growth; investment in human capital brings the best effects.	SF should support a more locally tailored combination of investment priorities, avoiding a focus on infrastructure.
Midelfart-Knarvik and Overman (2002)	SF affect industrial location by attracting R&D-intensive industries.	SF should help regions to specialise according to their competitive advantage.
Boldrin and Canova (2001)	No convergence in per capita GDP; small convergence in labour productivity.	SF is effective neither for growth nor for convergence.

the least developed regions, or that it is modestly effective. Other studies conclude that the effectiveness of Cohesion Policy has improved.

On the other hand, some studies conclude that Cohesion Policy would be more effective if it were more spatially concentrated in the most dynamic regions, while others argue that it should be more equally allocated between regions.

In general, the conclusions related to Cohesion Policy are usually less developed than the complex econometric analysis on which they are based. The studies often focus on the details of their econometric methodology and on the statistical robustness of the results, but usually do not sufficiently explain the complex economic mechanisms behind these relationships. Only a few of the analysed studies address the detail of Cohesion Policy. In a number of cases, the policy recommendations for Cohesion Policy appear oversimplified and may be difficult to implement in practice. In some other cases, the conclusions are not directly linked to the results of the econometric analysis, but repeat the usual recommendations for Cohesion Policy.

The conclusions usually concern Cohesion Policy EU-wide, or the whole group of Objective 1 regions. In the few cases in which the regressions lead to the results for individual regions, the results are not sufficiently differentiated (even when the analyses bring surprising results) because the analyses do not take account of regional specific factors to explain these results. This weakens the usefulness of these studies from the point of view of national or regional policymakers; the studies fail to provide convincing explanations of differences in the performance of regional economies.

Conclusions and suggestions for future work

The preceding sections have shown that progress has been made in recent years to improve the robustness of regression analysis of the impact of Cohesion Policy on economic growth. However, there are some issues that still need to be addressed to make future research more relevant for policymakers:

- The quality and consistency of data is essential. DG Regional and Urban Policy of the European Commission launched a study for a database on the ERDF and Cohesion Fund projects in the 2007–13 period, broken down by NUTS3 and by 86 priority themes; these data have also been integrated with the 2000–6 database. This new database is already publicly available for researchers to use.[1] The use of a dummy variable regarding the eligibility of a region for a certain category of Structural Funds instead of actual transfers should be avoided.
- The relevance of econometric analysis for policymakers would improve if the scope of the regression analysis were broader. For instance, it would be interesting to identify and test the existence of convergence clubs among the EU regions. It could also be useful to run separate regressions showing the impact of Cohesion Policy per member state and the impact of the main expenditure categories of payments (such as infrastructure, human capital, business support, etc.).
- Continued effort is needed to further improve the methodology of the studies. The modelling of the spatial dimension could be further improved to better reflect real interactions between regions. The choice of explanatory variables for the regressions is a difficult issue, but including some of the

variables omitted so far would be useful. Modern econometric methods, especially non-parametric estimation, also have considerable potential for use in regional econometric analysis, although their limitations need to be taken into account (data intensity, limited link to economic theory, etc.).
- The link between econometric analysis and the conclusions for Cohesion Policy drawn from these studies needs to be improved. Better knowledge of the details of Cohesion Policy would help researchers to draw more relevant conclusions about this policy. One of the possibilities would be a joint work of econometricians with academics and policymakers dealing with Cohesion Policy, in order to achieve synergies of knowledge.
- From the policymakers' perspective, the results of the econometric studies are not easy to understand for non-experts. Many of them use a very technical language, and the results are more difficult to interpret than, for instance, the results of macroeconomic models. The results of the regressions, and also their limitations, need to be more clearly explained.
- The econometric analysis of the impact of Cohesion Policy funds should be expanded beyond analysis of GDP growth.

Acknowledgements

The authors thank Laura de Dominicis and the participants of the Second EU Cohesion Policy Conference for their useful comments. The views expressed are those of the authors and may not be regarded as stating an official position of the European Commission.

Note

1 Ex Post Evaluations of the ERDF and CF in the 2007–2013 programming period, Work Package 13: Geography of Expenditures, ec.europa.eu/regional_policy/en/policy/evaluations/ec/2007-2013/#1.

References

Abreu, M., de Groot, H. L. F and Florax, R. J. G. M. (2005), 'Space and growth: a survey of empirical evidence and methods', *Région et Développement*, 21, 13–44.
Barrios, S. and Strobl, E. (2005), 'The dynamics of regional inequalities', Economic Papers No. 229, European Commission.
Barro, R. J. (2012), 'Convergence and modernisation revisited', NBER Working Paper 18295.
Becker, S. O., Egger, P. H. and von Ehrlich, M. (2010), 'Going NUTS: the effect of EU Structural Funds on regional performance', *Journal of Public Economics*, 94(1–2), 578–90.
Becker, S. O., Egger, P. H. and von Ehrlich, M. (2012a), 'Absorptive capacity and the growth effects of regional transfers: a regression discontinuity design with heterogeneous treatment effects', University of Warwick CAGE Working Paper 89.
Becker, S. O., Egger, P. H. and von Ehrlich, M. (2012b), 'Too much of a good thing? On the growth effects of the EU's Regional Policy', *European Economic Review*, 56(4), 648–68.

Boldrin, M. and Canova, F. (2001), 'Inequality and convergence in Europe's regions: reconsidering European regional policies', *Economic Policy*, 16(32), 205–53.

Crescenzi, R. and Giua, M. (2015), 'How does the net impact of the EU Cohesion Policy differ across countries?', paper presented at the RSA Conference *Challenges for the New Cohesion Policy in 2014–2020: An Academic and Policy Debate*, Riga, February.

Dall'Erba, S. and Le Gallo, J. (2008), 'Regional convergence and the impact of European Structural Funds 1989–1999: a spatial econometric analysis', *Papers in Regional Science*, 82(2), 219–44.

De Dominicis, L. (2014), 'Inequality and growth in European regions: towards a place-based approach', *Spatial Economic Analysis*, 9(2), 120–41.

Ederveen, S., de Groot, H. and Nahuis, R. (2006), 'Fertile soil for Structural Funds? A panel data analysis of the conditional effectiveness of European Cohesion Policy', *Kyklos*, 59(1), 17–42.

ESPON (2005), *ESPON Project 2.2.1: The Territorial Effects of the Structural Funds – Project Report*, Luxembourg: ESPON, available at: www.espon.eu/export/sites/default/Documents/Projects/ESPON2006Projects/PolicyImpactProjects/StructuralFundsImpact/fr-2.2.1-full_final-vers_aug2006.pdf (accessed 5 February 2016).

Esposti, R. and Bussoletti, S. (2008), 'Impact of Objective 1 funds on regional growth convergence in the European Union: a panel data approach', *Regional Studies*, 42(2), 159–73.

European Commission (2014), *Investment for Jobs and Growth: Sixth Report on Economic, Social and Territorial Cohesion*, Luxembourg: Publication Office of the European Union.

Fratesi, U. and Perucca, G. (2014), 'Territorial capital and the effectiveness of Cohesion Policy: an assessment for CEE regions', *Investigaciones Regionales*, 29, 165–91.

Le Gallo, J., Dall'Erba, S. and Guillain, R. (2011), 'The local versus global dilemma of the effects of Structural Funds', *Growth and Change*, 42(4), 466–90.

LeSage, J. P. and Fischer, M. (2008), 'Spatial growth regressions: model specification, estimation and interpretation', *Spatial Economic Analysis*, 3(3), 275–304.

Maynou, L., Saez, M., Kyriacou, A. and Bacaria, J. (2014), 'The impact of Structural and Cohesion Funds on Eurozone convergence, 1990–2010', *Regional Studies*, DOI:10.1080/00343404.2014.965137.

Midelfart-Knarvik, K. H. and Overman, H. (2002), 'Delocation and European integration: is structural spending justified?', *Economic Policy*, 17(35), 322–59.

Mohl, P. and Hagen, T. (2010), 'Do Structural Funds promote regional growth? New evidence from various panel data approaches', *Regional Science and Urban Economics*, 40, 253–365.

Pellegrini, G., Busillo, T., Muccigrosso, T., Tarola, O. and Terribile, F. (2013), 'Measuring the impact of the European Regional Policy on economic growth: a regression discontinuity design approach', *Papers in Regional Science*, 92(1), 217–33.

Puigcerver-Peñalver, M. (2007), 'The impact of Structural Funds policy on European regions' growth: a theoretical and empirical approach', *The European Journal of Comparative Economics*, 4(2), 179–208.

Ramajo, J., Marquez, M., Hewings, G. and Salinas, M. (2008), 'Spatial heterogeneity and interregional spillovers in the European Union: do cohesion policies encourage convergence across regions?', *European Economic Review*, 52(3), 551–67.

Rodríguez-Pose, A. and Fratesi, U. (2004), 'Between development and social policies: the impact of European Structural Funds in "Objective 1" regions', *Regional Studies*, 38(1), 97–114.

Rodríguez-Pose, A. and Garcilazo, E. (2013), 'Quality of government and the returns of investment: examining the impact of Cohesion expenditure in European regions', OECD Regional Development Working Papers, 2013/12.

Rodríguez-Pose, A. and Novak, K. (2013), 'Learning processes and economic returns in European Cohesion Policy', *Investigaciones Regionales*, 25, 7–26.

SWECO (2008), *Final Report: ERDF and CF Regional Expenditure*, Stockholm, Sweden: SWECO, available at: http://ec.europa.eu/regional_policy/sources/docgener/evaluation/pdf/expost2006/expenditure_final.pdf (accessed 5 February 2016).

Tomova, M., Rezessy, A., Lenkowski, A. and Maincent E. (2013), 'EU governance and EU funds: testing the effectiveness of EU funds in a sound macroeconomic framework', European Commission Economic Papers, 510.

5 Does Cohesion Policy affect regional growth?

New evidence from a semi-parametric approach

Nicola Pontarollo

Introduction

Cohesion Policy is the main instrument used to promote and achieve a balanced and lasting economic growth across the European Union (EU) and absorbs more than one-third of the EU's budget. Its impact on growth is still the subject of debate because existing empirical studies do not have consistent findings.[1] Among the most recent studies, Rodríguez-Pose and Novak (2013) and Pinho *et al.* (2015) find similar results: the returns on investment through Structural Funds improved between the second and third programming periods and have a positive impact on growth in richer countries and in better-off regions within countries. Using a Bayesian spatio-temporal econometric model, Maynou *et al.* (2016) state that Structural Funds have had a positive effect on the GDP growth per capita of recipient regions over the period 1990–2010. Finally, Rodríguez-Pose and Garcilazo (2015) show that regional institutional quality has a direct effect both on economic growth and in moderating the efficiency of the expenditure of Structural Funds.

This study is intended to contribute to the debate on the efficiency of Cohesion Policy expenditure from a new methodological perspective that consists of the analysis of the impact of Structural Funds devoted to three precise areas – productive environment, human capital and infrastructure – using a data-driven methodology that accounts for the possible heterogeneous response due to non-linearities. The analysis, which is performed on 202 regions of the EU15 countries over the programming period 2000–6, uses both GDP growth per capita (GDP/POP) and GVA per worker (GVA/EMP) as indicators for two main reasons: the first is the fundamental role of productivity in supporting lasting GDP growth per capita (Krugman, 1992), and the second is because, according to Porter (1990), "the only meaningful concept of competitiveness at the national level is productivity", which is one of the main objectives of the Lisbon Agenda. The analysis of growth through these two indicators also allows us to verify the degree to which Cohesion Policy has been reshaped as a consequence of the Lisbon Agenda. The main guidelines of this strategy were related to the importance of 'soft' investments, which, in this study, are basically the funds for productive environment and human capital. Information regarding the allocation of these funds across countries allows us to contextualise the results of the estimates and arrive at some policy recommendations for the possible redesign of Cohesion Policy for future programming periods.

The study is divided into four sections. In the first section, I perform an analysis of the allocation of Structural Funds in relation to the Lisbon Agenda and an outlook of European regional growth. In the second section, I present the economic model and econometric strategy used in the estimates. In the third section, I present the empirical results, while in the last section I set out some conclusions and policy recommendations.

The allocation of Structural Funds and European regional growth

The Lisbon Agenda – a strategy devised in 2000 that aimed to make the EU "the most competitive and dynamic knowledge-based economy in the world, capable of sustainable economic growth with more and better jobs and greater social cohesion" by 2010 (European Council, 2000) – shaped the nature of European regional support in the programming period 2000–6.

The main priority of the Lisbon Agenda was to improve the competitiveness of the EU, without sacrificing improved standards of living, labour market quality and environment quality. The guidelines of the Lisbon Agenda were oriented towards all of the member states, irrespective of whether they were developed or underdeveloped, and were non-binding in nature. In this respect, this strategy runs partially counter to the idea behind the implementation of Structural Funds, whose fundamental aim is cohesion, since they support a balanced development among regions by concentrating resources in areas defined by either relative poverty, peripherality or structural economic weaknesses (Barca, 2009). This is reflected in the amount of resources devoted to regions with a GDP per capita lower than 75 per cent of the EU average, which corresponds to 80 per cent of the total funds. In this chapter, I will consider total Structural Funds expenditure for the programming period 2000–6,[2] which comprises funds for Objective 1, Objective 2, Cohesion Funds, Urban and Interreg IIIA.[3]

Regarding the expenditure areas, these are reported in Figure 5.1. With the exception of Germany, the countries characterised by the majority of less developed regions – Portugal, Spain, Ireland, Italy and Greece – tend to concentrate on physical infrastructure. The European average for this area of intervention is 64.5 per cent and only Italy is below this threshold (54.9 per cent). The proportion of funds used for human resources is very low, with an average of just 2.2 per cent. The variance between different countries is not so strong, with northern countries tending to put more focus on this particular area. Finally, regarding the expenditure on productive environment, Greece, Ireland, Spain and Portugal are the only countries well below the European average of 33.3 per cent.

To sum up the investment strategies of EU countries with respect to the use of Structural Funds, we have seen that Greece, Ireland, Spain and Portugal tend to focus on infrastructure at the cost of productive environment. Italy has a more

Does Cohesion Policy affect regional growth? 71

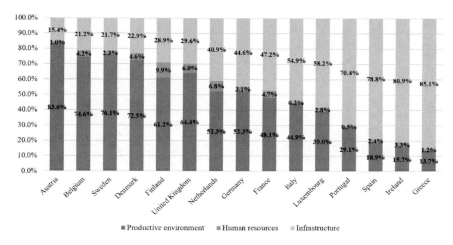

Figure 5.1 Funds by area of intervention.

balanced allocation but with a distinct preference for infrastructure that absorbs 55 per cent of total resources. The Netherlands, Germany and France allocate around a half of their resources to productive environment and the rest to infrastructure, while the rest of the countries devote more than 60 per cent of funds to productive environment.

The analysis of the distribution of Structural Funds helps us to understand the extent to which Cohesion Policy and the Lisbon Agenda work in the same direction. In this respect, we can note some shortcomings that undermine the effectiveness of the funds from the perspective of the Lisbon Agenda. The first problem concerns the very small proportion of the budget devoted to human resources and the excessive emphasis on infrastructure especially in countries with less developed regions. The primary focus of some countries on 'hard' investments (principally physical infrastructure) rather than on 'softer' investments (notably human capital and research capacity) that are at the heart of the Lisbon Agenda raises doubts about the effectiveness of the intervention financed by Structural Funds.

These doubts are related not only to the allocation and possible effects of Structural Funds but also to the sustainability of economic development in the medium and long term. In this regard, Figure 5.2 shows the density of the distribution of GDP growth per capita and GVA per worker over the 2000–6 period.[4] The mismatch of the two distributions highlights that there are regions that experience growth in GDP per capita but not in labour productivity. During the programming period in question, in some countries like Spain, GDP per capita increases while GVA per worker actually decreases due to a shift in employment patterns in the service and construction sectors (European Commission, 2007).

The twin-peaks configuration of productivity growth shows that there is a group of regions whose productivity does not increase (the left peak around 0 per cent), and another group of regions, the majority, whose productivity grows

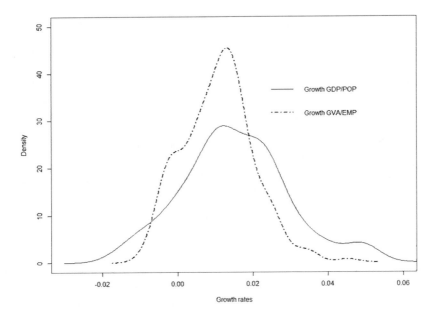

Figure 5.2 Density of GDP growth per capita and GVA per worker over the 2000–6 period.

at the rate of 1.8 per cent. In contrast, the distribution of GDP growth per capita is much more homogeneous and is concentrated between 1.8 per cent and 2 per cent. To strengthen this evidence, I have to stress that the correlation between growth of labour productivity and GDP per capita is 0.58, highlighting that – as shown in Figure 5.3 – the problem is not only specific to Spain. In Figure 5.3, we can observe the mismatch between the growth of GDP per person and GVA per worker over the period in question by country. Regardless of the actual growth rates of each individual country, the cases in which this mismatch is most pronounced are Finland, Luxembourg, Greece, Ireland, Spain and Italy; the latter four countries, together with Portugal, are the recipients of the greatest amounts of funds for their less developed regions.

To conclude, an in-depth analysis of the relationship between productivity and GDP growth per capita is not the main objective of this chapter, but their different paths make it important to estimate the impact of Structural Funds on each of them. The underlying idea, in fact, is to understand whether Structural Funds played a role in sustaining growth and, if so, whether they had a differentiated impact according to their area of intervention.

Economic model and econometric strategy

The impact of Structural Funds on the regional growth process of the EU15 countries over the 2000–6 programming period can be evaluated using a model that assumes the following form (Rodríguez-Pose and Fratesi, 2004):

Does Cohesion Policy affect regional growth? 73

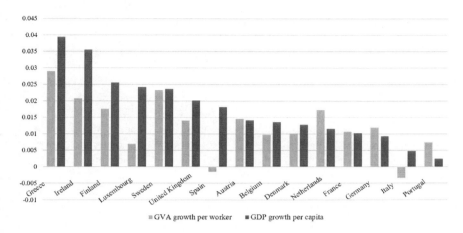

Figure 5.3 GDP growth per capita and GVA per worker over the 2000–6 period, by country.

$$\frac{\ln(Y_{i,T}) - \ln(Y_{i,0})}{T} = \beta \ln(Y_{i,0}) + \gamma \, F.prenv_i + \vartheta \, F.hcap_i + \phi \, F.infras_i + \varepsilon_i \quad (5.1)$$

where:

$$\frac{\ln(Y_{i,T}) - \ln(Y_{i,0})}{T}$$

is either the average regional growth rate of productivity (GVA/EMP) or GDP per capita (GDP/POP);

$\ln(Y_{i,0})$ is the natural logarithm of the level of regional GVA/EMP or GDP/POP in 2000, the initial year (the negative and significant coefficient addresses the existence of convergence);

$\ln(Y_{i,T})$ is the natural logarithm of the level of regional GVA/EMP or GDP/POP in 2006, the last year;

$F.prenv_i$ is the average funds allocated to productive environment in the programming period over the initial GVA or GDP;

$F.hcap_i$ is the average funds allocated to human capital in the programming period over the initial GVA or GDP;

$F.infras_i$ is the average funds allocated to infrastructure in the programming period over the initial GVA or GDP;

ε_i is an idiosyncratic error;
i is the region of which there are 202;
T is the interval of year of the sample, which are six.

Finally, the parameters β, γ, ϑ and ϕ have to be estimated.

From a theoretical point of view, Esposti and Bussoletti (2008) state that Structural Funds can affect long-term growth in various ways. They can increase the regional investment rate and/or total regional productivity by improving the initial level of technology or its growth rate, but they can also lead to an increase in the workforce growth rate, which in turn negatively influences the steady-state level. Barro (1990), on the other hand, observes that increased expenditure on public infrastructure may raise the efficiency of private capital, thereby speeding up convergence.

The empirical estimation strategy relies upon the General Additive Model (GAM) (Hastie and Tibshirani, 1986, 1990), a semi-parametric extension of Generalised Linear Models (GLMs), in which the only underlying assumptions made are that the functions are additive and that the components are "smooth". These kinds of data-driven models have been adopted to only a limited extent in the literature to explain non-linearity in growth, and they have not been used to test the effects of Structural Funds. At the European regional level, I can mention only the studies by Basile and Gress (2005), Basile (2008), Basile *et al.* (2012) and Fotopoulos (2012). Basile and Gress (2005) propose semi-parametric spatial autoregressive and spatial error models to analyse the growth behaviour of 156 European regions over the 1988–2000 period. Basile (2008) estimates a semi-parametric spatial Durbin model over the same period. Basile *et al.* (2012) use a semi-parametric lag and spatial Durbin model to analyse 249 regions of the EU27 countries over the period 1990–2004 to estimate the role of various types of proximity (relational, social and technological) on growth. Finally, Fotopoulos (2012) analyses regional development focusing on entrepreneurship with a partial linear model. The common point of these studies is that non-linearities are evident in all cases, regardless of the techniques used in the estimation.

Like GLMs, the GAM employed in this analysis uses a link function to establish a relationship between the mean of the response variable and a smooth function of the explanatory variables.

The GAM generalises the linear model by modelling the expected value of Y as

$$E(Y) = f(X_1; \ldots; X_p) = s_0 + s_1(X_1) + \ldots + s_p(X_p) \tag{5.2}$$

where $s_j(X_i)$, $i = 1; \ldots; p$ are smooth functions.

These functions are estimated in a non-parametric fashion and consist of a random component, an additive component and a link function relating these two components.

The estimating procedure of the GAM consists of two loops: the local scoring algorithm (outer loop) and a weighted backfitting algorithm (inner loop) used until convergence. The weighted backfitting algorithm provides a means of estimating each smooth function, keeping fixed the estimates for all of the others. During each iteration, an adjusted dependent variable and a set weight are computed, and then the smooth components are estimated using a weighted backfitting algorithm (for details, see Hastie and Tibshirani, 1990). The scoring algorithm stops when the deviance of the estimates stops decreasing. Any non-parametric smoothing method can be used to obtain $s_j(X_j)$. The procedure starts with a model in which all terms enter linearly and in a stepwise manner seeks to minimise Akaike Information Criterion by increasing or decreasing the degrees of freedom for each component (Chambers and Hastie, 1992).

Empirical results

In this section, I estimate the impact of Structural Funds on economic growth using the econometric approach specified above. The results are given in Table 5.1. The coefficients in the top half of the table refer to the linear estimation and do not consider non-linearity. The bottom half of the table shows the results of testing for the significant presence of non-linearity in the estimates. In instances of non-linearity, the implications in terms of effects could be quite different with respect to classical linear estimation. For testing, I adopt a test based on the effective degrees of freedom estimated for each smooth function. If the effective degrees of freedom equals 1, this implies that the smooth function can be approximated by a linear relationship (the top half of the table). In the bottom half of the table, I report only effective degrees of freedom greater than 1, which reflects the flexibility of the model.

Table 5.1 Estimation results of the semi-parametric model.

Model	1 Dep var. GDP/POP growth	2 Dep var. GVA/EMP growth
Parametric terms		
$\ln(Y)$	−0.00669	−0.01565
Expenditure on productive environment	−0.91593	−0.01110
Expenditure on human capital	28.13675***	4.74744
Expenditure on infrastructure	−0.51260*	−0.58895***
F-values for non-parametric terms		
$f(\ln(Y))$	2.5601* (3)	8.5603*** (3)
f(Expenditure on productive environment)	3.5274** (3)	1.6202 (3)
f(Expenditure on human capital)	4.5294*** (3)	6.5541*** (3)
f(Expenditure on infrastructure)	1.7471 (3)	9.3285*** (3)
AIC	−1179.4540	−1344.3890

Significance: * = 10%; ** = 5%; *** = 1%; standard errors in brackets.

The parametric part can be interpreted like a classic Ordinary Least Squared estimation. In contrast to the findings of Barro and Sala-i-Martin (1991) and Mankiw *et al.* (1992), we observe that for both models the parameters related to convergence are not linearly significant. The impact of Structural Funds is much more linear in Model 1, GDP per capita in the base year, where we have a positive and strongly significant effect for investments in human capital and a negative but weakly significant effect for expenditure on infrastructure. In the case of productivity growth, only expenditure on infrastructure has a significant impact and also, in this case, it is unexpectedly negative. These initial results show that, on average, investments in infrastructure, particularly concentrated in countries with less developed regions, seem incapable of creating the necessary conditions to exploit the potentials of these less developed regions in terms of the growth rates of both productivity and GDP per capita.

The significant non-linear estimates are shown in the bottom half of the table. In Model 1, funds for productive environment and human capital are non-linear with respect to GDP growth per capita, while in Model 2, funds for infrastructure are also non-linearly correlated to average growth.

Figures 5.4 and 5.5 show the non-linear marginal effects of the variables. The scale of the variables is on that of the linear predictors, but the smooth terms must sum to zero, and thus are presented in a mean-centred fashion. The parameter related to convergence has a concave shape in both models, but, while the negative slope is strongly evident for productivity, it is not for GDP/POP. In this last case, we have very weak convergence of less developed regions with a flex point around €25,000 that corresponds to the EU average, highlighting that more advanced regions are growing at levels comparable to less developed regions. Regarding productivity, regions below the €44,000 mark, which corresponds to 91 per cent of the EU productivity average, strongly converge; then, until €60,000, the marginal effect is null; and then, beyond this value, the impact of initial GVA per worker becomes positive. In this respect, the gap between more and less productive regions is not shrinking, with intermediate regions that have decreased their productivity levels.

Funds for productive environment are non-linear only in Model 1 where they have positive marginal effects until 0.15 per cent of GDP, at which point they become negative. From a policy point of view, we have a higher absorption capacity among the regions that receive the lowest amount of funds, which, as shown in Figure 5.1, roughly correspond to the countries with the majority of less developed regions. These countries devote a relatively small amount of funds to this area of intervention compared to other countries, which, probably due to their developed industrial structures, have difficulties in translating funds for productive environment into growth. The null impact on productivity growth, which contrasts with significant results for GDP/POP growth, probably depends on the nature and efficiency of firms financed by these funds, which, from what we observe from the data, seem incapable of translating investments into productive activities. On the other hand, according to the European Commission (2004: 51):

(a)

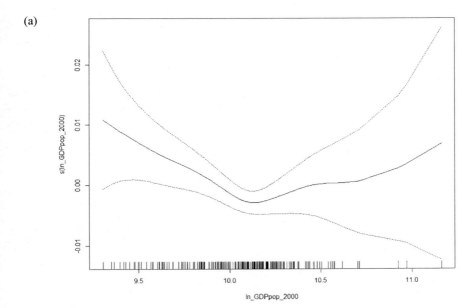

(b)

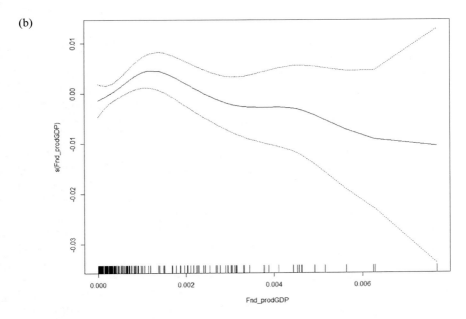

Figure 5.4 Estimation results for Model 1, non-parametric effects: (a) log(GDP/POP$_{2000}$); (b) Expenditure on productive environment; and (c) Expenditure on human capital.

(c)

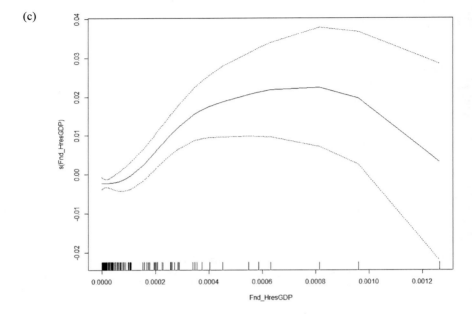

Figure 5.4 (continued)

[f]irms in less favoured regions suffer from being isolated from the best international R&D networks and research centres developing new technologies. Small and medium enterprises in these regions, in particular, have difficulty in finding out about the latest technological developments and how to use these and in making contact with suitable partners elsewhere.

Funds for human resources are positive and significant for the majority of regions with respect to the growth of both GDP per capita and GVA per worker. In the latter case, the impact is much stronger, as shown by the steeper slope. In both models, the curvature becomes negative at a certain point but, simultaneously, the marginal effects become insignificant. This finding is very important because it proves that, in spite of the very low expenditure on human resources, especially by less developed countries, these have a very strong effect in increasing competitiveness.

Finally, expenditure on infrastructure confirms the negative impact with respect to the growth of productivity in the non-linear estimates for around 70 per cent of regions. This result only partially confirms the findings of the linear part of the model, because the regions that receive the highest amount of funds show a positive impact for expenditure on infrastructure. This implies that richer regions (with lower funds for infrastructure) have a negative effect on the growth of both

(a)

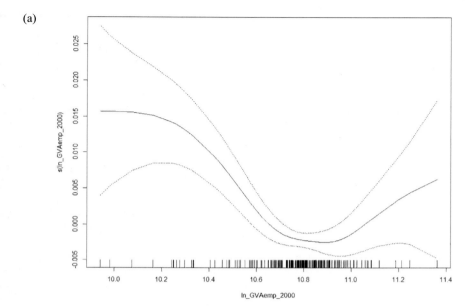

(b)

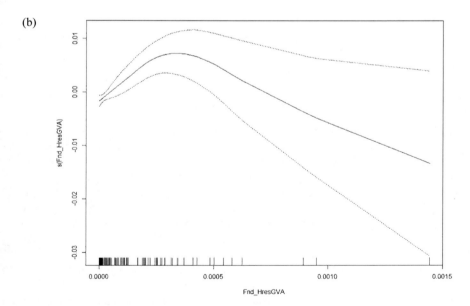

Figure 5.5 Estimation results for Model 2, non-parametric effects: (a) log(GVA/EMP$_{2000}$); (b) Expenditure on human capital; and (c) Expenditure on infrastructure.

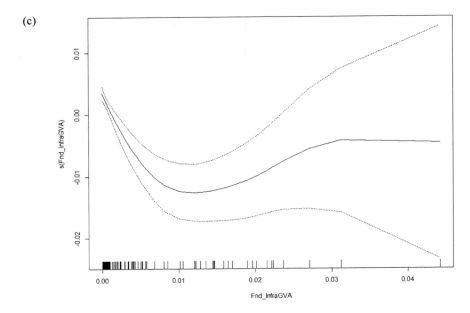

Figure 5.5 (continued)

GDP per capita and productivity, while in less developed regions, expenditure on infrastructure at least partially supports GVA growth per worker but has a weakly negative impact on GDP growth per capita.

Conclusions

In this chapter, by considering the Structural Funds disaggregated by areas of intervention, I have sought to investigate whether the aims of the Lisbon Agenda have been fulfilled by Cohesion Policy, and in particular whether expenditure has been devoted to 'softer' investments and whether the priorities financed by Structural Funds are in line with what is needed by regions in order to achieve the aim of convergence. The semi-parametric approach used in this study allows us to achieve this objective with a higher degree of detail with respect to classical linear models because, as might be imagined, expenditure on Cohesion Policy can have non-linear effects on growth.

An initial analysis reveals that in many regions the growth of productivity does not correspond to the growth of GDP per capita, raising doubts about the sustainability of the latter in the medium and long term. In this regard, I have been interested in investigating whether Structural Funds have a differentiated impact according to their area of intervention and, if so, what the policy implications of this eventuality might be.

The empirical findings show that, especially in Portugal, Spain, Ireland and Greece, and to a lesser extent Italy, Structural Funds have been used mainly to finance infrastructure, which runs at least partially counter to the aims of the Lisbon Agenda. If this translates into a positive impact for both growth of productivity and GDP per capita, it should not be a problem, but, according to the empirical results, this is not always the case. The positive impact on GVA growth per worker is achieved only with an investment of at least 1 per cent of GVA. The hypothesis that the development of transport infrastructure, while increasing accessibility, harms the industrialisation prospects of less developed areas (Puga, 2002) is not proven; however, we can observe that, in order to have a multiplier effect and to create good conditions for competitiveness, infrastructure policies cannot be fragmentary and they must be well funded, requiring at least 1 per cent of GVA. Isolated initiatives with low resource endowments do not have an effect, probably because they are not part of a planned and coordinated development strategy.

In order to avoid this problem, it is necessary to reshape regional policy, putting emphasis on a rationalisation of priorities to maximise the development potential of each region. To achieve this end, it is essential to reallocate resources in favour of human capital, particularly in less developed regions, where it is demonstrated that it has the highest returns, and to redesign intervention for productive environment with the aim of improving firms' competitiveness across all regions. In addition, as stated in the Fifth Cohesion Report (European Commission, 2010: xix–xx):

> Policies also tend to have inter-dependent effects. Without proper coordination, the impact of any one policy is likely to be severely diminished and might even be negative. The impact of policies cannot therefore be maximised if a fragmented approach is adopted and policy decisions are taken in isolation.

The institutional framework, thus, is implicitly recognised as a filter that has a crucial role in connecting the main policy objectives, in the context of EU growth strategy, to the real needs and characteristics of each region. This should ensure that spatially concentrated policies distribute their positive effects widely across both space and society.

Notes

1 See Pinho *et al.* (2015) for a complete review of the literature.
2 The data include resources from the European Regional Development Fund (ERDF) and Cohesion Fund devoted to Objective 1 regions and are drawn from SWECO (2008).
3 Objective 1 of the Structural Funds is the main priority of the EU's cohesion policy. Its aim is to "promote harmonious development" and to "narrow the gap between the development levels of the various regions". These Funds are allocated to help areas lagging behind in their development where the GDP per capita is below 75 per cent of the EU average. Objective 2 of the Structural Funds aims to revitalise all areas facing

structural difficulties, whether industrial, rural, urban or dependent on fisheries. Though situated in regions whose development level is close to the EU average, such areas are faced with different types of socio-economic difficulties that are often the source of high unemployment. Urban is the Community Initiative for sustainable development in the troubled urban districts of the EU. The Cohesion Fund part-finances action in the fields of the environment and transport infrastructure of common interest with a view to promoting economic and social cohesion and solidarity between member states with a GDP per capita below the threshold of 90 per cent of the EU average. Interreg IIIA objectives are to develop cross-border cooperation and to help the regions on the EU's internal and external borders to overcome the problems resulting from their isolation.

4 The data are from Cambridge Econometrics' database.

References

Barca, F. (2009), *An Agenda for a Reformed Cohesion Policy: A Place-Based Approach to Meeting European Union Challenges and Expectations*, Independent Report prepared at the request of Danuta Hübner, Commissioner for Regional Policy.

Barro, R. (1990), "Government spending in a simple model of endogenous growth", *Journal of Political Economy*, 98(1), 103–25.

Barro, R. J. and Sala-i-Martin, X. (1991), "Convergence across states and regions", *Brookings Papers on Economic Activity*, 1, 107–82.

Basile, R. (2008), "Regional economic growth in Europe: a semi-parametric spatial dependence approach", *Papers in Regional Science*, 87(4), 527–44.

Basile, R. and Gress, B. (2005), "Semi-parametric spatial auto-covariance models of regional growth in Europe", *Région et Développement*, 21, 93–118.

Basile, R., Capello, R. and Caragliu, A. (2012), "Technological interdependence and regional growth in Europe", *Papers in Regional Science*, 91(4), 697–722.

Chambers, J. M. and Hastie, T. J. (eds) (1992), *Statistical Models in S*, Pacific Grove, CA: Wadsworth.

Esposti, R. and Bussoletti, S. (2008), "Impact of Objective 1 funds on regional growth convergence in the European Union: a panel data approach", *Regional Studies*, 42(2), 159–73.

European Commission (2004), *Third Report on Economic and Social Cohesion*, Brussels: Commission of the European Communities.

European Commission (2007), *Growing Regions, Growing Europe: Fourth Report on Economic and Social Cohesion*, Brussels: Commission of the European Communities.

European Commission (2010), *Fifth Report on Economic, Social and Territorial Cohesion*, Brussels: Commission of the European Communities.

European Council (2000), "23 and 24 March Presidency Conclusion", available at: www.consilium.europa.eu/uedocs/cms_data/docs/pressdata/en/ec/00100-r1.en0.htm (accessed 7 June 2015).

Fotopoulos, G. (2012), "Non-linearities in regional economic growth and convergence: the role of entrepreneurship in the European Union regions", *The Annals of Regional Science*, 48(3), 719–41.

Hastie, T. J. and Tibshirani, R. J. (1986), "Generalized additive models", *Statistical Science*, 1(3), 295–318.

Hastie, T. J. and Tibshirani, R. J. (1990), *Generalized Additive Models*, London: Chapman & Hall.

Krugman, P. (1992), *The Age of Diminished Expectations: US Economic Policy in the 1980s*, Cambridge, MA: MIT Press.

Mankiw, N. G., Romer, D. and Weil, D. N. (1992), "A contribution to the empirics of economic growth", *Quarterly Journal of Economics*, 107(2), 407–37.

Maynou, L., Saez, M., Kyriacou, A. and Bacaria, J. (2016), "The impact of Structural and Cohesion Funds on Eurozone convergence, 1990–2010", *Regional Studies*, 50, 1127–1139.

Pinho, C., Varum, C. and Antunes, C. (2015), "Structural Funds and European regional growth: comparison of effects among different programming periods", *European Planning Studies*, 23(7), 1302–26.

Porter, M. E. (1990), "The competitive advantage of nations", *Harvard Business Review*, March–April, 74–91.

Puga, D. (2002), "European regional policies in the light of recent location theories", *Journal of Economic Geography*, 2(4), 373–406.

Rodríguez-Pose, A. and Fratesi, U. (2004), "Between development and social policies: the impact of European Structural Funds in 'Objective 1' regions", *Regional Studies*, 38(1), 97–114.

Rodríguez-Pose, A. and Garcilazo, E. (2015), "Quality of government and the returns of investment: examining the impact of Cohesion expenditure in European regions", *Regional Studies*, 49(8), 1274–90.

Rodríguez-Pose, A. and Novak, K. (2013), "Learning processes and economic returns in European Cohesion Policy", *Investigaciones Regionales*, 25(Primavera), 7–26.

SWECO (2008), *Final Report: ERDF and CF Regional Expenditure*, SWECO: Stockholm, available at: http://ec.europa.eu/regional_policy/sources/docgener/evaluation/pdf/expost2006/expenditure_final.pdf (accessed 1 February 2016).

Part II
The contribution of Cohesion Policy to smart, sustainable and inclusive growth

6 An evaluation of the impact of the construction of motorways and expressways in Poland during the period 2004–13 on accessibility and cohesion

Piotr Rosik, Marcin Stępniak and Tomasz Komornicki

Introduction

A modern network of collision-free roads is a characteristic feature of developed countries. The process of even regional distribution of high-quality transport infrastructure can lead to greater territorial cohesion at different spatial levels. The improvement in accessibility has come to be seen as an increasingly important criterion in the evaluation of road investments, and it is associated with the consideration of an improvement in cohesion as a prerequisite for a change in policy in the next financial framework.

Thanks to the possibility of using EU funds in two programming periods, 2004–6 and 2007–13, the development of motorways and expressways gained particular momentum in Poland, resulting in a four-fold increase in higher-standard roads. A decade has elapsed since the commencement of the first investment projects financed with the support of the Cohesion Policy Fund or under the Sectoral Operational Programme Transport (SOPT) in the years 2004–6, as well as later under the Operational Programme Infrastructure and Environment (OPI&E) in the years 2007–13. This is an opportune moment to attempt to evaluate the effects of a decade of efforts to create a network of motorways and expressways with the assistance of EU funding, paying particular attention to the impact of the 'big push' in road construction towards accessibility and territorial cohesion.

In this chapter, we propose an ex post evaluation of changes in the road potential accessibility of Polish municipalities as a method for evaluating Cohesion Policy. We provide an overview of the potential accessibility indicator methodology, with particular emphasis on two dimensions of accessibility: the spatial scale and the variation of the distance decay function. The road potential accessibility indicator used in the analysis is assessed on the basis of intranational accessibility (limited to travel destinations within Poland) and international accessibility (destinations in Poland and throughout Europe). The net effect of investments co-financed from EU funds on changes in intranational and international accessibility in the period 2004–13 is presented, with relative changes illustrated by a map showing changes at the municipal level.

88 Piotr Rosik et al.

Furthermore, we attempt to evaluate the impact of EU investment on territorial cohesion. This impact is measured using the Potential Accessibility Dispersion (PAD) index, which takes into account the standard deviation of the potential accessibility values across municipalities, using the population as the weighting variable. This is followed by a simulation of changes in intranational and international accessibility as a result of important investments within selected case studies. The chapter finishes with conclusions concerning how Cohesion Policy resources spent on road development can be used most effectively and efficiently in Poland in the next programming period, 2014–2020.

The potential accessibility indicator

The basic description of the potential accessibility indicator is as follows (see also Geurs and Van Eck, 2001; Spiekermann et al., 2014; Rosik et al., 2015):

$$A_i = \sum_j g(M_j) f(c_{ij}) \tag{6.1}$$

where A_i is the accessibility of unit i, $g(M_j)$ is the function determining the attractiveness of 'mass' (M_j) measured for instance in terms of the population of unit j, and $f(c_{ij})$ is a distance decay function representing the generalised cost (distance, time, cost or effort) needed to reach this 'mass'. In this chapter, we use municipal data at LAU-2 level and the population as a proxy of destination attractiveness in order to analyse the impact of infrastructure development on improving accessibility and territorial cohesion. Car travel time (t_{ij}) was chosen as a distance decay element. The shortest road travel times were calculated using a model described by Rosik (2012).

The impact on accessibility and cohesion is analysed at two geographical levels: intranational and international. The potential indicator at the international level is comprised of three components:

$$A_i = M_i f(t_{ii}) + \sum_j M_j f(t_{ij}) + \sum_k M_k f(t_{ik}) \tag{6.2}$$

Where $M_i f(t_{ii})$ is the self potential of municipality i and (t_{ii}) is the internal travel time calculated on the basis of the method proposed by Rich (1978; see also Gutiérrez et al., 2011). The sum of the self potential and the second component $\sum_j M_j f(t_{ij})$ is an intranational potential, where (t_{ij}) is the travel time between two Polish municipalities i and j. The sum of the intranational potential and the third component $\sum_k M_k f(t_{ik})$ is the international potential, where (t_{ik}) is the travel time, including border waiting time, between municipality i and one of the transport units encompassing the territory of the whole European continent outside of Poland.

The potential model is very sensitive to the particular distance decay function that is used (Haynes et al., 2003). Some authors suggest that the exponential function is very suitable for longer distances at the intranational and international level (Geurs and Van Eck, 2001). In practice, it is commonly used, in particular at the international level (Schürmann and Talaat, 2000; Spiekermann and Schürmann, 2007; Spiekermann *et al.*, 2014). Therefore, we adopt the exponential function:

$$f(t) = exp(-\beta t) \qquad (6.3)$$

The perceptions of the residents, workers and visitors in the study area need to be taken into account by adjusting the β parameter to the geographical level (Hilber and Arendt, 2004; Cheng and Bertolini, 2013). We assume that the more locally we look, the shorter the trip length and the sharper the distance decay (with higher β values). This procedure results in the use of $\beta = 0.02$ for short trips (intranational level) and $\beta = 0.005$ for long trips (international level). This corresponds to a situation in which, in the case of short trips, the attractiveness of a destination halves if the trip is 30 minutes, while in the case of long trips, the attractiveness of a destination halves after 90 minutes of travel.

The expansion of the Polish motorway network

Before 1989, the Polish transport system was characterised by freight traffic flows in an east–west direction between the Soviet Union and the German Democratic Republic and in a north–south direction between Polish harbours and the Upper Silesian coal region. After 1989, the decline in freight transport and the rapid increase in private mobility and motorisation led to car ownership of more than 450 motor vehicles per 1,000 inhabitants in 2010. In spite of the growing motorisation of society, the 1990s was a decade of further delay in major decisions concerning transport infrastructure investments (Stępniak et al., 2013).

Since 2000, Poland has been making up for lost time with the biggest national motorway construction programme in Europe. In 2000, about 500 km of motorways and expressways were in operation, whereas 14 years later, at the end of 2014, slightly less than 3,000 km of motorways and expressways are in use (Figure 6.1). The majority of new motorways and expressways have been constructed with the assistance of EU funds during the two EU programming periods 2004–6 and 2007–13. These sources include the Cohesion Policy Fund and the European Regional Development Fund with an average share of EU co-financing amounting to around 68 per cent of overall project costs (Rosik *et al.*, 2015).

Road traffic is particularly concentrated in areas of high population density: the Upper Silesia region, and the Poznań and Warsaw conurbations. The highest traffic volumes are observed on international roads: the existing motorway sections of the A4, A2 and A1 motorways, the S7 expressway (from Gdańsk through Warsaw to Kraków) and the S8 expressway (from Wrocław through Warsaw to the Polish–Lithuanian border) (Stępniak *et al.*, 2013).

90 *Piotr Rosik* et al.

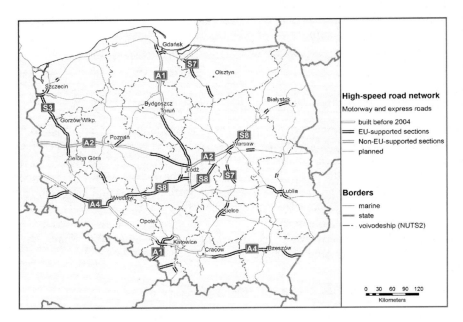

Figure 6.1 Polish high-speed road network.

Improving intranational potential accessibility as a result of investment from EU funds

The construction of motorways and expressways in the years 2004–13, co-financed from EU funds, has transformed the accessibility of many areas in Poland. In some voivodeships, these changes have reached the level of several tens of per cent. In Podkarpackie Voivodeship, for instance, road accessibility has risen by 27 per cent, and the main beneficiaries are the areas located along the A4 motorway. In relative terms, Podkarpackie is followed by Łódzkie Voivodeship, which has experienced a 21 per cent increase in accessibility as a consequence of the construction of sections of the A2 and A1 motorways and S8 expressway, and Lubuskie Voivodeship, where a 20 per cent increase was seen following the opening of the western section of the A2 and the northern part of the S3 expressway. In absolute terms, the most significant accessibility changes are due to investments co-financed from EU funds and pursued in Łódzkie and Śląskie Voivodeships.

The map of relative accessibility changes at the municipal level (Figure 6.2) also draws attention to the significant effects of improved local accessibility in border areas whose accessibility in the reference year (2004) was low. This is the result of new road connections created in these areas (for instance, the S22 in Braniewski Poviat). Such effects are also seen in those areas that have benefited from the construction of new road connections with nearby metropolitan areas (for instance, south of Śląskie Voivodeship, thanks to the construction of the A1

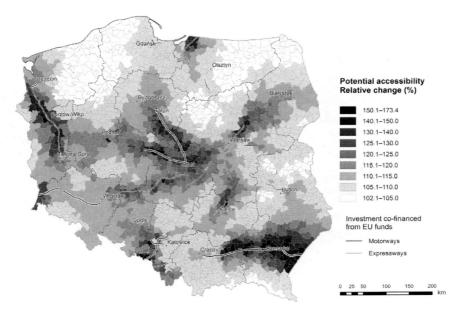

Figure 6.2 Relative changes in the intranational potential accessibility of Polish gminas in the years 2004–13 as a result of investments co-financed from EU funds.

motorway and S1 and S69 expressways), or with a provincial capital (for instance, the section of the S7 expressway between Skarżysko-Kamienna and Kielce). The effect of improved intranational accessibility was generally no greater than just over 12 per cent in many voivodeships, (the indicator of relative change for Poland as a whole was 13.9 per cent). Relative change has not exceeded 10 per cent in Lubelskie, Warmińsko-Mazurskie and Pomorskie Voivodeships. There are still large areas of the country that have hardly benefited at all from the construction of roads co-financed from EU funds. These are primarily Central Pomerania (together with the northern part of Wielkopolska), Masuria and the Suwałki region, the north-western areas of Mazowieckie Voivodeship, as well as the northern and central areas of Lubelskie Voivodeship.

The share of investments co-financed from EU funds in relation to the total investment in motorways and expressways in the years 2004–13 underlines the fact that investments financed under the SOPT, Cohesion Policy Fund or OPI&E were of great importance for the less developed eastern part of the country, and for eastern Poland in particular (Figure 6.3). They also accounted for over 90 per cent of the accessibility improvement in the centrally located area between Łódź, Kielce and Puławy, as well as locally in the western parts of the country. In turn, investments made from other sources have served to improve accessibility in Pomorskie Voivodeship, where the effects of substituting private funds in place of EU funds are clear due to the construction of the northern part of the A1 motorway with the use of the PPP formula.

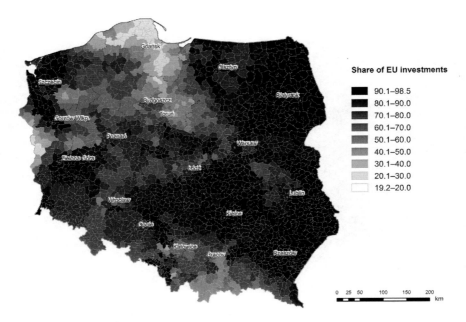

Figure 6.3 Share of EU investment in the total change in the intranational potential accessibility of Polish gminas in the years 2004–13.

Improving international potential accessibility as a result of investments from EU funds

The areas of western Poland, due to their geographical location (and the permeable frontier inside the Schengen area), have an inherently better accessibility taking into account destinations across the entire European continent (Rosik *et al.*, 2015). Therefore, if destinations across Europe are considered, the effectiveness of investments co-financed from EU funds changes, particularly in relative terms. It turns out that certain sections of roads are important for improving the travel speed along the main international transport corridors. When it comes to improvement across the entire area of the country in the international context, changes have benefited Podkarpackie (23.5 per cent), Mazowieckie (20.7 per cent), Łódzkie (19.8 per cent) and Podlaskie (19.6 per cent) Voivodeships most in relative terms, and Łódzkie and Śląskie Voivodeships most in absolute terms (Figure 6.4). Mazowieckie and Podlaskie Voivodeships have benefited owing to the construction of the central section of the A2 motorway and sections of the S8 expressway across Warsaw and along the Radzymin–Wyszków section. These investments have significantly shortened journeys to the west but also – following the opening of the next section of the S7 expressway between Warsaw and Kielce and the S8 expressway between Piotrków Trybunalski and Warsaw – in the direction of the Czech Republic and Slovakia. Improved international accessibility is

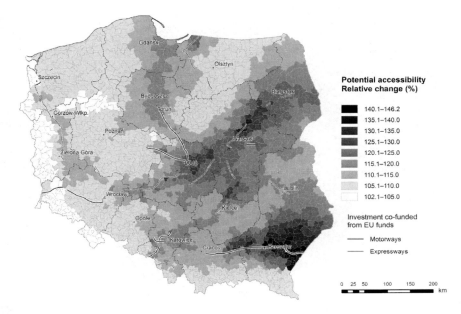

Figure 6.4 Relative changes in the international potential accessibility of Polish gminas in the years 2004–13 as a result of investments co-financed from EU funds.

also evident along the A1 corridor, in particular in the south, thanks to the key section Sośnica–Gorzyczki and, to a much lesser extent, along the S3 expressway. The S3 expressway is more important from the point of view of intranational trips, as it runs parallel to the western border.

The average improvement in the international accessibility of the country reached the level of 13.4 per cent. The value of the indicator was lower than 10 per cent in southern and western Poland. The result of improving the accessibility of eastern Poland is more evident when other investments irrespective of the source of funding are also taken into account (Figure 6.5). Private funds are a sort of substitute for EU funds as they contribute to improving the international accessibility of the Zielona Góra–Poznań–Toruń–Olsztyn axis and Bydgoszcz–Gdańsk (with an additional effect from the northern section of the A1 motorway). In turn, improved international accessibility in the eastern and southern voivodeships is largely the result of the use of EU funds. In some areas, the share of these measures in the improvement of international accessibility even exceeds 90 per cent.

The impact of road investments on territorial cohesion

Territorial cohesion can be measured using the PAD index, which takes into account the standard deviation of potential accessibility values across municipalities using population as the weighting variable (López *et al.*, 2008; Ortega *et al.*,

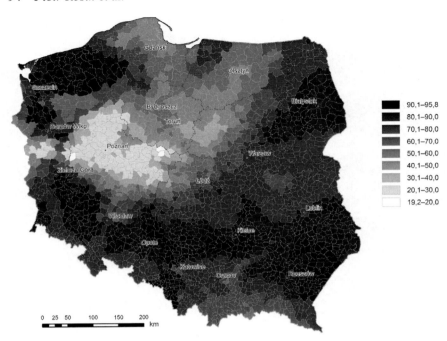

Figure 6.5 Share of EU investment in the total change in the international potential accessibility of Polish gminas in the years 2004–13.

2012; Stępniak and Rosik, 2013; Rosik *et al.*, 2015). The index is calculated using the following formula:

$$AD = \frac{SD_{A_i}}{\frac{\sum A_i * P_i}{\sum P_i}} \tag{6.4}$$

where A_i is the value of the potential accessibility indicator calculated for unit i, P_i is the population of unit i and SD_{Ai} is the standard deviation of A_i values weighted by population. The higher the PAD values, the greater the diversity of accessibility within the country.

The investments co-financed from EU funds have primarily improved the international accessibility of areas that have thus far suffered from poor accessibility from the so-called core of Europe (especially in eastern Poland). This leads to the conclusion that more emphasis has been placed on improving international accessibility than on improving intranational accessibility. Taking into account all investments (including those implemented with funding from other non-EU sources), the effect of improving spatial coherence in the international context is strengthened even further.

In the context of the country's internal cohesion, it can be argued that a deterioration (an increase of PAD values) and an increased diversity of accessibility of the country's regions have been observed since 2004. This is due to the fact that investments tend to focus on central Poland (for instance, Mazowieckie and Łódzkie Voivodeships), with a significantly lower level of interest in improving the situation in areas that are less accessible (mainly in eastern Poland). Among the Polish regions that were poorly accessible in 2004, only Pomerania (through the A1 link with central Poland) and Zachodniopomorskie (thanks to the northern section of the S3 expressway) have considerably benefited from investments (Table 6.1).

Simulations of changes in accessibility as a consequence of particular projects: a case study

An essential element of the analysis of improved accessibility following investment co-financed from EU funds is provided by simulations of the impact of individual sections on changes in accessibility at the intranational and international level. An analysis was conducted in relation to eight case studies co-financed by EU funds. Among the eight cases analysed, the greatest changes in accessibility (per 1 km of road) have been observed in three cases: the Sośnica–Gorzyczki section of the A1 motorway, the Szarów–Krzyż section of the A4 motorway and the Konin–Emilia section of the A2 motorway. In the international context, accessibility has been significantly improved along the Zgorzelec–Krzyż section of the A4 motorway (Figure 6.6). Noteworthy is the fact that despite its remoteness from the border, the construction of the centrally located Konin–Emilia section of the A2 has resulted in a change of international accessibility on a par with the Szarów–Krzyż section of the A4. The sections that run parallel to the border, such as the Szarów–Krzyż section of the A4 or the Szczecin–Gorzów Wielkopolski section of the S3, are more important from the intranational perspective than from the international point of view, while the construction of key sections of trans-European corridors, such as the central section of the A2, can result in significant changes in international accessibility. The remaining sections do not play a major role, either at an intranational or international level, as they have a strongly local character and are important for individual voivodeships or poviats.

Table 6.1 Territorial cohesion (measured by the PAD index) in the years 2004–13.

Accessibility	2013	2013 without EU investment		2004	
	Calculated value	Calculated value	Difference as compared to 2013	Calculated value	Difference as compared to 2013
Intranational	0.494	0.495	0.11%	0.489	−1.09%
International	0.299	0.319	6.70%	0.336	12.48%

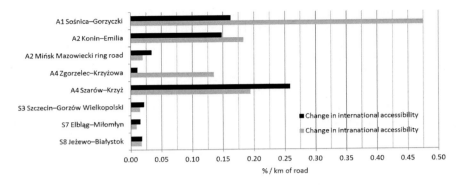

Figure 6.6 Relative changes in intranational and international accessibility for eight case studies.

Taking into account the spatial extent of the impact of the eight chosen investments, the effect of positive changes in intranational accessibility is clearly visible on a large scale in the Konin–Emilia section of the A2 motorway (the effects on the inhabitants of Szczecin and Bialystok, both in remote locations) (Figure 6.7).

In the international context, a positive effect is particularly noticeable for the Sośnica–Gorzyczki section of the A1 (this section is used by more than half of the Polish population travelling south to the Czech Republic, Austria, Italy or Croatia), the Konin–Emilia section of the A2 (with significantly improved accessibility for the inhabitants of Podlasie and the northern areas of Lubelskie Voivodeship) and the Zgorzelec–Krzyżowa section of the A4. The barrier of the external border of the Schengen area with Russia, Ukraine and Belarus is clearly noticeable. Despite a number of investments co-financed from EU funds and running perpendicular to the border (for instance, the Mińsk Mazowiecki ring road), international accessibility does not increase significantly in these directions. This can be explained primarily as the result of queues on the eastern border and the long waiting time at border crossings, which offset the positive effect of shortening the travel time within Poland (Figure 6.8).

Conclusions

Conclusions drawn from experience and empirical knowledge gained in the years 2004–13 are of key importance in drafting relevant recommendations. They are also important in ensuring the most efficient implementation of EU funds in the next programming period, 2014–20.

In the next programming period, the priority should be given to linking secondary centres with metropolitan areas. Such centres are voivodeship capitals in eastern Poland, but also a number of the other centres with considerable demographic and/or economic potential, located outside of the network of motorways and expressways (for instance, Koszalin, Słupsk, Kalisz and Płock) currently being constructed in the period up to 2015.

Impact of new roads in Poland 97

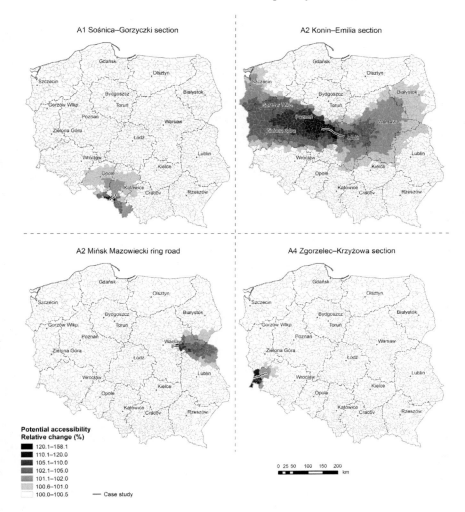

Figure 6.7 Relative changes in the intranational potential accessibility of Polish gminas as a result of the implementation of selected investments from EU funds.

A number of significant activities are planned in the forthcoming financial framework 2014–20 in relation to the construction of routes connecting major voivodeship and subregional capitals. Therefore, the hierarchy of priorities for future investments presents a potential problem to solve. It may prove crucial in the event of financing difficulties (as was the case in the current 2007–13 framework). Roads connecting voivodeship capitals with Warsaw seem to be perceived as priorities, with particular emphasis put on the S7, S8 and S17/S19 expressways (S19 between Lublin and Rzeszów), and the missing section of the A1 motorway in central Poland.

98 *Piotr Rosik* et al.

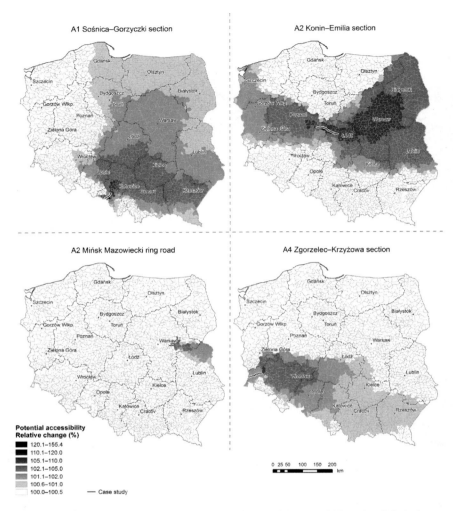

Figure 6.8 Relative changes in the international potential accessibility of Polish gminas as a result of the implementation of selected investments from EU funds.

The construction of ring roads along selected expressways (to be implemented after 2020) is in some cases additionally justified by increasingly heavy traffic. This is particularly important for the potentially large ring road around Warsaw provided for in the National Spatial Development Concept (NSDC, 2012), improving access to northern parts of Mazowieckie Voivodeship and characterised by a very high growth of heavy traffic.

The construction of sections of expressway towards tourist regions must also be a priority. These can be cul-de-sac sections constructed to maintain an appropriate level of concentration of heavy traffic. Furthermore, heavy traffic and its growth are additional arguments for giving priority to motorways and expressways leading to Poland's borders, which are also important routes for peripheral areas. This situation relates primarily to the S61 expressway to the Polish–Lithuanian border and a section of the S3 expressway from Zielona Góra through Legnica towards the Polish–Czech border. Other roads leading towards the Czech border (through the Kłodzko Valley) and the Slovak border (to Chyżne and through Nowy Sącz) are potential transit directions and at the same time fulfil potentially important functions related to the operation of tourism traffic (cf. Więckowski *et al.*, 2014).

The evolution of national transport policy in the years 2004–13 may be treated as a good prognostic sign for future strategic decisions. The hierarchy of functional linkages was prepared with a strengthened role for domestic and regional linkages. Nevertheless, greater emphasis is needed on policy consistency in the next programming period to overcome the obstacles to making infrastructure development more cohesion-oriented, including the construction of the comprehensive TEN-T connections or secondary networks, particularly in the peripheral regions.

Acknowledgement

This research received funds from the National Science Centre allocated on the basis of the decisions DEC-2012/05/E/HS4/01798 and DEC-2014/13/B/HS4/03397.

References

Cheng, J. and Bertolini, L. (2013), 'Measuring urban job accessibility with distance decay, competition and diversity', *Journal of Transport Geography*, 30, 100–9.

Geurs, K. T. and van Eck, J. R. R. (2001), *Accessibility Measures: Review and Applications*, Bilthoven, The Netherlands: National Institute of Public Health and the Environment.

Gutiérrez, J., Condeço-Melhorado, A., López, E. and Monzón, A. (2011), 'Evaluating the European added value of TEN-T projects: a methodological proposal based on spatial spillovers, accessibility and GIS', *Journal of Transport Geography*, 19(4), 840–50.

Haynes, R., Lovett, A. and Sünnenberg, G. (2003), 'Potential accessibility, travel time, and consumer choice: geographical variations in general medical practice registrations in Eastern England', *Environment and Planning A*, 35(10), 1733–50.

Hilber, R. and Arendt, M. (2004), 'Development of accessibility in Switzerland between 2000 and 2020: first results', conference paper, STRC 2004.

López, E., Gutiérrez, J. and Gómez, G. (2008), 'Measuring regional cohesion effects of large-scale transport infrastructure investments: an accessibility approach', *European Planning Studies*, 16(2), 277–301.

NSDC (2012), *National Spatial Development Concept 2030*, Warsaw: Ministry of Regional Development.

Ortega, E., López, E. and Monzón, A. (2012), 'Territorial cohesion impacts of high-speed rail at different planning levels', *Journal of Transport Geography*, 24, 130–41.

Rich, D. C. (1978), 'Population potential, potential transportation cost and industrial location', *Area*, 10(3), 222–6.

Rosik, P. (2012), 'Dostępność lądowa przestrzeni Polski w wymiarze europejskim', *Prace Geograficzne*, 233, IGiPZ PAN, Warsaw.

Rosik, P., Stępniak, M. and Komornicki, T. (2015), 'The decade of the big push to roads in Poland: impact on improvement in accessibility and territorial cohesion from a policy perspective', *Transport Policy*, 37, 134–46.

Schürmann, C. and Talaat, A. (2000), *Towards a European Peripherality Index: Final Report – Report for General Directorate XVI Regional Policy of the European Commission*, Berichte aus dem Inst. für Raumplan. der Univ. Dortmund 53.

Spiekermann, K. and Schürmann, C. (2007), *Update of Selected Potential Accessibility Indicators: Final Report*, Spiekermann & Wegener, Urban and Regional Research (S&W), RRG Spatial Planning and Geoinformation, Luxembourg: ESPON, available at: www.mdrl.ro/espon_cd2/Project_Reports/Scientific_briefing_and_networking/Map Update_final_report.pdf (accessed 1 April 2016).

Spiekermann, K., Wegener, M., Květoň, V., Marada, M., Schürmann, C., Biosca, O., Ulied Segui, A., Antikainen, H., Kotavaara, O., Rusanen, J., Bielańska, D., Fiorello, D., Komornicki, T., Rosik, P. and Stępniak, M. (2014), *TRACC Transport Accessibility at Regional/Local Scale and Patterns in Europe: Draft Final Report*, ESPON Applied Research.

Stępniak, M. and Rosik, P. (2013), 'Accessibility improvement, territorial cohesion and spillovers: a multidimensional evaluation of two motorway sections in Poland', *Journal of Transport Geography*, 31, 154–63.

Stępniak, M., Rosik, P. and Komornicki, T. (2013), 'Accessibility patterns: Poland case study', *EUROPA XXI*, 24, 77–93.

Więckowski, M., Michniak, D., Bednarek-Szczepańska, M., Chrenka, B., Ira, V., Komornicki, T., Rosik, P., Stępniak, M., Székely, V., Śleszyński, P., Świątek, D. and Wiśniewski, R. (2014), 'Road accessibility to tourist destinations of the Polish–Slovak borderland: 2010–2030 prediction and planning', *Geographia Polonica*, 87(1), 5–26.

7 Demographic implications of 2007–13 regional and Cohesion Policy actions in Latvia

Aleksandrs Dahs

Introduction

As may be concluded from various academic studies (Zvidriņš, 2009) and official reports prepared by the State Regional Development Agency (SRDA) (2013), at the regional level, Latvia, just like many other European Union (EU) member states and regions falling under the Convergence objective of 2007–13 Cohesion Policy, faces significant challenges of spatial heterogeneity and divergence in terms of both economic and demographic development. The continuous depopulation of rural areas and border regions, the growing influence of the capital city in internal migration and settlement processes and other region-specific demographic issues comprise the long list of the regional population development problems that the Latvian authorities have to address on a daily basis.

The pressing need to account for such processes in the regional policy response has been repeatedly underlined by many studies, including those carried out by Ferry and Vironen (2010) at the European Policies Research Centre and Fésüs *et al.* (2008) at the European Commission. It may also be concluded that understanding the effects of currently available policy instruments is crucial for planning future aid and investment measures aimed either fully or partially at tackling the regional demographic issues.

Statistical data reported by the Central Statistics Bureau (CSB) (2014) and the SRDA (2013) show that available national and/or municipal funding aimed at tackling the aforementioned population development issues remains scarce and is reliant upon the established social support and welfare structure, which cannot provide the solution to more fundamental socio-economic issues. Therefore, relevant regional aid instruments, capable of creating the necessary positive socio-economic conditions for demographic change, remain largely reliant on co-funding from EU Cohesion Policy instruments, which are subject to changing priorities of nationwide growth support measures and targeted regional aid. With all this in mind, I begin by briefly explaining some of the main regional demographic challenges in Latvia, and outline the available aid/support measures and other major impact factors capable of influencing the regional population development processes.

I subsequently attempt to measure both direct and spatially distributed (where applicable) regional demographic effects of the investments carried out under the Operational Programmes (OPs) of the Latvian national Cohesion Policy. The significance of these implications is also evaluated in comparison with other forms of regional socio-economic aid measures and forms of financial investment. By employing both classical and spatially adjusted models, as proposed by Anselin (1999), in conjunction with the analysis of the available data on regional and Cohesion Policy spending on the scale of local municipalities in the period 2009–13, I investigate the links between specific types of investments/policy instruments and their resulting effect on key regional demographic processes.

Finally, the results of the spatial econometric analysis allow me to confirm that, while the OPs of the Latvian national Cohesion Policy 2007–13 were not specifically designed to tackle the regional demographic issues, in comparison to all other available policy tools, investments undertaken under these programmes had some (indirect) impact on the local demographic processes, namely population change due to official migration, and the change in the missing registered population rate. However, the positive effect has been less significant than predicted by some of the national planning documents, including the National Development Plan 2007–13 elaborated by the Ministry of Regional Development and Local Government (2006). Further, it is determined that, depending on the type of investment/aid instrument used, its effect may be either localised (impacting only the target region) or spatially lagged (having effect not only in the target region but also having some measurable spillover into the neighbouring territorial units).

The conclusions of the study underline the need to re-evaluate some of the objectives and associated expectations of the national Population Development and Cohesion Policies. From the regional policy perspective, the analytical approach demonstrated in this chapter provides opportunities for better planning of future investment/aid priorities, and allows us to identify those forms of investment instrument that need to be applied locally and those that may be used in a more centralised manner in order to achieve higher efficiency, a desirable level of impact and better spatial coverage.

The available data and the associated limitations

Logic dictates that before conducting any model-based study, it is first necessary to identify the available data and understand the associated limitations. In addition, following the established methodology of spatial econometric analysis, it is necessary to define clearly the spatial frame of reference and the spatial weights to be employed in the study.

The reform of Latvian administrative territories in the years 1999–2009 has resulted in the completely new single-level system of local administrative units (LAU). There are only 119 units: 110 local municipalities or "Novadi" and 9 cities of republican significance.[1] The NUTS3 region structure of the country remained unchanged, with six statistical regions: Riga, Pieriga, Kurzeme,

Vidzeme, Zemgale and Latgale. For the purposes of this study, I use the available data on policy spending, aid and investment at the LAU level. Unfortunately, due to dramatic changes in territorial planning caused by the abovementioned reform, no such data is available before 2009, which thus limits the scope of the research to the 2009–14 period.

The main regional demographic indicators available for the analysis of Latvian LAUs have been previously identified in other studies on related topics (see, for example, Krišjāne and Bauls, 2007; Paiders, 2007; Eglīte, 2008; Zvidriņš, 2012). These include a change of estimated total population over the observed period of time (as estimated by the CSB), a change of registered total population due to natural movement and/or registered migration (as recorded by the Office of Citizenship and Migration Affairs (OCMA)), a change of population below the age of 15 or within the age of economic activity (15–74) and several other indicators.

In the case of Latvia, particular problems are posed by unregistered migration. It is often measured by comparing the census-based or estimated actual population data (provided by the CSB) with the size of declared population in the municipality (as given by the OCMA). It has been suggested in previous studies that the resulting difference between declared population and actual population – the missing declared population (MDP) – may be accepted as a crude estimation of the number of unregistered migrants currently located in different regions or other countries (Dahs, 2014a):

$$MDP = \frac{Declared\ population - Actual\ population}{Declared\ population} \qquad (7.1)$$

Figure 7.1 depicts several of the abovementioned regional demographic tendencies in Latvia during the time period under investigation.

In addition, with the purpose of capturing the dynamics of the observed changes, several indicators need to be recalculated and represented as change rates or change indexes (using the year 2011 as base – 100). Similarly, impact parameters, described below, need to be recalculated per capita (using the estimated official CSB population data), in order to ensure their comparability.

The number of possible impact variables is limited by the amount of data available at the municipal level. Table 7.1 provides an overview of the chosen impact factors that have been considered in this study. Data have been acquired via the Regional Development Indicator Module (RDIM) of the national Territorial Development and Planning Information System (2015), which accumulates the most up-to-date statistical information produced by the related ministries and government agencies. In all cases, the CSB estimates of the total actual population have been used for producing the per capita values.

Other factors considered in this study include the average collected personal income tax [*IncTax*] (representing the average income level of inhabitants) and its change over time, as well as average local unemployment rates [*Unemployed*].

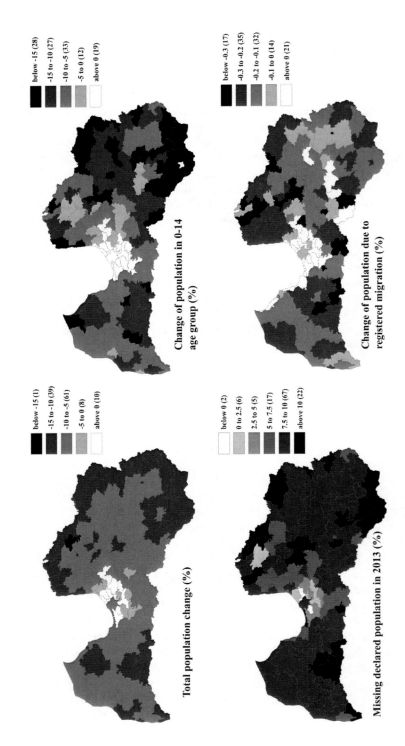

Figure 7.1 Regional demographic trends in Latvia in the years 2009–14.

Source: Author's elaboration based on CSB and OCMA data.

Table 7.1 Regional investment and policy instruments in Latvia in the years 2009–13.

Investment/aid instrument	Total per period (thousand EUR)	Average (per year and per capita) National average (EUR)	Maximum (EUR) (municipality)	Minimum (EUR) (municipality)
EU Structural and Cohesion Funds () (CF, ESF, ERDF) incl. national co-funding	2,893,179	278	811 (Ventspils City)	23 (Garkalnes novads)
Other EU funds (OF) (EFF, EAFRD, EAGF) incl. national co-funding	2,082,690	200	1,423 (Jaunpils novads)	4 (Rezekne City)
Foreign Direct Investment (FDI)	5,981,112	569	3,626 (Priekulu novads)	0 (Neretas novads)
Municipal spending on social support and social security (SocSup)	571,694	55	94 (Vilanu novads)	17 (Kekavas novads)

Source: Author's calculations based on CSB and RDIM data.

Figure 7.2 shows the spatial distribution of the EU funding across Latvian cities and municipalities during the period under investigation.

After examining the maps presented in Figure 7.2 and considering the relatively small size and interconnectedness of the local municipalities, it is impossible to deny that the regional demographic indicators in Latvia are (at least in part) subject to noticeable spatial autocorrelation. In order to better understand this term, some analogy may be drawn with the temporal autocorrelation in the time series analysis. Previous research into the spatial distribution of socio-economic indicators shows that when the observed phenomena are represented graphically on the map, spatial proximity usually results in some level of value similarity. This means that "high values tend to be located near other high values, while low values tend to be located near other low values, thus exhibiting positive spatial autocorrelation" (Voss *et al.*, 2006: 411).

The spatial autocorrelation may be caused either by spatial spillovers of the indicator under investigation (for instance, clustering of population around a regional economic centre) or by the spillovers of its impact parameters from/to the neighbouring regions. In order to factor the spatial spillovers between the municipalities into the econometric analysis, it is necessary to quantify the spatial relations by using some form of the spatial weights matrix (W) as explained by Ward and Gleditsch (2008: 13) or Anselin (2003). The easiest possible approach to capturing the general spatial relations of the observed territorial units is to use

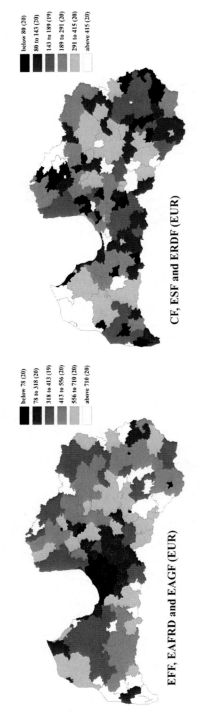

Figure 7.2 Average EU funds spent per year per capita in municipalities in the years 2009–13.

Source: Author's elaboration based on CSB and RDIM data.

the inverse values of geometric distances between the geographical coordinates of centroids or assigned central points of the regions under investigation. However, many authors, including Anselin (2003), show that with the availability of precise cartographic information, preferably in the form of compiled shapefiles, the more advanced connectivity matrices (representing the layered neighbourhood structure of the units with common borders, to the number of k layers) may be more precise and useful in representing the actual interactions between territories under investigation.

With this in mind, I have developed a square (n = 119) spatial connectivity weights matrix ($k = 1$) to be used in the spatially weighted regression (SWR) model estimations and bivariate spatial autocorrelation tests applied in the subsequent sections of this chapter.

Measuring direct and spatially distributed effects

This section provides the methodological basis for the quantitative analysis of both direct and spatially adjusted effects of the explanatory variables indicated above on the dynamics of the main regional demographic indicators during the period under investigation.

For measuring the direct effects, a proven and straightforward approach has been selected. I estimate a linear model for each of the demographic indicators:

$$Y = \alpha + \beta X + \varepsilon \qquad (7.2)$$

where vector Y stands for the particular indicator under investigation and matrix X denotes the main instruments/investments/factors considered instrumental in explaining the variance of Y. The significance of estimated coefficients β is then assumed to be the impact of the factor i under investigation. Selected results of this model's estimations are provided in Table 7.2 in the 'Results and findings' section.

Taking into account the suggested spatial autocorrelation of dependent variables, such an approach may be easily criticised from both a logical and a geographical point of view. It would be wrong to assume that individuals work (gain income), reside and obtain social services in the same municipalities with zero inter-regional mobility. In order to test the assumption that some spatial effects have a role as an external factor in the model, it is possible simply to test the model residuals for spatial autocorrelation by employing global Moran's I or any similar statistical test.

Therefore, in order to better study the links between investments/policy instruments and the regional demographic change, I estimate three of the most commonly used forms of spatially adjusted regression models:

1. the spatial lag model (SLM), which includes the spatially lagged values of the dependent variable as one of the explanatory factors (hereafter – Type 1 spatial spillover);

2   the spatial Durbin model (SDM), which incorporates the SLM and applies spatial weights to all explanatory variables, expecting that the influence of these factors is spilling over into the neighbouring territorial units (hereafter – Type 2 spatial spillover);
3   the spatial error model (SEM), which accounts for spatially dependent external influences through adding a spatially weighted error to the right-hand side of the model equation.

Anselin (2003) explains that the specification of the spatially adjusted regression model involves the incorporation of spatial weights matrices to account for the influence of neighbouring regions on the variable of interest in the region under review. Spatial weights for neighbour effects can be attributed to dependent (SLM) and independent (SDM) variables, as well as to error terms (SEM). The growing significance and necessity of such spatially adjusted models and other spatial methods in the regional demographic research has been excellently explained and proven by Matthews and Parker (2013).

For this particular study, the SLM may have the following form:

$$Y = pWY + \beta X + \varepsilon \tag{7.3}$$

where W is a pre-defined spatial weights matrix and coefficient p represents the impact of spatially lagged values of the dependent variable of the neighbouring regions, as defined by the matrix W.

The SDM may now be constructed by expanding the SLM structure (Equation 7.3) as follows:

$$Y = pWY + \beta X + \theta WX + \varepsilon \tag{7.4}$$

where the new coefficient θ denotes the impact of spatially lagged values of the predictor variables of the neighbouring regions, as defined by the matrix W.

The SEM is less sophisticated and may be built on the basis of the linear model (Equation 7.2):

$$Y = \beta X + \lambda W\varepsilon + \epsilon \tag{7.5}$$

Here, as explained by Ward and Gleditsch (2008: 55), the overall error has been decomposed into two components: vector ϵ, denoting a spatially uncorrelated error term that satisfies the normal regression assumption, and vector ε, indicating the spatial component of the error term. The coefficient λ now indicates the extent to which the spatial components of the error are correlated with one another for nearby observations, as defined by the matrix W.

In the next section of this chapter, the selected results of all three models are presented and discussed.

Results and findings

As explained above, I begin with the estimation of the linear model for each of the demographic indicators, incorporating all of the explanatory variables listed in the previous section in the right-hand side of Equation 7.2. Table 7.2 shows the estimation results, as well as the corresponding Moran's I test values for the model residuals (based on the $k = 1$ connectivity matrix).

From the LM estimations in Table 7.2, it can be seen that the average collected personal income tax is highlighted as the most significant predictor for total population change, change of population below working age and change of population due to registered migration. Unemployment levels appear to be just as significant for change of population below working age and change of population due to registered migration. Average per capita spending of other EU funds (EFF, EAFRD and EAGF) has been slightly significant for total population change, hinting at the role of these investments in the development of rural/coastal areas and the resulting improvement of economic and social conditions.

Low Moran's I values of the residuals for total population change and change of population below working age, combined with the high R-squared values, suggest that the LM is suitable in these cases and that the spatial models would not yield much improvement in the estimations.

Surprisingly, LM estimation shows that the only (moderately) significant factor for the reduction of the MDP rate in the regions is the average EU Structural and Cohesion Funds (SF&CF) investment per capita, which may be explained by the improvement in infrastructure and public services impacting individuals'

Table 7.2 Effects of regional investment/policy instruments on selected demographic indicators in the years 2009–13: linear model results.

Parameter	Indicator			
	Total population change	<15 population change	MDP change index	Population change due to registered migration
SF&CF	−0.00342	−0.00295	−0.00215 *	0.00036 *
OF	0.00248	−0.00152	0.00065	0.00015
FDI	−0.00015	−0.00032	0.00012	−0.00006
SocSup	−0.01447	−0.04147	0.01203	−0.00556 *
IncTax	0.04057 ***	0.08979 ***	−0.00147	0.00179 ***
Unemployed	0.17032	0.59820 ***	−0.02783	0.02615 **
R-squared	*0.80532*	*0.83928*	*0.11095*	*0.26709*
Moran's I of residuals	0.07103	0.07679	0.16280	0.13681

Significance codes: 0–0.001 ***; 0.001–0.01 **; 0.01–0.05 *; 0.05–0.1 '; 0.1–1 no code.

Source: Author's calculations based on CSB and RDIM data.

choices regarding temporary (or unregistered) employment abroad or in a different region. However, the very low R-squared value for this estimation indicates that the model is missing several key impact factors. In addition, the moderately high Moran's I value of the residuals indicate that these missing external factors must be noticeably spatially correlated. This is also relevant for the last indicator.

Average EU SF&CF investment per capita also has a moderately significant positive impact on change of population due to registered migration, which can be easily explained by the benefits of improved infrastructure and public services for the registered residents of the particular municipality actively involved in the SF&CF projects.

Table 7.3 provides the estimation results of the three types of SWR model, estimated using the methodology widely explained in the literature and demonstrated by Bivand (2002).

As expected, all three types of spatially weighted model bring only slight improvements to the model fit results for the first two indicators under investigation. The SLM results demonstrate a moderate to significant role of the spatially lagged dependent variable for the first three indicators, resulting in a 0.1–0.5 improvement in R-squared values.

The moderate negative influence of the SF&CF investment on total population change in conjunction with the present positive effects on the migration-related indicators (MDP and registered migration) suggests that these funds were applied more intensively in the regions with highly negative population change due to natural movement, and were unable to improve the situation over such a short time period.

The SDM shows a very good fit for change of population due to registered migration (indicated by a high logarithmic likelihood value), which suggests the important role of Type 2 spatial spillovers of the EU SF&CF as well as municipal social support spending. This is logical, as both of these factors provide known benefits (social services, social aid, public infrastructure, etc.) for the inhabitants officially registered in the particular municipality or residing in the direct vicinity. The SDM also hints at the moderately significant spatially distributed effects of the EU SF&CF on both change of population below working age (possibly due to investment in education, medical and social care facilities in rural centres) and reduction of MDP.

By demonstrating a high significance of the spatially correlated error term, the SEM confirms and underlines the presence of one or more unaccounted external spatially correlated factors impacting the MDP rate in the local municipalities. This highlights the need for additional in-depth study of this important social, economic and demographic phenomenon.

Although very useful in understanding the nature of regional demographic processes, the analytical approach presented in this section should be further expanded by the inclusion of individual-level data and wider use of qualitative information regarding the socio-economic situation in the particular groups of municipalities. Some use of historical information and historical population data, as demonstrated by Dahs (2014b), is also highly advisable.

Conclusions

First, confirming the conclusions of previous studies, the LM estimations show that personal income (represented by average collected personal income tax) remains the most significant predictor for such regional demographic indicators as total population change, change of population below working age and change of population due to registered migration. Furthermore, unemployment levels appear to be just as significant for change of population below working age and change of population due to registered migration.

Second, judging by the overall estimation results, it is possible to conclude that, in terms of regional demographic change, EU SF&CF have had a moderately significant direct and partly significant spatially distributed impact on the migration-related indicators under investigation (MDP and registered migration). On the other hand, the per capita spending of agriculture-related funds (EFF, EAFRD and EAGF) has been slightly significant for total population change, hinting at the role of these investments in the development of rural or coastal areas and the resulting improvement in economic and social conditions.

Third, from the SDM estimation results, one may draw a conclusion about noticeable spatial spillovers of the EU SF&CF as well as municipal social support spending in relation to change of population due to registered migration. A similar conclusion may be drawn concerning a spatially distributed effect of the EU SF&CF on both change of population below working age and the reduction of MDP. Both of these observations suggest that these instruments may be applied in a more centralised manner (in other words, concentrating on regional development centres), while sustaining sufficient spatial coverage.

Finally, further comparison of the linear and spatial model estimations (particularly the SEM) for the MDP indicator allows us to assume the existence of an unknown highly spatially correlated factor (or series of factors) influencing the individual decisions regarding temporary or unregistered migration for economic or other purposes. This underlines the necessity to conduct further qualitative and quantitative studies of this complex process, using both classical and spatially adjusted tools.

Acknowledgements

This chapter was supported by the Latvian National Research Programme 5.2, "Economic Transformation, Smart Growth, Governance and Legal Framework for the State and Society for Sustainable Development: A New Approach to the Creation of a Sustainable Learning Community" (EKOSOC-LV).

Table 7.3 Effects of regional investment/policy instruments on selected demographic indicators in the years 2009–13: SWR model results (SLM, SDM and SEM using connectivity matrix, k = 1).

Parameter		SLM				SDM					SEM			
	Indicator	Total pop. change	<15 pop. change	MDP change index	Pop. change due to reg. migration	Total pop. change	<15 pop. change	MDP change index	Pop. change due to reg. migration		Total pop. change	<15 pop. change	MDP change index	Pop. change due to reg. migration
Direct effects (β)	SF&CF	−0.00303	−0.00196	−0.00222**	0.00037*	−0.00269*	−0.00271	−0.00191*	0.00033		−0.00342*	−0.0244	−0.00219**	0.00036*
	OF	0.00270**	−0.00152	0.00082	0.00016	0.00221**	−0.00103	0.00045	0.00009		0.00277**	−0.0160	0.00088	0.00016
	FDI	−0.00017	−0.00035	0.00015	−0.00006	−0.00014	−0.00044	0.00019	−0.00006		−0.00020	−0.00050	0.00021	−0.00006
	SocSup	−0.01769	−0.04791	−0.00099	−0.00571*	−0.01354	−0.02827	0.00934	−0.00546*		−0.01715	−0.04752	0.00540	−0.00584*
	IncTax	0.03729***	0.08229***	0.00925	0.00175***	0.03456***	0.08428***	−0.00370	0.00153***		0.04070***	0.08943***	−0.00164	0.00180***
	Unemployed	0.18204**	0.60759***	−0.02508	0.02622**	0.19273	0.70316**	−0.03733	0.02908		0.17321	0.62119***	−0.01880	0.02679**
Spatially lagged indicators (θ)	SF&CF	–	–	–	–	0.00161	−0.01102	0.00205	0.00041		–	–	–	–
	OF	–	–	–	–	−0.00338	0.00174	−0.00156	−0.00002		–	–	–	–
	FDI	–	–	–	–	−0.00123	0.00372	−0.00074	0.00000		–	–	–	–
	SocSup	–	–	–	–	0.05663	0.07473	0.04897	0.01356*		–	–	–	–
	IncTax	–	–	–	–	0.00054	0.00527	0.00063	−0.00007		–	–	–	–
	Unemployed	–	–	–	–	−0.12681	−0.32300	−0.06214	−0.02845		–	–	–	–
Spatial	ρ (spat. lag. dep. var.)	0.16922*	0.14102	0.30717**	0.05530	–	–	–	–		–	–	–	–
	λ (spat. error)	–	–	–	–	–	–	–	–		0.19713	0.20248	0.36608**	0.08630
Model fit	R²	0.81196	0.84364	0.16622	0.26862	–	–	–	–		0.80957	0.84309	0.18908	0.27050
	Log. likelihood	–	–	–	–	−256.43	−355.88	−210.30	−33.09		–	–	–	–

Significance codes: 0–0.001 ***; 0.001–0.01 **; 0.01–0.05 *; 0.05–0.1 `; 0.1–1 no code.

Source: Author's calculations based on CSB and RDIM data.

Note

1 "Cities of republican significance" is the official designation for the urban municipalities meeting specific criteria outlined by the Law on Administrative-Territorial Reform of the Republic of Latvia.

References

Anselin, L. (1999), "Interactive techniques and exploratory spatial data analysis", in P. Longley, M. Goodchild, D. Maguire and D. Rhind (eds), *Geographical Information Systems: Principles, Techniques, Management and Applications*, Cambridge, UK: GeoInformation International, pp. 253–66.
Anselin, L. (2003), "Spatial externalities, spatial multipliers, and spatial econometrics", *International Regional Science Review*, 26(2), 153–66.
Bivand, R. (2002), "Spatial econometrics functions in R: classes and methods", *Journal of Geographical Systems*, 4(4), 405–21.
Central Statistics Bureau of Latvia (CSB) (2014), *CSB Database* (online), http://dati.csb.gov.lv (accessed 2 December 2014).
Dahs, A. (2014a), "Measuring the impact of spatial factors in regional demographic development of Latvia", *New Challenges of Economic and Business Development 2014, Conference Proceedings*, pp. 85–96.
Dahs, A. (2014b), "Historical regional demographic divergence in Latvia: lessons of the common past with Eastern Partnership countries", *Baltic Journal of European Studies*, 4(2), 119–33.
Eglīte, P. (2008), "Nedeklarētās izceļošanas sekas un to rosinātā rīcība: Darbaspējīgo skaita mazināšanās Latvijā un iespējamie risinājumi", *Apcerējumi par Latvijas iedzīvotājiem*, 13(1), 16–34.
Ferry, M. and Vironen, H. (2010), "Dealing with demographic change: regional policy responses, s.l.", European Policy Research Centre, Paper No. 72.
Fésüs, G., Rillaers, A., Poelman, H. and Gáková, Z. (2008), "Regions 2020: demographic challenges for European regions, s.l.", background document to European Commission Staff Working Document No. SEC(2008) 2868.
Krišjāne, Z. and Bauls, A. (2007), "Migrācijas plūsmu reģionālās iezīmes Latvijā", *Paaudžu nomaiņa un migrācija Latvijā, Stratēģiskās analīzes komisijas zinātniski pētnieciskie raksti*, 4(15), 130–43.
Matthews, S. A. and Parker, D. M. (2013), "Progress in spatial demography", *Demographic Research*, 28(10), 271–312.
Ministry of Regional Development and Local Governments of the Republic of Latvia (2006). *National Development Plan 2007–2013*, Riga, Latvia: MRDLG.
Paiders, J. (2007), "Ekonomisku un sociālu kvantitatīvu indikatoru pielietošana reģionālās attīstības un politikas mērījumos", *Latvijas Zinātņu akadēmijas Vēstis. A daļa: Sociālās un humanitārās zinātnes*, 61(6), 16–31.
Regional Development Indicator Module (RDIM) (2015), *RDIM Database* (online), http://raim.gov.lv/pub/#/ (accessed 10 May 2015).
State Regional Development Agency (SRDA) (2013), *Attīstības centru ietekmes areālu noteikšana un analīze: Plānošanas reģionu, republikas pilsētu un novadu pašvaldību attīstības raksturojums*, Riga, Latvia: Ministry of Environmental Protection and Regional Development.

Voss, P. R., White, K. C. and Hammer, R. B. (2006), "Explorations in spatial demography", in W. A. Kandel and D. L. Brown (eds), *Population Change and Rural Society*, Netherlands: Springer, pp. 407–429.
Ward, M. D. and Gleditsch, K. S. (2008), *Spatial Regression Models*, Thousand Oaks, CA: Sage.
Zvidriņš, P. (ed.) (2009), *Demogrāfiskā attīstība Latvijas reģionos*, Riga, Latvia: LU Akadēmiskais apgāds.
Zvidriņš, P. (2012), "Demographic development in the Baltic Sea Region", *Latvijas Zinātņu Akadēmijas Vēstis – A 66*, 5(6), 49–61.

8 The policy challenge in smart specialisation

A common approach meets European diversity

Henning Kroll

Introduction

Triggered by the work of the Knowledge for Growth Expert Group (David *et al.*, 2009; Foray *et al.*, 2009, 2011), smart specialisation was developed as an academic concept in the mid- to late-2000s (McCann and Ortega-Argilés, 2011). It originated from the acknowledgement that neither laissez-faire strategies nor simple support for high-tech industries will be sufficient to prompt a turnaround in Europe's industries (Ahner and Landabaso, 2011; Foray *et al.*, 2011; Ortega-Argilés, 2012; McCann and Ortega-Argilés, 2014a). As was suggested, Europe's problems with translating technologies into products are not so much due to its industrial structure (Van Ark *et al.*, 2008) than to *intrinsic* deficiencies within many sectors (O'Mahony and Van Ark, 2003; Draca *et al.*, 2006; Wilson, 2009). Against this background, it was argued that policy support should to a greater extent focus on *general purpose technologies* (Rodrik, 2004; Enkel and Gassmann, 2010; Foray, 2012; Landabaso, 2012) that could help transform industries onto a broader basis (Landabaso, 2014; McCann and Ortega-Argilés, 2014b) rather than being targeted at selected high-tech sectors. As was argued further, such areas of support could best be determined in a joint process of "discovery" with those who, in their everyday work, develop products and apply technology (Hausman and Rodrik, 2003; Foray *et al.*, 2012; Coffano and Foray, 2014; OECD, 2014).

Even before the concept of smart specialisation had been formulated, regional economists and economic geographers had addressed issues of regional development through concepts that shared some of the smart specialisation debate's notions, while being more consciously sensitive to the diversity of regional contexts. As early as 2006, Cooke and Asheim (Asheim *et al.*, 2006) not only devised an approach to *constructing regional advantage*, but also provided suggestions for potential ways of realising it in different settings. In this context, a need for place-based approaches was advocated not least on the grounds of differences between institutions (Tödtling and Trippl, 2005; Barca *et al.*, 2012; Asheim, 2013). Moreover, many European regions had actually embraced place-based policy approaches for decades, so that routines for participatory and evidence-based strategy definition had been tested and proven there long before the onset of the smart specialisation debate (Lagendijk, 2012; Capello, 2014; Kroll *et al.*,

2014). While the smart specialisation debate thus provided new momentum and a better rationale and overall framework for a new take on regional policy, in many regions relevant concepts, practices and even tools for implementation stood ready to be incorporated (Foray, 2014).

Conceptual background

RIS3: a rash translation from concept to policy?

As McCann and Ortega-Argilés (2011) and Foray (2014) have vividly described, the months following the delivery of the Knowledge for Growth report witnessed an energetic embracing of the smart specialisation concept by the European Commission's Directorate General for Regional and Urban Policy (Foray *et al.*, 2012). Soon, a high-level decision was taken that it should be applied in all European regions, irrespective of their economic – and institutional – strength, and the submission of regional innovation strategies for smart specialisation ("RIS3" documents) as well as the establishment of a related governance structure was declared an ex ante conditionality for funding from the European Structural and Investment Funds. As this chapter will argue, this unusually swift translation of a still nascent academic notion into a hands-on policy approach (Foray *et al.*, 2011; Foray, 2014) did not leave enough time to suitably adapt the resulting policy agenda based on an "in-depth understanding" of Europe's diverse "regional institutional arrangements" to which successful "development strategies [should be] tailored" (Rodríguez-Pose, 2013: 1042).

Policy failures: past and present

As Foray *et al.* (2011) have argued, part of the failure of regional innovation policy during the 2007–13 programming period was due to what they call a persistent and "stifling policy dogma": the prevalent notion that regional innovation policy should not discriminate in terms of the sectoral or technological fields that should receive priority support. In practice, this approach often met with weak institutions and became prone to rent-seeking, clientelism and other undesirable processes of decision-making (Rodríguez-Pose, 2013). As has been convincingly argued, bad faith actions and corruption (Acemoglu and Robinson, 2000; Farole *et al.*, 2011; Rodríguez-Pose *et al.*, 2014) took a substantial toll on the success of generalist regional innovation policies. These failures are often discussed by advocates of the RIS3 agenda as being the result of inadequate action, based on a lack of comprehension or goodwill, which could, in principle, be remedied by *better* RIS3 processes (Coffano and Foray, 2014).

Unfortunately, however, recent empirical analysis (Iacobucci, 2014) and an increasing number of case studies (Reid *et al.*, 2012; Reid and Stanovnik, 2013; Komninos *et al.*, 2014) demonstrate that the RIS3 process has so far failed to prompt this general turnaround and Iacobucci (2014) paints a rather bleak picture of the draft RIS3 documents submitted to the European Commission. Moreover,

Iacobucci (2014) and Boschma (2014) cast doubt on the notion that bottom-up processes will as such be conducive to making "tough choices" and increase the efficacy of support policy. While acknowledging that entrepreneurs are in a better position than officials to identify opportunities, Iacobucci (2014: 118) strongly cautions that "a bottom-up process [may] inevitably result in a proliferation [of] specialisation domains, rather than in their more effective identification". Apparently, regions with known institutional weaknesses and weak governance systems are indeed facing difficulties in focusing their strategies (Reid *et al.*, 2012; Reid and Stanovnik, 2013; Komninos *et al.*, 2014). As many case studies suggest, regional frameworks can thus hardly be analysed based on the premise that there is "a regional government" that simply has to "perform well", for two reasons:

1 Successful policies depend on the capacities of actors as much as on institutions. Many regional entities, however, do not possess the necessary material, human or professional resources to adequately deal with complex strategic processes.
2 Even with sound competencies in developing innovation strategies, regional governments are not atomic actors. In more autonomous regions, moreover, regional policy is often subject to complex, intra-administrative negotiations of claims between local ministries and agencies.

In my view, therefore, the acknowledgement of these two *internal* aspects of regional governance is crucial – not least because they not only constitute an external, limiting framework for policymakers but can, in principle, also be amended by them.

Research questions

In brief, this chapter will address two main research questions:

1 It will seek to confirm whether there is indeed a persistent policy failure by evaluating whether final RIS3 strategies still lack focus in terms of the number of priorities.
2 It will analyse in which type of European regions policymakers see positive cost–benefit assessments of bottom-up RIS3 processes and what motivates this appraisal.

Across both areas, an institutional and governance perspective will be taken by juxtaposing groups of regions that differ in both respects.

Methodology

This study builds on the new empirical basis of two successive questionnaire-based online surveys with policymakers conducted in the three-month period from July to September 2013 and the four-month period from May to August

2014. The population of potential respondents was built on data from the European Commission's S3 Platform (owners of RIS3 processes) and the Inforegio website (ERDF managing authorities). Even for the 2013 survey, more than 500 potential respondents could be identified. In 2014, with more knowledge about the full teams working on RIS3, the baseline population could be extended to nearly 1,000.

In 2013, more than 70 of the targeted addressees completed the questionnaire in full and more than 130 answered notable sections of it. In 2014, the respective figures were similar, with 80 complete and 160 partially complete responses. In 2013, 43 questionnaires could be identified as coming from Central Europe (DE, FR, BE, NL, LU, AT), 10 from Northern Europe (DK, SE, FI), 25 from Southern Europe (ES, PT, IT, GR) and 22 from Eastern Europe, leaving a certain gap in coverage only with regard to a mere five responses from Ireland and the UK. The following year, 25 questionnaires could be identified as coming from Central Europe, 11 from Northern Europe, 20 from Southern Europe, 30 from Eastern Europe and only 7 from Ireland and the UK.

Results

Regarding the first research question, the 2013 data suggested that nearly half of all respondents found the number of potential RIS3 priority fields in their region rather limited, while only 30 per cent saw a broad range of choices. Hence, the starting conditions for a development of focused strategies through conscious choices seemed not to be detrimental as such. At first sight, the results of the 2014 survey confirm this expectation with more than 80 per cent of all regions indicating that they defined fewer than five "RIS3 priorities". However, this impression is qualified by further analyses that distinguish the average number of priorities by regional type. As Table 8.1 illustrates, the surprising result of doing so is that the number of priorities and in particular sub-priorities is significantly higher in regions where one has reason to assume that the number of actual economic fields of strength is in reality more limited. This applies to both regions in Eastern Europe and former "convergence regions". Thus, the data seem to corroborate Iacobucci's (2014) claim that many economically weaker regions are outlining a number of priorities that are inadequate given their actual techno-economic potentials.

Beyond the nominal focus on a certain number of priorities, the survey inquired about actual changes to policy delivery (Komninos *et al.*, 2014). As Table 8.2 illustrates, in 2013, only about 40 per cent of respondents indicated that the RIS3 agenda was likely to spur substantial adaptations to their local policy mix. In line with this, an "increase of efficacy of support policy due to a clearer focus of allocations" was identified as the main positive outcome of the RIS3 process by a mere 22 per cent of respondents in 2014. Beyond the issue of regional distribution, these findings provide further grounds for doubting the initial impression that the RIS3 agenda has indeed prompted a stronger focus of support policies across the board.

Table 8.1 Number of RIS3 priorities as indicated in strategy.

	Main priorities (average)	Sub-priorities (average)
By member state group		
Central Europe	3.56	2.40
Southern Europe	4.06	2.94
Eastern Europe	3.70	6.90
By target category		
Regional competitiveness and employment (GDP per capita above 75% EU average)	3.14	3.58
Convergence (GDP per capita below 75% EU average)	3.54	5.29

Note: For member state ANOVA significance at the 1 per cent level (both); for regional type ANOVA significance at the 5 per cent level (both).

Table 8.2 Expected and actual changes to policy based on RIS3.

Predictions of likely adaptations (in 2013 survey)			Conclusions on main benefit of RIS3 (in 2014 survey)		
Substantial adaptations	9	9.9%	Collection of evidence on future opportunities	35	47.3%
Notable amendments	29	31.9%	Increase of efficacy due to focus of allocations	16	21.6%
Minor adaptations	33	36.3%	Renewal of the regional planning culture	15	20.3%
No adaptations expected	20	22.0%	Methodological improvement of governance	4	5.4%
			Other	4	5.4%
n =		91		74	

Regarding the second research question, we at first find prevalent claims that successful, bottom-up consultation processes have been implemented according to requirements. Even in 2013, about three out of five respondents suggested that additional stakeholders from the enterprise sector and the research sector and further external experts could be involved in a more inclusive process. Moreover, the findings suggested that the process was indeed taking a fairly "hands-on", pragmatic course, drawing on well-established methods such as working groups (78 per cent of respondents), expert hearings (60 per cent) and general public discourses (55 per cent). On the surface, once more, the degree of realisation of RIS3 objectives thus appeared quite high.

When respondents were asked about the processes' results in 2014, however, a fairly different picture emerged. Overall, more than two-thirds stated that RIS3 processes had generated novel insights to an at best moderate extent (Table 8.3). Apparently, their straightforward benefit in terms of "discovery" (in other words, novelty of findings) was limited, as was suggested might be the case by Boschma (2014) and Iacobucci (2014). Nonetheless, respondents from a surprisingly high proportion of all of the regions – more than half – indicated that the benefits of the RIS3 process outweighed its costs. Apparently, factors other than mere "discovery" came into play in prompting this assessment. This impression is confirmed by the finding that there is no significant correlation between the extent of discoveries and the overall assessment reported. When exploring the data beyond the notion of "discovery", however, one finds that more than two-thirds of the respondents indicated that the RIS3 process has triggered the introduction of *new elements of governance* into the regional policy process, and more than 90 per cent asserted that these will be maintained. Beyond the "discovery" of new knowledge, a degree of institutional change thus appears to be a relevant impact of RIS3 processes.

Again, no direct, significant correlation can be identified between the degree of novelty of the process and the overall degree of satisfaction with the local RIS3 efforts. When adding an interaction term that combines the introduction of novel processes with a positive outcome in terms of findings, the coefficient takes a positive sign and comes closer to tentative significance. While, apparently, the introduction of a novel process is not *per se* reason enough to trigger a favourable assessment, the *combination* of process-related novelty and actual "discoveries" does yield that result. Likewise, cases in which the degree of institutional change is high yet are unaccompanied by actual "discoveries" will lead to a more negative assessment of the cost–benefit ratio of the exercise (Table 8.4, Model 1).

In the remainder of this chapter, I will shed some more light onto this diversity by analysing the findings from the perspective of country groups. As Table 8.5 illustrates, RIS3 processes with their bottom-up character were identified as a substantial novelty to a much greater extent in Southern and Eastern European regions than in the established democratic governance systems of Central Europe, where fewer than 10 per cent of respondents considered this approach new. Accordingly, regions from these countries more commonly reported a greater degree of novelty in their findings. Central European regions, in contrast, built on earlier findings with "moderate" amendments rather than learning things of which they had so far been entirely unaware. In this respect, Southern and Eastern Europe profited from the RIS3 agenda in a similar way.

Table 8.3 Outcome of RIS3 process: novel insights vs. novel routines.

To what degree has the RIS3-inspired consultation process generated novel insights not available before? (2014)			To what degree are bottom-up consultation processes new to the planning tradition of your region? (2014)		
Very low degree	2	2.6%	Entirely new	5	6.4%
Low degree	12	15.8%	New in many respects	13	16.7%
Moderate degree	39	51.3%	New in some respects	41	52.6%
High degree	18	23.7%	Not at all new	19	24.4%
Very high degree	5	6.6%			
n =	76			78	

Table 8.4 Determinants of the overall assessment of RIS3 processes.

dV: Cost–benefit assessment (1–5)	Model 1 (OLS)			Model 2 (OLS)		
	Coeff.	Std. err.	p-value	Coeff.	Std. err.	p-value
Novelty of findings (1–5)	−0.221	0.324	0.497	−0.050	0.330	0.881
Novelty of process (1–5)	−0.743	0.513	0.153	−0.460	0.523	0.382
INT novelty of findings * process	0.209	0.146	0.157	0.130	0.149	0.384
DUM Eastern Europe				−0.632	0.306	0.043
DUM Central, North, British Isles				−0.221	0.320	0.492
Constant	−1.608	1.017	0.119	1.855	1.032	0.077
Observations	65			64		
R² within	0.0574			0.1242		
F	0.3037			0.1626		

Note: Reference country group for dummies = Southern Europe.

Table 8.5 Outcomes of RIS3 process by member state group.

	Central Europe	Southern Europe	Eastern Europe	Contingency coefficient
Novelty of process/routines				
Not at all or only in some respects new	**78.3%**	55.6%	65.5%	**0.054**
In many respects or totally new	8.7%	**38.9%**	**31.0%**	
Novelty of findings				
High/very high degree of novelty	**8.7%**	38.9%	37.9%	0.390
Moderate degree of novelty	56.5%	44.4%	41.4%	
Low/very low degree of novelty	21.7%	**11.1%**	**13.8%**	
Main effect/benefit				
Clearer focus of allocations	**38.1%**	23.5%	6.9%	**0.041**
Better understanding of potentials	14.3%	**58.8%**	**48.3%**	
Renewal of planning culture	19.0%	5.9%	**34.5%**	
Technical improvement through methodological input	9.5%	0.0%	3.4%	
Overall cost/benefit assessment				
Benefits outweighed costs	43%	**76%**	38%	0.133
Benefits equalled costs	5%	12%	**38%**	
Costs outweighed benefits	14%	6%	**17%**	

Note: Contingency coefficients calculated based on tables excluding "n/a" or missing data points; percentages calculated including these. Data of particular interest highlighted in bold.

The question of RIS3's key benefit, however, also reveals a central difference between Southern and Eastern Europe in terms of the nature of the RIS3 process. In Southern Europe, the "renewal of the local planning culture" was even less commonly mentioned than in Central Europe, while in Eastern Europe, more than a third of all regions considered that aspect to be the main benefit of the RIS3 agenda. Interestingly, regions in this group were also those that most commonly reported that the costs of the process outweighed or at best equalled its benefits.

Apparently, regions in which bottom-up approaches constituted a fairly novel take on governance had to invest significant effort to renew the regional planning culture to make RIS3 processes work in the first place. Arguably, this cost them a lot of energy so that their overall cost–benefit assessment became – as a tendency – more negative.

Again, this finding can be confirmed with a tentative regression analysis that illustrates that both the novelty of findings and process-based novelty lose relevance when dummies for country groups are introduced. Instead, the only remaining finding is that respondents from Eastern Europe's institutionally weak environments are significantly less likely to consider their local RIS3 activities worthwhile than others (Table 8.4, Model 2).

Summary and discussion

With regard to the first research question, this chapter finds that, formally, there is in fact a distinct thematic focus in many of the by now developed RIS3 strategies. Nonetheless, there is equally strong evidence that many weaker regions have failed to adapt their strategic ambitions to the locally available economic options and that "strategic priorities" often take the character of recommendations.

With regard to the second research question, this chapter finds that, for many regions, the implementation and exploitation of bottom-up consultation processes proved a challenging effort. Moreover, its success has been notably influenced by the capacities of local governance systems. In many regions of Southern and Eastern Europe, the requirements of the RIS3 agenda required the establishment of novel routines. Achieving this was often in itself considered a valuable contribution. As theory suggests, however, the institutional framework also determined whether findings, once made, could be fruitfully exploited. While, on average, Southern European regions have been able to do so, the general mismatch between RIS3 ideas and local governance systems in Eastern Europe more often prompted situations in which the potential for freshly gained RIS3 knowledge was lost.

In summary, the context sensitivity of RIS3 implementation can be illustrated by distinguishing three main groups of regions:

1 *Newcomers.* To (often) Eastern European regions, the RIS3 agenda represented an entirely novel approach to policy-making. New suggestions on governance practices met with hard institutional obstacles in terms of traditional planning cultures and centralist governance systems, which made it difficult to implement them. Although most RIS3 processes were in the end completed, more effort had to be invested in setting them up than elsewhere. Also, it remains uncertain if their "discoveries" will be translated into action (Komninos *et al.*, 2014).

2 *Active beneficiaries.* To (often) Southern European regions, the RIS3 agenda brought a new impetus to governance systems where bottom-up approaches were so far less prevalent in economic and S&T policy while the overall

institutional framework was more suitable than in the first group. Many of these polities had used participatory strategies before, while at the same time their routines of governance left room for improvement. Not least because budgetary pressure increased their willingness to accept any process to improve efficacy in policy-making, this group of regions profited most. Importantly, their benefit appears to have been based on the reshaping of malleable governance routines as much as on actual findings.

3 *Drivers*. Many Central and Northern European regions with long experience and strong capacities in strategy-building did not gain substantial new insights through their RIS3 processes. In fact, many of them provided input to the RIS3 agenda, rather than drawing significant lessons from it. Nonetheless, even they tended to report having been inspired to amend their routines of governance. Quite often, the RIS3 agenda was credited with helping to overcome fragmentation and improve coordination even in *per se* already well-functioning policy systems.

On the one hand, this study thus concludes that the pursuit of the RIS3 agenda's generalist objectives will necessarily evolve differently in different "systems" (Foray and Rainoldi, 2013) – in other words, in different institutional arrangements and frameworks of governance. On the other hand, it provides evidence that RIS3 processes have in turn made a notable contribution to changes and amendments in routines and practices of governance – of which some may hopefully be long lasting.

Policy conclusions

The practical application of the RIS3 agenda constitutes a showcase of European regional diversity. Indeed, there is reason to doubt that the often promoted positive messages from RIS3 best practice cases can be considered as representative or universally applicable. In line with the literature, this study suggests that diversity in implementation is strongly determined by differences in general institutions and, more importantly, regionally specific modes of governance. At the same time, it demonstrates that not all institutional arrangements and routines are cast in stone and that it may in fact be one of the key merits of the RIS3 agenda to not accept them as given. While this study underlines that smart specialisation "by the book" could often not be achieved, RIS3 processes helped to promote key notions of participatory policy and evidence-based thinking in many regions. Arguably, this conscious "structuration" of regional governance by RIS3 processes is the agenda's most substantial contribution, laying the foundations for future, more effective regional policies. In the long run, this may well prove more valuable than a one-off shift in allocations according to formal priorities. To conclude, the RIS3 agenda should be followed up in a place-sensitive manner. When continuing RIS3-inspired policy efforts across the programming period, there may be as much value in asking what a specific regional polity can (next) achieve as in asking what, theoretically, it should do.

Acknowledgements

While the conclusions and opinions outlined in this chapter are entirely my own, I am indebted to Prof. Knut Koschatzky for financing this research from internal means at Fraunhofer ISI as well as to my colleagues Andrea Zenker, Esther Schnabl and Emmanuel Muller, who substantially contributed to building the quantitative database for this study.

References

Acemoglu, D. and Robinson, J. A. (2000), "Political losers as a barrier to economic development", *American Economic Review*, 90(2), 126–30.

Ahner, D. and Landabaso, M. (2011), "Regional policies in times of austerity, *European Review of Industrial Economics and Policy*, 2, itopics, available at: http://revel.unice.fr/eriep/index.html?id=3238 (accessed 8 February 2016).

Asheim, B. (2013), "Smart specialization: old wine in new bottles or new wine in old bottles?", presentation at the ERSA Conference, Palermo, 28 August.

Asheim, B., Annerstedt, J., Blazek, J., Boschma, R., Brzica, D., Dahlstrand Lindholm, A., Del Castillo Hermosa, J., Laredo, P., Moula, M. and Piccaluga, A. (2006), *Constructing Regional Advantage: Principles, Perspectives, Policies*, report prepared by an independent expert group, chaired by Prof. Phil Cooke for the DG for Research, Brussels: European Commission.

Barca, F., McCann, P. and Rodríguez-Pose, A. (2012), "The case for regional development intervention: place-based versus place-neutral approaches", *Journal of Regional Science*, 52(1), 134–52.

Boschma, R. (2014), "Constructing regional advantage and smart specialisation: comparison of two European policy concepts", *Scienze Regionali, Italian Journal of Regional Science*, 13(1), 51–68.

Capello, R. (2014), "Smart specialisation strategy and the new EU Cohesion Policy reform: introductory remarks", *Scienze Regionali, Italian Journal of Regional Science*, 13(1), 5–15.

Coffano, M. and Foray, D. (2014), "The centrality of entrepreneurial discovery in building and implementing a smart specialisation strategy", *Scienze Regionali, Italian Journal of Regional Science*, 13(1), 33–50.

David, P., Foray, D. and Hall, B. (2009), "Measuring smart specialisation: the concept and the need for indicators", Knowledge for Growth Expert Group, available at: cemi.epfl.ch/./Measuring% 20smart%20specialization (accessed 10 November 2014).

Draca, M., Sadun, R. and van Reenen, J. (2006), "Productivity and the ICTs: a review of the evidence", in R. Mansell, C. Avgerou, D. Quah and R. Silverstone (eds), *The Oxford Handbook of Innovation and Communication Technologies*, Oxford, UK: Oxford University Press, pp. 100–47.

Enkel, E. and Gassmann, O. (2010), "Creative imitation: exploring the case of cross-industry innovation", *R&D Management*, 40(3), 256–70.

Farole, T., Rodríguez-Pose, A. and Storper, M. (2011), "Cohesion Policy in the European Union: growth, geography, institutions", *Journal of Common Market Studies*, 49(5), 1089–111.

Foray, D. (2012), *Smart Specialisation and the New Industrial Policy Agenda, Innovation for Growth*, i4g Policy Brief No. 8, Brussels: European Commission.

Foray, D. (2014), *Smart Specialisation: Opportunities and Challenges for Regional Innovations Policy*, London: Routledge.

Foray, D. and Rainoldi, A. (2013), *Smart Specialisation Programmes and Implementation Report*, EUR 26002 EN, S3 Policy Brief Series, No. 02/2013, Seville, Spain: European Commission, JRC-IPTS.

Foray, D., David, P. A. and Hall, B. H. (2009), *Smart Specialisation: The Concept*, Knowledge Economists Policy Brief No. 9, June, Brussels: European Commission, available at: http://ec.europa.eu/invest-in-research/pdf/download_en/kfg_policy_brief_no9.pdf (accessed 7 February 2016).

Foray, D., David, P. A. and Hall, B. H. (2011), "Smart specialization: from academic idea to political instrument/the surprising career of a concept and the difficulties involved in its implementation", MTEI-WORKING_PAPER-2011-001, Lausanne, Switzerland: École Polytechnique Federale de Lausanne.

Foray, D., Goddard, J., Goenaga Beldarrain, X., Landabaso, M., McCann, P., Morgan, K., Nauwelaers, C. and Ortega-Artilés, R. (2012), *Guide to Research and Innovation Strategies for Smart Specialisation (RIS3)*, Brussels: European Commission, Smart Specialisation Platform.

Hausman, R. and Rodrik, D. (2003), "Economic development as self-discovery", *Journal of Development Economics*, 72(2), 603–33.

Iacobucci, D. (2014), "Designing and implementing a smart specialisation strategy at regional level: some open questions", *Scienze Regionali, Italian Journal of Regional Science*, 13(1), 107–26.

Komninos, N., Musyck, B. and Reid, A. I. (2014), "Smart specialisation strategies in south Europe during crisis", *European Journal of Innovation Management*, 17(4), 448–71.

Kroll, H., Muller, E., Schnabl, E. and Zenker, A. (2014), "From smart concept to challenging practice: how European regions deal with the Commission's request for novel innovation strategies", Working Paper Policy and Region No. R2/2014, Karlsruhe, Germany: Fraunhofer ISI.

Lagendijk, A. (2012), "Smart specialization strategies: how can it benefit the Brainflow regions", presentation at the Brainflow Thematic Exchange of Experience Meeting, Arnheim.

Landabaso, M. (2012), "What public policies can and cannot do for regional development", in P. Cooke, M. D. Parrilli and J. L. Curbelo (eds), *Innovation, Global Challenge and Territorial Resilience*, Cheltenham, UK: Edward Elgar, pp. 364–81.

Landabaso, M. (2014), "Time for the real economy: the need for new forms of public entrepreneurship", *Scienze Regionali, Italian Journal of Regional Science*, 13(1), 27–40.

McCann, P. and Ortega-Argilés, R. (2011), "Smart specialisation, regional growth and applications to EU Cohesion Policy", Economic Geography Working Paper, University of Groningen.

McCann, P. and Ortega-Argilés, R. (2014a), "The role of the smart specialisation agenda in a reformed EU Cohesion Policy", *Scienze Regionali, Italian Journal of Regional Science*, 13(1), 15–32.

McCann, P. and Ortega-Argilés, R. (2014b), "Smart specialisation, regional growth and applications to EU Cohesion Policy", *Regional Studies*, DOI:10.1080/00343404.2013.799769.

OECD (2014), *Innovation-Driven Growth in Regions: The Role of Smart Specialisation*, Preliminary Version, Paris: OECD.

O'Mahony, M. and Van Ark, B. (eds) (2003), *EU Productivity and Competitiveness: An Industry Perspective – Can Europe Resume the Catching-Up Process?* Luxembourg: European Communities.

Ortega-Argilés, R. (2012), "The transatlantic productivity gap: a survey of the main causes", *Journal of Economic Surveys*, 26(3), 395–419.

Reid, A. and Stanovnik, P. (2013), *The Development of a Smart Specialisation Strategy (S3) for Slovenia*, report to the European Commission, DG Research & Innovation, Brussels: European Commission.

Reid, A., Komninos, N., Sanchez, J. and Tsanakas, P. (2012), *RIS3 National Assessment: Greece – Smart Specialisation as a Means to Foster Economic Renewal*, report to the European Commission, DG Regional Policy, Brussels: European Commission.

Rodríguez-Pose, A. (2013), "Do institutions matter for regional development?", *Regional Studies*, 47(7), 1034–47.

Rodríguez-Pose, A., di Cataldo, M. and Rainoldi, A. (2014), "The role of government institutions for smart specialisation and regional development", JRC-IPTS Working Papers JRC88935, Institute for Prospective and Technological Studies, Joint Research Centre.

Rodrik, D. (2004), *Industrial Policy for the Twenty-First Century*, CEPR Discussion Paper Series No. 4767, London: Centre for Economic Policy Research.

Tödtling, F. and Trippl, M. (2005), "One size fits all? Towards a differentiated regional innovation policy approach", *Research Policy*, 34(8), 1203–19.

Van Ark, B., O'Mahony, M. and Timmer, M. (2008), "The productivity gap between Europe and the United States: trends and causes", *Journal of Economic Perspectives*, 22(1), 25–44.

Wilson, D. J. (2009), "IT and beyond: the contribution of heterogeneous capital to productivity", *Journal of Business and Economic Statistics*, 27(1), 52–70.

9 Resilience and involvement

The role of the EU's Structural and Investment Funds in addressing youth unemployment

Elizabeth Sanderson, Peter Wells and Ian Wilson

Introduction

This chapter explores the role of the EU's Structural and Investment Funds (ESIF) in addressing youth unemployment. Successive European Council conclusions have stated the need for concerted action between the EU institutions and member states to address youth unemployment (Council of the European Union 2011, 2014a; European Commission 2013, 2014). While such calls are welcome, concern has been voiced that the proposals do not go far enough, either in the resources to be deployed or in recognising the scale of structural reforms to labour markets that may be required (Eichhorst *et al.*, 2013; Lahusen *et al.*, 2013).

This chapter looks beyond the now well-established repertoire of ESIF interventions, set out in the European Commission's call for action on youth unemployment (European Commission, 2013) and its memo on how the EU Social Fund (ESF) can support the Youth Guarantee (European Commission, 2014). The call for action recommends the front-loading of actions to address youth unemployment (including the Youth Employment Initiative) as well as longer-term structural reforms, notably around VET (Vocational Education and Training) and practices to encourage hiring by SMEs.

In response to the EU policy positions for the use of the ESIF, this chapter considers evidence on two possible areas for intervention: the involvement of young people in the design and delivery of programmes, and the development of young people's personal resilience as a determinant of successful labour market outcomes. The focus throughout the chapter is on young people furthest from the labour market.

This chapter presents interim findings from a large-scale evaluation of a €130 million seven-year programme (called Talent Match) in England, which is being funded by the UK's Big Lottery Fund (the main distributor of lottery funding in the UK). The programme runs from 2013 to 2020, and differs from approaches seen in many Structural Funds and national programmes in that it is administered and delivered by civil society organisations working as part of youth-led partnerships (with 'youth' defined as those aged 18–24). The programme and its evaluation are at an early stage.

The chapter is structured as follows. First, it considers the challenge of youth unemployment, drawing out evidence to highlight the complexity and severity of the challenge. Second, brief details about the Talent Match programme and its evaluation are outlined. Third, evidence on youth involvement and resilience are considered. A discussion then draws out the implications of the evidence for the ESIF.

The challenge of youth unemployment

With the so-called 'Great Recession', which began in 2008, there was a sharp rise in unemployment across the EU. This increase in unemployment was unevenly distributed both spatially (at both member state and sub-national levels) and by sub-group.

The number of young people (aged 15–24) in the EU28 who were unemployed rose to 5.6 million in 2012 (Eurostat, 2014). Youth unemployment is also concentrated in those areas with a high general level of unemployment. The youth unemployment rate exceeded 50 per cent in 24 NUTS2 regions in 2012, double the number of regions than in 2011. These regions were located in Spain, Greece, France (and its overseas territories) and Italy. There were 111 regions across the EU that had a youth unemployment rate of 25 per cent or more, and thus were eligible for funding under the Youth Employment Initiative. However, there were also regions with relatively low youth unemployment rates. These were predominantly in Germany, Austria and the Netherlands.

Youth unemployment increased more rapidly from 2008 than the overall level of unemployment. In countries such as the UK, it peaked in 2011, albeit at a lower rate than in the recessions of the 1980s and 1990s. It is important to note that since those previous recessions, the proportion of young people in the labour force has fallen, with rising participation in higher education.

The rise in youth unemployment in the 'Great Recession' was experienced across the EU and remains much worse in southern Europe, such that Simmons and Thompson (2013: 1) suggest that: 'Unemployment amongst young people is now at levels without modern historical precedent'. Moreover, focusing solely on unemployment statistics provides only a *partial* perspective on the position of young people vis-à-vis employment. Furthermore, there are concerns about the position of young people *in employment* across the EU. First, there are higher levels of *under-employment* among those young people in relatively stable employment (including those with higher-level qualifications). Second, a 'low-pay, no-pay' cycle persists for those young people who are moving in and out of unstable employment (often with low or no qualifications) (Shildrick *et al.*, 2012).

There were signs that the relative position of young people in the labour market was deteriorating before the 'Great Recession' (Gordon, 1999), suggesting that high levels of youth unemployment are not solely a consequence of recession, albeit they were exacerbated by it. Rather, the root cause goes beyond the state of the economy to underlying structural issues in the youth labour market (Breen, 2005; Cinalli and Giugni, 2013; House of Lords European Union Committee, 2014; Moffat and Roth, 2014).

Structural changes in European labour markets provide some explanations for why young people are faring relatively badly in the labour market. For the UK, 'the sorts of jobs that young people, particularly non-graduates, used to go into are declining. Those that are left are increasingly contested by older and more experienced workers' (UKCES, 2014: 8). Cinalli and Giugni (2013) argue there are at least three youth unemployment 'regimes' in Europe: a conservative regime (in particular countries such as the UK), a Mediterranean regime and a social democratic regime. And so for the UK and other 'conservative regime' countries, the structure of employment is changing to take on the shape of a so-called 'hourglass economy'.

Evidence suggests that in recent years a number of factors, including an increase in the number of small businesses with limited resources, have resulted in a move towards the expectation that people should be 'work-ready' rather than trained 'on the job' (House of Lords European Union Committee, 2014). This disadvantages young people. The UK Employer Skills Survey 2013 shows that while the majority of employers find young recruits well prepared for the world of work, a significant minority do not. The main reasons for dissatisfaction do not relate to literacy or numeracy skills, but rather to a lack of experience and poor attitude (UKCES, 2014). This suggests that so-called 'soft skills' and work experience are becoming especially vital for young people in order to gain first employment as a precursor to sustained employment.

A key focus of this chapter is on young people furthest from the labour market. In broad terms, EU variations in youth unemployment are explained by a range of factors, including economic performance, institutional or regime factors (such as labour market regulation, transition mechanisms from school to work, school quality and qualification quality, and models of VET) (Breen, 2005; Cahuc et al., 2013) and how these together play out in local labour markets (including factors such as transport and social networks) (Green and White, 2007).

A range of psychological factors – including self-efficacy, confidence, motivation and aspirations – are also important in making a successful and sustained transition into employment (or further education and training). For example, in the context of a job search, self-efficacy refers to individuals' judgements about their abilities to successfully perform search activities, such as looking for and applying for opportunities and performing at interviews, and so on (Green et al., 2011). Research suggests that self-efficacy is a key psychological variable affecting job search behaviour and subsequent employment, albeit personal, behavioural and environmental factors play a moderating role. As Brandt and Hank (2014) find, early life experience, including ill health in childhood, can influence self-efficacy and thus is a predictor of labour market outcomes in later life.

The evidence presented suggests that a holistic approach is required for successful activation policies. There is increasing policy attention given to the empowerment of young people in the design and delivery of programmes (as a response to perceived and actual deficits in the legitimacy of public and private institutions) (Dunne et al., 2014), and to the personal resilience of young people in securing successful labour market outcomes. These factors stem from markedly different understandings of the policy problem: one focused on problems with institutions and structures; the other with issues of agency and the problematisation of individuals. Whether the attention given to either is warranted as a response to youth unemployment is considered in the following sections.

Talent Match and its evaluation

Talent Match is a strategic programme of the Big Lottery Fund. The Big Lottery Fund is the main distributor of national lottery funding in the UK, with a particular focus on disadvantage and the support of civic society. The £108 million (€130 million) programme runs from 2013 to 2020 with a main delivery phase from 2014 to 2018. It is a multi-annual grant-funded programme targeted at 21 local areas (Local Enterprise Partnerships in England with high concentrations, or hotspots, of long-term youth unemployment). The aim of the programme is to support around 25,000 people aged 18–24, with at least 20 per cent securing sustainable employment.

The programme intends to improve the pathways for those furthest from the labour market. To this end, the investment is designed around an analysis of the causes of these young people's circumstances, a set of principles or issues it wishes interventions in each of the areas to address, and a set of features that each intervention should embody.

Three aspects of the programme set it apart from other mainstream provision in the UK:

1 Young people are actively involved in the design of partnership strategies and the delivery of projects.
2 There is a strong emphasis on a youth work perspective to deliver the programme, rather than a more traditional work-first or employment focus. It is here where the greater attention to intrinsic factors is considered.
3 Partnerships are coordinated by civil society organisations, including a mix of lead organisations. Some are local organisations while others are major national charities.

The first two aspects are considered in more detail in this chapter.

The evaluation of Talent Match involves a range of methods to make a full economic assessment of the impact of the programme. It includes the collection of longitudinal data on beneficiaries as well as comparator work. These methods are supported by qualitative research (with local partnerships and beneficiaries) and analysis of secondary data (particularly at the local level but also benchmarking to UK surveys). The evaluation does not include randomised control trials, in part due to the heterogeneity of the interventions and for ethical reasons. For the purposes of this chapter, the evaluation evidence presented is intended to provide initial insights into the programme, rather than a full economic assessment.

The involvement of young people

The involvement of young people in the decision-making processes related to service design and delivery can take various forms, and it is important to note that different levels and forms of participation are valid for different groups of young people and for different purposes. Honesty and clarity about the extent of, and limits to, young people's involvement has been found in the literature to be as important, if not more so, than the level of involvement (see, for example, Carnegie UK Trust, 2008). Nonetheless, since the mid-2000s, there has been a growing emphasis on the involvement of service users in the service provision, variously termed co-design, co-production and co-delivery (Bovaird, 2007).

Evidence shows that young people can become involved in service design at both a strategic and an operational level. For example, they may take a strategic role in planning new service developments, in developing organisational policies or in evaluating existing services. Or they may have a more operational focus in, for example, designing services and developing resources including videos and leaflets, or they may be involved in the delivery of the services themselves or in training others to deliver them (Kirby *et al.*, 2003). There is a large body of literature on methods used to engage young people (see, for example, Thomas and O'Kane, 2000; Sinclair, 2004; Halsey *et al.*, 2006), with the appropriateness of different methods largely being seen to reflect both the purpose of engagement and the characteristics of the young people involved.

These trends have led to various attempts to develop a theory of youth participation and conceptualise different types of participation. Evidence from the application of Hart's ladder of participation (Hart, 1992) or modifications thereof show that it is often difficult to distinguish at the operational level which precise 'rung' activities are on and that the main benefits of the model are in prompting organisations to think critically about how they involve young people and in identifying and avoiding 'non-participation' (Treseder, 1997; Bovaird, 2007). In practice, it is more beneficial to divide the types of involvement of young people in decision-making processes related to service provision into three groups:

1. processes in which young people are consulted, but professional staff make decisions;
2. processes of co-production, in which young people and professional staff work together; and
3. processes that are wholly, or mostly, led by young people with professional staff providing support.

Co-production in decision-making – in which service users and professional staff work together, with both groups having substantial input and approximately equal power in the decision-making process – has become increasingly common (Bovaird, 2007). However, evidence of this type of work between young people beyond school age and professional staff remains relatively rare. Evidence suggests that the most common methods used for co-production in decision-making are group discussions, forums, councils and conferences – in other words, methods that bring together young people and service providers face-to-face to promote in-depth discussion and learning (Kirby et al., 2003; Bovaird, 2007).

Placing young people at the heart of Talent Match is its defining characteristic for most people involved in the programme (Wells and Powell, 2014). It represents an ambitious and innovative approach with very few examples of similar approaches in past employment interventions for the 18–24 age group. The extent of partnerships' previous experience of involving young people in co-design varies greatly. For some, it is a new experience involving a steep learning curve and a great deal of testing and learning, while for others, the key issue is adapting already existing ways of working to the specific challenges of Talent Match.

The following are the main findings from the Talent Match programme with regard to partnership experiences of involving young people, and focus in particular on a phase of the programme concerned with the design of partnership strategies and interventions:

- The involvement of young people was not 'all or nothing'. Identifying areas where young people's involvement was crucial was important, but so too was identifying those areas where their involvement was less beneficial, or where there was less interest. The form of involvement had to be determined by young people in conjunction with partnerships, and it had to be recognised that this would take different forms.
- Moving beyond simply consulting young people to facilitating young people's leadership was found to be challenging. This recognised that many of those involved had faced considerable barriers and challenges (for example, mental health issues such as anxiety and learning difficulties which feed into a lack of confidence in formal settings). However, it was also noted that Talent Match represented something of a 'different approach' due to its youth-led approach and that this was implemented by civil society organisations.
- 'Buy-in from young people and organisations' was found to be a key issue. It required clear communication of the rationale for involving young people and the benefits of doing so. This again was reflected in the youth-led approach, and this approach was embedded in the organisations delivering the programme.
- Co-development and co-production can be significantly hindered by both a lack of resources and a lack of ownership among those engaged. Successful engagement with young people took a great deal of time and effort. This involved considerable 'up-front' costs for the programme.
- Some young people – including those with disabilities, issues with confidence and previously poor relationships with authority figures – required additional

support if they were to be effectively engaged, but engagement with these groups was particularly important for Talent Match, given its focus on those furthest from the labour market.
- Participation in formal decision-making processes was a new experience for the majority of young people. Various initiatives can make this less daunting. These include providing dedicated time and space for young people to contribute, ensuring that there are enough young people involved that they do not feel outnumbered, and paying attention to the language and methods used in presenting information.
- The establishment of youth boards and groups tasked with particular responsibilities was found both to encourage engagement in a broad sense and to develop the personal, social and work-related skills of the young people involved. However, in terms of the total target number of young people to be supported by the programme, those involved actively in forums such as decision-making groups was relatively small.

Approaches to involving young people are evolving and will continue to evolve as Talent Match proceeds. However, it is worth summarising some of the key challenges that are likely to persist in Talent Match and other similar programmes:

- The proportions of those directly involved are small compared to the total number of beneficiaries.
- Involvement is resource-intensive, far more so than the norm for labour market programmes.
- The group engaged is not homogeneous, which raises questions as to the extent to which it is *representative* of a wider population.
- Involvement needs to be continually refreshed to address attrition as young people move on or out of their current situations and may cease to be involved.

Intrinsic factors: the role of 'grit' and resilience

EU funds have traditionally focused on extrinsic factors such as qualifications and experience in their attempts to tackle youth unemployment. There is however a growing consensus that intrinsic factors are also fundamental in determining positive employment outcomes for young people. The Young Foundation (McNeil *et al.*, 2012) points to a growing evidence base linking social and emotional capabilities, such as determination, self-control, persistence and self-motivation, to positive outcomes for young people. Studies have linked intrinsic capabilities such as 'grit' and resilience to successful life outcomes. Research has shown that possessing grit, defined as perseverance and passion for long-term goals, can be linked to successful outcomes including educational attainment (Duckworth *et al.*, 2007), while resilience has also been identified as a factor in determining positive outcomes. Benard (2004) points to 'personal resilience strengths' and their association with healthy development and life success.

This growing evidence base suggests that there may be a need to extend the focus of EU funds to a more explicit consideration of intrinsic factors. The traditional focus has been on 'harder' extrinsic factors, which are generally easier to measure and quantify. While intrinsic measures are less straightforward to capture, this should not prevent them from being considered. Intrinsic and extrinsic outcomes are invariably linked. For example, providers may value a programme in terms of numbers of young people gaining employment through it, but this approach fails to acknowledge that some extrinsic employment outcomes may not have been achieved without developing a young person's social and emotional capabilities first.

Talent Match genuinely aims to develop interventions that are holistic and person-centred and take a long-term approach. Accordingly, the programme evaluation appreciates that intrinsic factors need to be captured as well as conventional hard outcomes such as numbers entering employment, training or formal education. If a young person has not yet gained employment but their social and emotional capabilities have developed, they may be closer to achieving employment than previously, while also improving their life in other ways.

The Talent Match evaluation uses an extensive monitoring system designed to collect standard monitoring data from all partnerships on all beneficiaries. This Common Data Framework allows monitoring of:

- who has participated in Talent Match;
- what they have done;
- what difference it has made to them; and
- what impact it has made on their labour market outcomes.

A number of questions explore intrinsic factors, with established psychological 'well-being' measures a key component. At each stage of data collection, young people are asked four subjective questions regarding their well-being:

1 Overall, how satisfied are you with your life nowadays?
2 Overall, to what extent do you feel the things you do in your life are worthwhile?
3 Overall, how happy did you feel yesterday?
4 Overall, how anxious did you feel yesterday?

These questions are taken from the UK's Office for National Statistics' (ONS) Annual Population Survey and have been designed to provide an alternative fuller picture of society beyond the usual socio-economic measures.

Figure 9.1 shows data collected at three time points: when an individual enters the Talent Match programme (the baseline), at three months and at six months. By way of comparison, data are also shown for individuals who only complete the baseline ('baseline only') and for a similarly aged group from the wider population (16–24-year-olds). The positive findings are that those individuals participating in the programme for at least six months report on average that their well-being has improved.

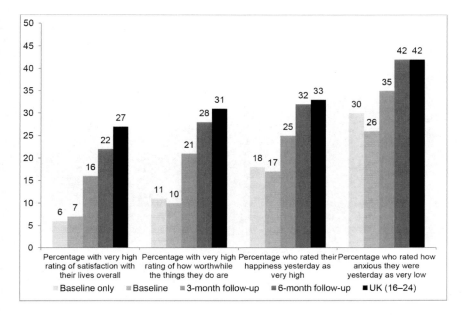

Figure 9.1 Changes in the self-reported well-being of programme beneficiaries.

Figure 9.2 shows how individual well-being scores have changed for those progressing through the programme for at least six months. Sizeable proportions across all four measures reported a higher score at the initial follow-up stage with notable proportions also reporting a positive change at the six-month stage. However, almost one-third (31 per cent) actually reported a more negative score for how anxious they felt yesterday at the three-month stage and almost the same proportion again gave a negative score at the six-month stage. Although the anxiety measure showed the worst results for the proportions reporting negative changes, there were nonetheless significant negative changes against the other measures too. These results suggest that while the interventions have tended to yield positive interim outcomes in terms of reported well-being, there is some evidence that well-being for many within the study group is far more fragile than expected. Indeed, engagement in the programme may surface an individual's previously hidden vulnerability.

We should qualify the significance of these data. They are intended to reveal a possible issue rather than to explore the extent to which the Talent Match programme affects these well-being measures. This will come later through analysis of matched comparator groups.

These and other data highlight the low levels and fragility of well-being among unemployed young people and may suggest shortcomings in current support provided to disadvantaged young people. This chimes with cohort

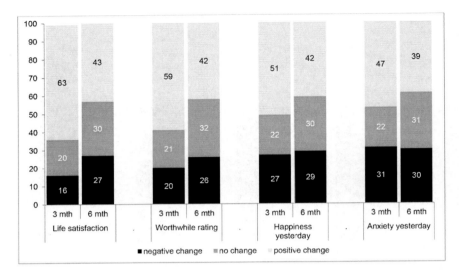

Figure 9.2 Self-reported well-being: individual change.

studies such as that of Brandt and Hank (2014), who confirm the existence of scarring effects, and how their causes may lie in childhood and not simply early adulthood. This raises questions for the role that EU funds play in complementing what have traditionally been member state responsibilities, ostensibly through primary and secondary education systems. The objective appears to be the ability to address both extrinsic and intrinsic factors as young people progress, something that should perhaps be considered in the allocation of future EU funds.

Discussion and conclusion: implications for the EU Structural and Investment Funds

While the interim findings presented here are from a particular labour market context (the UK), they may also be of relevance to countries with similar 'conservative' welfare regimes, though not to Mediterranean welfare regimes with very high levels of youth unemployment.

Involvement and resilience are concerned a priori with two very different understandings of youth unemployment. Youth involvement is situated very much within a structural and political critique of labour markets, and associated in particular with the view that voice in all market and social activity is fundamental to an inclusive society. Conversely, personal resilience is concerned with individual agency, either as a necessary part of progression in the labour market, or as a possible critique of youth unemployment in which young people are blamed or stigmatised for being unemployed.

Involvement and resilience activities may be eligible for support under the ESF (European Commission, 2014) – for instance, as part of outreach and capacity-building activities or activation schemes that involve individual action planning.

The findings from Talent Match suggest that youth involvement is very much seen as a capacity-building activity. The evaluation found that the involvement of young people did increase the legitimacy of programmes among both beneficiaries and funders. However, it was not without challenges, such as the retention of young people once programmes moved to delivery, the fact that young people could reflect but not represent the views of a wider population of young people, and the need for young people to receive support to be involved.

The findings suggested that effective involvement increased the legitimacy of programmes, especially for those involved in partnership working. This was through the development of their skills, experience, and social and professional networks.

At this stage of the Talent Match programme, we have not sought to relate specific interventions to the development of personal resilience and self-efficacy. The numbers supported by the programme are too small to do this at present.

What we have explored for a small set of measures is how resilience develops through the initial engagement in the programme. In part, the findings are positive. The support for young people seems to have been reflected in some overall positive improvements in terms of general well-being. However, it should be stressed that overall levels of well-being on initial engagement in the programme are (worryingly) low compared to the general population. This is perhaps not a surprise, but does provide some insight into the extent of the challenges that labour market programmes face in addressing youth unemployment among the hardest to reach.

The findings also raise concerns that the well-being of around a third of those engaged in the programme worsened in the six months after initial engagement. This may be because the intervention in effect surfaces or reveals what were hidden or latent issues facing a young person. What we cannot yet know is how well-being changes as the young person continues on the programme, enters the labour market or remains outside the labour market.

It is here that there is some convergence between youth involvement, personal resilience and the role that youth work may play in job activation (Council of the European Union, 2014b; Dunne *et al.*, 2014). The relationships between job activation, access to rights and personal self-efficacy are complex and probably lie outside traditional linear models of work-first type programmes.

References

Benard, B. (2004), *Resiliency: What We Have Learned*, San Francisco: WestEd.
Bovaird, T. (2007), 'Beyond engagement and participation: user and community coproduction of public services', *Public Administration Review*, 67(5), 846–60.

Brandt, M. and Hank, K. (2014), 'Scars that will not disappear: long-term associations between early and later life unemployment under different welfare regimes', *Journal of Social Policy*, 43(4), 727–43.

Breen, R. (2005), 'Explaining cross-national variation in youth unemployment: market and institutional factors', *European Sociological Review*, 21(2), 125–34.

Cahuc, P., Carcillo, S., Rinne, U. and Zimmermann, K. F. (2013), 'Youth unemployment in old Europe: the polar cases of France and Germany', *IZA Journal of European Labor Studies*, 2(18), 1–23.

Carnegie UK Trust (2008), *Empowering Young People: Final Report of the Carnegie Young People Initiative*, London: Carnegie Trust.

Cinalli, M. and Giugni, M. (2013), 'New challenges for the welfare state: the emergence of youth unemployment regimes in Europe?', *International Journal or Social Welfare*, 22(3), 290–9.

Council of the European Union (2011), *Council Conclusions: Promoting Youth Employment to Achieve the Europe 2020 Objectives*, Luxembourg: European Commission.

Council of the European Union (2014a), *18-Month Programme of the Council (1 July 2014–31 December 2015)*, 11258/14, Brussels: European Commission.

Council of the European Union (2014b), *Draft Resolution of the Council and of the Representatives of the Governments of the Member States, Meeting within the Council, on a European Union Work Plan for Youth for 2014–2015*, 9523/14, Brussels: European Commission.

Duckworth, A. L., Peterson, C., Matthews, M. D. and Kelly, D. R. (2007) 'Grit: perseverance and passion for long-term goals', *Journal of Personality and Social Psychology*, 92(6), 1087–101.

Dunne, A., Ulicna, D., Murphy, I. and Golubeva, M. (2014), *Working with Young People: The Value of Youth Work in the EU*, Brussels: European Commission.

Eichhorst, W., Hinte, H. and Rinne, U. (2013), 'Youth unemployment in Europe: what to do about it?', IZA Policy Paper No. 65, Leibniz Information Centre for Economics.

European Commission (2013), *Working Together for Europe's Young People: A Call to Action on Youth Unemployment*, COM(2013) 447 final, Brussels: European Commission.

European Commission (2014), 'The EU Youth Guarantee', memo, 8 October.

Eurostat (2014), *Eurostat Regional Yearbook 2014*, Luxembourg: Eurostat.

Gordon, I. (1999), 'Move on up the car dealing with structural unemployment in London', *Local Economy*, 14(1), 87–95.

Green, A. and White, R. (2007), *Attachment to Place: Social Networks, Mobility and Prospects for Young People*, York, UK: Joseph Rowntree Foundation.

Green, A. E., de Hoyos, M., Li, Y. and Owen, D. (2011), *Job Search Study: Literature Review and Analysis of the Labour Force Survey*, DWP Research Report 726, London: Department for Work and Pensions.

Halsey, K., Murfield, J., Harland, J. and Lord, P. (2006), *The Voice of Young People: An Engine for Improvement? Scoping the Evidence.*, London: National Foundation for Educational Research.

Hart, R. A. (1992), *Children's Participation: from Tokenism to Citizenship*, Innocenti Essays No. 4, Florence: UNICEF.

House of Lords European Union Committee (2014), *Youth Unemployment in the EU: A Scarred Generation?* 12th Report of Session 2013–14, HL Paper 164, London: The Stationery Office.

Kirby, P., Lanyon, C., Cronin, K. and Sinclair, R. (2003), *Building a Culture of Participation: Involving Children and Young People in Policy, Service Planning, Delivery and Evaluation*, London: Department for Education and Skills.

Lahusen, C., Schulz, N. and Graziano, P. R. (2013), 'Promoting social Europe? The development of European youth unemployment policies', *International Journal of Social Welfare*, 22(3), 300–9.

McNeil, B., Reeder, N. and Rich, J. (2012), *A Framework of Outcomes for Young People*. London: Department for Education/The Young Foundation.

Moffat, J. and Roth, D. (2014), 'Cohort size and youth unemployment in Europe: a regional analysis', Joint Discussion Paper Series in Economics, No. 40-2014, Leibniz Information Centre for Economics.

Shildrick, T., MacDonald, R., Webster, C. and Garthwaite, K. (2012), *Poverty and Insecurity: Life in Low-Pay, No-Pay Britain*, Bristol, UK: Policy Press.

Simmons, R. and Thompson, R. (2013), 'Reclaiming the disengaged: critical perspectives on young people not in education, employment or training', *Research in Post-Compulsory Education*, 18(1–2), 1–11.

Sinclair, R. (2004), 'Participation in practice: making it meaningful, effective and sustainable', *Children & Society*, 18(2), 106–18.

Thomas, N. and O'Kane, C. (2000), 'Discovering what children think: connections between research and practice', *British Journal of Social Work*, 30(6), 819–36.

Treseder, P. (1997), *Empowering Children and Young People: Training Manual*. London: Save the Children and Children's Rights Office.

UKCES (2014), *Precarious Futures? Youth Unemployment in an International Context*, Wath-upon-Dearne and London: UK Commission for Employment and Skills.

Wells, P. and Powell, R. (2014), *Evaluation of the Talent Match Programme: 2014 Annual Report*, London: Big Lottery Fund.

10 Whatever happened to gender mainstreaming?

Lessons for the EU's 2014–20 Structural and Investment Funds

Leaza McSorley and Jim Campbell

Introduction

The concept of gender mainstreaming was adopted by the EU in the mid-1990s and became a requirement for EU Cohesion Policy delivered through the 2000–6 Structural Funds programme, which continued into the 2007–13 period. Gender mainstreaming implied the need to recognise that additional resources targeted at stimulating economic development and growth did not benefit men and women equally. Policy interventions could no longer be assumed to be gender neutral. Therefore, in order to maximise the economic impact of policies designed to stimulate regional development, they needed to be more 'gender aware'.

This chapter explores the impact of gender mainstreaming on projects funded under the Structural Funds in Scotland in the 2007–13 period. A cross-section of ESF- and ERDF-funded projects that supported labour market participation was investigated. The main issues examined included the extent to which the participants understood and were aware of gender mainstreaming and whether they undertook any gender-based monitoring and evaluation. The case of Scotland is then contextualised within the experience of the EU as a whole, highlighting the relevance for achieving Europe 2020 targets. Finally, the chapter discusses what lessons we can learn from this experience and whether gender mainstreaming can deliver in terms of increasing female employment opportunities.

Gender mainstreaming and Structural Funds

The EU has progressively promoted equality between women and men. Article 119 of the Treaty of Rome established the principle of equal pay for equal work for women and men. Since then, EU policy has evolved incrementally through various Directives and Action Programmes as the objectives have expanded from equal pay to equal opportunities (Pollack and Hafner-Burton, 2000).

The concept of gender mainstreaming was formally adopted by the EU as part of the Treaty of Amsterdam in 1997 (Guerrina, 2005). At the time, it seemed to offer the potential to achieve greater gender equality in the labour market (Walby, 2005). There was also a recognition at the time that previous attempts to achieve greater gender equality had failed:

[a]t the beginning of the 1990s, gender equality policy entered a period of crisis. In light of studies released by expert networks on gender equality, the gender equality policy Community and member states' representatives began to acknowledge that, despite more than 15 years of active and interventionist Community action, inequalities between women and men in the workplace and on the labour market had not significantly diminished.

(Jacquot, 2010: 122)

By building gender equality considerations into the core of policy formulation and decision-making, the likely consequences for both men and women can be assessed as an integral and continuing part of those processes. Unintended consequences and/or effects that could undermine or prevent the achievement of stated policy aims for either men or women can be identified, avoided or monitored from the earliest stages (McKay and Gillespie, 2007). This approach is now central to the EU's policy for equal opportunities and employment as well as being a key feature of its regional policy (European Commission, 2010).

The rationale for pursuing gender mainstreaming via the Structural Funds is as much about promoting economic efficiency as it is about promoting equity.

The main aim of the Structural Funds to reduce economic and social disparities and to establish the conditions which will assure the long-term development of the regions depends upon the fullest participation of the active population in economic and social life. Failure to overcome the constraints to the equal and full participation of women and men means that the development objectives of growth, competitiveness and employment cannot be fully achieved, and also that the investments made in human resources (e.g. in raising education and qualification levels) are not exploited efficiently.

(Braithwaite *et al.*, 1999: 5)

If the less developed regions are to improve their comparative economic performance, then they have to make more efficient use of the resources available to them, particularly human resources. Within the EU, women account for the majority of the labour market that is inactive and unemployed (Rees, 2000: 181). In addition, there is a recognition of the need to expand the total number of people of working age in paid employment in order to accommodate the ageing population and the resulting fiscal consequences. The desire to increase women's participation in the formal labour market was also a key feature of the European Employment Strategy and the subsequent Lisbon Agenda (Rubery, 2005), and now of the Europe 2020 targets. However, the key question is whether gender mainstreaming can be any more successful than previous attempts to achieve gender equality. As Rees states, "Gender mainstreaming is hard to define but harder to implement" (Rees, 2005: 570).

Case study: Scottish Structural Funds 2007–13

The main aim of the case study was to explore the extent to which gender mainstreaming featured in the 2007–13 Scottish Structural Funds programmes and to highlight any lessons in terms of what worked and what did not work, which could inform the 2014–20 Scottish Structural Funds programme.[1] The case study builds upon previous work undertaken by the authors into the impact of gender mainstreaming in western Scotland (Campbell *et al.*, 2009).

A number of ERDF and ESF projects in both the Lowlands and Uplands (LUPS) and Highlands and Islands (H&I) areas were selected for study. All projects were active labour market projects designed to get people into work or support them in work. A total of 19 projects were initially contacted and 13 agreed to be interviewed. Projects were selected to provide a cross-section of regional areas, a mix of public-, private- and voluntary-sector projects and a mix of ERDF and ESF funding.

The majority of participants who agreed to be interviewed were located within the LUPS area (eight), with five from the H&I region. In terms of types of Structural Funds, nine of the participants interviewed were in receipt of ESF funding, compared to four with ERDF funding. Of the 13 participants interviewed, 3 were from the private sector, 7 from the public sector and 3 from the voluntary sector. The participants could be split into two distinct group: those projects that had a clear equal opportunities focus, of which there were six (five ESF and one ERDF), known as Group 1; and those projects that did not have a specific equal opportunities objective, of which there were seven (four ESF and three ERDF), designated as Group 2.

The interviews were undertaken in order to elicit information about:

- understanding of gender mainstreaming;
- access and monitoring;
- the impact of the Great Recession;
- the main legacy of these projects in terms of gender mainstreaming;
- recommendations for the 2014–20 funding period.

Understanding of gender mainstreaming

The research findings showed that overall understanding of gender mainstreaming was varied across all of the projects. This ranged from participants who displayed a great depth of understanding of gender issues and proactively embedded these considerations within their daily activities, to participants who were completely unaware of gender mainstreaming as a concept and took a more passive approach. This difference of understanding and integration was somewhat obvious when both groups' answers were compared. On the whole, Group 1 displayed greater overall understanding of equal opportunities and gender mainstreaming compared to Group 2. Despite the disparity in understanding, all of the projects had some form of equal opportunities policy in place.

As would be expected, gender mainstreaming formed a central part of Group 1's overarching thinking, whereby gender equality became part of that natural thought process. These participants displayed an informed approach and recognised that in order to understand gender mainstreaming, analysing labour market statistics and gathering demographic intelligence were fundamental to identifying where the gaps were. Nonetheless, two participants within Group 2 also demonstrated a great depth of understanding and awareness of gender mainstreaming within their daily activities.

However, the majority of those in Group 2 were totally unaware of gender mainstreaming as a concept. These projects, which were ERDF-funded infrastructure projects or provided business support services, did not consider gender to be an issue for them. This was very much the case with private-sector projects or those projects that were providing some form of business enterprise and innovation support services. For them, businesses were genderless, and they viewed gender mainstreaming solely in terms of complying with equal opportunities requirements. The majority of Group 2 participants viewed gender mainstreaming as a legal and administrative hurdle they had to overcome.

Some of the participants within Group 1 with experience in previous funding periods stated their concerns that the horizontal theme of equal opportunities was not as prominent as it had been in the 2000–6 period. Some felt it was becoming eroded. They felt that issues relating to gender had been subsumed within the broader horizontal theme of equal opportunities. This has resulted in what they felt was a lack of direction and less prominence afforded to the pursuit of equality within the 2007–13 funding period.

Access and monitoring

Across all of the projects, there was a distinct lack of the systematic data-gathering that would facilitate a gender analysis of the impact of the projects. The Group 1 participants did make some attempt to gather statistics that would enable them to have a better awareness of the impacts of the projects. However, despite this, there was no real evaluation of the impact of gender mainstreaming across all of the projects.

Many participants from Group 1 and a couple from Group 2 noted that it would be useful to have some practical advice, to be able to draw on experience from other organisations and to have the opportunity to share best practice. The majority of Group 1 noted that the current claim forms submitted to the Scottish Government were not sufficiently extensive in terms of the information that they were required to report on. It did not allow for the inclusion of details of what was being done at a project level to tackle the horizontal themes or gender issues. By contrast, Article 60B monitoring visits, which were mid-term evaluations, provided a good point at which projects could take stock of what they could do over the next 18 months. The visits also provided them with the opportunity to show the managing authority what they had done to address horizontal themes and what they were going to do in the future.

The impact of the Great Recession

The Great Recession had an impact on projects both in terms of increasing the difficulty of attracting match funding due to public expenditure reductions as well as resulting in increasing demand for those projects that had an employability dimension due to the rise in unemployment particularly amongst young people.

Following the onset of the Great Recession in 2007–8 and the resulting public expenditure cuts, the reduced availability of match funding proved restrictive to a large number of projects within Group 1. They reported that it was "more and more difficult to get public funding".

Some of the participants, across both groups, involved in providing support for individuals to find employment opportunities noted a direct impact from the Great Recession. They experienced huge difficulties securing placements for beneficiaries and employment opportunities within organisations. For Group 2, the changing economic climate provided challenges for those projects that were looking for businesses, particularly small and medium-sized enterprises, to invest in innovation, competitiveness and business start-ups. In other words, engagement with the private sector was more challenging in the aftermath of the Great Recession.

There was a recognition across both groups that demand for their services had increased as a result of the Great Recession. In most cases, it was reported that demand had far exceeded their initial expectations at the outset of the project. Every participant interviewed observed that there had been a significant increase in the number of requests since the start of the Great Recession.

For those providing employment opportunities and employability support, across both groups, there was an observation that the type of people accessing their services was changing. For example, there was an increase in the number of university graduates approaching them for support.

The main legacy of these projects in terms of gender mainstreaming

In terms of legacy, there were concerns from the equal opportunities-focused projects that this objective would be further downgraded in the 2014–20 funding period. On the positive side, however, there was some evidence to suggest that there was some spillover from the funded project to the organisation as a whole in relation to gender mainstreaming. This applied equally to Group 1 and Group 2.

One of the issues discussed with the participants was whether gender issues have been incorporated into other activities outside of the funded projects. For the most part, participants within both groups were very positive in response to this particular question. Participants, particularly within Group 1, stated that as a result of work within the project they had been involved in, they had been "able to inform our organisation on the wider work, whether it's been around other activities"; "it is being embedded within our other work"; "we are learning so much from the projects". Two participants from Group 2 observed that they were beginning to influence the organisations within which they were situated: "Gender issues are now at a senior management level and we are now looking at how they can improve our own internal policies".

However, despite the encouraging rhetoric from both groups, participants from Group 2 were largely unable to provide practical examples of how consideration of gender issues had been incorporated within other work they did as an organisation. Group 1 participants, on the other hand, provided a wealth of practical examples of their awareness-raising activity through workshops, providing case studies and running focus groups.

What worked well for projects across both groups was the opportunity to use ESF funding to build and develop capacity for their own organisations. Money had been used to serve far more than its original objectives; it had forced some organisations to look at their own internal activities, procedures and policies. What had not worked so well, perhaps, was the fact that gender mainstreaming and tackling gender issues had not been particularly high on the agenda for many organisations within Group 2. Work is still required to ensure that projects without an equal opportunities focus develop a better understanding and appreciation of gender mainstreaming.

In terms of the availability of pre-application advice, many participants from both groups felt that this was absolutely invaluable. The provision of workshops in the 2000–6 period, and to some extent in the current funding period, encouraged potential applicants to have those discussions in advance of final application deadlines.

Going forward into the 2014–20 programme, concerns were raised by a number of participants within Group 1 about whether there would continue to be a horizontal theme on equal opportunities and how that would actually work in practice as the Structural Funds (ESF and ERDF) are combined with Rural Development Fund and Fisheries Funds. They felt that there was a lack of clarity about where equal opportunities would stand within the next funding period and that there was a real danger that the equality strand would disappear. For those participants involved in both the 2000–6 and 2007–13 periods, comments were raised that the application and monitoring of the horizontal themes seemed secondary to everything else within the programme.

Summary of research findings

The research findings are based upon a relatively small sample of the projects funded under the 2007–13 Scottish Structural Funds Programmes. Nonetheless, certain conclusions can be drawn based upon the interviews:

- For participants without a specific equal opportunities focus, there was a lack of understanding about the concept of gender mainstreaming. In addition, those participants that did have an equal opportunities objective felt that the move to mainstreaming had downgraded the importance of gender equality issues compared to the 2000–6 funding period.

- There was a consensus across both groups that the level of support and information available to projects to ensure that they took cognisance of the equal opportunities agenda was significantly less than that available in the 2000–6 funding period.
- There was a lack of the systematic data-gathering that would enable a gender analysis of the impacts of the projects. Consequently, there was no real evaluation of the impact of gender mainstreaming.
- Mid-term evaluation visits were viewed as being a more useful opportunity to discuss and develop gender mainstreaming activities than reporting at the funding claim or final evaluation stages.
- The Great Recession had an impact on projects both in terms of increasing the difficulty of attracting match funding and increasing demand for those projects with an employability dimension.
- In terms of legacy, there were concerns from the equal opportunities-focused participants that this objective would be further downgraded in the 2014–20 funding period. On the positive side, however, there was some evidence to suggest that there was some spillover from the funded projects to the organisations as a whole in relation to gender mainstreaming.

European Structural and Investment Funds Regulations 2014–20

The European Structural and Investment Funds (ESIF) Regulations 2014–20 set out a number of articles and clauses that specifically relate to gender issues:

> In the context of its effort to increase economic, territorial and social cohesion, the Union should, at all stages of implementation of the ESI Funds, aim at eliminating inequalities and at promoting equality between men and women and integrating the gender perspective, as well as at combating discrimination based on sex, racial or ethnic origin, religion or belief, disability, age or sexual orientation.
> (European Commission, 2013: Paragraph 13)

This commitment also works vice versa; eliminating inequalities and promoting equality will enhance efforts to increase economic, territorial and social cohesion.

At a strategic level, the regulations clearly set out the ambition of the ESIF to implement gender mainstreaming and tackle gender inequalities. However, at an operational level, the detail is weaker. Articles and clauses do require partnerships and multi-level governance in all member states to include representative gender organisations (European Commission, 2013: Article 5). They also require that:

> The Member States and the Commission shall ensure that equality between men and women and the integration of gender perspective are taken into account and promoted throughout the preparation and implementation of programmes, including in relation to monitoring, reporting and evaluation.
> (European Commission, 2013: Article 7)

Nonetheless, analysis of the Thematic Objectives and Investment Priorities (along with their ex ante conditionalities and criteria for fulfilment) shows that only a few of the Thematic Objectives have stated gender-specific Investment Priorities. The ESF has explicit objectives in relation to gender mainstreaming and achieving gender equality targets, but the other funds have no such obvious targets. The implication is that gender considerations are mainstreamed within the other funds – but with no visible specific strategy, actions or targets, it may send out the message that gender mainstreaming is no longer an objective.

For example, the Thematic Objective 'Supporting the shift towards a low-carbon economy in all sectors' will use ERDF and the Cohesion Policy Fund to deliver its Investment Priorities. The low-carbon economy will require new skills and expertise to exploit the potential of ESIF investments. The skill level varies greatly between member states and regions but, for this priority to be delivered, a skills match is required. The Commission has long advised on the looming skills gap in the low-carbon sector:

> The education, training and employment policies of the Member States must focus on increasing and adapting skills and providing better learning opportunities at all levels, to develop a workforce that is high skilled and responsive to the needs of the economy. Similarly, businesses have an acute interest in investing in human capital and improving their human resource management. Moreover, gender equality is a key factor to responding to new skills needs.
>
> (European Commission, 2008: 3–4)

This proactive approach, strategic leadership and clear guidance need to be implemented for the Thematic Objective of a low-carbon economy to ensure an appropriately skilled labour force can be provided to meet the need for skills in this sector in the forthcoming funding period of 2014–20.

The ESIF has been designed to support the Europe 2020 targets and therefore will have an important role to play in enabling the EU to reach its target of a 75 per cent employment rate for the 20–64 age group. In order to achieve that goal, the female employment rate will need to increase from its 2014 level of 63.5 per cent (Eurostat, 2015). In 2014, the male employment rate in the EU28 for the 20–64 age group was 75 per cent, giving a gender employment gap in that year of 11.5 per cent, compared to 16.1 per cent in 2004 (Eurostat, 2015). Thus there has been some improvement in narrowing the gender employment gap, although this masks wide disparities between the member states. Throughout the EU, there are significant variations to the headline female employment rate. Greece had the lowest female employment rate in 2014 at 44.3 per cent (compared to a male employment rate of 62.6 per cent), whereas Sweden had the highest female employment rate of 77.6 per cent (and a male employment rate of 82.2 per cent) (Eurostat, 2015).

The European Commission is committed to "promoting equality as part of the Europe 2020 strategy" (European Commission, 2010). A key element of that commitment is to increase the female employment rate. However, the Commission recognises that it is not sufficient to simply increase the number of women in employment if that also means increasing the number of women in low-paid and low-skilled employment. In addition to increasing the female employment rate, gender equality also requires action to be taken to reduce the gender pay gap and also gender-based occupational segregation. Part of the reason for the persistence of the gender pay gap in the EU, which stood at 16.4 per cent in 2012 (European Commission, 2014), is that women tend to be concentrated in occupations that are regarded as low skilled and therefore tend to be poorly paid, and in addition women tend to be under-represented at senior management and decision-making levels.

Recommendations

The ESIF has an important role to play in tackling these issues and delivering greater gender equality within the EU. However, in order to do so, policymakers need to be aware that interventions funded under the ESIF are not gender neutral and if gender mainstreaming is to be implemented more effectively in the 2014–20 period, then the following actions are necessary:

- Resources need to be committed to providing leadership and oversight of gender mainstreaming as a horizontal theme. This is especially true for non-ESF funds, where there appears to be a lack of conditionalities for ensuring that gender mainstreaming is implemented.
- Projects require clearer practical guidance on what is involved in gender mainstreaming – for example, the provision of awareness-raising workshops on gender mainstreaming at the pre-application stage as well as the establishment of Gender Equality Champions within the projects' managing authorities and strategic delivery partners. Particular focus should be on supporting member states and regions that have not received funding in previous periods.
- Funded projects need to gather gender-disaggregated data and indicators. There is a need to better understand differences in how men and women access and benefit from the ESIF.
- Gender equality and gender mainstreaming should be given greater prominence as objectives in the 2014–20 funding period.
- Thematic Objectives and Investment Priorities (along with their ex ante conditionalities and criteria for fulfilment) require clearly stated gender equality and mainstreaming targets. Although the Regulations clearly set out gender equality and mainstreaming requirements, these are not followed through sufficiently in the Thematic Objectives and Investment Priorities.
- A more robust appraisal of projects is needed to ensure that gender equality objectives are met, particularly at the mid-term evaluation stage.

The ESIF 2014–20 cannot assume that gender mainstreaming lessons have been learned from the 2000–6 and 2007–13 funding periods. New member states, new regions receiving funding and the consolidation of funding in older member states may mean that institutional learning is lost. This implies that continued leadership and guidance – not just at a strategic level but at an implementation level – should be an ongoing resource commitment for the ESIF. This sustained commitment to gender mainstreaming is needed to ensure not only that the ESIF delivers on its targets but also that the objectives of Europe 2020 can be met.

Note

1 This case study research was funded by ESF Technical Assistance funding and commissioned by the Scottish Government.

References

Braithwaite, M., Fitzgerald, R. and Fries, R. (1999), *Mainstreaming Equal Opportunities for Women and Men into the Structural Funds: Findings of a Survey of Current Practice in Germany, France and UK*, DG XVI Regional Policy and Cohesion, Brussels: European Commission.

Campbell, J., Fitzgerald, R. and McSorley, L. (2009), "Structural Funds and gender equality: the impact of gender mainstreaming in Western Scotland", *Local Economy*, 24(2), 140–50.

European Commission (2008), *Communication from the Commission to the European Parliament, the Council, the European Economic and Social Committee and the Committee of the Regions: New Skills for New Jobs – Anticipating and Matching Labour Market and Skills Needs*, COM(2008) 868/3, Brussels: European Commission.

European Commission (2010), *Strategy for Equality between Women and Men 2010–2015*, DG Employment, Social Affairs and Equal Opportunities, Brussels: European Commission.

European Commission (2013), "Regulation (EU) No. 1303/2013 of the European Parliament and of the Council", *Official Journal of the European Union*, L347.

European Commission (2014), *Tackling the Gender Pay Gap in the EU*, Brussels: European Commission, available at: http://ec.europa.eu/justice/gender-equality/files/gender_pay_gap/140319_gpg_en.pdf (accessed 10 February 2016).

Eurostat (2015), "Employment rates by sex", available at: http://ec.europa.eu/eurostat/web/lfs/data/main-tables (accessed 11 June 2015).

Guerrina, R. (2005), *Mothering the Union: Gender Politics in the EU*, Manchester: Manchester University Press.

Jacquot, S. (2010), "The paradox of gender mainstreaming: unanticipated effects of new modes of governance in the gender equality domain", *West European Politics*, 33(1), 118–35.

McKay, A and Gillespie, M. (2007), "Gender mainstreaming or 'mainstreaming gender'? A question of delivering on gender equality in the new Scotland", in M. Keating (ed.), *Scottish Social Democracy: Progressive Ideas for Public Policy*, Brussels: PIE Peter Lang, pp. 191–212.

Pollack, M. and Hafner-Burton, E. (2000), "Mainstreaming gender in the European Union", *Journal of European Public Policy*, 7(3), 432–56.

Rees, T. (2000), "The learning region? Integrating gender equality in regional economic development", *Policy and Politics*, 28(2), 179–91.

Rees, T. (2005), "Reflections on the uneven development of gender mainstreaming in Europe", *International Feminist Journal of Politics*, 7(4), 555–74.

Rubery, J. (2005), "Reflections on gender mainstreaming: an example of feminist economics in action?", *Feminist Economics*, 11(3), 1–26.

Walby, S. (2005), "Gender mainstreaming: productive tensions in theory and practice", *Social Politics*, 12(3), 321–42.

11 The absorption of Structural and Investment Funds and youth unemployment
An empirical test

Jale Tosun, Stefan Speckesser, Carsten Jensen and Jacqueline O'Reilly

Introduction

Youth unemployment in Europe has been exacerbated by the economic crisis of 2008, although antecedents of youth vulnerability were evident earlier in some countries (O'Reilly and Lain, 2010; Bell and Blanchflower, 2011; Berlingieri *et al.*, 2014). EU measures to reduce youth unemployment involve adding value to national policies through measures such as the Youth Employment Initiative (YEI), launched in 2013 and designed to support young people not in education, employment or training (NEETs) in EU regions where the youth unemployment rate in 2012 was above 25 per cent (Chabanet, 2014; Nafilyan and Speckesser, 2014; O'Reilly *et al.*, 2015). The YEI represents a direct response to current challenges and needs to be examined in a broader context related to the effectiveness of the Structural Funds in general and the European Social Fund (ESF) and the European Regional Development Fund (ERDF) in particular. The ESF was set up in 1957 and is the main financial instrument used by the EU and its member states to create employment opportunities and support measures for unemployed people. The ERDF was established in 1973 and aims to strengthen economic and social cohesion in the EU. It has ramifications for unemployed young people to the extent that it provides funding for new business start-ups and entrepreneurship as well as support for job creation and for small and medium-sized enterprises in taking on apprentices, trainees and placements (House of Lords, 2014: 22; see also Mendez *et al.*, 2014).

Our interest in the ESF and the ERDF rather than in the YEI is motivated by two considerations. The first is that these two funding programmes are substantial in terms of their volume. For the funding period 2014–20, the ESF has been allocated about €72 billion and the ERDF about €183 billion as compared to the €6 billion of the YEI (House of Lords, 2014: 23). The second reason is more pragmatic and refers to the fact that the YEI has only recently been launched, which makes it impossible to currently assess its effectiveness.

In theoretical terms, this chapter concentrates on the individual member states' absorption behaviour concerning the ESF, the ERDF and total Structural Funds (Bachtler *et al.*, 2014; Tosun, 2014) and the impact of the absorption performance on changes in youth unemployment levels. Empirically, the analysis concentrates on the absorption behaviour of the EU member states between 2000 and 2011, which allows for capturing possible effects of the economic and financial crisis (see, for example, Choudhry et al., 2012; Tosun et al., 2014). The relationship between fund absorption and youth unemployment levels is tested by econometric methods, while controlling for further demographic characteristics of the member states, the effect of the business cycle and variables characterising the labour market and bargaining regime (Hörisch and Weishaupt, 2012; O'Higgins, 2012; Choudhry et al., 2013; Caporale and Gil-Alana, 2014; Scruggs et al., 2014).

We show that the long-term absorption behaviour matters. Member states can only make an effective use of Structural Funds if they develop and maintain a sufficiently high absorption capacity. It is not only the volume of the financial means that is important but also the provision of assistance in absorbing EU funding in a sustained fashion.

Youth unemployment in the EU

The extent of youth unemployment in the EU between 2000 and 2013 is illustrated in Figure 11.1 showing the longer-term antecedents of youth unemployment, where the rate fluctuated but never fell below 15 per cent, and the recent sharp increase since 2008–9 (O'Higgins, 2012). In addition, young people have been more vulnerable than older workers (aged 25 and over); in 2013, the EU average

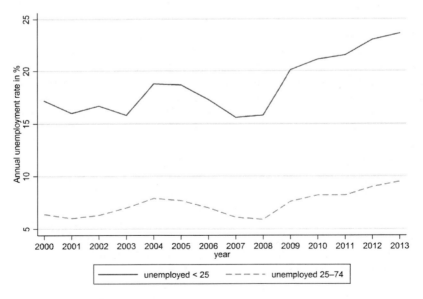

Figure 11.1 Annual youth unemployment rates, 2000–13.
Source: Data from Eurostat (2015).

youth unemployment rate was two and a half times higher than the unemployment rate for older workers.

However, the heterogeneous experience across the EU both for those inside the Eurozone monetary system and those outside is captured in Figure 11.2. Before the Great Recession (2005–8), the median youth unemployment rates and ratios were lower in the non-Eurozone countries. Second, for both country groups the increase in median youth unemployment due to the crisis is visible from the box plots. Third, however, the variation in the youth unemployment rates across the individual member states of the Eurozone has grown visibly, while it has remained constant in non-Euro states.

Finally, it is instructive to explore the regional variation in youth unemployment rates. Figure 11.3 presents the box plots for the three EU member states with the lowest youth unemployment levels (Austria, Germany and the Netherlands) and the highest proportion of unemployed young people (Greece, Italy and Spain) in 2013. The figure shows that the countries confronted with high youth unemployment rates also have a large variation at the NUTS2 level, while the regional variation is low in Austria, Germany and the Netherlands.

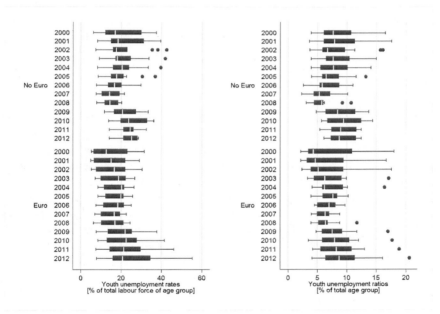

Figure 11.2 Youth unemployment in EU28 member states, 2000–12.

Source: Data from Eurostat (2015).

Note: Dots indicate outliers; "Euro" = members of the Eurozone (Austria, Belgium, Cyprus, Estonia, Finland, France, Germany, Greece, Ireland, Italy, Latvia, Lithuania, Luxembourg, Malta, the Netherlands, Portugal, Slovakia, Slovenia and Spain; membership varies over time); "no Euro" = other EU members (Bulgaria, Croatia, Czech Republic, Denmark, Hungary, Poland, Romania, Sweden and the UK).

154 *Jale Tosun* et al.

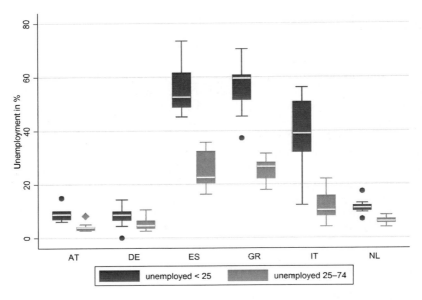

Figure 11.3 Youth unemployment in NUTS2 regions in six selected EU member states, 2013.
Source: Data from Eurostat (2015).

Thus, the exploratory analysis of youth unemployment rates in Europe has revealed two important types of disparity. First, there is significant variation between countries in the degree to which young people participate in the labour market. Second, in countries that are affected by high levels of youth unemployment, there is notable variation between the regions. The main objective of EU Cohesion Policy is specifically to "promote economic and social cohesion across Europe by reducing disparities between regions and countries" (Bachtler and Mendez, 2007: 537). This raises the question that this chapter is interested in addressing – namely, how effective EU Cohesion Policy has been in facilitating the labour market participation of young people.

Motivating the hypotheses

The likelihood of experiencing unemployment is a function of both individual and institutional factors. At the individual level, higher and better education is the main factor reducing the risk of becoming unemployed. Low-qualified and unqualified young people are most at risk of becoming unemployed (Isengard, 2003). Once they have experienced unemployment, young people show a higher probability of unemployment later in life (Berlingieri *et al.*, 2014: 22). Furthermore, the social embeddedness of individuals matters. Freitag and Kirchner (2011), for instance, show that higher levels of social capital limit the degree of vulnerability to unemployment.

However, individual risk factors are affected or even caused by institutional factors – even when it comes to individual-level preferences for education and training (Busemeyer and Jensen, 2012). The most important institutional determinants of (youth) unemployment are educational systems, welfare state structures, labour market institutions and the alignment of labour market needs and educational outcomes (Hörisch and Weishaupt, 2012; Berlingieri *et al.*, 2014; O'Reilly *et al.*, 2015). Labour market flexibility, O'Higgins (2012) argues, contributed significantly to the negative consequences felt by young people during the economic and financial crisis. Choudhry *et al.* (2012), by contrast, argue that a high proportion of part-time employment and active labour market policies reduce unemployment and improve labour market performance. Finally, studies have shown that there exist long-term relationships between youth unemployment, Gross Domestic Income (GDP) and inflation (Choudhry *et al.*, 2013; Caporale and Gil-Alana, 2014).

How the EU can help to overcome youth unemployment is insufficiently informed by evidence. To close this knowledge gap, we examine the potential effects of EU Cohesion Policy. We claim that the absorption of EU funds may help to reduce youth unemployment. The causal mechanism underlying this general expectation is that EU funds lead to economic growth, which then translates into higher demand for labour and leads to higher employment levels. However, the necessary precondition for the EU financial means to become effective is that they are made available to the individual member states, which happens through the process of funds absorption (see, for example, Bachtler *et al.*, 2014; Tosun, 2014). The better the absorption performance, the more resources the national governments can employ to tackle youth unemployment.

The ESF provides financial means to keep young people in education by combating early school-leaving and by providing opportunities for re-entry into formal training or education. Transition from school to work is facilitated through mentoring and personal advice, additional training and work placements, including traineeships and apprenticeships. From 2007 to 2012, 20 million young people under 25 years benefited from the ESF through training or mentoring. National governments use ESF funding to improve education and vocational training (European Commission, 2014). We expect that countries with a higher absorption of ESF investment will show a better performance regarding the integration of young people in labour markets.

- Hypothesis 1A: Higher absorption of ESF funding leads to lower youth unemployment ratios.
- Hypothesis 1B: Higher absorption of ESF funding leads to a lower increase in youth unemployment ratios.

The ERDF aims to strengthen economic and social cohesion in the EU by correcting imbalances between its regions. ERDF investments can also potentially help to increase the labour market participation of young people, but in a way that is different than the ESF. The ERDF focuses its investment in the new funding of small and medium-sized enterprises. The European Commission (2013) acknowledges entrepreneurship as an important source of economic growth and the creation of new employment and seeks to promote entrepreneurial behaviour (see also, for example, Van Der Zwan et al., 2013). We therefore expect that the absorption of ERDF investment should also have a positive impact on economic growth and job creation.

- Hypothesis 2A: Higher absorption of ERDF funding leads to lower youth unemployment ratios.
- Hypothesis 2B: Higher absorption of ERDF funding leads to a lower increase in youth unemployment ratios.

Finally, since the causal mechanism through which funds absorption is expected to be effective is the stimulation for economic growth (Mohl and Hagen, 2010), we also hypothesise that not only does ESF and ERDF absorption matter for the labour market integration of young people but also the absorption of the Structural Funds in general.

- Hypothesis 3A: Higher absorption of Structural Funds leads to lower youth unemployment ratios.
- Hypothesis 3B: Higher absorption of Structural Funds leads to a lower increase in youth unemployment ratios.

Explanations of the data

Our focal variable is *absorption*, which captures the percentage proportion of funds paid out to the individual member states. We estimate six specifications in order to test the hypotheses:

- The first two specifications refer to the absorption of the ESF in the programming period 2000–6, which concluded in 2011 (European Commission, 2012).
- The second two specifications provide the same test for the absorption of the ERDF in 2000–6.
- The final two models estimate the effect of the total absorption of Structural Funds in 2000–6 on youth unemployment ratios – that is, the ESF and the ERDF along with the European Agricultural Guidance and Guarantee Fund and the Financial Instrument for Fisheries Guidance, which represent the other two of the four structural policy instruments. However, it should be noted that the ESF and the ERDF make up, in terms of financial volume, the great bulk of EU Structural Funds (for an overview, see Mendez et al., 2014).

The data for our focal explanatory variable poses several methodological challenges which need to be considered. First of all, there is an overlap of five years (2007–11) in the two programming periods. From this, it follows that the Western European member states could absorb funds from two sources during the entire observation period and ten Central and Eastern European member states (those that joined the EU in 2004) could do so for most of the observation period (2004–2011). Another problem is that the Central and Eastern European member states only became entitled to use the Structural Funds upon EU accession in 2004, resulting in a significant reduction in the available data points for the empirical analysis. The data situation is even worse for Bulgaria and Romania, which only became entitled to the Structural Funds in 2007 (see also, for example, Bachtler et al., 2014; Tosun, 2014). Therefore, the analysis must rely on a comparatively small number of observations, which forces us to make use of a small number of control variables.

Since further macro-economic and institutional characteristics of the national economies are likely to affect the relationship between absorption of funds and youth unemployment, we test our hypotheses controlling for the effects of further characteristics resulting from the business cycle such as GDP growth, aggregate unemployment and the specific year, the proportion of 15- to 24-year-olds as a percentage of the population, and the main features of the labour market and wage-bargaining regime.

Testing of the hypotheses

We now provide empirical tests of the hypotheses based on a panel dataset of EU member states for the period 2000–11 (for the programming period 2000–6). We provide full descriptive analyses in Table 11.A1 in the Appendix, which shows the great variation in dependent variables (unemployment ratios), absorption and further demographics. The empirical models test the impact of absorption, conditional on further country characteristics, formulated as:

$$Y_{it} = f(ABS_{it}, DBC_{it}, LMI_{it}) \qquad (11.1)$$

Where $Y_{i,t}$ is the dependent variable (youth unemployment ratio) in any of the member states i in a year t depending on:

- $ABS_{i,t}$: absorption of the ESF, the ERDF and total Structural Funds;
- $DBC_{i,t}$: a country's demographics and the state of the economy, in particular the proportion of 15- to 24-year-olds as a percentage of the total population, the growth rate of the GDP and the aggregate unemployment rate of the total labour force; this data is taken from the European Commission's annual macro-economic database (AMECO) and from Eurostat data;
- $LMI_{i,t}$: variables describing the labour market regimes, including the flexibility of the labour market (part-time work and fixed-term employment as a percentage of total employment) and the wage-setting system (level and coordination of bargaining and government intervention in wage bargaining); quantitative and qualitative data on characteristics of the wage-bargaining

regime were taken from Visser's Database on Institutional Characteristics of Trade Unions, Wage Settings, State Interventions and Social Pacts (ICTWSS; Visser, 2013).

Given the limited number of observations available from the data, these variables capture most of the time-variant economic and institutional circumstances affecting youth unemployment, in particular the impact of the business cycle (Anxo et al., 2001; Schmid et al., 2001; Hujer et al., 2002; Bassanini and Duval, 2006).

The empirical models tested are of the following form:

$$Y_{i,t} = \beta_0 + \beta_j ABS_{i,t}^j + \sum_{k=1}^{0} \delta_k DBC_{i,t}^k + \sum_{l=0}^{n} \theta_l LMI_{i,t}^l + \alpha_i - u_{i,t} \tag{11.2}$$

with an intercept and ABS, the variable on specific absorption j, demographic and other context variables specified in a linear additive way. In addition, our specification as a Fixed Effects model allows us to capture any time-invariant effect α_i of unobserved characteristics that are intrinsic to the different countries and represent level differences in the outcome variable. $u_{i,t}$ is an error term of the empirical model.

Including dummy variables for years removes time effects, which are constant across countries. Finally, the variables summarising absorption and circumstances change over time and across countries. The parameter estimates for these variables from the empirical model show impacts of absorption on youth unemployment, which would result from a variation in policy variables, all other things being equal.

We specify the models as dynamic models, which include the lagged level of the endogenous variable (to capture dynamics). Because of this specification and the potential risk that the absorption variable is itself endogenous as it may depend on youth unemployment levels in previous years, we estimate the models using the Generalised Method of Moments estimator proposed by Arellano and Bond (1991) and Blundell and Bond (1998). This approach estimates the Fixed Effects model in "first differences" of dependent and independent variables, instrumenting the differences in lagged dependent variables with suitable lags of their own levels and other available instruments.

Table 11.1 shows the estimated effect of absorption on youth unemployment ratios (see also Tables 11.A2–11.A7 in the Appendix). Coefficients found for both the absorption of the ESF and total Structural Funds on the level of youth unemployment show significant effects (Hypotheses 1A and 3A), with the coefficient for ESF absorption showing a slightly larger effect size. The effect of ERDF absorption, which also has a negative sign, is not significant (Hypothesis 2A). In contrast to youth unemployment ratios, absorption did not show significant effects on the growth of youth unemployment ratios (Hypotheses 1B, 2B and 3B).

The analysis shows that absorption behaviour of the member states helps to reduce youth unemployment, although this affects levels on a year-by-year basis

Table 11.1 Effect of ESF, ERDF and total Structural Funds absorption on levels of youth unemployment.

	Coef.	Std. Err.	z
Absorption ESF			
Effect on youth unemployment ratio (H1A)	**−1.948**	0.974	−2.000
Effect on growth of youth unemployment ratio (H1B)	2.054	1.368	1.500
Absorption ERDF			
Effect on youth unemployment ratio (H2A)	−1.205	0.708	−1.700
Effect on growth of youth unemployment ratio (H2B)	0.515	1.252	0.410
Absorption total Structural Funds			
Effect on youth unemployment ratio (H3A)	**−1.750**	0.852	−2.050
Effect on growth of youth unemployment ratio (H3B)	2.289	1.693	1.350

Source: European Commission, Eurostat database, ICTWSS4.0, AMECO, authors' calculations.
Note: Bold denotes significance at 5% or higher.

rather than effecting long-term change in youth unemployment. What is important to note here is that the member states must make a sustained effort to absorb the Structural Funds in order to be provided with an effective means of tackling youth unemployment. Even if the EU is providing funding, the member states are ultimately responsible for absorbing and using the resources, which ties our study in with the literature on the implementation of Structural Funds (see, for example, Rodríguez-Pose and Fratesi, 2004; Bachtler and McMaster, 2007; Milio, 2007; Bache and Chapman, 2008; Bachtler et al., 2014; Tosun, 2014).

Conclusion and policy implications

Since 2008, youth unemployment and the proportion of NEETs has reached alarming levels in some EU member states. While most of the means for tackling youth unemployment are in the member states' hands, the EU can address this problem at an international level through Cohesion Policy. In this study we have assessed to what extent the ESF, the ERDF and the Structural Funds in general may support activities designed to help to integrate young people into the labour market.

Our findings show that the cumulative absorption of Structural Funds – irrespective of whether it is the ESF, the ERDF or the Structural Funds in total – does indeed have a significant effect on youth unemployment. Exhausting funds would indeed reduce youth unemployment levels. However, in terms of the magnitude, the effect of ESF absorption is greater than for ERDF and total funds absorption. Since the ESF is tailored most directly towards enhancing employment, this finding resonates with our theoretical reasoning.

At this stage, however, we view our results as early and indicative. We propose that a similar analysis should be undertaken for a longer period (for example, 2000–13) and at lower levels of aggregation, for which the European Labour Force Survey delivers an appropriate set of outcome variables on the labour market of young people and further control variables for regional demography and employment structures (see, for example, Mohl and Hagen, 2010).

Despite the preliminary character of our findings, we support the use of Structural Funds in the overall instrument mix aiming to combat youth unemployment. However, it is important to note that it is not the annual changes in the absorption of funds that help to reduce youth unemployment but the accumulation of the funds. From this, it follows that the effect of the Structural Funds depends on the long-term absorption behaviour of the member states, and thus that it is the absorption capacity of the individual member states that is likely to eventually determine the extent to which they can make use of the EU's Structural and Investment Funds to address youth unemployment. Our findings suggest that the provision of the funds matters, but that the administrative support provided to member states to ensure they attain high fund accumulation levels is also significant. We therefore invite researchers and policymakers to pay enhanced attention to the role of administrative capacity when discussing solutions to youth unemployment in Europe.

Acknowledgements

This chapter is an outcome of the two EU-funded collaborative research projects CUPESSE (Cultural Pathways to Economic Self-Sufficiency and Entrepreneurship; Grant Agreement No.613257; www.cupesse.eu) and STYLE (Strategic Transitions of Youth Labour in Europe; Grant Agreement No. 613256; www.style-research.eu). Simon Schaub and Jason Franz deserve credit for research assistance.

Appendix

Table 11.A1 Description of the dataset.

	N	Mean	SD	Min.	Max.
Dependent variables					
Unemployment ratio 15–24-year-olds	312	7.60	3.25	2.20	18.90
Key policy variables					
Absorption ESF	251	0.68	0.26	0.00	1.00
Absorption ERDF	249	0.69	0.26	0.00	1.00
Absorption total Structural Funds	227	0.66	0.25	0.09	0.97
Country demographics and business cycle					
15–24–year–olds as % of population	312	13.34	2.50	7.44	24.79
Growth rate of the per capita GDP p.a.	312	2.37	4.09	−16.59	13.27
Aggregate unemployment rate	312	8.49	3.94	1.90	21.40
Year	312	2005.50	3.46	2000.00	2011.00

Labour market and wage-bargaining regime					
Part–time employment rate	309	14.30	9.51	1.70	49.10
Fixed–term employment rate	311	10.90	6.89	1.00	34.00
Main level of bargaining company	311	0.48	0.50	0.00	1.00
Main level of bargaining intermediate	311	0.41	0.49	0.00	1.00
Main level of bargaining centralised	311	0.11	0.32	0.00	1.00
Coordination of bargaining centralised (0 = fragmented, mixed, intermediate)	310	0.35	0.48	0.00	1.00

Source: European Commission, Eurostat database, ICTWSS4.0, AMECO, authors' calculations.

Table 11.A2 Effect of ESF absorption on levels of youth unemployment (H1A).

Independent variables	Coef.	Std. err.	z	P > z
Lagged dependent variable	0.074	0.069	1.070	0.284
Absorption ESF	−1.948	0.974	−2.000	0.045
Aggregate unemployment	0.612	0.043	14.320	0.000
Growth of GDP per capita	−0.068	0.024	−2.820	0.005
15–24-year-olds as % of population	−0.110	0.102	−1.080	0.281
Part-time employment rate	−0.002	0.078	−0.020	0.983
Fixed-term employment rate	−0.126	0.054	−2.320	0.021
Main level of bargaining company	−0.757	0.505	−1.500	0.134
Main level of bargaining intermediate	−0.433	0.387	−1.120	0.263
Coordination of bargaining centralised (0 = fragmented, mixed, intermediate)	0.141	0.121	1.170	0.242
Year 2000	−0.887	1.075	−0.830	0.409
Year 2001	−1.427	1.287	−1.110	0.268
Year 2002	−1.311	1.126	−1.160	0.244
Year 2003	−1.340	1.040	−1.290	0.198
Year 2004	−0.774	0.873	−0.890	0.376
Year 2005	−1.033	0.703	−1.470	0.142
Year 2006	−0.770	0.615	−1.250	0.210
Year 2007	−0.587	0.416	−1.410	0.158
Year 2008	−0.293	0.352	−0.830	0.405
Year 2009	−0.104	0.324	−0.320	0.748
Year 2010	−0.036	0.163	−0.220	0.825
Observations/statistics				
N	156			
Groups	18			
Number of instruments	93	N by G: min	0	
Wald chi^2(21)	1290	avg	9	

(contiuned)

Table 11.A2 (continued)

Independent variables	Coef.	Std. err.	z	P > z
Prob > chi^2	0	max	11	
Arellano–Bond test for AR(1) in first differences: z	−1.8700	Pr > z		0.0610
Arellano–Bond test for AR(2) in first differences: z	−1.4700	Pr > z		0.1430
Sargan test of overid. restrictions	chi^2(72) = 122.77	Prob > chi^2		0.0000
Hansen test of overid. restrictions	chi^2(72) = 0.00	Prob > chi^2		1.0000

Source: European Commission, Eurostat database, ICTWSS4.0, AMECO, authors' calculations.

Table 11.A3 Effect of ESF absorption on youth unemployment growth (H1B).

Independent variables	Coef.	Std. Err.	z	P > z
Lagged dependent variable	−0.074	0.059	−1.260	0.208
Absorption ESF	2.054	1.368	1.500	0.133
Aggregate unemployment	−0.021	0.053	−0.400	0.687
Growth of GDP per capita	−0.273	0.032	−8.640	0.000
15–24-year-olds as % of population	−0.088	0.084	−1.040	0.298
Part-time employment rate	−0.030	0.101	−0.300	0.766
Fixed-term employment rate	−0.122	0.113	−1.070	0.282
Main level of bargaining company	−0.782	0.632	−1.240	0.216
Main level of bargaining intermediate	−0.586	0.549	−1.070	0.286
Coordination of bargaining centralised (0 = fragmented, mixed, intermediate)	0.177	0.381	0.470	0.641
Year 2001	1.228	1.241	0.990	0.322
Year 2002	1.898	1.050	1.810	0.071
Year 2003	1.907	1.037	1.840	0.066
Year 2004	1.721	0.864	1.990	0.046
Year 2005	1.324	0.888	1.490	0.136
Year 2006	1.231	0.879	1.400	0.161
Year 2007	0.357	0.626	0.570	0.568
Year 2008	−0.052	0.409	−0.130	0.899
Year 2009	0.457	0.356	1.290	0.198
Year 2010	0.687	0.399	1.720	0.086

Observations/statistics

N	149			
Groups	18			
Number of instruments	81	N by G: min	0	
Wald chi^2(20)	4912	avg	8	
Prob > chi^2	0	max	10	
Arellano–Bond test for AR(1) in first differences: z	−3.4700	Pr > z		0.0010

Arellano–Bond test for AR(2) in first differences: z	−1.6200	Pr > z	0.1050
Sargan test of overid. restrictions	chi² (61) = 118.27	Prob > chi²	0.0000
Hansen test of overid. restrictions	chi²(61) = 0.00	Prob > chi²	1.0000

Source: European Commission, Eurostat database, ICTWSS4.0, AMECO, authors' calculations.

Table 11.A4 Effect of ERDF absorption on levels of youth unemployment (H2A).

Independent variables	Coef.	Std. Err.	z	P > z
Lagged dependent variable	0.108	0.078	1.390	0.164
Absorption ERDF	−1.205	0.708	−1.700	0.089
Aggregate unemployment	0.594	0.058	10.310	0.000
Growth of GDP per capita	−0.070	0.034	−2.080	0.038
15–24-year-olds as % of population	−0.109	0.097	−1.130	0.260
Part-time employment rate	0.010	0.086	0.110	0.912
Fixed-term employment rate	−0.143	0.060	−2.380	0.017
Main level of bargaining company	−0.824	0.499	−1.650	0.099
Main level of bargaining intermediate	−0.447	0.383	−1.170	0.244
Coordination of bargaining centralised (0 = fragmented, mixed, intermediate)	0.159	0.121	1.310	0.191
Year 2000	−0.542	0.728	−0.740	0.456
Year 2001	−0.964	0.957	−1.010	0.313
Year 2002	−0.893	0.794	−1.130	0.261
Year 2003	−0.917	0.741	−1.240	0.216
Year 2004	−0.267	0.559	−0.480	0.632
Year 2005	−0.607	0.528	−1.150	0.251
Year 2006	−0.347	0.436	−0.800	0.426
Year 2007	−0.262	0.310	−0.840	0.398
Year 2008	−0.166	0.325	−0.510	0.610
Year 2009	0.003	0.305	0.010	0.992
Year 2010	0.008	0.139	0.060	0.955
Observations/statistics				
N	154			MS
Groups	18			Year
Number of instruments	93	N by G: min	0	
Wald chi²(21)	381	avg	9	
Prob > chi²	0	max	11	
Arellano–Bond test for AR(1) in first differences: z	−2.0000	Pr > z	0.0450	
Arellano–Bond test for AR(2) in first differences: z	−0.8400	Pr > z	0.4010	
Sargan test of overid. restrictions	chi²(72) = 132.53	Prob > chi²	0.0000	
Hansen test of overid. restrictions	chi²(72) = 0.00	Prob > chi²	1.0000	

Source: European Commission, Eurostat database, ICTWSS4.0, AMECO, authors' calculations.

Table 11.A5 Effect of ERDF absorption on youth unemployment growth (H2B).

Independent variables	Coef.	Std. Err.	z	P > z
Lagged dependent variable	−0.059	0.058	−1.010	0.313
Absorption ERDF	0.515	1.252	0.410	0.681
Aggregate unemployment	−0.036	0.048	−0.740	0.461
Growth of GDP per capita	−0.282	0.032	−8.850	0.000
15–24-year-olds as % of population	−0.099	0.090	−1.100	0.271
Part-time employment rate	−0.039	0.100	−0.390	0.697
Fixed-term employment rate	−0.132	0.117	−1.130	0.259
Main level of bargaining company	−0.792	0.667	−1.190	0.235
Main level of bargaining intermediate	−0.624	0.579	−1.080	0.281
Coordination of bargaining centralised (0 = fragmented, mixed, intermediate)	0.211	0.372	0.570	0.571
Year 2001	0.261	1.044	0.250	0.802
Year 2002	1.044	0.879	1.190	0.235
Year 2003	1.049	0.868	1.210	0.227
Year 2004	0.880	0.589	1.490	0.135
Year 2005	0.473	0.738	0.640	0.522
Year 2006	0.477	0.634	0.750	0.451
Year 2007	−0.068	0.504	−0.140	0.892
Year 2008	−0.226	0.369	−0.610	0.541
Year 2009	0.306	0.342	0.900	0.371
Year 2010	0.627	0.385	1.630	0.103
Observations/statistics				
N	149			
Groups	18			
Number of instruments	81	N by G: min	0	
Wald chi^2(20)	448	avg	8	
Prob > chi^2	0	max	10	
Arellano–Bond test for AR(1) in first differences: z	−3.3000	Pr > z	0.0010	
Arellano–Bond test for AR(2) in first differences: z	−1.6900	Pr > z	0.0910	
Sargan test of overid. restrictions	chi^2(61) = 118.25	Prob > chi^2	0.0000	
Hansen test of overid. restrictions	chi^2(61) = 0.00	Prob > chi^2	1.0000	

Source: European Commission, Eurostat database, ICTWSS4.0, AMECO, authors' calculations.

Table 11.A6 Effect of total Structural Funds absorption on levels of youth unemployment (H3A).

Independent variables	Coef.	Std. Err.	z	P > z
Lagged dependent variable	0.085	0.085	1.000	0.316
Absorption total Structural Funds	−1.750	0.852	−2.050	0.040
Aggregate unemployment	0.610	0.062	9.910	0.000
Growth of GDP per capita	−0.065	0.033	−1.990	0.046
15–24-year-olds as % of population	−0.071	0.082	−0.860	0.388
Part-time employment rate	0.003	0.082	0.030	0.975
Fixed-term employment rate	−0.115	0.059	−1.940	0.053
Main level of bargaining company	−1.120	0.386	−2.910	0.004
Main level of bargaining intermediate	−0.647	0.295	−2.200	0.028
Coordination of bargaining centralised (0 = fragmented, mixed, intermediate)	0.121	0.135	0.900	0.368
Year 2000	−0.974	0.864	−1.130	0.260
Year 2001	−1.491	1.029	−1.450	0.147
Year 2002	−1.375	0.860	−1.600	0.110
Year 2003	−1.340	0.795	−1.690	0.092
Year 2004	−0.639	0.597	−1.070	0.285
Year 2005	−0.938	0.576	−1.630	0.103
Year 2006	−0.617	0.472	−1.310	0.191
Year 2007	−0.403	0.303	−1.330	0.184
Year 2008	−0.193	0.309	−0.620	0.533
Year 2009	−0.015	0.275	−0.060	0.955
Observations/statistics				
N	138			
Groups	18			
Number of instruments	81	N by G: min	0	
Wald chi^2(20)	241	avg	8	
Prob > chi^2	0	max	10	
Arellano–Bond test for AR(1) in first differences: z	−2	Pr > z	0	
Arellano–Bond test for AR(2) in first differences: z	−0.8500	Pr > z	0.3940	
Sargan test of overid. restrictions	chi^2(61) = 117.81	Prob > chi^2	0.0000	
Hansen test of overid. restrictions	chi^2(61) = 0.00	Prob > chi^2	1.0000	

Source: European Commission, Eurostat database, ICTWSS4.0, AMECO, authors' calculations.

Table 11.A7 Effect of total Structural Funds absorption on youth unemployment growth (H3B).

Independent variables	Coef.	Std. Err.	z	P > z
Lagged dependent variable	−0.085	0.092	−0.920	0.360
Absorption total Structural Funds	2.289	1.693	1.350	0.176
Aggregate unemployment	0.022	0.064	0.340	0.732
Growth of GDP per capita	−0.229	0.024	−9.620	0.000
15–24-year-olds as % of population	−0.056	0.065	−0.850	0.393
Part-time employment rate	−0.052	0.091	−0.580	0.565
Fixed-term employment rate	−0.146	0.108	−1.360	0.175
Main level of bargaining company	−1.021	0.507	−2.020	0.044
Main level of bargaining intermediate	−0.572	0.466	−1.230	0.220
Coordination of bargaining centralised (0 = fragmented, mixed, intermediate)	0.073	0.289	0.250	0.802
Year 2002	0.749	0.308	2.430	0.015
Year 2003	0.732	0.478	1.530	0.125
Year 2004	0.359	0.789	0.460	0.649
Year 2005	0.077	0.737	0.100	0.917
Year 2006	−0.114	0.773	−0.150	0.883
Year 2007	−1.080	1.237	−0.870	0.383
Year 2008	−1.209	1.523	−0.790	0.427
Year 2009	−0.506	1.628	−0.310	0.756
Year 2010	−0.589	1.517	−0.390	0.698
Observations/statistics				
N	131			
Groups	18			
Number of instruments	70	N by G: min	0	
Wald chi²(19)	235	avg	7	
Prob > chi²	0	max	9	
Arellano–Bond test for AR(1) in first differences: z	−3	Pr > z	0	
Arellano–Bond test for AR(2) in first differences: z	−1.4900	Pr > z	0.1370	
Sargan test of overid. restrictions	chi²(51) = 110.61	Prob > chi²	0.0000	
Hansen test of overid. restrictions	chi²(51) = 0.00	Prob > chi²	1.0000	

Source: European Commission, Eurostat database, ICTWSS4.0, AMECO, authors' calculations.

References

Anxo, D., Carcillo, S. and Erhel, C. (2001), "Aggregate impact analysis of active labour market policy in France and Sweden: a regional approach", in J. de Koning and H. Mosley (eds), *Labour Market Policy and Unemployment: An Evaluation of Active Measures in France, Germany, the Netherlands, Spain and Sweden*, Cheltenham, UK: Edward Elgar, pp. 49–76.

Arellano, M. and Bond, S. (1991), "Some tests of specification for panel data: Monte Carlo evidence and an application to employment equations", *The Review of Economic Studies*, 58(2), 277–97.

Bache, I. and Chapman, R. (2008), "Democracy through multilevel governance? The implementation of the Structural Funds in South Yorkshire", *Governance*, 21(3), 397–418.

Bachtler, J. and McMaster, I. (2007), "EU Cohesion Policy and the role of the regions: investigating the influence of Structural Funds in the new member states", *Environment and Planning C: Government and Policy*, 26(2), 398–427.

Bachtler, J. and Mendez, C. (2007), "Who governs EU Cohesion Policy? Deconstructing the reforms of the Structural Funds", *Journal of Common Market Studies*, 45(3), 535–64.

Bachtler, J., Mendez, C. and Oraže, H. (2014), "From conditionality to Europeanization in Central and Eastern Europe: administrative performance and capacity in cohesion policy", *European Planning Studies*, 22(4), 735–57.

Bassanini, A. and Duval, R. (2006), "Employment patterns in OECD countries: reassessing the role of policies and institutions", OECD Economics Department Working Papers 486, Paris (OECD).

Bell, D. N. and Blanchflower, D. G. (2011), "Young people and the Great Recession", *Oxford Review of Economic Policy*, 27(2), 241–67.

Berlingieri, F., Bonin, H. and Sprietsma, M. (2014), *Youth Unemployment in Europe Appraisal and Policy Options*, Mannheim/Stuttgart: Centre for European Economic Research/Robert Bosch Foundation, available at: www.bosch-stiftung.de/content/language1/downloads/RBS_ZEW-Studie_Jugendarbeitslosigkeit_Online_einzel.pdf (accessed 20 December 2014).

Blundell, R. and Bond, S. (1998), "Initial conditions and moment restrictions in dynamic panel data models", *Journal of Econometrics*, 87(1), 115–43.

Busemeyer, M. R. and Jensen, C. (2012), "The impact of economic coordination and educational institutions on individual-level preferences for academic and vocational education", *Socio-Economic Review*, 10(3), 525–47.

Caporale, G. M. and Gil-Alana, L. A. (2014), "Youth unemployment in Europe: persistence and macroeconomic determinants", *Comparative Economic Studies*, 56(4), 581–91.

Chabanet, D. (2014), "Between youth policy and employment policy: the rise, limits and ambiguities of a corporatist system of youth representation within the EU", *Journal of Common Market Studies*, 52(3), 479–94.

Choudhry, M. T., Marelli, E. and Signorelli, M. (2012), "Youth unemployment rate and impact of financial crises", *International Journal of Manpower*, 33(1), 76–95.

Choudhry, M. T., Marelli, E. and Signorelli, M. (2013), "Youth and total unemployment rate: the impact of policies and institutions", *Rivista Internazionale di Scienze Sociali*, 121(1), 63–86.

European Commission (2012), *23rd Annual Report on Implementation of the Structural Funds (2011)*, COM(2012) 633 final, Brussels: European Commission, available at: www.europarl.europa.eu/document/activities/cont/201301/20130109ATT58733/20130109ATT58733EN.pdf (accessed 20 December 2014).

European Commission (2013), *Entrepreneurship 2020 Action Plan: Reigniting the Entrepreneurial Spirit in Europe*, COM(2012) 795 final, Brussels: European Commission, available at: http://eur-lex.europa.eu/LexUriServ/LexUriServ.do?uri=COM:2012:0795:FIN:EN:PDF (accessed 20 December 2014).

European Commission (2014), *EU Measures to Tackle Youth Unemployment*, Brussels: European Commission, available at: http://ec.europa.eu/social/main.jsp?catId=1036 (accessed 20 December 2014).

Eurostat (2015), "Harmonised unemployment by sex – age group 15–24", Luxembourg: Eurostat, available at: http://ec.europa.eu/eurostat/tgm/table.do?tab=table&init=1&language=en&pcode=teilm011&plugin=1 (accessed 23 January 2015).

Freitag, M. and Kirchner, A. (2011), "Social capital and unemployment: a macroquantitative analysis of the European regions", *Political Studies*, 59(2), 389–410.

Hörisch, F. and Weishaupt, T. (2012), "It's the youth, stupid! Explaining labour market policy reactions to the crisis", *Zeitschrift für Vergleichende Politikwissenschaft*, 6(2), 233–53.

House of Lords (2014), *Youth Unemployment in the EU: A Scarred Generation?* London. House of Lords, available at: www.publications.parliament.uk/pa/ld201314/ldselect/ldeucom/164/164.pdf (accessed 2 January 2015).

Hujer, R., Zeiss, C., Caliendo, M. and Blien, U. (2002), "Macroeconometric evaluation of active labour market policies in Germany: a dynamic panel approach using regional data", IZA Discussion Paper Series.

Isengard, B. (2003), "Youth unemployment – individual risk factors and institutional determinants: a case study of Germany and the United Kingdom", *Journal of Youth Studies*, 6(4), 357–76.

Mendez, C., Bachtler, J. and Wishlade, M. F. (2014), *EU Cohesion Policy and European Integration: The Dynamics of EU Budget and Regional Policy Reform*, Aldershot, UK: Ashgate.

Milio, S. (2007), "Can administrative capacity explain differences in regional performances? Evidence from Structural Funds implementation in southern Italy", *Regional Studies*, 41(4), 429–42.

Mohl, P. and Hagen, T. (2010), "Do EU Structural Funds promote regional growth? New evidence from various panel data approaches", *Regional Science and Urban Economics*, 40(5), 353–65.

Nafilyan, V. and Speckesser, S. (2014), *Estimating the Long-Term Social Benefits of a Programme Aiming to Re-engage NEETs in Education*, Brighton, UK: Institute for Employment Studies, available at: www.ieb.ub.edu/files/PapersWSEE2014/Nafilyan.pdf (accessed 20 December 2014).

O'Higgins, N. (2012), "This time it's different: youth labour markets during 'the Great Recession'", *Comparative Economic Studies*, 54(2), 395–412.

O'Reilly, J. and Lain, D. (2010), *Labour Market Transitions in Comparative Perspective: Policy Briefing from EU Research Findings*, Brighton: Centre for Research on Management and Employment, available at: http://workcaresynergies.eu/wp-content/uploads/2010/12/WCS%20v9.pdf (accessed 20 December 2014).

O'Reilly, J., Eichhorst, W., Gabos, A., Hadjivassiliou, K., Kurakova, L., Lain, D., Lesckhe, J., McGuinness, S., Nazio, T., Ortlieb, R., Russell, H. and Villa, P. (2015), "Five characteristics of youth unemployment in Europe: flexibility, education, migration, family legacies and EU policy", *Sage Open*, DOI: 10.1177/2158244015574962.

Rodríguez-Pose, A. and Fratesi, U. (2004), "Between development and social policies: the impact of European Structural Funds in Objective 1 regions", *Regional Studies*, 38(1), 97–113.

Schmid, G., Speckesser, S. and Hilbert, H. (2001), "Does active labour market policy matter? An aggregate analysis for Germany", in J. de Koning and H. Mosley (eds), *Labour Market Policy and Unemployment: An Evaluation of Active Measures in France, Germany, the Netherlands, Spain and Sweden*, Cheltenham, UK: Edward Elgar, pp. 77–114.

Scruggs, L., Jahn, D. and Kuitto, K. (2014), *Comparative Welfare Entitlements Dataset 2: Version 2014-03*, University of Connecticut/University of Greifswald, available at: http://cwed2.org/ (accessed 20 December 2014).

Tosun, J. (2014), "Absorption of Regional Funds: a comparative analysis", *Journal of Common Market Studies*, 52(2), 371–87.

Tosun, J., Wetzel, A. and Zapryanova, G. (2014), "The EU in crisis: advancing the debate", *Journal of European Integration*, 36(3), 195–211.

Van Der Zwan, P., Verheul, I., Thurik, R. and Grilo, I. (2013), "Entrepreneurial progress: climbing the entrepreneurial ladder in Europe and the United States, *Regional Studies*, 47(5), 803–25.

Visser, J. (2013), *Data Base on Institutional Characteristics of Trade Unions, Wage Setting, State Intervention and Social Pacts 1960–2010 (ICTWSS 4.0)*, Amsterdam: University of Amsterdam AIAS, available at: www.uva-aias.net (accessed 20 December 2014).

Part III
The administration and delivery of Cohesion Policy

12 Administrative and political embeddedness

How to improve the institutional environments dealing with the management and implementation of EU Structural and Investment Funds? The experience of new member states[1]

Neculai-Cristian Surubaru

Introduction

Time and time again, administrative capacity has been identified as a key feature of the successful management and implementation of EU funds. However, the capacity of national authorities to implement European funding instruments varies from country to country and from region to region. The integration of Central and Eastern European countries into the EU has contributed to an increase in this variation. Different styles of management, issues of public administration and a lack of experience have generally affected the ability of new member states to manage funding. Many studies have examined the administrative capacity of EU member states vis-à-vis European Cohesion Policy implementation (Boeckhout *et al*., 2002; Horvat and Maier, 2004; Sumpíková *et al*., 2004; Milio, 2007; Bachtler and McMaster, 2008; Bachtler *et al*., 2013; Ferry, 2013; Petzold *et al*., 2015). Recently, new correlations have emerged between the quality of governance in EU countries and their capacity and performance to absorb EU funds (Boijmans, 2013; Charron *et al*., 2014). As a consequence, it is often hinted that "good governance" can play an important role in this respect (European Commission, 2014). As emphasized by the sixth European Cohesion report, good governance may be an underlying condition necessary for sustained economic and social development, as well as for a modern public administration (European Commission, 2014: 160–1). However, little remains known about the formal and informal dimensions of domestic governance and the role and influence of political factors over formal mechanisms for the management of EU Structural Funds (SF). At the same time, there is little discussion about the institutional environment in which Managing and Control Institutions[2] are embedded.

Consequently, this chapter investigates the extent to which domestic governance interferes with the development of administrative capacity. It questions, in theoretical and practical terms, how issues of domestic governance may affect administrative capacity processes and the domestic institutional actors in charge of the implementation. The chapter provides a snapshot of some of the domestic barriers affecting the management of EU funding. It does so by developing the concept of administrative and political embeddedness in order to explain why the environment in which Managing and Control Institutions are situated matters.

Reflections are based on an analysis of qualitative evidence gathered from two new member states, Bulgaria and Romania. More than 60 in-depth, semi-structured interviews were carried out over the course of 2013 and 2014, with representatives from Managing and Control Institutions in both countries as well as with Brussels-based officials. Several interviewees provided valuable evidence on how the domestic political and administrative environment shapes the overall administrative capacity of the countries and determines shortcomings at the different stages of the absorption process. It is this type of evidence that may help us to grasp some of the mechanisms that affect national implementation systems. This evidence was corroborated with a detailed analysis of key primary documents such as national implementation reports, audit reports and external evaluations, as well as of a digest of media coverage on EU funds in both countries and the reports of different civil society stakeholders on the subject.

The chapter is structured as follows. After a brief presentation of some of the theoretical debates on administrative capacity and governance, the main section defines and provides empirical instances of administrative and political embeddedness. The concluding section sketches several recommendations for how to counteract the effects of these factors. Some of the measures discussed may be essential to improve the performance of policy instruments such as the EU Structural and Investment Funds during the 2014–20 period.

Administrative capacity and governance: an ever-growing link

Administrative capacity is a key concept in the specialized literature dealing with Cohesion Policy implementation and with the governance of Structural and Cohesion Funds. Its theoretical development can enable policymakers and practitioners to further understand why some Managing and Control Institutions or beneficiaries have been more successful than others in implementing EU-funded projects. There is a growing body of evidence with regard to the implementation of SF based on the experience of Central and Eastern European countries (Horvat and Maier, 2004; Sumpíková *et al.*, 2004; Bachtler *et al.*, 2013; Ferry and McMaster, 2013; Dabrowski, 2014; Surubaru, 2014). Similarly, at the national level in the two countries under discussion, several analysts have examined the key obstacles and deficiencies for SF implementation (Georgescu, 2008; Zaman and Georgescu, 2009; Berica, 2010; Cace *et al.*, 2010; Stefanov *et al.*, 2010; Zaman and Cristea, 2011; Tsachevsky, 2012; Hristova Kurzydlowski, 2013).

On the one hand, there are more and more studies that seek to define what administrative capacity is in relation to the management of EU funds (Boeckhout *et al.*, 2002; Milio, 2007; Petzold *et al.*, 2015), although there is no universally accepted definition of the term (Addison, 2009). Some see administrative capacity as the "organizational structures, adequacy and quality of human resources and administrative adaptability" employed by states at the different stages of the absorption process (Bachtler *et al.*, 2013: 14). Others envision administrative capacity as "an essential component of good governance, although not limited only to it" (Marinov, 2011: 20). With all this, the boundaries and inter-linkages between administrative capacity and governance are still an important source of debate.

On the other hand, the growing debate on the governance of EU funds and the potential impact of Cohesion Policy has recently been acknowledged by the Barca report (2009), which provided evidence to policymakers of the increasing role of governance. Other reports have stressed that there is a need for strong continuity of staff working in the specialized bodies dealing with EU funds and a quality-oriented administration (World Bank, 2006: xii). In order to foster this, there needs to be a smooth relationship between the administrative and the political level (World Bank, 2006: xii).

Specifically, Charron *et al.* (2014) argue that there is a strong link between the quality of regional governance and administrative capacity. Rodríguez-Pose (2013) points to the way in which formal and informal institutional settings influence the environment for policy implementation. In addition, Dotti (2013) argues that the weakness of the EU institutional framework, combined with differential multi-level governance settings across the EU, as well as domestic political context and factors, adds to the complexity of managing the funds. Studying the Italian case, Milio (2008) is among the few scholars who have pointed to the importance of domestic political factors for creating an environment conducive to the successful implementation of the policy. More recently, it has been suggested that good governmental capacity accounts for a better absorption performance, specifically for the European Regional Development Funds (Tosun, 2014). Finally, political support has been identified as a key variable that may explain the differences in capacity and performance within and between new member states (Surubaru, 2014).

In parallel, the immense body of literature on post-Communist politics and transition underlines the strong grip of informal networks and clienteles on economic and political outputs (Dimitrova, 2010; Ganev, 2013). Moreover, the importance of administrative traditions and political leadership (Eriksen, 2007) and the slow pace of public-sector reforms (Verheijen, 1999) have crippled the potential for developing strong institutions. Consequently, 25 years since the fall of the Communist system, it may be argued that socio-political conditions and weak institutions have provided a significant handicap for new member states as regards the management of external aid. With all this, the strong variation between Central and Eastern European countries when it comes to the overall absorption of funding remains puzzling. For instance, Estonia, Lithuania and Poland are among the most efficient with regard to the absorption of funds. Researching how administrative capacity may interact with domestic governance and institutional arrangements has become a critical area of inquiry in order to understand issues of performance.

The underlying assumption of this inquiry is that the political and administrative spheres affect the different stages of the absorption process. Understanding how technocratic issues specific to the absorption of EU funds may interact with domestic political factors can help us to specify how the latter impact on administrative capacity. Whether positive or negative, political factors do play a key role and should be more properly accounted for in analyses of the implementation of EU Cohesion Policy, as advocated by several authors (Milio, 2008; Surubaru, 2014).

Administrative and political embeddedness: what is it and how is it manifested?

This chapter's main contribution is to highlight instances of what is defined as administrative and political embeddedness in relation to EU Cohesion Policy management. "Embeddedness", be it administrative or political, is an ill-defined concept in political science and public administration. Several authors have used it in relation to management, business and organizational science (Cohen *et al.*, 1969; Uzzi, 1997; Welch and Wilkinson, 2004; Moran, 2005). Knill (1998) has developed the concept in relation to the issue of administrative traditions and national capacities for public administration reforms, as a means of explaining variation in the implementation of EU legislation. More recently, Chardas (2012) has used the concept to explain some of the problems that the Greek authorities have faced in implementing EU Cohesion Policy, linking the concept with socio-economic environments.

In order to assess the usefulness of this concept empirically, this section presents qualitative evidence on how domestic institutional and political environments affect the daily work of EU funds administrators in Bulgaria and Romania. These are two of the countries that have had numerous problems in the management of the funding, but that have also drifted apart in terms of performance. In the two sub-sections that follow, the empirical analysis concentrates principally on Managing Authorities as the primary stakeholders involved in the implementation of Operational Programmes (OPs). Several examples are presented in relation to what is referred to in the literature as administrative capacity-building and processes (Boeckhout *et al.*, 2002; Milio, 2007; Bachtler *et al.*, 2013; Petzold *et al.*, 2015). The two sub-sections provide concrete illustrations of how both administrative and political embeddedness is manifested and how it affects the work of the Bulgarian and Romanian authorities in charge of EU funds management.

Administrative embeddedness

Administrative embeddedness is widely defined here as the dependency of Managing and Control Institutions, from a bureaucratic and procedural point of view, on their institutional hosts. Often, Managing Authorities (MAs) have relied on the bureaucratic and procedural support of the ministries in which they resided. Several problems emerged concerning the interaction of the two sides, which ultimately led to deficiencies in administrative capacity-building and generally for the process of EU funds management.

First, given that MAs acted as independent departments within the state administration led to animosities between different types of civil servants. Giving a special status to administrators in charge of EU funding was seen as a way to strengthen their capacity. However, in some cases this also alienated the wider administration and generated a "state-within-a-state" phenomenon:

> Because we operated under different rules, we operated within the ministry as a state within a state. Acting like that alienated us from the administration, and it took a lot of effort. It could be done. I've done it. But it took a lot of effort. This is a process that depends on people.
> (Former Director of Bulgarian Managing Authority #2)

The above clearly illustrates the inter-dependence between the two categories of civil servants. On the one hand, several hundred administrators created an elite type of public administration body, with a higher degree of expertise and incentives. On the other, regular civil servants had to assist the former in their daily activities, particularly on legal, procedural and human resources matters. However, because MAs were part of the wider administration, they often had to wait for support. In some ministries, EU funds administrators did not receive any "priority treatment" as compared to other departments, which could have slowed down the absorption process (Director of Romanian Managing Authority #3; Director of Bulgarian Managing Authority #1).

Another example of dependency on the host institution, and with concrete implications for the development of administrative capacity, was that in some Romanian ministries the wider ministerial apparatus was responsible for the use of technical assistance funding. One Director of a Romanian Managing Authority (#2) expressed how poorly the management of this funding was understood:

> With regard to new resources, we manage the technical assistance axis equivalent to €10 million. This was another difficult aspect given that it was difficult to explain at the beginning of the programming period that these funds need to be spent. The MA is not a credit co-ordinator. It is a department in a big ministry with many other departments and which has one or several credit co-ordinators. It was difficult that they [the Ministry] needed to co-finance [technical assistance projects] with 25 per cent [from the overall budget of the project] in order for the MA to develop, on the one hand to train its personnel, and on the other hand to provide the technical conditions and to use certain work techniques, to go and train and inform beneficiaries

through all sorts of events. The Commission only came in 2011 and decided to co-finance [these type of projects] with 85 per cent [of the overall budget].

Second, administrative embeddedness presumed a legal dependency on the institutional host. The fact that MAs were based in a national ministry meant that they did not have judicial status and could only be represented in various judicial processes by a minister. On the one hand, this was often useful because the ministry could engage and assume responsibility in various legal proceedings on behalf of the MA. On the other, as mentioned by a Former Director of a Bulgarian Managing Authority (#2): "It was never understood that the MAs need certain operational independence and legal independence. They considered that yes, they will be directorates and the minister will do everything and decide everything". The technical and operational legitimacy of MAs may have been damaged as a consequence of their lack of judicial status.

Third, the general discrepancies in terms of salaries between staff from Managing and Control Institutions and staff from domestic host structures provoked internal rows and processes of contestation from the latter, who often had to provide crucial support to EU funds administrators in various stages of the absorption process. The fact that state experts working on EU funds were paid much more highly than most other civil servants triggered tensions, as related by an official involved in the process:

> There was always a tension. For example, if you work in a structure like the Central Co-ordination Unit (CCU) and you want some help from the legal department of the ministry, there is always a chance for some experts to say: "You have a double salary, deal with it yourself". The trouble is that two years ago this measure was removed from the Government because of this tension. Because we are in the European Union you have to apply the same approach to the whole administration.
> (Head of Unit in the Bulgarian Central Co-ordination Unit #1)

Furthermore, as emphasized by one local Bulgarian Mayor (#1), another problem was the lack of alignment between salaries, standards and work-related conditions of the indirectly involved stakeholders: "The problem is that the salaries in the Bulgarian administration are not in accordance with the quality and efficiency and motivation that the European projects require". Furthermore, for a long period of time, there were significant discrepancies between and within similar structures managing OPs. This reflected the configuration and internal arrangements of the host institutions for each and every MA or Intermediate Body (IB). For instance, within the Romanian Human Resources Operational Programme, until 2014, there were problems with disparities between salaries of staff in the different IBs. The Ministry of Labour had its own territorially spread IBs, at the NUTS2 level, covering the priority axes related mainly to employment and training. The Ministry of Education had one central IB that managed the education priority axis. Although situated in Bucharest, it operated at the regional level through staff working in affiliation with Education Inspectorates. As emphasized by someone working in these institutions, the differences in salaries and workloads, within the same Operational Programme, were very high:

> Hierarchically we addressed [reported to] Bucharest and the Intermediate Body there. As in [to] us. The IB addressed or had to address [report to] the Ministry of Education. The Ministry of Labour could not do anything to us. We were the Ministry of Education and they were the Ministry of Labour. This was one of the problems. This is how [the system] was thought. We did not receive any financial bonuses, they received financial bonuses. Then they could reach 50 million LEI [approx. €1,200] or in some months even 60–70 million LEI [approx. €1,300–1,400] and we had the same money 17–18 million LEI [approx. €400]. For so many years it went on like this, apart from the fact that the workload was totally different [the quantity of work was higher for the latter].
>
> (Head of Romanian North-East Intermediate Body)

Overall, a general lack of financial incentives caused many other problems during the implementation stage of the projects. Quite often, domestic internal restrictions and salary caps affected the motivation among personnel and increased staff turnover. In the context of political instability and institutional turmoil, as well as in light of the effects of the austerity measures adopted by the governments of Emil Boc (2008–12), many administrators from Romanian MAs were tempted by the prospect of working in consultancies for salaries two or three times higher (Director of Romanian Managing Authority #2). The austerity measures entailed cuts of 25 per cent in the wages of all public-sector employees. Given that they applied equally to administrators managing EU funding, they were widely seen as 'contextual blockages' with important negative consequences for staff morale (Director in Romanian Audit Authority #1; Romanian MA Programme Evaluations Officer #3; Former Romanian EU Affairs Minister). Restrictions on hiring new staff was also a systemic problem, found in both countries, that affected all OPs, predominantly those in which the level of technical expertise required was high (for example, Environment and Transport) (Romanian MA Programme Evaluations Officer #1).

Overall, the fact that these institutions were administratively embedded in the national structures increased their vulnerability. However, added to this, political embeddedness also proved a negative factor for many of the staff involved in the absorption process.

Political embeddedness

Administrative embeddedness was manifested mainly at the legal/bureaucratic level and had a concrete operational dimension attached to it. Political embeddedness entails a stronger political component. Very often, internal political dynamics and interests could affect the work of the Managing and Control Institutions.

First, being judicially dependent often made it difficult for MAs to react quickly to various developments. As pointed out by a Romanian Expert (#2), this was particularly the case when administrators required a validation at the political level:

> The fact is that MAs were part of the ministries because they lack a judicial status. In general, to engage a ministry as a judicial actor is much more difficult. Although most communications were between MAs, if strategic issues arose, they could even reach the minister.

This enforced a dependency on politicians and limited the room for manoeuvre of administrators, as emphasized by a Former Director of a Bulgarian Managing Authority (#2):

> By the way, an important perspective, one other fact that regards MAs as structures of the administration is the fact that being a director I am not of a public body under Bulgarian law. I had a status of a director as a civil servant relationship. But still, as a public body, judicially in relation with other bodies outside the ministry, I don't have entity [judicial status]. The entity [judicial status] is carried by the minister and the deputy minister, they are the [judicial] entities under Bulgarian [law and] administration. It creates problems because I cannot do a lot of my job without the minister.

One key argument for an enhanced political dependency was that these Managing and Control Institutions need to be politically accountable. Nevertheless, interviewees signalled that due to this, and the administrative tradition affiliated to it, many of the institutions involved in the process did not take the initiative and often waited for political leadership and guidance (Bulgarian Expert #2; Romanian Expert #1). This increased the importance of decisions taken by political representatives such as ministers, deputy ministers (Bulgaria) or secretaries of state (Romania). As a consequence, internal politics has played an equally important role in the management of the funds. One of the interesting examples given was that counsellors or political aides of ministers often acted as 'veto players'. They had the role of intermediaries between EU funds administrators and the minister. They also had the ability to convince politicians of the utility of different courses of action. However, if counsellors followed their own agenda or different political interests, then they could influence the opinion of the minister in a negative manner (Director of Romanian Managing Authority #2).

Despite all this, some have argued that over the years, relations between politicians and administrators improved, especially at the local level, where politicians often saw the political opportunities associated with EU funds developments:

> We have cooperated well and we discovered that it can be done. You can have a good relation with different politicians, of different colours and

different types. In 15 years a lot of them changed. Some were more difficult than others and we cooperated well with them given the same reasons and because we did our job well and because they couldn't intervene. They don't have the necessary levers to intervene and do what they want. Here there are some rules they need to respect. We did our job and we protected them as well.

(Director in Romanian North-East Development Agency)

Yet, Romanian Regional Development Agencies tended to be institutional exceptions. Given their non-governmental and contractual status, they were separate from the overall institutional system, which allowed them to employ staff on a meritocratic basis, adopt a private-sector-oriented approach and improve their internal processes. Their success was widely recognized by both national and European officials. Such administrators could notice differences between the operation of their organization operated and that of those institutions embedded in the wider public administration.

Another key issue highlighted was that the lack of assumed responsibility went hand in hand with bureaucratization and unnecessary paperwork (Director in Romanian North-East Development Agency). Not only was there a dependency on procedural aspects but also on the official signing and validation of these documents. As stressed by an administrator, this caused significant delays in the process: "The following scenario is illogical: when the credit co-ordinators [elected officials] determine delays because they are gone for three weeks. Everything is blocked and no one can sign for them. This leads to delays" (Former Director of Romanian Intermediate Body #1).

Furthermore, there were also significant differences between ministries concerning the level of involvement of political actors. Several interviewees argued that some ministries provided a better working environment than others:

Yes, the Ministry of Regional Development has the investment logic and the necessary structures. You are not asked. You don't have to defend an Additional Act [amendment to a signed contract]. You make a payment and you send it to the credit officer. In the Ministry of the Interior, there were secretaries of state who required explanations for the payments we made. If there were ineligible payments, we had to argue why. Issues that didn't make sense and that took a lot of time.

(Director of Romanian Managing Authority #2)

Given the wider context and governance-related conditions in which these institutions had to operate, issues of administrative and political embeddedness affected their strategic abilities to carry out their work. Often, the strategic capacity of the public administration as a whole was poor or subject to political interference. For instance, in Romania the lack of a governmental commitment, as well as a general decrease in administrative capacity after 2007, affected the ability of the public administration to think strategically (EC Head of Sector #1; Former Romanian EU Affairs Minister). All of these examples show that the wider administrative and political context in which these institutions were situated was often key for their operational functioning.

It must be mentioned at this point that administrative and political embeddedness not only characterized Managing and Control Institutions but also public beneficiaries, in particular the structures managing EU funds at the municipality level which, in Bulgaria and Romania, are generally part of the local or regional public administration apparatus. Many municipalities had to rely on the decisions taken by mayors or municipal councils (Bulgarian EU Funds Co-ordinator for South-West Region #1; Bulgarian Municipality EU Funds Director #2). In addition, projects had to develop in line with the development strategies of the municipalities (Bulgarian Mayor #1; Romanian Expert #1). All of this added considerable pressure and increased the complexity of the management process.

Conclusions and recommendations

Drawing on evidence from the management and implementation of Cohesion Policy in Bulgaria and Romania, this chapter has argued that in order to comprehend what affects administrative capacity-building processes and performance, we must examine more thoroughly the administrative and political environments in which institutions responsible for EU funds management are embedded. Administrative and political embeddedness entails not only the settings and characteristics of local institutional environments and processes but also a general dependency of institutions managing EU funding on their host environment from several points of view (for example, financial and human resources, judicial support, technical expertise, political support). Consequently, embeddedness can affect the room for manoeuvre of Managing and Control Institutions and their inner workings and performance.

There was reasonable qualitative evidence, corroborated by various other official documents (Bulgarian Council of Ministers, 2013; Government of Romania, 2014) and independent evaluations (KPMG Romania *et al.*, 2010), to suggest that host institutional environments can often have a detrimental effect on the functioning of Managing and Control Institutions. In this respect, the very fact that administrators were dependent on the resources or willingness of domestic administrations and political representatives or did not receive sufficient support for everyday activities is a strong indication of the phenomenon of embeddedness. However, the above scenarios are by no means representative of all Managing and Control Institutions in the EU28 countries. They provide a glimpse of the internal workings and inter-dependencies of the institutional ecosystems analysed. It may be that many of these patterns of cooperation between, on the one hand, EU funds administrators and regular civil servants, and on the other, between EU funds administrators and national political actors may be found in other cases as well.

Overall, the fact that in some cases Managing and Control Institutions were dependent on the political leadership of their host institution may broadly reflect the political and organizational culture of those institutions. On paper, the MAs had the necessary independence, yet in practice, given administrative and political embeddedness, their functions were often limited. Capacity-building processes need to be tackled not only within MAs but also in relation to the host administrative and institutional environments in which the MAs are situated. In other words, addressing the needs of the institutional ecosystems that host Managing and Control Institutions can potentially improve their functioning. In this respect, several measures can mitigate the role of the domestic institutional hosts and improve capacity and performance-related processes.

First and foremost, the importance of the domestic institutional environments must be acknowledged in both theoretical and practical terms. Keeping the two separate or disregarding the roles and differences in domestic institutional environments diminishes the ability of scholars and practitioners to understand the complexity of EU funds management processes. As argued, the inconsistencies and inefficiencies of the general environment in which MAs operated often hindered the development of an adequate capacity and led to poor performance. In this respect, measures that seek to build capacity should target not only Managing and Control Institutions but also domestic institutional environments (for example, central ministries that host or act as MAs). Generally, it has been up to the Administrative Capacity OP in both Bulgaria and Romania to seek to improve the quality of domestic public administration. However, more co-ordinated measures are needed, as are synergies between the Administrative Capacity and Technical Assistance OPs, in order to address administrative capacity for the administration as a whole. For instance, financial incentives may also be provided to staff who are tangentially involved in the management of EU funding. This may be done through an enhanced use of technical assistance funding (for example, the development of training curricula for EU funds and normal administrators), irrespective of national political judgements on the utility of such funding. Overall, a more targeted and uniform use of technical assistance could help to ensure more adequate capacity for OP implementation and help to boost administrative capacity-building processes.

Second, to counteract political influence and embeddedness, several courses of action may be needed. In this respect, better defined arrangements within Managing and Control Institutions may help to clarify the role and prerogatives of administrators and politicians. For instance, political agreements or memorandums may be useful in order to ensure administrative stability and safeguard senior and middle management staff from negative interference or practices of political clientelism. Another solution may be to enhance the legal protection of personnel working in MAs and IBs, balancing provision regarding their political and administrative accountability. Overall, one of the key principles behind these actions would be to restrict the prerogatives of political representatives to only those dimensions of the absorption process that entail a political contribution. Empowering administrators with regard to all procedural aspects in ministries hosting MAs and IBs may be another avenue worth pursuing. Decreasing the administrative dependence of administrators on the signing and approval of documents may be a concrete example that can be introduced in future EU regulations.

Finally, more measures are needed to tackle an increased politicization of the use of EU funds. In recent years, many political representatives have sought to use EU funds to their advantage. Political clienteles have generated many bottlenecks in the selection and implementation of projects in Bulgaria and Romania, especially in the area of public procurement, which has often triggered funding suspensions and financial corrections from Brussels (Surubaru, 2014). To counter this, the independence of project selection must be reinforced and EU funds administrators need to track, prevent and eliminate potential conflicts of interest. Support for beneficiaries, transparency at all stages of the process, more protection for whistle-blowers and accessible open data for researchers could also help to achieve this.

Notes

1 This chapter is based on a paper presented at the 2nd EU Cohesion Policy Conference, Riga, Latvia, 4–6 February 2015. The author is grateful for a research grant provided by the Ratiu Family Charitable Foundation in support of data collection.
2 'Managing and Control Institutions' will henceforth refer to all of the main institutions that are part of the management and control systems of EU funding: Managing Authorities, Intermediate Bodies, the Certifying and Payment Authority, the Audit Authority and other public institutions involved in the EU funds management and control process.

References

Addison, H. J. (2009), "Is administrative capacity a useful concept? Review of the application, meaning and observation of administrative capacity in political science literature", LSE Research Paper, available at: http://personal.lse.ac.uk/addisonh/Papers/AC_Concept.pdf (accessed 15 February 2016).
Bachtler, J. and McMaster, I. (2008), "EU Cohesion Policy and the role of the regions: investigating the influence of Structural Funds in the new member states", *Environment and Planning C: Government and Policy*, 26(2), 398–427.
Bachtler, J., Mendez, C. and Oraže, H. (2013), "From conditionality to Europeanization in Central and Eastern Europe: administrative performance and capacity in Cohesion Policy", *European Planning Studies*, 22(4), 1–23.
Barca, F. (2009), *An Agenda for a Reformed Cohesion Policy: A Place-Based Approach to Meeting European Union Challenges and Expectations*, report prepared at the request of the EU Commissioner for Regional Policy Danuta Hübner, Brussels: European Commission.
Berica, C. (2010), "Factors that influence the low rate of Structural Funds absorption in Romania", CES Working Papers II (4).
Boeckhout, S., Boot, L., Hollanders, M., Reincke, K.-J., de Vet, J. M., Figueiredo, A. M. F. and Oporto Portugal Quaternaire (2002), "Key indicators for candidate countries to effectively manage the Structural Funds", Netherlands Economic Institute, Regional and Urban Development, available at: www.evaluace.cz/dokumenty/hodnot_zpr_eu/souhrnna_studie.pdf (accessed 15 February 2016).

Boijmans, P. (2013), "The secrets of a successful administration for Cohesion Policy", presentation given at the RSA European Conference, Tampere, Finland, 6 May.

Bulgarian Council of Ministers (2013), *Strategic Report of the Republic of Bulgaria for 2012 on the Implementation of Structural and Cohesion Funds*, ec.europa.eu/regional_policy/how/policy/doc/strategic_report/2012/bg_strat_report_2012.zip (accessed 15 February 2016).

Cace, C., Nicolaescu, V., Cace, S. and Iova, C. (2010), "Capacity of Phare and Structural Funds absorption: pre-accession versus post-accession", *Revista de Cercetare si Interventie Sociala*, 28, 78–96.

Chardas, A. (2012), "State capacity and 'embeddedness' in the context of the European Union's Regional Policy: the case of Greece and the third Community Support Framework (CSF)", *Southeast European and Black Sea Studies*, 12(2), 221–42.

Charron, N., Dijkstra, L. and Lapuente, V. (2014), "Regional governance matters: quality of government within European Union member states", *Regional Studies*, 48(1), 68–90.

Cohen, A. M., Robinson, E. L. and Edwards, J. L. (1969), "Experiments in organizational embeddedness", *Administrative Science Quarterly*, 14(2), 208–21.

Dabrowski, M. (2014), "EU Cohesion Policy, horizontal partnership and the patterns of sub-national governance: insights from Central and Eastern Europe", *European Urban and Regional Studies*, 21(4), 364–83.

Dimitrova, A. (2010), "The new member states of the EU in the aftermath of enlargement: do new European rules remain empty shells?" *Journal of European Public Policy*, 17(1), 137–48.

Dotti, N. F. (2013), "The unbearable instability of Structural Funds' distribution", *European Planning Studies*, 21(4), 596–614.

Eriksen, S. (2007), "Institution building in Central and Eastern Europe: foreign influences and domestic responses", *Review of Central and East European Law*, 32(3), 333–69.

European Commission (2014), *Investment for Jobs and Growth: Promoting Development and Good Governance in EU Regions and Cities – Sixth Report on Economic, Social and Territorial Cohesion*, L. Dijkstra (ed.), Directorate General for Regional and Urban Policy, Brussels: European Commission.

Ferry, M. (2013), "The achievements of Cohesion Policy: evidence and methodological challenges from an EU10 perspective", European Policies Research Centre, University of Strathclyde WP8 Task 1: "Growth–Innovation–Competitiveness: Fostering Cohesion in Central and Eastern Europe" (GRNCOH), available at: www.grincoh.eu/working-papers?get=4dbe2d66d9a6e53c1265b9188beff39e (accessed 15 February 2016).

Ferry, M. and McMaster, I. (2013), "Cohesion Policy and the evolution of Regional Policy in Central and Eastern Europe", *Europe–Asia Studies*, 65(8), 1502–28.

Ganev, V. I. (2013), "Post-accession hooliganism: democratic governance in Bulgaria and Romania after 2007", *East European Politics & Societies*, 27(1), 26–44.

Georgescu, G. (2008), "Determinants of increasing EU funds absorption capacity in Romania", *Annales Universitatis Apulensis Series Oeconomica*, 2(10), 1–8.

Government of Romania, Ministry of European Funds (2014), *Partnership Agreement*, Document No. RO16M8PA001.1.1.

Horvat, A. and Maier, G. (2004), "Regional development, absorption problems and the EU Structural Funds", paper presented at the European Regional Science Association (ERSA) conference, available at: http://ideas.repec.org/p/wiw/wiwrsa/ersa04p591.html (accessed 15 February 2016).

Hristova Kurzydlowski, D. (2013), "Programming EU funds in Bulgaria: challenges, opportunities and the role of civil society", *Studies of Transition States and Societies*, 5(1), 22–41.

Knill, C. (1998), "European policies: the impact of national administrative traditions", *Journal of Public Policy*, 18(1), 1–28.

KPMG Romania, GEA S&C and Pluriconsult (2010), A *Formative Evaluation of Structural Instruments in Romania: Final Report*, evaluation conducted for the Authority for Coordination of Structural Instruments (ACIS), July.

Marinov, A. (2011), "Problems in defining the administrative capacity concept", *Public Policies Bulgaria*, 2(1), 15–24, available at: http://ejpp.eu/index.php/ejpp/article/viewFile/17/11 (accessed 15 February 2016).

Milio, S. (2007), "Can administrative capacity explain differences in regional performances? Evidence from Structural Funds implementation in southern Italy", *Regional Studies*, 41(4), 429–42.

Milio, S. (2008), "How political stability shapes administrative performance: the Italian case", *West European Politics*, 31(5), 915–36.

Moran, P. (2005), "Structural vs. relational embeddedness: social capital and managerial performance", *Strategic Management Journal*, 26(12), 1129–51.

Petzold, W., Guderjan, M., Smeriglio, A., Tourtouri, M., Surubaru, N.-C., Salemink, K., Idczak, P., Monsson, C. K., Bajtalan, H., Garau, C., Soultanova, M., Usai, A., Medeiros, E., Szulc, T., Trienes, M., Jaansoo, A., Lange, E., Yalcin, G., Modro, G. and Venineaux, J.-M. (2015), "Future research on European Union Cohesion Policy: a master class during the OPEN DAYS 2014", *Regional Studies, Regional Science*, 2(1), 184–203.

Rodríguez-Pose, A. (2013), "Do institutions matter for regional development?" *Regional Studies*, 47(7), 1034–47.

Stefanov, R., Mineva, D. and Mantcheva, D. (2010), *Expert Evaluation Network Delivering Policy Analysis on the Performance of Cohesion Policy 2007–2013, Task 2: Country Report on Achievements of Cohesion Policy*, report to Directorate General for Regional and Urban Policy, Brussels: European Commission.

Sumpíková, M., Pavel, J. and Klazar, S. (2004), "EU funds: absorption capacity and effectiveness of their use, with focus on regional level in the Czech Republic", paper presented at the 12th NISPAcee Conference, available at: http://unpan1.un.org/intradoc/groups/public/documents/nispacee/unpan018547.pdf (accessed 15 February 2016).

Surubaru, N.-C. (2014), "Similar, yet different: performance variation in the management and implementation of Structural Funds in Bulgaria and Romania (2007–2013) – going beyond the administrative capacity nexus?", paper presented at the 44th Annual Conference of the University Association of Contemporary European Studies, Cork, Ireland.

Tosun, J. (2014), "Absorption of Regional Funds: a comparative analysis", *JCMS: Journal of Common Market Studies*, 52(2), 371–87.

Tsachevsky, V. (2012), "Five years of Bulgaria's membership into the European Union: the slow absorption of EU funds slackens Bulgaria's Europeanisation", Pan-European Institute 2/2012, Turku School of Economics.

Uzzi, B. (1997), "Social structure and competition in interfirm networks: the paradox of embeddedness", *Administrative Science Quarterly*, 42(1), 35–67.

Verheijen, T. (1999), *Civil Service Systems in Central and Eastern Europe*, Cheltenham, UK: Edward Elgar.

Welch, C. and Wilkinson, I. (2004), "The political embeddedness of international business networks", *International Marketing Review*, 21(2), 216–31.

World Bank (2006), "EU-8 – administrative capacity in the new member states : the limits of innovation?" World Bank Document No. 36930, available at: http://documents.banquemondiale.org/curated/fr/2006/12/7440666/eu-8-administrative-capacity-new-member-states-limits-innovation (accessed 15 February 2016).

Zaman, G. and Cristea, A. (2011), "EU Structural Funds absorption in Romania: obstacles and issues", *Romanian Journal of Economics*, 32, 60–77.

Zaman, G. and Georgescu, G. (2009), "Structural Fund absorption: a new challenge for Romania?", *Journal for Economic Forecasting*, 6(1), 136–54.

List of selected interviews

Bulgarian Expert #2, 19 May 2014
Bulgarian EU Funds Co-ordinator for South-West Region #1, 26 May 2014
Bulgarian Mayor #1, 5 June 2014
Bulgarian Municipality EU Funds Director #1, 4 June 2014
Director of Bulgarian Managing Authority #1, 30 April 2014
Director in Romanian Audit Authority #1, 14 April 2014
Director of Romanian Managing Authority #2, 7 March 2014
Director of Romanian Managing Authority #3, 14 April 2014
Director in Romanian North-East Regional Development Agency, 17 April 2014
European Commission (EC) Head of Sector #1, 16 October 2013
Former Director of Bulgarian Managing Authority #2, 16 May 2014
Former Director of Romanian Intermediate Body #1, 19 March 2014
Former Romanian Minister of EU Affairs, 27 March 2014
Head of Romanian North-East Intermediate Body #1, 17 April 2014
Head of Unit of Bulgarian Managing Authority #1, 7 May 2014
Romanian Expert #1, 18 March 2014
Romanian Expert #2, 11 April 2014
Romanian MA Programme Evaluations Officer #1, 12 March 2014
Romanian MA Programme Evaluations Officer #3, 11 April 2014

13 Corruption in EU Funds?
Europe-wide evidence of the corruption effect of EU-funded public contracting

Mihály Fazekas and István János Tóth

Introduction

There is an intense public and policy debate over whether EU Structural and Cohesion Funds (henceforth EU Funds) contribute to lower levels of corruption and better governance or conversely fuel government favouritism and erode institutional quality. This debate is fed by striking negative examples: the Italian mafia hijacking highway projects, or the European Commission freezing Structural Funds payments in countries such as Romania, Bulgaria and Hungary. Some of these examples suggest the involvement of high-level politics and organised criminal groups, raising the possibility that the EU in fact extensively finances large-scale corruption in a number of countries. As EU Funds constitute a considerable proportion of GDP in many member states, especially in Central and Eastern Europe (CEE) where they amount to between 1.9 per cent and 4.4 per cent of annual member state GDPs (KPMG, 2012) and well above 50 per cent of public investment, this debate is crucial for the future of the EU and its territorial cohesion as well as the quality of institutions across Europe more broadly.

However, there has been little academic research on this topic, which deprives policymakers of crucial evidence underpinning future policy decisions. In order to address this gap in the evidence base, this chapter sets out to assess systematically the impact of EU Funds spending on institutionalised grand corruption risks across the whole EU. The chapter focuses on the 27 EU member states with sufficiently sizeable public procurement spending funded by the EU – that is, the EU28 countries except for Malta[1] – over the 2009–14 period. EU Funds are spent in various ways that make it impossible to arrive at a blanket assessment of their impact on corruption. We look specifically at public procurement spending by public or semi-public organisations (i.e. state-owned enterprises) financed from EU Funds, which predominantly means the use of Cohesion and Structural Funds. This approach has the advantage that we can compare projects that are similar in most respects except for the source of financing: predominantly EU or predominantly national. Moreover, there is exceptionally good comparative data available on large public procurement tenders in all countries at the level of individual contracts. Our approach is a major departure from prior studies in this area, as it utilises a large-scale micro-level quantitative database, which allows us to paint a detailed picture of mechanisms at the analytical level where corruption takes place, while also being broad enough to evaluate whole systems of governance.

Theory

In spite of the considerable public and policy interest in corruption risks in EU Funds spending, there has been remarkably little scientific research conducted into the question to date (Dimulescu *et al.*, 2013; Beblavy and Sičáková-Beblavá, 2014; Fazekas *et al.*, 2014). There are, however, two bodies of literature that speak to this issue: the political science literature on aid dependence and the Europeanisation literature in political science.

The literature looking at the effect of development aid on quality of institutions, and corruption is extensive. It can only suggest the main mechanisms at play, as EU Funds are spent in Europe in very different institutional contexts and funding volumes than development aid is spent in developing countries. Nevertheless, according to this literature, foreign aid can have a positive effect on governance by providing clear policy goals such as improving the civil service and helping countries to overcome the lack of resources for state-building (Knack, 2001). However, development aid can also destroy institutions and impede state-building in much the same way that natural resources can (Djankov *et al.*, 2008). It can weaken accountability and the development of civil society by breaking the link between domestic revenues (i.e. taxation) and government services. It can also damage administrative capacity in three ways:

1 reallocating talented bureaucrats from domestic institutions to aid organisations;
2 providing additional organisational goals that undermine institutional cohesion; and
3 increasing the pool of public resources available for rent-seeking, which easily translates into additional corruption in contexts with weak administrative capacity (Bräutigam, 2000).

Meanwhile, the Europeanisation literature presents three good reasons for believing that EU Funds support good government:

1 One of the most important remaining post-accession levers that Brussels has at its disposal for disciplining new member states is EU Funds and the threat of withdrawing them (Epstein and Sedelmeier, 2009). This should motivate recipient countries to manage funds to a high EU standard, if needed, even better than national funds.
2 The disbursement of EU Funds is more heavily regulated, making corruption more costly and motivating recipient organisations to invest in administrative capacity.

3 Extensive monitoring of and controls on EU Funds in addition to the national audit frameworks (for example, OLAF or the European Court of Justice) make the detection and punishment of corruption more likely than in projects funded with domestic funds (European Commission, 2003; European Court of Auditors, 2012, 2013).

However, there are also three arguments in the Europeanisation literature that external funding such as EU Funds damages the quality of government and increases corruption:

1 EU Cohesion and Structural Funds are spent on investment projects where public officials have wide discretion (for example, project design and budgeting). From the wider literature, it is clear that discretionary spending is more likely to involve corruption than non-discretionary spending such as pensions (Mauro, 1998; Tanzi and Davoodi, 2001).
2 EU funding provides a large additional pool of public resources for rent extraction, which is in effect unlimited as most recipient countries struggle to draw 100 per cent of allocated funds (Mungiu-Pippidi, 2013).
3 EU Funds, like any external funding, weaken the link between domestic civil society, taxation and policy performance.

In the context of public procurement, 'institutionalised grand corruption' refers to the allocation and performance of public procurement contracts by bending prior explicit rules and principles of good public procurement in order to benefit a closed network while denying access to all others (World Bank, 2009; Fazekas et al., 2014).

From the above discussion, the following null hypothesis results:

H_0: EU Funds decrease institutionalised grand corruption across the EU.

The above discussion also suggests that in countries and regions with diverse institutional quality, the effect may also differ due to the relative strength of each causal mechanism linking EU Funds to public procurement corruption. While no systematic analysis of determinants is presented due to lack of space, it is suggested that more corrupt countries and regions are less willing to cooperate with EU authorities and more prone to rent-seeking, which tips the balance towards more corruption in EU Funds.

Data and variables

Data used

The database we used, Tenders Electronic Daily (henceforth TED), derives from public procurement announcements of the 2009–14 period in the EU27 countries (i.e. the EU28 countries minus Malta) and is the online version of the Supplement to the *Official Journal of the European Union*, dedicated to EU public procurement (DG GROWTH, 2015). TED is a comprehensive database containing details of all public procurement procedures conducted under the EU Public Procurement Directive – that is, all contracts exceeding set contract value thresholds (for example, €135,000 for services and goods contracts). The database was released by the European Commission, which has also conducted a series of data quality checks and enhancements. TED contains variables appearing in both calls for tenders and contract award notices, which provide a rich picture of the procurement process up until contract award by disclosing contract values, the number of bidders, the names of the winning firm and the deadline for submission, to name only a few key variables available.[2] Each country's public procurement legislation operates within the framework of the EU Public Procurement Directive and so the legislation of different countries is therefore, by and large, comparable. TED contains the details of over 2.8 million contracts for the 27 EU member states considered.

Variables used in the analysis

Use of EU Funds

The spending of EU Funds in public procurement can be directly identified in each contract award announcement, which records the use or non-use of EU Funds along with reference to the corresponding EU programme. However, no information is published as to the proportion of EU funding within the total contract value. Hence, we had to employ a yes/no categorisation of each contract awarded. Public procurement from EU Funds falls under the same procurement rules and thresholds as other funding sources. Common national and EU legal frameworks for public procurement warrant a meaningful comparison between EU-funded and non-EU-funded public procurement procedures. The crucial difference between contracts funded from EU Funds and those funded by national governments lies in the additional monitoring and controls and different motivation structures associated with spending EU Funds. While the use of EU Funds differs greatly between countries, there are a large number of observations for matching contracts in each case (see Table 13.A1 in the Appendix). The full database used for this analysis can be downloaded at digiwhist.eu/resources/data.

Indicators of institutionalised grand corruption

Developing comparative indicators of institutionalised grand corruption in public procurement for all EU27 countries represents the primary methodological innovation of this chapter. The approach follows closely the corruption risk measurement methodology developed by the authors in that it makes use of a wide range of public procurement 'red flags' (Fazekas *et al.*, 2014, forthcoming; Charron *et al.*, 2015).

The measurement approach exploits the fact that for institutionalised grand corruption to work, procurement contracts have to be awarded recurrently to companies belonging to the corrupt network. This can only be achieved if legally prescribed rules of competition and openness are circumvented. By implication, it is possible to identify both the input side of the corruption process (i.e. fixing the procedural rules for limiting competition) and also the output side (i.e. signs of limited competition). By measuring the degree of unfair restriction of competition in public procurement, a proxy indicator of corruption can be obtained.

First, the simplest indication of restricted competition in line with our theoretical definition is when only one bid is submitted for a tender in an otherwise competitive market, which typically allows for awarding contracts above market prices and extracting corrupt rents (output side). Hence, single-bidder contracts as a percentage of all of the awarded contracts is the most straightforward measure we used.

Second, a more complex indication of high-level corruption also incorporates characteristics of the tendering procedure that are in the hands of public officials who conduct the tender and suggests deliberate competition restriction (input side) (Fazekas *et al.*, 2013). This composite indicator, which we call the corruption risk index (CRI), represents the probability of corrupt contract award in public procurement, defined as follows:

$$CRI^i = \Sigma_j w_j * CI_j^i \qquad (13.1)$$

$$\Sigma_j w_j = 1 \qquad (13.2)$$

$$0 \leq CRI^i \leq 1 \qquad (13.3)$$

$$0 \leq CI_j^i \leq 1 \qquad (13.4)$$

where CRI^i stands for the corruption risk index of contract i, CI_j^i represents the jth elementary corruption indicator observed in the tender of contract i and w_j represents the weight of elementary corruption indicator j. Elementary corruption indicators can be either corruption inputs or outputs. CRI = 0 indicates minimum corruption risk, while CRI = 1 denotes maximum corruption risk observed. Based on qualitative interviews about corruption in the public procurement process, a review of the literature (OECD, 2007; World Bank, 2009; PricewaterhouseCoopers, 2013) and regression analysis, we identified the following five components of the CRI in addition to single bidding (Table 13.1):

1   A simple way to fix tenders is to avoid the publication of the call for tenders in the official public procurement journal, as this makes it harder for competitors to prepare a bid. This is only considered in non-open procedures, as in open procedures publication is mandatory.
2   While open competition is relatively hard to avoid in some tendering procedure types such as open tender, others such as invitation tenders are by default much less competitive; hence using less open and transparent procedure types can indicate the deliberate limitation of competition, hence corruption risks.

Table 13.1 Summary of elementary corruption risk indicators.

Procedural phase	Indicator name	Indicator values
Submission	Call for tenders publication	0 = call for tender published in official journal 1 = NO call for tender published in official journal
	Procedure type	0 = open procedure types 1 = non-open procedure types (e.g. accelerated restricted procedure)
	Length of submission period	Number of days between publication of call for tenders and submission deadline (for short submission periods, weekends are deducted)
Assessment	Weight of non-price evaluation criteria	Sum of weights for evaluation criteria that are NOT related to prices
	Length of decision period	Number of days between submission deadline and contract award announcement
Outcome	Single bidder contract (valid/received)	0 = more than 1 bid received 1 = only 1 bid received

3 If the advertisement period (i.e. the number of days between publishing the call for tenders and the submission deadline) is too short to allow for the preparation of an adequate bid, it can serve corrupt purposes, whereby the issuer informally tells the well-connected company about the opportunity well in advance.

4 Different types of evaluation criteria are prone to manipulation to different degrees; subjective, hard-to-quantify criteria often accompany rigged assessment procedures as they create room for discretion and limit accountability mechanisms.

5 If the time taken to decide on the submitted bids is excessively short or lengthened by legal challenge, it can also signal corruption risks. Snap decisions may reflect premediated assessment, while legal challenge and the correspondingly lengthy decision period suggests outright violation of laws.

For continuous variables above such as the length of the advertisement period, thresholds had to be identified in order to reflect the non-linear character of corruption. This is because most values of continuous variables can be considered as reflections of diverse market practices, while some sets of outlier values are more likely associated with corruption. Thresholds were identified using regression analysis, in particular analysing residual distributions (for more on this, see Fazekas *et al.*, forthcoming).

We restricted the sample in two ways:

1 *Competitive markets*: We only examined tenders in markets with at least ten contracts awarded during the 2009–14 period, where markets are defined by product type (CPV[3] level 3) and location (NUTS[4] level 1) within each country.
2 *Regulated tenders*: We only used those tenders that are above EU thresholds in order to avoid the noise of contracts that are too small and voluntary reporting, which follows erratic patterns across countries and over time.

These together removed 17 per cent of the observations.

In addition to the identification of thresholds in continuous variables, regression analysis was also used to identify 'red flags' which are most likely to signal corruption rather than any other phenomena such as low administrative capacity. Ultimately, those variables and variable categories that were selected are large and significant predictors of single-bidder contracts. The regression set-up controlled for four likely confounders of bidder numbers:

1 institutional endowments measured by type of issuer (for example, municipal or national);
2 product market and technological specificities measured by CPV division of products procured;
3 contract size (log contract value in euros);
4 regulatory changes as proxied by year of contract award.

The logic of regression analysis is as follows. If, in a certain country, not publishing the call for tenders in the official journal for open procedures is associated with a higher probability of a single-bidder contract award, it is likely that avoiding the transparent and easily accessible publication of a new tender is typically used for limiting competition. This would imply that a call for tenders not published in the official journal becomes part of the analysed country's CRI. Taking another example, if we found that leaving only 5 or fewer days for bidders to submit their bids is associated with a higher probability of a single-bidder contract award compared to periods longer than 20 calendar days (a more or less arbitrary benchmark category), this would indicate that extremely short advertisement periods are often used for limiting competition. This would then provide sufficient grounds to include the 'Five or fewer days' category of the decision period variable in the CRI of the country in question. Following this logic, in addition to the outcome variable in these regressions (single-bidder), only those variables and variable categories that are in line with a rent extraction logic and proven to be significant and powerful predictors were included in the CRI.

Once the list of elementary corruption risk indicators was determined with the help of the above regressions, each of the variables and variable categories received a component weight. As we lacked the detailed knowledge of which elementary corruption technique is a necessary or sufficient condition for corruption to occur, we assigned equal weight to each variable and the sizes of regression coefficients were only used to determine the weights of categories within variables.

For example, if there were four significant categories of a variable, then they would get weights 1, 0.75, 0.5 and 0.25, reflecting category ranking according to coefficient size. The component weights were normed so that the observed CRI fell between 0 and 1.

Each of the two corruption risk indicators has its pros and cons. The strength of the single-bidder indicator is that it is very simple and straightforward to interpret. However, it is also more prone to gaming by corrupt actors due to its simplicity. The strength of the CRI is that while individual strategies of corruption may change as the environment changes, they are likely to be replaced by other techniques. Therefore, the composite indicator is a more robust proxy of corruption over time than a single-variable approach. In an international comparative perspective, a further strength of the CRI is that it balances national specificities with international comparability by allowing for the exact formulation of the components to vary, thereby reflecting differences in local market conditions. The main weakness of the CRI is that it can only capture a subset of corruption strategies in public procurement, arguably the simplest ones; hence it misses out on sophisticated types of corruption such as corruption combined with inter-bidder collusion.

Validity of corruption risk indicators

While the validity of both corruption risk measures predominantly stems from their direct fit with the definition of high-level corruption in public procurement, it is also underpinned by their association with widely used survey-based macro-level corruption indicators as well as with further micro-level objective indicators of corruption risks.

Both corruption risk indicators (2009–14 averages per NUTS region using the number of nationally funded contracts) correlated as expected with the regional European Quality of Institutions index, population corruption perceptions and self-reported bribery of the same regional representative survey of 2013 (Charron et al., 2010) (Table 13.2).

Table 13.2 Bivariate Pearson correlation between 'objective' measures of regional corruption and survey-based indicators for NUTS2 regions that awarded at least five contracts in the 2009–14 period.

Variable	% single-bidder contracts	Regional CRI	N
% single-bidder contracts		0.51*	178
Regional CRI	0.51*		178
EQI (2013)	−0.41*	−0.11	171
Corruption perception	0.34*	0.12	172
Reported bribery	0.34*	0.20*	172

Source: TED and Charron et al. (2015).

Note: * = significant at the 5% level.

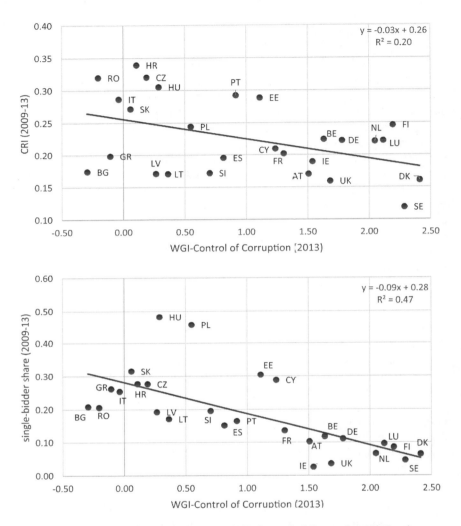

Figure 13.1 Bivariate relationship between WGI-Control of Corruption (2013 point estimate) and the CRI and the share of single-bidder contracts (2009–13 period averages).

Source: TED and Kaufmann *et al.* (2010).

At the national level, one simple indication that the corruption indices were valid was their association with widely acknowledged and used corruption indices such as the World Bank's Control of Corruption indicator (Figure 13.1: top panel for the CRI, bottom panel for the share of single-bidder contracts). While validity tests were confirmatory in both cases, the association was much stronger for the single-bidder indicator than for the CRI.

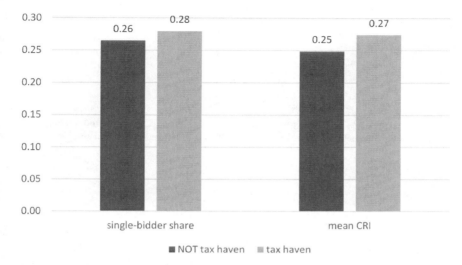

Figure 13.2 Average corruption risks of public procurement suppliers registered abroad, EU26, 2009–14 ($N_{contract} = 27,888$).
Source: TED
Note: We excluded Croatia and Malta due to the small number of observations.

In addition to macro-level evidence of validity, two micro-level 'objective' risk indicators were inspected for further testing validity: procurement suppliers' country of origin and contract prices. It was expected that contracts that carry a higher corruption risk are won by companies registered in tax havens as their secrecy allows for hiding illicit money flows (Shaxson and Christensen, 2014). In line with our expectations, there was a marked and significant difference with regards to both indicators (Figure 13.2).

We also expected corruption to drive prices up. A simplistic, albeit widely used, indicator of price in the absence of reliable unit prices is the ratio of actual contract value to initially estimated contract value (Coviello and Mariniello, 2014). As expected, both the single-bidder indicator and the CRI were associated with a higher price ratio. Single-bidder contracts were associated with a 9 per cent higher contract value, while contracts with one unit higher CRI were associated with a 17 per cent higher contract value (Table 13.3).

Results

In the absence of random assignment of EU funding, the causal effect of EU Funds on corruption risks was estimated by matching tenders without EU funding (control group) with tenders funded by EU Funds (treatment group) and comparing the two groups in terms of corruption risks, measured by the CRI

Table 13.3 Linear regression explaining relative contract value, EU27, 2009–14.

Dependent variable	Relative contract value (contract price/estimated price)	
Independent variables		
Single-bidder contract	0.092	
CRI		0.173
Sign.	0.000	0.000
Each regression contains constant		
Controls: sector of contracting entity, type of contracting entity, year of contract award, country of contract award, main product market of procured goods and services, contract value		
N	543,355	543,355
R^2	0.143	0.115

Source: TED.

and the single-bidder share. Comparing tenders that were as similar as possible in every relevant respect except funding source allowed for the identification of a causal impact of EU Funds on corruption risks. The obvious limitation of this approach was that we could not measure all of the confounding factors; hence we could not fully account for all of the systematic differences between EU-funded and nationally funded contracts that contribute to corruption risks. We used state-of-the-art matching methods that are widely employed in the programme evaluation literature (Imbens and Wooldridge, 2009).

Matching is superior to the simple, unmatched comparison of group means as long as the selection of EU-funded projects is itself not driven by corrupt considerations such as deliberately channelling EU Funds to markets where hiding corruption is easier. If the selection is predominantly strategic, driven by corruption, the simple comparison is more appropriate than matching. As it is unclear to what degree EU Funds selection is driven by corrupt considerations, we considered the matched results as a lower-bound estimate and the simple comparison as an upper-bound estimate of the causal impact.

A simple, unmatched comparison of the average single-bidder share and the CRI suggested that EU-funded procurement carries higher corruption risks than nationally funded procurement across the whole of the EU (Tables 13.4 and 13.5). These effects are substantial: increases of 38 per cent and 16 per cent for the single bidder share and the CRI respectively compared to nationally funded contracts.

In order to balance the different composition of EU-funded and nationally funded contracts, we employed a propensity score-matching algorithm[7] that matched contracts on control variables.[8] The corruption risks of any contract are determined on the one hand by the characteristics of the contract itself (for example, the type of service or goods procured, such as a consultancy report) and on the other, by the institutional environment in which it is awarded (for example, weaker control institutions in a country). Both of these had to be

Table 13.4 Unmatched and matched comparisons of EU-funded and non-EU-funded contracts' single-bidder share, EU27[5] totals, 2009–14.

	Unmatched comparison	Propensity score-matching (cross-country)	Propensity score-matching (within-country)
Non-EU-funded	0.247	0.242	0.281
EU-funded	0.340	0.340	0.338
Diff. (EU-funded − non-EU-funded)	**0.093**	**0.098**	**0.057**
95% conf. interval – lower bound	0.091	0.094	0.054
95% conf. interval – upper bound	0.096	0.101	0.061
N non-EU-funded	1,407,301	123,678	121,338
N EU-funded	123,696	123,696	121,338

Source: TED.

Table 13.5 Unmatched and matched comparisons of EU-funded and non-EU-funded contracts' CRI, EU27[6] totals, 2009–14.

	Unmatched comparison	Propensity score-matching (cross-country)	Propensity score-matching (within-country)
Non-EU-funded	0.225	0.260	0.254
EU-funded	0.262	0.262	0.261
Diff. (EU-funded − non-EU-funded)	**0.037**	**0.003**	**0.008**
95% conf. interval – lower bound	0.036	0.001	0.006
95% conf. interval – upper bound	0.038	0.004	0.009
N non-EU-funded	1,407,300	123,678	121,338
N EU-funded	123,696	123,696	121,338

Source: TED.

controlled for in the matching process to arrive at a balanced comparison. In terms of characteristics of contracts matched, the following five variables were used:

- the main market of procured goods and services (using CPV two-digit categorisation once again);
- the log value of the contract;
- the year of contract award;
- the type of procuring organisation (for example, local body or public utility);
- the main sector in which the procuring organisation operates (e.g. education, healthcare).

In terms of institutional characteristics, we controlled for the country in which the contracting authority resides, which captures the macro-institutional factors determining corruption risks. This was done in two alternative ways:

1   We allowed for a degree of flexibility where some contracts could be matched to a contract in another country as long as it improved matching on contract-level characteristics (cross-country matching).
2   We restricted matching only to contracts in the same country at the expense of poorer matching on contract-level characteristics and in fact removing some EU-funded contracts due to a lack of sufficient matches (within-country matching).

While these two variants did not deliver substantially different results, the more restrictive approach is preferable as national-level effects are likely to override contract-level effects. Tables and Figures demonstrating the quality of matching procedures can be found in the Appendix.

The propensity score-matching procedures, taking into account confounding factors, revealed a similar picture to the unmatched comparison, although effect magnitudes change somewhat, in particular for CRI comparisons. For the single-bidder indicator, the cross-country propensity score-matching resulted in a similarly strong effect (0.1), while the within-country propensity score-matching delivered a slightly smaller effect (0.06) (Table 13.4). Both of these effects are substantial in relative terms: they indicate that corruption risks would have been 20–40 per cent lower had the same contracts been financed from national funds rather than EU Funds.

For the CRI, both propensity score-matching algorithms delivered a substantially smaller effect size than the simple comparison: the cross-country matching showed an increase of corruption risks due to EU Funds of 0.003, while the within-country matching resulted in a somewhat larger effect (0.01) (Table 13.5). Both of these effects are small in relative terms: they indicate that corruption risks would have been 1–3 per cent lower had the same contracts been financed from national funds rather than EU Funds.

In sum, for all of the specifications, the negative effect of EU funding on corruption risks (i.e. worsening corruption) stayed by and large the same. The stronger negative effect when measuring corruption risks by the single-bidder share rather than by the CRI is in line with prior research looking at CEE national datasets (Fazekas *et al.*, 2014). This suggests that it is market outcomes that are particularly negatively influenced by EU funding, whereas formal requirements such as the use of open procedure or publishing the call for tenders are more positively influenced.

It must be noted that a large portion of the control group was discarded in order to achieve a tight comparison between treatment and control groups, while even some EU-funded contracts were excluded by the within-country propensity score-matching algorithm, as no sufficiently close match was found. Missing values of control variables were included as separate values in each matching algorithm; however, due to their large numbers in some countries, they may have influenced the reliability of the results in ways that are not clear. As data quality is best for the biggest beneficiaries of EU funding, such bias is expected to be minor. For the EU-wide average effect, we did not apply any country weights; hence each country contributed to the overall mean in proportion to the number of EU-funded contracts it has been awarded. This made the performance of the Polish EU funding system the single most important factor in determining the overall EU mean as Polish EU-funded contracts make up roughly one-third of all EU-funded contracts in the database.

Based on these results, we can reject H_0 – that is, the moderating effect of EU Funds on grand corruption in public procurement across the whole EU. EU-funded public procurement contracts carry a greater risk of corruption than domestically funded ones whether or not tenders' characteristics are matched. The different effect magnitudes given by using the single-bidder share and the CRI indicate the different effect of EU Funds on the outcomes of competition and the characteristics of the contracting process. This is hardly a surprise given the predominant focus of EU monitoring on bureaucratic inputs rather than competitive outcomes.

The change in effect magnitude when controlling for confounding factors highlights that the contexts in which EU Funds are spent exercise a considerable impact on corruption risks. In order to directly explore this variability at the national level, EU-funded and nationally funded contracts' shares of single bidders were plotted by country (Figure 13.3). It is apparent that most countries cluster around the line representing parity between corruption risks in EU-funded and nationally funded public procurement, though there are some

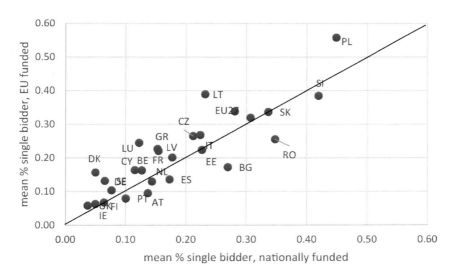

Figure 13.3 Single-bidder shares of EU-funded and nationally funded public procurement contracts by country, EU26,[9] 2009–14 (applying within-country matching).

Source: TED.

Note: The dashed line indicates where the single-bidder shares are equal in EU-funded and national funded contracts. We excluded Croatia and Malta due to the small number of observations.

notable exceptions representing wide deviations between EU funding and national funding such as Poland or Bulgaria.

While no comprehensive explanation of such heterogeneous effect can be offered here due to lack of space, it is suggested that regions with higher levels of corruption risks in general are also less able to control the additional corruption risks attached to EU Funds (for example, additional discretionary spending). Plotting the CRI difference between EU-funded and nationally funded contracts on matched samples and the unmatched mean total CRI at the regional level (Figure 13.4) suggests that the increase of the general level of corruption in a region increases the relative underperformance of EU Funds; that is, corruption risks in EU Funds increase further compared to national funds.

Conclusions

While much additional work is needed, this chapter has already demonstrated that it is feasible and fruitful to use detailed, contract-level data for tracking corruption risks over time across EU countries. Such monitoring can be done in real time if the necessary investment into database development is made. Findings indicate that EU funding increases corruption risks in some EU member states albeit not in others, while on average having a negative effect across the EU. This effect is particularly large where general corruption risks in the region are

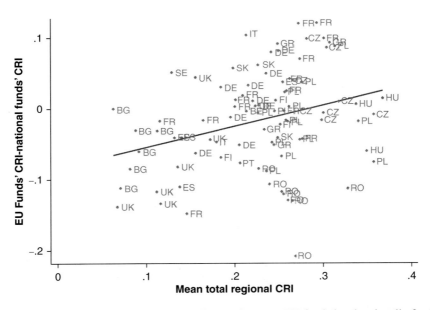

Figure 13.4 Scatter plot of the CRI difference between EU-funded and nationally funded contracts and the mean total regional CRI, by NUTS2 regions that awarded at least 200 EU-funded contracts in the 2009–14 period.

Source: TED.

high. Relative prices in EU-funded contract awards (the ratio of actual contract value to initially estimated contract value) (Coviello and Mariniello, 2014) are also higher than nationally funded ones on the matched samples (price increase of 0.4 per cent), which implies that approximately €9.9 billion of EU taxpayers' money is lost per annum. When interpreting the results, it is worth keeping in mind that corruption is a diverse phenomenon that could only partially be captured with the selected 'red flags'. Further work should use more precise measurement based on richer data.

Appendix

Table 13.A1 Use of EU Funds in the EU27, for markets that awarded at least ten contracts worth above €125,000 in the 2009–14 period.

Country	N of contracts awarded	% of contracts funded by the EU	% of spending through EU-funded public procurement
AT	13,147	1.4%	1.6%
BE	24,901	7.8%	18.2%
BG	33,023	6.8%	33.9%
CY	4,465	4.7%	8.3%
CZ	27,432	38.8%	18.5%
DE	138,477	5.0%	7.6%
DK	22,553	0.8%	1.4%
EE	7,308	21.9%	14.6%
ES	69,022	13.8%	16.3%
FI	8,729	8.8%	11.0%
FR	391,673	4.9%	9.4%
GR	12,963	29.8%	64.5%
HR	4,056	0.6%	0.3%
HU	28,111	21.8%	62.8%
IE	4,338	8.0%	15.7%
IT	74,579	2.8%	4.6%
LT	32,902	11.7%	5.7%
LU	2,264	9.4%	91.0%
LV	56,036	20.1%	38.8%
NL	22,146	3.5%	1.8%
PL	523,797	8.8%	28.1%
PT	6,145	28.4%	54.7%
RO	86,602	3.8%	29.2%
SE	27,235	1.2%	3.1%
SI	29,707	3.9%	35.3%
SK	12,902	13.1%	38.5%
UK	105,389	5.0%	2.0%
Total	**1,769,902**	**8.0%**	**14.0%**

Source: TED.

Table 13.A2 Summary of balance in the unmatched and the two matched samples (using Stata 12.0 ps test command).

Sample	Ps R²	LR chi²	p > chi²	MeanBias	MedBias	B	R	%Var
Unmatched	0.396	391175	0.000	11.0	7.6	186.5*	1.59	99
Propensity score-matching (cross-country)	0.070	25682	0.000	5.3	3.3	64.1*	1.83	95
Propensity score-matching (within-country)	0.110	40114	0.000	5.6	3.0	82.0*	1.38	98

Source: TED.

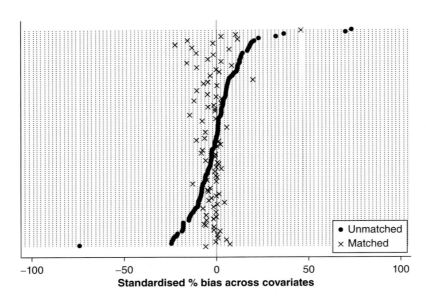

Figure 13.A1 Overview of bias remaining after matching per variable, propensity score-matching (cross-country).

Source: TED.

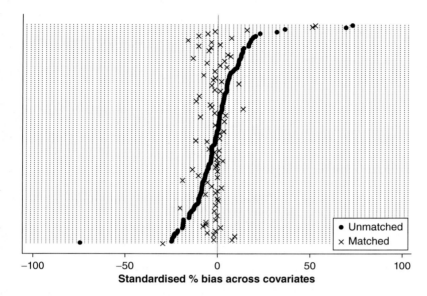

Figure 13.A2 Overview of bias remaining after matching per variable, propensity score-matching (within-country).

Source: TED.

Notes

1 Malta is too small a country with small public procurement markets, making it unsuitable for the corruption risk measurement methodology.
2 For full list of variables available see: http://digiwhist.eu/publications/towards-a-comprehensive-mapping-of-information-on-public-procurement-tendering-and-its-actors-across-europe/.
3 CPV = Common Procurement Vocabulary. For more information, see http://simap.ted.europa.eu/en/web/simap/cpv.
4 NUTS = nomenclature of territorial units for statistics. For more information, see http://ec.europa.eu/eurostat/web/nuts/overview.
5 Croatia is excluded from the matched comparisons as it didn't have a sufficient pool of non-EU-funded project to generate a sufficient quality matching.
6 Croatia is excluded from the matched comparisons as it didn't have a sufficient pool of non-EU-funded project to generate a sufficient quality matching.
7 We used the Stata 12.0 psmatch2 algorithm.
8 Coarsened exact matching was also conducted, leading to a much tighter matching at the expense of discarding most of the EU-funded contracts due to lack of sufficient matches. By implication, the resulting sample was not reliable enough to characterise the whole of the EU anymore. Detailed results can be obtained from the authors.
9 The EU28 minus Malta and Croatia.

References

Beblavy, M. and Sičáková-Beblavá, E. (2014), 'The changing faces of Europeanisation: how did the European Union influence corruption in Slovakia before and after accession?', *Europe-Asia Studies*, 66(4), 536–56.
Bräutigam, D. A. (2000), *Aid Dependence and Governance*, Stockholm, Sweden: Almqvist & Wiksell International.
Charron, N., Dijkstra, L. and Lapuente, V. (2010), 'Mapping quality of government in the European Union: a study of national and sub-national variation', Quality of Government Institute Working Paper No. 2010:22, University of Gothenburg.
Charron, N., Dahlström, C., Fazekas, M. and Lapuente, V. (2015), 'Carriers, connections and corruption risks in Europe', Quality of Government Institute Working Paper No. 2015:6, University of Gothenburg.
Coviello, D. and Mariniello, M. (2014), 'Publicity requirements in public procurement: evidence from a regression discontinuity design', *Journal of Public Economics*, 109, 76–100.
DG GROWTH (2015), *Tenders Electronic Daily (TED) Structured Dataset (2009–2014)*, supplement to the *Official Journal of the European Union*, Brussels.
Dimulescu, V., Pop, R. and Doroftei, I. M. (2013), 'Corruption risks with EU funds in Romania', *Romanian Journal of Political Science*, 13(1), 101–23.
Djankov, S., Montalvo, J. and Reynal-Querol, M. (2008), 'The curse of aid', *Journal of Economic Growth*, 13(3), 169–94.
Epstein, R. A. and Sedelmeier, U. (eds) (2009), *International Influence Beyond Conditionality: Postcommunist Europe After EU Enlargement*, London: Routledge.
European Commission (2003), *A Comprehensive EU Policy Against Corruption*, Brussels: European Commission.
European Court of Auditors (2012), *Annual Report on the Implementation of the Budget Concerning Financial Year 2011*, Luxembourg: European Court of Auditors.
European Court of Auditors (2013), *Are EU Cohesion Policy Funds Well Spent on Roads?*, Luxembourg: European Court of Auditors.
Fazekas, M., Tóth, I. J. and King, L. P. (2013), 'Corruption manual for beginners: inventory of elementary "corruption techniques" in public procurement using the case of Hungary', Corruption Research Center Budapest Working Paper No. CRC-WP/2013:01), Corruption Research Centre, Budapest.
Fazekas, M., Tóth, I. J. and King, L. P. (forthcoming), 'Anatomy of grand corruption: a composite corruption risk index based on objective data', *European Journal of Criminal Policy and Research*.
Fazekas, M., Chvalkovská, J., Skuhrovec, J., Tóth, I. J. and King, L. P. (2014), 'Are EU funds a corruption risk? The impact of EU funds on grand corruption in Central and Eastern Europe', in A. Mungiu-Pippidi (ed.), *The Anticorruption Frontline: The ANTICORRP Project, Vol. 2.*, Berlin: Barbara Budrich Publishers, pp. 68–89.
Imbens, G. W. and Wooldridge, J. M. (2009), 'Recent developments in the econometrics of program evaluation', *Journal of Economic Literature*, 47(1), 5–86.
Kaufmann, D., Mastruzzi, M. and Kraay, A. (2010), 'The Worldwide Governance Indicators: methodology and analytical issues', Working Paper No. 5430, Washington, DC: World Bank.
Knack, S. (2001), 'Aid dependence and the quality of governance: cross-country empirical tests', *Southern Economic Journal*, 68(2), 310–29.
KPMG (2012), *EU Funds in Central and Eastern Europe 2011*, Warsaw: KPMG.

Mauro, P. (1998), 'Corruption and the composition of government expenditure', *Journal of Public Economics*, 69, 263–79.
Mungiu-Pippidi, A. (ed.) (2013), *Controlling Corruption in Europe: The Anticorruption Report 1*, Berlin: Barbara Budrich Publishers.
OECD (2007), *Integrity in Public Procurement: Good Practice from A to Z*, Paris: OECD.
PricewaterhouseCoopers (2013), *Identifying and Reducing Corruption in Public Procurement in the EU*, Brussels: PricewaterhouseCoopers and Ecorys.
Shaxson, N. and Christensen, J. (2014), *The Finance Curse: How Oversized Financial Centres Attack Democracy and Corrupt Economies*, Chesham, UK: Tax Justice Network.
Tanzi, V. and Davoodi, H. (2001), 'Corruption, growth, and public finances', in A. K. Jain (ed.), *The Political Economy of Corruption*, New York: Routledge, pp. 89–110.
World Bank (2009), *Fraud and Corruption Awareness Handbook*, Washington DC: World Bank.

14 Efficient implementers and partners

What do we miss in our understanding of how Cohesion Policy administrators work?

Andrey Demidov

Introduction

National bureaucrats are undoubtedly one of the main factors that ensure efficient and successful implementation of Cohesion Policy. That their contribution to unproblematic EU policy implementation is crucial is supported by a huge body of research literature (Hille and Knill, 2006; Haverland and Romeijn, 2007; Toshkov, 2007; Steunenberg and Toshkov, 2009). There is also a strong agreement among EU officials and policy practitioners that Cohesion Policymakers and implementers matter when it comes to effective allocation and disbursement of funds. However, both academics and practitioners often discuss bureaucrats in the member states as major obstructors of policy implementation and, consequently, major contributors to its failures. State officials are portrayed as driven by their own narrow strategic interests, unfamiliar with the EU norms and standards of policy making or, even if they are familiar, still unable to fully commit to these standards and principles. Alternative explanations of implementation failures produced by the state officials focus on capacities and resources of these actors.

The practical implementation of the Partnership Principle for Structural Funds, one of the crucial principles of Cohesion Policy, is frequently referred to as an example of the above-mentioned mechanisms of 'bureaucratic menace', low capacities or shallow socialization that result in failed implementation. The small albeit growing body of literature on partnership registers that despite large democratic appeal of this requirement and the openly expressed commitment of the member states to its implementation, current practice has resulted in rivalry and confusion within member states' administrative structures (Bauer, 2002), opened up room for the flourishing of informality rather than transparency (Piattoni, 2006) and seriously affected the accountability of the whole policy making process (Milio, 2007). In CEE member states, both scholars and practitioners view partnership as especially problematic despite its great promises (Batory and Cartwright, 2011; Cartwright and Batory, 2012; Dąbrowski, 2014, 2013; Potluka and Liddle, 2014). The ongoing contestation over this principle, with actors clashing with each other over the appropriate ways and formats of its implementation, is seen as a clear sign of failure, and national state officials are seen as the main causes of this failure.

Two bodies of research literature analytically support these arguments. More structural explanations of Europeanization, transposition and compliance link the failure of partnership to noticeable 'misfits' between member states' institutional and administrative traditions, and the idea of policy making communicated through the concept of partnership (Borzel and Risse, 2003; Bruszt, 2008). In a more sociological reading of Europeanization, such a 'misfit' manifests itself at the normative level as a clash of different understandings. In both cases, bureaucrats are portrayed as perpetuating specific habits, traditions and norms of policy making, which they bring to bear on partnership. The main clash occurs between the idea of a centralized government and a strong, uncontested role for state bureaucracies in policy making and the idea of more horizontal interactions between multiple actors. More centralized polities, including CEE member states, are perceived as inherently infertile soils for the entrenchment of partnership as opposed to more corporatist states (Borzel, 1999; Heinelt and Lang, 2011). State officials in those contexts are seen as merely unfamiliar with and resistant to any forms of collaboration with civil society actors or economic and social partners. The sociological reading of Europeanization also suggests that attempts to educate and socialize state officials into EU norms and standards such as partnership inevitably fail, and the results remain shallow and superficial (Paraskevopoulos and Leonardi, 2004). In line with the second argument, state officials' faithfulness to the EU norms and standards of policy making is purely discursive and does not translate into an in-depth commitment and, consequently, a thoroughgoing implementation of the EU rules (Dąbrowski, 2008, 2012).

By contrast, actor-centered explanations found in the literature on public policy and partnerships in public policy making attribute the failure of partnership to facets of bureaucratic behaviour such as the strategic abuse of the idea of partnership, low administrative capacities[1] of state representatives or contingently realized preferences and interests (Sullivan et al., 2006). From this perspective, partnership 'fails' at the micro contextual level of individual partnership arrangements or practices due to either insufficient capacity to deal with additional complexities brought about by the partnership or to deliberate bureaucratic menace and open resistance.

The present chapter seeks to break with these widespread interpretations. It argues that, formulated within certain analytical traditions, these explanations trivialize the complexity of bureaucratic action and do not shed much light on our understanding of how national state officials work and what their input in Cohesion Policy implementation is. Additionally, by mechanically reproducing the templates of 'misfits', 'shallow internalization' or 'strategic abuse', both analytical positions provide empirically problematic explanations of the practical implementation of partnership and the role of state officials in it. By contrast, empirical data on partnership implementation in the CEE member states illustrate that partnership is hugely contested by the involved actors rather than sabotaged or neglected, a situation fuelled by the vagueness of the EU Regulations on partnership and the lack of any clear-cut benchmarks of its proper implementation. The contestation over partnership essentially indicates that actors get involved in advancing certain understandings. The latter cannot be simply reduced to representations and reflections of either specific narrow interests or cultural templates or scripts. Existing explanations, by contrast, oscillate between two extremes and view state officials as representatives of bigger structures like institutional and administrative traditions and cultures, or as driven by specific institutional interests.

This chapter argues that analysis of how state officials *relate* rather than *respond* to the requirement of partnership and interpretive reconstruction of the meanings-in-use of partnership would reveal a lot more about what role state officials play in partnership implementation. Drawing on the assumptions of interpretive analysis, namely its focus on actors' lived experience and their own conceptualizations of the world around them, the chapter goes beyond presuming what shapes the position of the state officials on partnership in the CEE member states and, consequently, does away with the current limited conception of partnership implementation. Thus, it identifies the meanings of partnership shared by state officials across four countries: Hungary, Slovakia, Slovenia and Poland. The data from 26 conversational interviews, policy documents and participant observations demonstrate that the meanings of partnership are shaped by a complex interplay of state officials' previous experiences of pre-accession and enlargement, the productive role of Cohesion Policy practice and self-perceptions and institutional identities. As a result of these conditions, partnership is understood as a practice aimed at:

- collecting policy input;
- ensuring transparency through updating both the EU and societal actors about policy developments;
- carrying out certain obligations towards partners.

The chapter begins by positioning the implementation of the Partnership Principle within a broader history of relations between the EU and the new member states and the entrenchment of the specific practice of Cohesion Policy making to provide the empirical background. It proceeds by reconstructing the meanings-in-use of partnership through interpretive analysis of the major themes found in actors' elaborations on partnership and mapping how these meanings translate into existing practices.

Cohesion Policy and its implementers

The practice of Cohesion Policy making in the countries under scrutiny is a product of not only existing national administrative traditions and ways of doing things. The structuring role of the EU and long-lasting effects of the pre-accession process also need to be taken into consideration. The existing literature on enlargement and pre-accession reconstructs in detail the dynamics and the effects of relations between the EU and the candidate countries. Scholars agree that in handling pre-accession, the European Commission (EC) chose to prioritize timely transposition and compliance to ensuring meaningful implementation of transposed rules and norms (Brusis, 2002; Hughes *et al.*, 2004). In relation to Cohesion Policy, another important feature of the pre-accession process was a quick rolling back of the EC on its initial plans. The most notorious example of such a move is the unfinished decentralization/regionalization process when the EC, contrary to what it required before when it was concerned with the issue of absorption capacity, encouraged the candidate countries to recentralize Cohesion Policy management and curtail planned devolution (Hughes *et al.*, 2004). The low administrative capacity of the candidate countries' administrations was used as an argument against further regionalization. Candidate countries' administrations were seen as unprepared for the arrival of the Structural Funds, and the governments, in the course of negotiations over Chapter 21 of the *acquis* on Cohesion Policy, were strongly advised to strengthen their bureaucracies.

Excessive centralization and the striking complexity of the systems of institutions that were installed in the candidate countries to implement Cohesion Policy are seen in the literature as the major effects of this turbulence of the pre-accession negotiations. Scholars note that 'defensive bureaucratization' – in other words, the desire to ensure compliance with the EU requirements through the creation of new administrative units – was the natural and immediate reaction in the candidate countries (Dezséri and Vida, 2011). The EU's 'conceptual division and practical differentiation between decision-making and implementation' as stages of Cohesion Policy implementation (Leonardi, 2005: 69) was complemented by candidates' own efforts to secure themselves against additional criticisms or sanctions.

Several features of the system that emerged bear particular importance. First, the system demonstrates functional polarization between two major groups of actors: the so-called coordination authorities (the central Managing Authorities, in the EU Cohesion Policy jargon) and the line ministries or the policy implementers. According to the existing practice, these bodies serve different functions. The coordination authorities deal exclusively with the process of programming and planning, including drafting and preparation of all programmatic policy documents such as partnership agreements (previously NSRF), Operational Programmes (OPs), reports and so on. In addition, these bodies' main function is to oversee the EU rules, including the so-called horizontal priorities such as gender equality or non-discrimination and, most importantly, the Partnership Principle. The latter makes them important translators and promoters of the EU discourses on partnership. By contrast, the line ministries are entrusted with direct implementation which, in turn, implies the translation of general policy priorities into concrete actions and policies, the selection of projects, the monitoring of their implementation and financial reporting.

Second, another feature of the system is the presence of multiple veto players. Numerous intermediary and controlling bodies (such as ministries of finance and audit commissions), let alone formal and informal political groups at the higher level, are involved in Cohesion Policy implementation in different ways. With regard to partnership, this means that other actors can potentially easily affect its implementation by insisting on following certain rules or procedures. For instance, ministries of finance are just such veto players. Their involvement in the monitoring of the EU rules on procurement and contracting can significantly limit the discretion of the coordination authorities, the central Cohesion Policy actors.

However, in practice, the seemingly neat and clear division of competences proves to be very hazy, complicated and fragmented on closer inspection. State officials involved in Cohesion Policy implementation are represented by multiple types of organizations with different or, conversely, overlapping functions, aspirations, institutional identities and self-perceptions. Additionally, Cohesion Policy practice itself prioritizes certain relational dynamics of intensive political struggles and rivalries over the policy's goals and mechanisms, both within the group and between the state officials and external actors.

The next section takes a closer look at how these effects and the complex realities of state officials' positions and work impact the meanings of partnership.

Partnership and policy input

Elaborations of coordination authorities' officials on partnership are structured around several themes. The quotation below, taken from an interview with a Hungarian official, provides initial entry points into their understandings:

> Most of the people who dealt with the Partnership Principle at that time thought it was a beautiful phenomenon from the EU. *We had in mind that it can be useful for policy-making. We expected that if we could organize it in a good way, it would help us to collect and spread the information* . . . To understand the whole story better – the politicians were not deciding on goals at the abstract level but they were deciding on projects . . . *but we needed legitimacy* . . . the EU says 'growth and jobs', the politicians stamp it. *This is beautiful but this has not been a politically discussed and legitimized document. So some of us were thinking of partnership as input from society in order to know where all these goals come from.*[2]

The excerpt illustrates in a straightforward manner how the position of state officials within the system of Cohesion Policy making structures their understandings of partnership. Partnership was seen as a 'beautiful phenomenon from the EU' which would assist state officials in acquiring the necessary policy information. Being already 'in mind', this interpretation was further strengthened by the officials' first encounters with Cohesion Policy making practice, when they were thrown into a completely new, unfamiliar and extremely complex context of policy documents preparation. In this new context, state officials, especially those from the coordination authorities whose responsibilities were, in fact, their whole countries and not policy sectors, faced a complex problem of suddenly becoming important decision-makers lacking a proper and clearly defined mandate. This state of affairs was exacerbated by the sheer lack of relevant policy content. Partnership offered a way out of both impasses. It was seen as an opportunity to 'get the bottom-up information about *the real needs that we do not have*'[3] (as one Slovenian respondent put it), to access partners' expertise and to ensure legitimacy. Naturally enough, public consultations – organized either physically across countries or in an online format in which the policy documents were opened up for external commentaries – appeared as the most convenient tool to acquire policy content and legitimacy and, as a result, became closely associated with 'real' partnership.

Empirical data illustrate a striking homogeneity in the ways in which coordination authorities decided to deal with the partnership requirement across the four analysed countries – be it the Slovakian Ministry of Health, which organized consultations with the partners to collect policy input on the new OP; the Slovenian Ministry of Economic Development, which decided to start the new programming period of 2014–20 with consultations in all 12 regions; or the Marshall's Offices in the Polish regions, which did exactly the same in order to prepare regional OPs. Contrary to expectations, no variation across policy areas or, alternatively, across regions within a single member state has been found.

The urge to hunt for expertise also structures how state officials from the line ministries interpret partnership. Despite occupying a structurally different position within national administrations and naturally enjoying direct access to policy information and expertise, these officials nevertheless experienced a similar lack of policy input with the arrival of Cohesion Policy and its particular goals and priorities. In fact, novel policy priorities brought in by the EU put line ministries' officials in similar situations of a lack of knowledge and understanding of the real content behind the EU priorities. Partnership thus emerged as an opportunity to access the necessary policy content. However, the problem of a lack of policy information was even more acute as the line ministries have been made responsible for project selection, implementation and monitoring, a function that made the channelling of necessary expertise a higher priority.

These concerns have been projected onto partnership. Partnership, for instance, gets directly equated with the so-called 'project partnership' or the existence or formation of a coalition of various actors willing and, importantly, capable of implementing certain projects. In this interpretation, partnership is associated with smooth and non-conflictual relations between project implementers that ensure an unproblematic and undisruptive journey through the project cycle. Conflictual relations, by contrast, were directly associated with unprofessional conduct by respondents.

Any attempts by the partners to disrupt the dynamics of partnership revolving around expertise and input provision are, in fact, met with strong resistance. The latter normally occurs when societal partners appeal to issues of representation or citizens' participation and try to argue for an expansion of their rights or competences. These attempts to 'rock the boat' are especially condemned by state officials who strongly oppose having this discussion in such clearly political terms. Justifying their uncompromising position, they appeal to the depoliticized image of a 'real' partner to which they especially eagerly want partners to conform. According to this representation, societal partners should refrain from making any political claims, which is equated with 'working in their narrow interests' and even 'biting your whole hand off'.[4] Most interestingly, any claims made by societal partners that are not based on supposedly objective data, facts or information, such as the ones made frequently by environmental organizations, are associated with 'non-strategic claims', labelled as 'politicization' and stigmatized as 'complaining' and 'whining'.[5] 'Real' partners are expected to possess knowledge and expertise, as the quote below vividly exemplifies:

> [b]y 'partnership' I mean *the ability to see the wider context, the ability to think at the strategic level, the ability to read all the documents, to comment on them and also to be able to make the linkages with other policies.*[6]

This quote illuminates the core of officials' expectations. Societal partners are not seen as members of civil society, an interpretation that the EC used to insist on; instead, they are supposed to almost mirror the state officials themselves, at least in terms of possessing the same complex expert knowledge of the finer points of EU Cohesion Policy.

Despite functional differences between state officials from both camps, one can capture the common ground in interpretations of partnership. Partnership is understood as a system of relations with partners in which partners' primary role is the provision of expertise and policy input. It is important to note that in contesting the role of societal partners, state officials also provide specific normative input into emerging understandings of European civil society stripped of any political meanings.

Selection of partners and procedural formats

As was shown above, the clear interest of state officials in obtaining policy expertise and input also shapes their understandings of the procedural format of partnership. The EU Regulations remain rather vague regarding the procedural aspect of partnership and its formats, apart from having the provisions about the Monitoring Committees (MCs). Moreover, the EU Regulations explicitly refer to member states' legal and administrative traditions as guiding principles for state officials. In this light, it is especially interesting that state officials of coordination authorities in all four countries primarily opted for the format of public consultations and the collection of comments on the drafts of documents online. The example of Hungary represents an extreme version of such 'consultative' logic. The National Development Agency, an institution established to deal exclusively with Cohesion Policy, organized an almost direct democracy experiment when it announced that it would be collecting comments and suggestions for the new OPs for the 2007–13 period from everyone who was willing to provide these comments. What shapes such an interpretation of partnership apart from an explicit interest in eliciting otherwise rare policy input? Respondents' elaborations on 'real' partnership also revealed the structuring effect of their professional dispositions.

Pushing for the consultative format of partnership, state officials seem to address and reconcile another group of concerns that are brought to life by the peculiarities of their work – namely, their liminal position between the tiers of governance and numerous actors including the EC, the higher echelons of national authorities and societal partners. Such a liminal position puts two interrelated groups of pressures on them, which translate into concerns about, first, transparency and, second, neutrality. Numerous utterances similar to *'what we really care about is whether this is in line with the EU priorities, the Regulations, primarily'*[7] not only signify that state officials refer to the 'EU rules' as a convenient argument during disputes. The position of being squeezed between, on the one hand, the EU – whose interests they are supposed to guard by overseeing compliance and whose feedback is seen as legitimizing their actions and, to an extent, their existence – and, on the other, national higher authorities and societal partners, exerts immense political pressure and makes the search for points of intersection of various interests the major priority. In such a situation, neutrality and loyalty become issues of primary importance, as, within the complex dynamics of Cohesion Policy making, ensuring compliance with the EU rules may easily be interpreted as a betrayal of national interests, especially when such compliance can lead to withdrawal of EU Funds. Neutrality naturally becomes an especial concern in this context.

The stories about how state officials addressed the remarks, comments and suggestions collected through the exercise of consultations constituted a very important part of their narratives about 'true' partnership and served to demonstrate their impartiality as moderators of these encounters and, most importantly, the transparency of their work. Responding to partners' remarks or preparing reports that would indicate how suggestions were dealt with were referred to as practices of 'real' partnership that seem to sustain the image of state officials as transparent, effective and, most importantly, politically neutral actors insulated from any influences. As directly put by one Hungarian respondent, 'the reason we organized partnership like that was that it is very important *to keep the Agency open so that the public knows what is going on here*'.[8]

Public consultations and providing online access to the policy documents are seen as the best means of ensuring transparency and neutrality. Explaining the reasons behind the choice of these institutional formats, state officials especially emphasized equality of access and treatment as principles that can only be guaranteed by public consultations. As stressed several times by the representative of the Polish Ministry for Regional Development, 'we *do not have any hand in choosing* the partners; if partners come to our Managing Authorities and say they would like to participate, they are accepted'.[9] Against the background of being 'limited by [your] responsibility',[10] consultations appear to be the only way of resolving issues such as partnership outreach, political pressures from actors such as municipalities and regions and never-ending problems of proper representation when it comes to societal partners. The latter can only be effectively resolved by applying no selection criteria and allowing everyone to take part in the consultations.

Furthermore, public consultations allow for the most convenient solution to the problem of insufficient transparency: informing the wider public about policy developments and actions. This is confirmed by very frequent equation of partnership with pro-active effort on the part of state officials to share with the partners how the whole policy process develops. Respondents traded numerous stories of how partnership is practised through the organization of visits around the country and the installation of billboards with the relevant information about funds allocation in Hungary or the especially conscientious attitude to informing the partners about how their comments were acted upon in Poland.[11] This exercise of informing did not come across as a purely performative practice, though. By contrast, respondents' elaborations demonstrated that state officials take this to be a fundamental part of their job. Such an attitude is especially manifest in the practice of the MCs, the whole purpose of which has been interpreted by state officials as being to inform the public about recent developments, approved allocations or changes in budget priorities. In this light, neglect of the MCs by societal partners leaves state officials rather perplexed.

It is important to mention that bureaucrats from the line ministries contest these procedural formats. Approaching partnership similarly as a process of channelling or, to be more precise, acquiring policy content, these officials nevertheless have little incentive to engage in public consultations, although they responsibly take part in them. The officials from the line ministries opt for more closed formats of partnership or various working groups and committees with selected partners. The major reason for this is that the closed format allows for more efficient networking with future project implementers, a crucial orientation in their work. As expressed by one Polish official, 'we invited these people because *the better you know the ones who will be using this money, the less trouble implementation brings*, as you know who to trust'.[12] Such a need impacts their view of partners as those who are professionally capable of engaging in notoriously cumbersome EU project management. Professionalism, working ethics and, most importantly, the credible reputation of partners become the most important selection criteria. As a result, partnership in the line ministries is practised as a series of more or less institutionalized interactions with selected organizations. Reliance on personal connections with partners, acquired through either previous professional experiences or learning-by-talking within established groups and committees characterizes the practical implementation of partnership in the line ministries.

Partnership and empowerment

Interpretations of partnership as a communicative process during which partners are expected to channel relevant policy information and expertise while state officials ensure wide access and equality of treatment are complemented by certain representations of dynamics of relations with partners. Apart from 'informing' the public and 'listening to what they say',[13] state officials conceive of partnership as a set of specific obligations on their part. A closer look at discursive interventions that contain references to these obligations shows that it is not only instrumental considerations that inform their judgments and actions but also certain deep-seated beliefs and understandings. One Hungarian respondent revealed an aspect of these beliefs by saying that *'we wanted* [partners] *to feel as if they were managing the program with us . . . as if partners were really in charge of it . . . they were treating it as their own program and they wanted to shape it.* As far as I remember, *we did not get that impression from our social partners'*.[14] The respondent confirmed that there is an expectation that partners will demonstrate professional conduct, as previously discussed. Such understandings seem to directly inform further actions that are framed as manifestations of 'true' partnership – namely, the initiatives of state officials to train partners, including sending them abroad to 'learn how to be a partner'.[15]

State officials associate partnership with their own pro-active position on strengthening and empowering partners. In their narratives of successful or 'real' partnership, respondents regularly moved away from describing why partnership did not work, mentioning the unprofessionalism of partners and their apathy or, conversely, complaining conduct, to reporting on what had been done on their part to fix partnership dynamics. Establishing communication or, in other words, providing an opportunity to have a say and be listened to was perceived by them as the first step in them enacting partnership. The second step involves creating conditions in which the partners can express themselves, be it organizing public consultations, inviting partners into the MCs or even adjusting procedural routines of the MCs for the sake of letting partners talk. However, the most important indicators of acting in the spirit of partnership are measures taken to ensure the capacity-building of partners, a complex of policy initiatives aimed at the organizational strengthening of societal partners implemented through either direct unconditional financial aid or various schemes of financial assistance. Such empowerment can take many forms. State officials repeatedly gave examples of the measures they took to support the partners: '*sending them to Austria to study*'[16] (Hungary); training partners and establishing a system of financial support for their activities as '*input providers through reimbursement of their costs*'[17] (Poland); creating and financing country-wide networks of NGOs or even activities at the EU level targeted at convincing the EC to simplify the administrative and technical requirements for projects (Slovenia).

Two other themes within this big field of interventions aimed at strengthening partners stand out as further clarifying state officials' understandings of partnership. First, there is a certain expectation that the above-described aid is not, in fact, totally unconditional. As very straightforwardly put by a Polish respondent, 'Sometimes they are not as supportive as they should be. *I agree to pay their administrative costs, travel and other expenses but, in exchange, [they should] give us something which is important*'.[18] This quote displays an important aspect of understandings of partnership – it is seen as an exchange of benefits for expertise, empowerment for policy input. Second, some remarks conveyed the message that the achievement of 'real' partnership may be deferred until the investment in and empowerment of partners have themselves been achieved. In describing what has been done for partners, some respondents straightforwardly pointed out that 'when it comes to Cohesion Funds, of course, *partners should have their capacity fixed* first . . . *we first need to make them stronger* so they could really implement some measures'.[19] Moreover, the underdeveloped professionalism of partners is presented as the reason why, for instance, the proportion of partners in the MCs is limited to 50 per cent of the total membership. This is done to avoid the situation, as one Hungarian respondent put it, of placing a 'loaded gun into their hands'[20] or, as echoed in the interview with his Polish colleague, 'blocking something that we know will be implemented improperly'.[21]

These interventions should not be read as proving the pure rational reasons underpinning state officials' understandings, although references to the provision of assistance in exchange for expertise and an unwillingness to open up institutional structures of partnership for wider representation can lead to these conclusions. In reality, at a deeper level, these references conveniently fit into an overall understanding of partnership as a system of rigid power relations between state officials, who are responsible for overall implementation and compliance with the EU rules, and partners, actors who, in officials' eyes, are not restricted by external conditions and monitoring, like state officials, yet who need to understand this positionality of state officials. Strengthening and empowering partners is sincerely viewed as, first, an obligation incumbent upon officials, although of limited scope, and, second, an indication of acting in the spirit of partnership.

Conclusions

This chapter has sought to provide an interpretive explanation of situated meanings of partnership and the meaning-making practices of state officials in their particular contexts, rather than to impose any external conceptualization. The empirical data bring attention to the powerful structuring effect of the practice of Cohesion Policy on interpretations of partnership, coupled with previous experiences of pre-accession and their own institutional identities and self-perceptions. Occupying the position of producers of innovative policy content who need to comply with the EU rules and, at the same time, navigate between various demands and pressures at both transnational and national levels, state officials transpose this experience and the outcomes of their interpretive engagement with these conditions onto the image of partnership. Partnership is therefore seen as a solution to the problem of scarce policy content and expertise, legitimacy, and expectations of transparency and neutrality. Moreover, the whole discourse and experience of Cohesion Policy as a depoliticized and highly technocratic exercise shapes understandings of partnership as a technical exchange of information rather than as a series of politically coloured debates. Seeing themselves as chief technical implementers, though inevitably engaging in highly political encounters, state officials push for a particular institutional format of partnership. They see that public consultations organized according to the principles of universal access and equality of treatment ensure the timely and smooth provision of the necessary policy information and do not jeopardize their image as transparent and neutral implementers, both domestically and in the eyes of the EU.

It should be mentioned, however, that actors successfully reconcile these understandings triggered by the conditions of their profession with their pre-existing beliefs. The latter relates to beliefs about state officials' obligation towards societal partners in terms of capacity-building measures. However, as has been shown, this orientation – which, as might be expected, dates back to times before the arrival of EU Cohesion Policy – gets interlinked with the understanding of societal partners as providers of expertise. Capacity-building, in this light, is seen as making societal partners into more professional experts capable of playing the role of reliable policy informants.

The obvious limitation of this study is its narrow focus on the implementation of one particular requirement, namely the Partnership Principle. Perhaps it does not come as a huge surprise that partnership is contested given the highly normative nature of this concept as related to issues of political participation, transparency and civil society. However, the apparent clarity and uncontested character of other Cohesion Policy requirements, or other EU requirements more generally, should not be taken for granted either. Such principles as gender equality, non-discrimination or even additionality and complementarity, while clear and unproblematic at first sight, do in fact have an underlying normative quality that is very often dismissed and serve as a fruitful space for contestation, a social practice and process during which actors engage in renegotiating and reconceptualizing that normative quality (Wiener, 2014). How state officials interpret partnership demonstrates the normative underpinnings of actors' behaviour, a finding that not only challenges existing conventional explanations of bureaucratic behaviour but also reopens the discussion of what can be done to ensure better administrative input and, as a result, better overall policy implementation.

Notes

1 References to low administrative capacities can also be found in research that attempts to provide a macro account, such as, for instance, research on transposition of and compliance with the EU directives (Toshkov, 2008; Steunenberg and Toshkov, 2009).
2 Interviewee SO HU, 26 March 2013, emphasis mine.
3 Interviewee SO SK, 24 July 2013, emphasis mine.
4 Interviewee SO PL, 14 June 2013.
5 Interviewee SO SL, 7 September 2012.
6 Interviewee SO SK, 24 July 2013, emphasis mine.
7 Interviewee SO SL, 5 April 2012, emphasis mine.
8 Interviewee SO HU, 12 June 2012, emphasis mine.
9 Interviewee SO PL, 14 June 2013, emphasis mine.
10 Interviewee SO SK, 24 July 2013.

11 In Hungary, at the end of the direct democracy experiment referred to above, the NDA sent more than 4,000 personal letters to everyone who had left a comment, explaining how their comment or suggestion would be taken into consideration or why this would not happen.
12 Interviewee SO PL, 16 March 2012, emphasis mine.
13 Interviewee SO SK, 12 November 2012.
14 Interviewee SO HU, 29 April 2013, emphasis mine.
15 Ibid.
16 Interviewee SO HU, 29 April 2013, emphasis mine.
17 Interviewee SO PL, 14 June 2013, emphasis mine.
18 Ibid., emphasis mine.
19 Interviewee SO SL, 7 September 2012, emphasis mine.
20 Interviewee SO HU, 29 April 2013.
21 Interviewee SO PL, 14 June 2013.

References

Batory, A. and Cartwright, A. (2011), 'Re-visiting the Partnership Principle in Cohesion Policy: the role of civil society organizations in Structural Funds monitoring', *Journal of Common Market Studies*, 49(4), 697–717.
Bauer, M. W. (2002), 'The EU "Partnership Principle": still a sustainable governance device across multiple administrative arenas?', *Public Administration*, 80(4), 769–89.
Borzel, T. (1999), 'Towards convergence in Europe? Institutional adaptation to Europeanization in Germany and Spain', *Journal of Common Market Studies*, 37(4), 573–96.
Borzel, T. and Risse, T. (2003), 'Conceptualising the domestic impact of Europe', in K. Featherstone and C. Radaelli (eds), *The Politics of Europeanization*, Oxford, UK: Oxford University Press, pp. 57–82.
Brusis, M. (2002), 'Between EU requirements, competitive politics, and national traditions: re-creating regions in the accession countries of Central and Eastern Europe', *Governance*, 15(4), 531–59.
Bruszt, L. (2008), 'Multi-level governance – the eastern versions: emerging patterns of regional developmental governance in the new member states', *Regional and Federal Studies*, 18(5), 607–27.
Cartwright, A. and Batory, A. (2012), 'Monitoring Committees in Cohesion Policy: overseeing the distribution of Structural Funds in Hungary and Slovakia', *Journal of European Integration*, 34(4), 323–40.
Dąbrowski, M. (2008), 'Structural Funds as a driver for institutional change in Poland', *Europe-Asia Studies*, 60(2), 227–48.
Dąbrowski, M. (2012), 'Shallow or deep Europeanisation? The uneven impact of EU Cohesion Policy on the regional and local authorities in Poland', *Environment and Planning C: Government and Policy*, 30(4), 730–45.
Dąbrowski, M. (2013), 'Europeanizing sub-national governance: partnership in the implementation of European Union Structural Funds in Poland', *Regional Studies*, 47(8), 1363–74.
Dąbrowski, M. (2014), 'EU Cohesion Policy, horizontal partnership and the patterns of sub-national governance: insights from Central and Eastern Europe', *European Urban and Regional Studies*, 1(1), 1–20.
Dezséri, K. and Vida, K. (2011), 'Cohesion policy in the new member states: unfolding new modes of governance?', in U. Diedrichs, W. Reiners and W. Wessels (eds), *The Dynamics of Change in EU Governance*, Cheltenham, UK: Edward Elgar, pp. 132–48.

Haverland, M. and Romeijn, M. (2007), 'Do member states make European policies work? Analyzing the EU transposition deficit', *Public Administration*, 85(3), 757–78.

Heinelt, H. and Lang, A. (2011), 'Regional actor constellations in EU Cohesion Policy: differentiation along the policy cycle', *Central European Journal of Public Policy*, 5(2), 4–29.

Hille, P. and Knill, C. (2006), '"It's the bureaucracy, stupid": the implementation of the acquis communautaire in EU candidate countries, 1999–2003', *European Union Politics*, 7(4), 531–52.

Hughes, J., Sasse, G. and Gordon, C. (2004), 'Conditionality and compliance in the EU's eastward enlargement: Regional Policy and the reform of sub-national government', *Journal of Common Market Studies*, 42(3), 523–51.

Leonardi, R. (2005), *Cohesion Policy in the European Union: The Building of Europe*, London: Palgrave Macmillan.

Milio, S. (2007), 'Can administrative capacity explain differences in regional performances? Evidence from Structural Funds implementation in southern Italy', *Regional Studies*, 41(4), 429–42.

Paraskevopoulos, C. J. and Leonardi, R. (2004), 'Introduction: adaptational pressures and social learning in European Regional Policy – cohesion (Greece, Ireland and Portugal) vs. CEE (Hungary, Poland) countries', *Regional & Federal Studies*, 14(3), 315–54.

Piattoni, S. (2006), 'Informal governance in Structural Policy', *Perspectives on European Politics and Society*, 7(1), 56–74.

Potluka, O. and Liddle, J. (2014), 'Managing European Union Structural Funds: using a multilevel governance framework to examine the application of the Partnership Principle at the project level', *Regional Studies*, 48(8), 1434–47.

Steunenberg, B. and Toshkov, D. (2009), 'Comparing transposition in the 27 member states of the EU: the impact of discretion and legal fit', *Journal of European Public Policy*, 16(7), 951–70.

Sullivan, H., Barnes, M. and Matka, E. (2006), 'Collaborative capacity and strategies in area-based initiatives', *Public Administration*, 84(2), 289–310.

Toshkov, D. (2007), 'In search of the worlds of compliance: culture and transposition performance in the European Union', *Journal of European Public Policy*, 14(6), 933–59.

Toshkov, D. (2008), 'Embracing European Law: compliance with EU directives in Central and Eastern Europe', *European Union Politics*, 9(3), 379–402.

Wiener, A. (2014), *A Theory of Contestation*, Berlin: Springer.

15 Funds for the wealthy and the politically loyal?

How EU Funds may contribute to increasing regional disparities in East Central Europe

Gergő Medve-Bálint

Introduction

Since the early 2000s, transfers from the European Union (EU) have become the most important resources for regional development programmes in the Eastern member states. However, because of the recent involvement of these countries in the EU's Cohesion Policy, we know little about the territorial distribution of the funds. Questions about which regions and localities have benefited the most from the grants and what factors influenced the domestic allocation of funds have so far remained largely unanswered. An inquiry into these issues bears both theoretical and practical relevance because it reveals whether EU grants did indeed benefit the backward regions to narrow internal development gaps. Accordingly, the chapter investigates the determinants of the spatial distribution of the funds in Hungary and Poland in the 2007–13 programming period.[1]

The chapter analyses two countries from East Central Europe (ECE), Hungary and Poland, for which territorial-administrative structures differ markedly. Although both are unitary states, Hungary is strongly centralized, while Poland has adopted one of the most decentralized systems in ECE in which the regional governments (voivodeship or *województwo*) possess notable decision-making powers (Dąbrowski, 2014). Furthermore, the central government dominates territorial administration in Hungary, whereas in Poland power is shared between the central state and the sub-national level. Lastly, the Polish units of local government (*gmina*) are far bigger in both size and population than the municipalities in the highly fragmented Hungarian system.

In spite of the above differences, the following analysis reveals that in both countries the same factors show a similar relationship with the territorial distribution of EU grants. In particular, the lack of differentiation between the more and the less prosperous regions in terms of fund eligibility has enabled unequal internal competition for the funds, which has primarily benefited the wealthier regions and localities. This suggests that the concentration principle of the EU's Cohesion Policy, which stipulates that the funds should be spent in the most backward regions of the member states, has not been fulfilled. On the contrary, EU funds have contributed to intra-regional disparities and failed to reduce inter-regional inequality. Moreover, central governments have exercised notable control over the distribution of funds, which has allowed for political bias in funding decisions. The chapter finds that in both countries political loyalty towards the central government has been positively associated with the per capita amount of funds spent at the local and the regional level.

The next section offers a brief review of the literature and formulates the hypotheses. The chapter proceeds by introducing the data and the analytical approach; then it goes on to discuss the empirical results. Besides summarizing the findings, the conclusion also offers policy recommendations.

Literature review and hypotheses

Distributive policies are often exposed to political manipulation (Weingast *et al.*, 1981), which is commonly referred to as "pork barrel politics". In advanced Western democracies, the allocation of infrastructure investments (Castells and Solé-Ollé, 2005; Cadot *et al.*, 2006) and regional grants (Milligan and Smart, 2005) has been found to be influenced by the incumbents, who wish to maximize electoral success.

Empirical research has shown that political considerations also play a role in the allocation of EU funds. For instance, Kemmerling and Bodenstein (2006) showed that in the 2000–6 period, the sub-national regions that received more EU grants where left-wing parties were more popular or where there was a strong pro-EU vs. anti-EU cleavage. By analysing 12 EU member states over the 1989–99 period, Bouvet and Dall'Erba (2010) found that sub-national leaders' political alignment with the central government was positively related to the funds spent in the regions. The authors' results also suggested that national governments were inclined to use EU funds to secure votes in those regions where their position was weaker (2010: 524). Dellmuth and Stoffel (2012), however, highlighted an opposite mechanism: German federal states tended to reward those districts with more EU funds where their support was higher.

Contrary to the above works, Dellmuth (2011) did not detect a significant role of regional partisan politics in the allocation of EU funds. She concluded that economic affluence and the constitutional status of the regions were the key determinants of the size of transfers; although poorer regions received more grants, in constitutionally weak regions past records of fund absorption were positively associated with the grants. Bodenstein and Kemmerling (2011) partially confirmed these results as their analysis showed that Objective 1 regions[2] in decentralized states were able to secure more grants in the 2000–6 period than regions in unitary countries. The authors explained this with reference to the greater lobbying power of the federalist regions compared to the constitutionally weak ones.

While pork barrel politics may influence the distribution of EU grants within ECE as well, the above empirical works offer only limited guidance about the determinants of fund distribution, for three reasons:

1 All of the Eastern regions, without differentiation, have been eligible for EU grants. What is more, with few exceptions, they have qualified for the highest level of support (Objective 1 in the 2004–6 period and Convergence Regions in the 2007–13 period).
2 The Eastern members are all unitary states in which the decision-making power is concentrated at the central level; thus, a distinction between constitutionally weak and strong regions would not make sense in the case of ECE. Even in Poland, where decentralization has advanced the furthest, the autonomy of the regional administrations is considerably bounded.
3 Unlike most Western EU members, all of the ECE countries exercise strong central control over the implementation and management of EU grants. This is because the European Commission has prioritized effective fund management over decentralization in ECE (Grabbe, 2001; Bachtler and McMaster, 2007; Ferry and McMaster, 2013), which has strengthened centralized control over the distribution of EU funds.

These conditions may lead to the following two consequences:

1 The uniform fund eligibility of the ECE regions may create an unequal competition for EU grants where the relatively advanced regions would secure more funds than the most backward ones. This expectation is based on the absorption literature, which suggests that economically better-off places and those with higher institutional quality are likely to absorb more development funds (see, for instance, Ederveen *et al.*, 2006; Milio, 2007; Le Gallo *et al.*, 2011). In short, if the same rules apply to both the advanced and the backward regions, then the more developed ones are likely to enjoy a competitive advantage over the less prosperous ones.
2 Centralized fund management may produce a strong political bias in the distribution of funds. This assumption is based on the work of Kemmerling and Stephan (2002), who argue that in centralized decision-making systems the incumbents' political preferences may play a greater role in determining fund allocation than in decentralized systems.

To date, only Bloom and Petrova (2013) have attempted to identify the determinants of the distribution of EU grants in Eastern Europe from a comparative perspective. Examining a sample of EU-financed projects, they analysed fund allocation in Latvia and Bulgaria at the municipal level. The authors found that in both countries the wealthier localities were able to secure higher per capita EU grants. They also revealed that the local vote shares for the ruling parties were positively associated with the funds, which suggested that central governments had indeed engaged in pork barrel politics. The authors claimed that the centralized management of the funds may have been responsible for this, because in such circumstances politicians have greater influence on funding decisions. Political factors have also been reported to play a role in the distribution of EU funds in Hungary (Csengődi *et al.*, 2006; Kálmán, 2011), Latvia (Kule *et al.*, 2011),

Romania (Ion, 2014) and Poland (Dąbrowski, 2012). However, none of the above studies incorporated local- and regional-level economic and political factors simultaneously into the analysis; thus, they do not provide a nuanced view of the mechanisms of EU fund distribution in ECE. This chapter aims to contribute to the literature by addressing these shortcomings.

The two country cases

Although the 2007–13 Polish Cohesion Policy programmes were planned and adopted during the coalition government led by the Law and Justice (PiS) party, implementation began shortly before the Civic Platform (PO) and its junior ally, the Polish People's Party (PSL), won the early elections in November 2007. The PO–PSL government maintained its parliamentary majority after the 2011 elections and so remained in power during the whole programming period. While the PSL is traditionally more popular in the poorer eastern and agricultural areas, the cities and the western and south-western regions represent the key constituency of the PO. Contrary to the Polish case, in Hungary the implementation of the 2007–13 programmes has been shared by two governments; until the landslide victory of the right-wing Fidesz at the 2010 parliamentary elections, a socialist government was in power.

In terms of their territorial system, the two countries differ to a certain extent. Poland has considerably decentralized its territorial administration, yet the role of the regional administrations (voivodeships) in the management and implementation of EU funds remains limited. Although in the 2007–13 period the centralized system was somewhat relaxed, the central government retained the power to certify payments of the Regional Operational Programmes (ROPs), and the majority of EU funds were still allocated through centrally managed programmes (Dąbrowski, 2012). Hungary has adopted an even more restrictive approach in that in 2006 the socialist government assigned the responsibility for managing all of the sectoral programmes to a central agency (the National Development Agency); thus, the regional actors had even more limited influence on funding decisions than before (Pálné Kovács et al., 2004). In 2010, the Fidesz government further centralized and politicized the system when it replaced the entire management of the agency and subordinated the operations to the Ministry of National Development (Buzogány and Korkut, 2013).

In the 2007–13 period, three sectoral Operational Programmes (OPs) were executed in Poland through which 69 per cent of the country's total EU funding was disbursed. Besides the OPs, all 16 of the NUTS2-level voivodeships, which qualified as Convergence Regions, had their own ROPs. Altogether, the budget of the ROPs amounted to 24.9 per cent of the whole EU contribution. In addition, a multi-regional OP called Development of Eastern Poland, which represented 3.4 per cent of the total EU support, was also introduced. This programme sought to provide assistance for the five most backward eastern voivodeships[3] (Ferry and McMaster, 2013). Hungary's fund allocation was divided among seven sectoral and seven regional OPs. The budget of the sectoral programmes represented 63.3 per cent of the total funding, and 34.8 per cent was dedicated to the regional OPs. Six NUTS2 units qualified as Convergence Regions, whereas the Central Hungary region, which incorporates the capital city of Budapest and the county Pest, received EU grants as a Competitiveness and Employment Region.

Data and methodology

EU-supported projects are typically implemented in localities nested within sub-national regions. The analysis therefore simultaneously estimates regional- and local-level effects on the distribution of EU grants. The dependent variable refers to the local level and is operationalized as the amount of EU grants per capita spent in a locality. There are 2,478 such units of local administration (*gminas*) in Poland and 3,151 (*helyi önkormányzat*) in Hungary. The analysis draws on data from the 2007–13 budgetary cycle. In the Polish case, the hypotheses are tested on 101,529 projects, of which the location is indicated at the *gmina* level in the official records and which were contracted until April 2014.[4] As for Hungary, the dataset contains 63,696 projects that were contracted until June 2014.[5] It is important to note that the Polish NUTS2 units (voivodeships) and the Hungarian NUTS3 units (counties or *megye*) constitute the regional level of the analysis.

Regarding the Polish explanatory factors, they represent socio-economic and political characteristics of both the *gminas* and the voivodeships in 2007, at the beginning of the funding period.[6] The local-level political variables show the outcomes of the last two local and parliamentary elections. The share of votes for the PO and the PSL in the 2007 and 2011 general elections reveals the local popularity of the two parties that formed the governing coalition after both elections. Furthermore, binary variables indicate whether PSL- or PO-nominated mayors won both the 2006 and the 2010 local elections. Interestingly, while the PO was more successful at the parliamentary elections, the PSL demonstrated greater local embeddedness, which may be explained by the historical presence of the party's predecessors in the agrarian eastern territories (Zarycki, 2000: 865).

Similarly, the Hungarian indicators also account for the local- and the regional-level socio-economic and political factors.[7] However, because at the 2010 parliamentary elections the centre-right Fidesz gained a landslide victory over the former incumbent, the Hungarian Socialist Party (MSZP), the dependent variable distinguishes between grants awarded during the socialist and the conservative governments, and the same distinction applies to the independent variables. Thus the reference year of the socio-economic indicators is 2007 for funds awarded in the socialist period, but 2010 for the grants distributed during the term of the conservative government.

Regarding the political variables, besides the local and the regional vote shares of the winning coalition parties at the 2006 (the MSZP and its junior ally, the liberal Alliance of Free Democrats or SZDSZ) and 2010 elections, additional factors need to be considered because of the peculiarities of the Hungarian political system. While Poland adopted a system of proportional representation whereby members of parliament (MP) are elected exclusively through party lists, Hungary has a mixed electoral system with both proportional and majoritarian elements. In the 2006 and 2010 parliamentary elections, 176 MPs were elected in single-member constituencies, while 210 seats were allocated through territorial and national party lists. The role of the MPs who are elected in single-member districts is relevant here because they are more dependent on local support, which means that they tend to be more constituency-oriented relative to those who gain their mandate through party lists. This relationship has been empirically demonstrated in Western contexts (Heitshusen *et al.*, 2005; Pilet *et al.*, 2012) and, as a recent analysis shows, it also applies to Hungary (Papp, 2013).

In this vein, a government MP elected in a single-member district may engage in lobbying for his or her constituency, and these efforts may positively influence the amount of EU funds spent in the localities that the MP represents. Because the Hungarian single-member districts cover multiple local governments, this indicator does not strictly belong to the local level, thus it is introduced as a regional factor.[8] However, it is considered only for the period of the socialist–liberal coalition because it does not show variation during the term of the conservative government; in 2010, Fidesz won 173 out of the 176 single-member districts.

Further political variables need to be introduced because of the peculiarities of the Hungarian system. Unlike in Poland, MPs in Hungary were until recently allowed to undertake roles in local and regional administrations. In particular, serving both as an MP (irrespective of whether the mandate has been gained in a single-member district or through a party list) and as a mayor has been a common practice for many of the Hungarian legislators. Consequently, if the leader of a local government is also a member of the parliament, then this dual service is likely to be associated with more development support spent in the locality. The political colour of the mayors (independent or affiliated with the governing or the opposition parties) may also affect the distribution of funds, so this aspect is also considered in the analysis. Finally, it is important to note that the capital city of Budapest was dropped from the observations because disaggregated data on EU funds are unavailable for the city's 23 districts, which are themselves local governments. Including Budapest would also bias the results because the city serves both as a local government and a NUTS3 region, which in this case makes it impossible to distinguish between local- and regional-level factors.

Because per capita EU funds are expected to vary across both the local governments and the regions, the data structure requires multi-level modelling, which is a suitable method for analysing nested data (Hox, 2010). To test the hypothesized effects, a series of multi-level regressions are estimated where the data have a hierarchical structure in that the local governments are nested within the 16 NUTS2 regions in Poland and the 19 NUTS3 counties in Hungary.

While in the case of Poland simple linear multi-level regressions can be applied because all of the *gminas* have secured some EU funding in the observed period, the Hungarian data represent certain complications because several local governments remained without EU grants. During the period of the socialist government, 44 per cent of the localities were left without a single EU-funded project, while in the period of the Fidesz government, the proportion of such localities was 29 per cent. The dependent variable contains a lot of zero values, so ordinary least squares estimators would be biased and inconsistent. However, this type of censored or limited dependent variable can be conveniently modelled with Tobit regression (Tobin, 1958; Wooldridge, 2012). Because the local governments are nested within the NUTS3 regions, multi-level Tobit regressions are estimated.

Results and discussion

Tables 15.1, 15.2 and 15.3 report the parameter estimates of the multi-level regressions.[9] The results confirm that both economic and political factors played a role in the distribution of EU funds and, in most cases, the direction of the relationship of these indicators with the dependent variable confirms the hypotheses.[10]

As for the effect of the Polish local-level socio-economic variables (Table 15.1), tax revenue per capita and the number of private companies per 1,000 inhabitants are positively and significantly related to the EU funds (for descriptive statistics, see Table 15.A1 in the Appendix). All else being equal, more funds were spent in *gminas* with greater economic output. The local unemployment rate, however, shows a significant negative association with the funds. This implies that if all other conditions are the same, per capita EU grants will, on average, be higher where unemployment rates are lower. Population size is also positively related to the outcome, but this relationship is significant only if the indicator of private companies is excluded from the model. Lastly, the density of civil society organizations does not show significant association with EU funds. The effects of the local governments' socio-economic characteristics on the dependent variable thus reinforce the assumption about the economic logic that presumes that funds tend to concentrate in the wealthier places, if all other conditions are equal.

The coefficients of the local political variables reveal that while the electoral popularity of the PO was positively associated with EU funds, votes for the junior coalition partner, the PSL, were negatively related to per capita grants. Because the PO was more popular in richer localities, whereas the strongholds of the PSL were typically poorer rural areas, one may doubt that these variables truly measure a political rather than a latent economic effect. Such concerns can be mitigated because these variables have a statistically significant relationship with EU funds in spite of the significant effects of the other socio-economic indicators. Moreover, even though the vote shares correlate with per capita tax revenue and private companies, the Cronbach's alpha scores of these items[11] suggest that the political variables measure a concept (party popularity) that is distinct from or at least not directly related to the economic situation of the localities.

The regional-level effects refine the previous findings. While the quality of the regional government index shows a positive but not consistently significant sign

Table 15.1 Results of the linear multi-level models for Poland (DV: EU funding per capita in 2007–13).

	Model 1 B	Model 1 SE	Model 2 B	Model 2 SE	Model 3 B	Model 3 SE	Model 4 B	Model 4 SE
Constant	7.762***	.058	7.748***	.053	7.787***	.045	7.757***	.058
Gmina-level fixed effects								
Population size	.082**	.039	.023	.048	.033	.047	.084**	.037
Tax revenue	.560***	.044					.563***	.045
Private companies per 1,000 inhabitants			.429***	.110	.561***	.088		
Unemployment rate	−.014**	.007	−.019***	.005	−.020***	.006	−.014**	.007
NGOs per 1,000 inhabitants	.009	.069	.048	.078	.050	.084	.006	.069
PO vote share (2011)	.007**	.003	.012***	.003			.008***	.003
PSL vote share (2011)					−.006*	.003		
PO mayor (2006 and 2010)	−.016	.066	−.088	.065	−.046	.068	−.022	.062
PSL mayor (2006 and 2010)	.020	.065	.033	.062	.025	.062	.019	.065
Regional-level fixed effects								
GDP per capita	.315*	.169	.436***	.149	.323	.201	.284*	.168
Regional unemployment rate	.080**	.036	.090**	.038	.096**	.042	.077**	.036
Quality of government index	.591	.430	.602*	.337	.565*	.288	.534	.423
Eastern region	.280**	.110	.344***	.121	.229*	.118	.300***	.110
PO–PSL seat share (2010)	−.001	.006	−.001	.006	.003	.006	.000	.006
Cross-level interactions								
Population * GDP							−.292***	.061
Random effects								
Gmina-level variance	.842***		.881***		.887***		.839***	
Regional-level variance	.014***		.013***		.014***		.014***	
−2Log likelihood	−6,625		−6,736		−6,756		−6,616	
Wald Chi-square	1,382.4***		338.8***		883.9***		3,172.9***	

Note: Unstandardized coefficients, robust standard errors. * $p < .1$; ** $p < .05$; *** $p < .01$. The 2007 local-level vote shares produce identical results.

across the models, the regions' political alignment with the central government does not show any relationship to the outcome. However, the other regional indicators reveal an interesting pattern. Regional GDP per capita shows a positive and significant coefficient in all of the specifications, which implies that on average more funds were spent in *gminas* located in richer voivodeships, all else being equal. At the same time, the indicator of regional unemployment and the dummy for the most backward eastern regions are positively and significantly associated with EU grants.

This suggests that regional factors draw funds in opposite directions. In practice, their effects cancel each other out because localities in the most backward regions did not receive a substantially higher amount of funds than those in the more developed areas. The average EU grant per capita in the 708 *gminas* of the five poorest voivodeships was equal to 4,567 PLN (€1,142), whereas it was marginally lower, 4,476 PLN (€1,119) in the other 1,770 *gminas*.

Model 4 also tested for the cross-level effect between local population and regional GDP per capita. The negative interaction term would imply that the concentration of EU funds in more populated (i.e. urban) localities is stronger in poorer than in rather more affluent voivodeships, if all other conditions are the same. However, this effect is statistically not different across the voivodeships because the confidence intervals (not reported here) overlap even if the poorest and the richest regions are compared. All else being the same, *gminas* with fewer inhabitants tend to receive less funds per capita regardless of whether they are located in a prosperous or a backward region.

Tables 15.2 and 15.3 display the results of the Hungarian models for the funds distributed during the socialist and conservative governments respectively (for descriptive statistics, see Table 15.A2 in the Appendix). The coefficients reveal that the effects of most of the local socio-economic factors benefit the wealthier localities: population size, the density of private companies and the local governments' own budget revenue per capita are positively and significantly related to EU funds. Moreover, the absence of NGOs has a significant negative association with the dependent variable, which implies that per capita grants are, on average, lower in those local governments that lack civil society organizations.[12] Only local unemployment rates draw funds into the underprivileged localities, but the positive relationship between unemployment rate and EU funds applies only to the period of the socialist–liberal coalition; the significance of this effect disappears during the Fidesz government.

These results suggest that, all else being the same, the richer and the more populous localities and those with greater economic activity manage to accumulate more grants. This is in line with the Polish results and provides strong empirical evidence for the presence of an economic bias in fund distribution. Uniform fund eligibility is disadvantageous precisely for those localities that are in the greatest need of development support.

Although most of the local socio-economic indicators pull funds to the more developed localities, the regional-level factors moderate these effects. All else being equal, higher regional wealth is associated with lower funds per inhabitant,

Table 15.2 Results of the multi-level Tobit models for Hungary (DV: EU funding per capita awarded during the socialist government).

	Model 5		Model 6		Model 7		Model 8	
	B	SE	B	SE	B	SE	B	SE
Constant	4.091***	.355	4.060***	.356	3.962***	.350	4.024***	.349
Local-level effects								
Population size (2007)	3.476***	.162	3.459***	.162	4.122***	.184	4.131***	.184
Own revenue (2007)	1.198***	.195	1.202***	.195	1.216***	.194	1.216***	.194
Private companies per 1,000 inhabitants (2007)	1.523**	.350	1.521***	.349	1.704***	.351	1.715***	.350
Unemployment rate (2007)	.066**	.029	.060**	.029	.064**	.029	.061**	.029
No NGOs (2007)	−4.392***	.793	−4.429***	.795	−3.572***	.797	−3.545***	.797
MSZP–SZDSZ vote share (2006)	−.009	.015	−.008	.015	−.015	.015	−.015	.015
Government mayor (2006)	−1.475**	.671	−1.465**	.671	1.384	.887	1.391	.887
Opposition mayor (2006)	−1.265**	.546	−1.261**	.546	.922	.675	.925	.675
Mayor also government MP (2006)	−1.464	1.490	−1.522	1.490	−1.270	1.473	−1.978	1.691
Mayor also opposition MP (2006)	−.809	1.326	−1.316	1.797	−1.168	1.784	−1.174	1.785
Regional-level effects								
GDP per capita (2007)	−3.538**	1.425	−3.956***	1.444	−3.229**	1.397		
Regional unemployment rate (2007)							.234**	.100
Government vote share (2006)	.187**	.072	.182**	.072	.190***	.071	.173**	.071
MSZP–SZDSZ MP (2006)	−.139	.358	−.168	.358	.038	.356	.034	.356

(continued)

Table 15.2 (continued)

	Model 5		Model 6		Model 7		Model 8	
	B	SE	B	SE	B	SE	B	SE
Interaction effects								
Population * government mayor					−2.312***	.433	−2.318***	.433
Population * opposition mayor					−2.140***	.340	−2.147***	.340
Population * government vote share					−.089***	.027	−.088***	.027
Population * mayor also government MP					.988	1.065	.999	1.066
Own revenue * GDP			1.556*	.843				
Random effects								
Sigma_u (random intercept SD)	1.143***	.232	1.144***	.232	1.113***	.226	1.098***	.228
Sigma_e (overall SD)	7.094***	.134	7.091***	.134	7.022***	.132	7.022***	.132
Rho	.025	.010	.025	.010	.024	.010	.024	.010
N (uncensored)	3,135 (1,767)		3,135 (1,767)		3,135 (1,767)		3,135 (1,767)	
−2Log likelihood	−13,783		−13,779		−13,714		−13,714	
Wald Chi-square	1,052.3***		1,054.1***		1,096.2***		1,097.9***	

Note: Unstandardized coefficients. * p < .1; ** p < .05; *** p < .01.

Table 15.3 Results of the multi-level Tobit models for Hungary (DV: EU funding per capita awarded during the conservative government).

	Model 9		Model 10		Model 11		Model 12	
	B	SE	B	SE	B	SE	B	SE
Constant	7.333***	.275	7.280***	.264	7.450***	.220	7.519***	.169
Local-level effects								
Population size (2010)	2.229***	.122	2.210***	.122	2.725***	.138	2.745***	.135
Own revenue (2010)	1.596***	.146	1.601***	.146	1.526***	.145	1.509***	.145
Private companies per 1,000 inhabitants (2010)	.544**	.267	.571**	.266	.606**	.261	.518**	.256
Unemployment rate (2010)	−.014	.021	−.022	.021	−.006	.020	−.022	.020
No NGOs (2010)	−2.580***	.568	−2.596***	.567	−1.907***	.569	−1.901***	.567
Fidesz vote share (2010)	.004	.013	.003	.013	−.004	.012	−.001	.012
Government mayor (2010)	.085	.312	.063	.311	.452	.331	.425	.331
Opposition mayor (2010)	−.744	.862	−.665	.860	.735	1.016	.784	1.016
Mayor also government MP (2010)	−2.301***	.782	−2.313***	.781	3.381**	1.433	3.352**	1.432
Regional-level effects								
GDP per capita (2010)	−3.860**	1.314	−4.413***	1.270	−3.231***	1.051		
Regional unemployment rate (2010)							.315***	.058
Government vote share (2010)	−.154**	.061	−.146**	.058	−.162***	.048	−.143***	.038

(continued)

Table 15.3 (continued)

	Model 9		Model 10		Model 11		Model 12	
	B	SE	B	SE	B	SE	B	SE
Interaction effects								
Population * government mayor					−.943***	.229	−.941***	.229
Population * opposition mayor					−1.516***	.543	−1.574***	.542
Population * government vote share					.136***	.019	.135***	.019
Population * mayor also government MP					−1.871***	.505	−1.879***	.504
Own revenue * GDP			2.571***	.629				
Random effects								
Sigma_u (random intercept SD)	1.029***	.216	.975***	.209	.743***	.187	.450***	.167
Sigma_e (overall SD)	5.875***	.096	5.863***	.096	5.799***	.095	5.798***	.095
Rho	.030	.012	.027	.011	.016	.008	.006	.004
N (uncensored)	3,151 (2,234)		3,151 (2,234)		3,151 (2,234)		3,151 (2,234)	
−2Log likelihood	−15,911		−15,894		−15,814		−15,803	
Wald Chi-square	1,027.4***		1,048.4***		1,163.5***		1,274.2***	

Note: Unstandardized coefficients. * $p < .1$; ** $p < .05$; *** $p < .01$.

while a higher regional unemployment rate is related to more per capita grants for the locality. Thus, if two local governments show exactly the same features, then the one that lies in a poorer region or where the regional unemployment rate is higher will be likely to secure more funds.

But to what extent do the regional conditions modify the effect of the local indicators? The significant positive cross-level interaction between local government revenue and regional GDP (Models 6 and 10) reveals that among equally poor local governments, those that lie in a poorer region would earn more funds. Thus, in terms of per capita grants, regional prosperity is disadvantageous whereas regional backwardness is beneficial for poor local governments. To put it differently, the gap between per capita EU grants secured by the relatively rich and the poorer local governments is greater in more prosperous than in backward regions. In spite of this mitigating effect, wealthy local governments remain the greatest beneficiaries of the funds in each region regardless of its level of development.

The regional-level political variables reveal an interesting pattern. While *ceteris paribus* a higher regional vote share for the government at the 2006 elections is associated with more EU grants spent in the corresponding localities, the relationship is negative in the case of the regional electoral popularity of Fidesz at the 2010 elections. This suggests that the left-wing government rewarded its relative strongholds with more funds, which corresponds to the argument of Kemmerling and Bodenstein (2006) who claim that left-leaning areas would receive more development support. At the same time, Fidesz steered resources to those regions where its support was somewhat lower and where it had to face greater political competition, which is in line with the findings of Bouvet and Dall'Erba (2010).

Because of the different political circumstances during the two parliamentary cycles, both strategies seem rational. In the 2006–10 period, the government faced a powerful opposition, the popularity of which was rising steeply. In this situation, the socialists may have anticipated some limited rewards by adopting a defensive approach and trying to maintain their support in the strongholds by pumping in more EU funds there. Conversely, after the 2010 parliamentary elections, Fidesz became the most powerful party. The lowest regional vote share for Fidesz (45 per cent) was nearly twice as high than the best regional result of the second-placed socialists (25 per cent). Having established a dominant position, the Fidesz government chose to provide more funds to those regions where its popularity was relatively low.

The political effects are further elaborated in Models 7, 8, 11 and 12, which estimate the cross-level interaction between local population size and the regional vote shares. The estimates reveal that during the socialist government especially, the lowly populated localities had a higher chance of receiving funds if they were located in regions where the government was more popular. Conversely, during the Fidesz government, those small local governments that belonged to counties where the governing party was less popular were likely to secure more funds, all else being equal. Relative to large localities, the less populous ones possess fewer capabilities for securing funds, so it is not surprising that the regional political factor had greater influence in the smaller localities.

The other political variables that demonstrate a notable association with EU funds are the partisanship of the mayors and the parliamentary presence of government-nominated local leaders. At first, it is puzzling that the dummies for mayors with a party affiliation show a negative sign in those models that estimate only their main effects (Models 5 and 6) during the socialist period. The reason for this counterintuitive result is that as population size increases, the chance for a local government to secure grants rises. Furthermore, the vast majority of the most populous localities, which are predicted to have the highest amount of per capita EU grants, tend to elect partisan mayors. However, in both periods, the top beneficiaries of the funds were typically small and middle-sized localities with independent mayors. Partisan mayors are thus rare among the localities with the best grant-securing performance. At the same time, the most populous localities, whose record of securing EU funds is inferior compared to the top group, are almost exclusively led by partisan mayors. This is the reason why, after controlling for the positive main effect of population size, the local leaders' party affiliation produces a negative sign unless the interaction terms are also introduced.

Accordingly, the interaction between the mayors' party affiliation and the population size of the localities (Models 7, 8, 11 and 12) reveals that the partisanship of local leaders modifies the effect of population size. More specifically, among equally small localities, those that elect partisan mayors are likely to secure more funds. This is because in lowly populated localities the local government is usually the sole entity capable of preparing project applications. In such circumstances, a partisan mayor may rely on a broad political network that gives access to influential decision-makers. Because similar connections are presumably unavailable for independent local leaders, it is more difficult for them to mobilize support for the projects. Models 11 and 12 also show that during the conservative government the presence of a Fidesz-affiliated mayor who was also serving as an MP generated greater per capita funds for the locality, all else being equal. As the corresponding interaction terms suggest, this factor also greatly mitigated the negative effect of population size, especially in the case of small localities.

Overall, the spatial distribution of funds suggests that EU grants have not concentrated in the most backward areas in Hungary. In the entire programming period, 951 localities received some EU support in the six poorest counties, which, on average, amounted to 618,000 HUF (€2,060) per capita. In contrast, the mean funds per inhabitant reached 491,000 HUF (€1,637) in the other 1,471 localities benefitting from the grants. The difference between the means of these two groups is only marginally significant.[13] This suggests that the regions with the greatest need for development grants did not enjoy clear advantages over the more advanced areas.

Conclusion

The above analysis suggests that mechanisms similar to those in Western Europe may determine the distribution of EU grants in ECE; both an economic and a political bias seem to influence the distribution of funds. On the one hand, uniform fund eligibility promotes the relatively more prosperous areas, but, on the other hand, central government control allows for political considerations to play a role in funding decisions.

Both in Poland and Hungary the richer localities have absorbed higher per capita EU grants. Local affluence thus shows a strong positive association with the amount of EU funds spent in a locality. While in both countries the regional-level economic factors modify the effect of the local variables to a certain extent, this impact is not unambiguous because regional economic circumstances seem to pull funds in opposite directions. This is the reason why neither the most underprivileged nor the most advanced regions have been clear beneficiaries of the EU's support.

In addition, while per capita funds are positively associated with the local popularity of the main governing party in Poland, the Hungarian analysis revealed that both local and regional political factors have influenced the flow of funds. In Hungary, EU grants have been steered either to the strongholds of the incumbent party (during the socialist government) or to regions where the incumbent party was less popular (during the conservative government). Furthermore, the partisanship of local government leaders and their presence in the parliament seems to bring additional EU funds, especially to smaller localities.

All things considered, the distribution of EU funds does not satisfy the concentration principle of the EU's Cohesion Policy. Instead, the more affluent localities have benefited more from the grants, which means that EU support has contributed to intra-regional disparities and at the same time failed to reduce inter-regional development gaps. While it may not be possible to eliminate political bias entirely from the fund distribution process, economic bias could perhaps be mitigated if, instead of applying an EU-wide benchmark, the fund eligibility of the regions was determined according to their internal development positions. This would allow for greater differentiation between the more advanced and the less prosperous areas and would possibly lower the relevance of the economic effects on fund distribution.

Appendix

Table 15.A1 Descriptive statistics of the Polish variables (original scales, N = 2,478).

	Min.	Max.	Mean	SD	Skewness	Kurtosis
EU funds per capita	48.6 PLN	143,286 PLN	4,502 PLN	8,098 PLN	7.2	80.2
Population size (2007)	1,370	1,706,624	15,382	50,700	19.9	558.4
Tax revenue (2007)	72.1 PLN	18,447 PLN	384.9 PLN	445.6 PLN	27.6	1,092.9
Own revenue (2007)	239.4 PLN	33,299 PLN	932.8 PLN	909.3 PLN	19.8	659.7
Private companies per 1,000 inhabitants (2007)	21.8	375.9	66.5	30.6	2.4	16.8
Unemployment rate (2007)	1.3%	31.2%	8.9%	4.1%	.76	3.7
NGOs per 1,000 inhabitants (2007)	.24	8.9	2.2	.83	1.3	7.1
PO vote share (2007)	2.4%	69.6%	29.9%	13.7%	.15	2.1
PO vote share (2011)	1.73%	70.3%	29.1%	13.5%	.08	1.9
PSL vote share (2007)	1.63%	72.7%	16.8%	10.8%	1.0	4.2
PSL vote share (2011)	1.1%	76.6%	16.3%	10.9%	.98	3.9
GDP per capita (2007)	20,895 PLN	49,350 PLN	29,937 PLN	8,408 PLN	1.3	3.9
Regional unemployment rate (2007)	5.1%	10.7%	7.4%	1.7%	.39	1.9
Quality of government index	−.22	.29	−.02	.12	.42	3.4
PO–PSL seat share (2006)	36.7%	60.6%	48.4%	6.3%	.29	1.9
PO–PSL seat share (2010)	42.4%	70.0%	56.3%	7.3%	−.21	2.4

Table 15.A2 Descriptive statistics of the Hungarian variables (original scales without Budapest, N = 3,151).

	Min.	Max.	Mean	SD	Skewness	Kurtosis
EU funds per capita (2007)	0 HUF	14,906,647 HUF	131,552 HUF	557,848 HUF	13.9	264.7
EU funds per capita (2010)	0 HUF	40,177,768 HUF	284,201 HUF	1,259,739 HUF	19.9	503.7
Tax revenue (2007) (N = 3,090)	7 HUF	776,206 HUF	15,358 HUF	32,768 HUF	10.7	193
Tax revenue (2010) (N = 3,150)	0 HUF	604,618 HUF	16,657 HUF	32,447 HUF	7.9	98.8
Own revenue (2007)	27 HUF	863,583 HUF	28,798 HUF	40,808 HUF	8.2	125.6
Own revenue (2010)	4 HUF	716,051 HUF	34,226 HUF	45,514 HUF	5.9	59.6
Private companies per 1,000 inhabitants (2007) (N = 3,143)	0	446	70.6	41.3	2.1	11.0
Private companies per 1,000 inhabitants (2010)	4	645	141	70.5	1.4	7.1
Unemployment rate (2007) (N = 3,144)	0%	48.8%	11.3%	7.9%	1.2	4.6
Unemployment rate (2010)	0%	51.1%	13.3%	7.9%	1.2	4.5
Population size (2007)	16	206,073	2,690	9,240	12.3	201.8
Population size (2010)	13	205,468	2,673	12.3	12.3	200.9
MSZP–SZDSZ vote share (2006) (N = 3,143)	0%	99.4%	43.4%	12.1%	.05	3.1
Fidesz vote share (2010)	20.8%	98.6%	60.6%	11.1%	-.04	3.1
GDP per capita (2007)	1,143,000 HUF	2,811,000 HUF	1,858,100 HUF	408,445 HUF	.71	3.1
GDP per capita (2010)	1,201,000 HUF	3,138,000 HUF	1,948,591 HUF	434,986 HUF	1.0	4.1
Regional unemployment rate (2007)	2.8%	13.4%	8.2%	3.4%	.03	1.8
Regional unemployment rate (2010)	4.5%	15.9%	10.3%	3.4%	-.04	1.9
Government vote share (2006)	41.4%	55.4%	48.1%	22.2%	.12	1.7
Government vote share (2010)	46.0%	63.2%	54.9%	25.0%	-.39	2.3

Notes

1 The chapter analyses the distribution of Structural Funds and does not consider projects financed from the Cohesion Fund.
2 In the 2000–6 period, Objective 1 regions were those where GDP per capita was below 75 per cent of the EU average. They were eligible for the highest amount of EU support. In the 2007–13 period, the Convergence Regions replaced this category.
3 The five NUTS2 regions that received funds from the multi-regional OP were Warmińsko-Mazurskie, Podlaskie, Lubelskie, Podkarpackie and Świętokrzyskie.
4 Source: official website on the European funds in Poland (*Portal Funduszy Europejskich*), List of Beneficiaries, www.funduszeeuropejskie.2007-2013.gov.pl/ NaborWnioskow/Strony/Naborwnioskow.aspx?strona=1&zakladka=4.
5 Source: Department for Monitoring and Evaluation of the Prime Minister's Office.
6 Indicators at the *gmina* level: total own tax revenue per inhabitant, private companies per 1,000 inhabitants, unemployment rate, population size, per capita number of foundations, associations and social organizations. Indicators at the regional level: the voivodeships' GDP per capita, regional unemployment rate, share of PO and PSL representatives in the regional councils after the last two local elections (2006 and 2010), the quality of regional government index (Charron *et al.*, 2014), a dummy variable indicating whether the voivodeship received funds from the Development of Eastern Poland OP.
7 Indicators at the local level: population size, the local government's per capita tax and own budget revenue, private companies per 1,000 inhabitants, unemployment rate, a dummy variable showing the presence of civil organizations. Indicators at the regional level: GDP per capita, unemployment rate. The quality of government index is not available for the Hungarian counties, so it cannot be included in the models.
8 Besides the capital city of Budapest, the most populous towns in Hungary incorporate more than one single-member districts. In their case, the dummy variable indicates whether a government-affiliated candidate won a mandate in the parliamentary elections in at least one of those city districts.
9 There is a strong association between the Polish indicators of local government affluence but the strength of the same relationships was weaker in the Hungarian case. In order to avoid problems of collinearity, these indicators were treated separately in the Polish models. Furthermore, as expected, the share of votes for the PO and the PSL are also strongly negatively correlated, so these measures were also used separately. Those regional-level variables that demonstrated relatively strong associations were treated separately as well.
10 Both the Polish and the Hungarian dependent variables were logarithmically transformed to normalize their distribution. A similar transformation was carried out on those continuous indicators that also demonstrated considerable right-skew (transformed Polish variables: tax revenue per capita, private companies per 1,000 inhabitants, population size, NGOs per 1,000 inhabitants, regional GDP per capita; transformed Hungarian variables: local government revenue per capita, private companies per 1,000 inhabitants, population size, regional GDP). To facilitate the interpretation of the results, all of the continuous explanatory variables were centred on the country means.
11 The alpha score of the three indicators (PO vote shares (taking either the 2007 or the 2011 values), per capita tax revenue, private companies) is 0.11 but the score for the two indicators of tax revenue and private companies is .68. Pairing PO vote shares either with tax revenue or private companies produces even lower alpha scores (below 0.1). Replacing PO vote shares with PSL vote shares does not influence the results.
12 This finding is different from the one obtained in the Polish case. However, in a strict sense, the two variables are not comparable to each other because the Hungarian measure of NGO presence is a simple binary indicator whereas the Polish one shows the number of registered non-profit organizations per 1,000 inhabitants. In this respect,

there is a qualitative difference between the two variables, which may also explain the differences in the results.

13 Assuming equal variances across the two groups, the independent samples t-test is significant at the 90 per cent confidence level: $t(2420) = 1.948$, $p < .1$.

References

Bachtler, J. and McMaster, I. (2007), "EU Cohesion Policy and the role of the regions: investigating the influence of Structural Funds in the new member states", *Environment and Planning C: Government and Policy*, 26(2), 398–427.

Bloom, S. and Petrova, V. (2013), "National subversion of supranational goals: 'pork-barrel' politics and EU regional aid", *Europe-Asia Studies*, 65(8), 1599–620.

Bodenstein, T. and Kemmerling, A. (2011), "Ripples in a rising tide: why some EU regions receive more Structural Funds than others", *European Integration Online Papers (EIoP)*, 16(Article 1), available at: http://eiop.or.at/eiop/texte/2012-001a.htm (accessed 22 February 2016).

Bouvet, F. and Dall'Erba, S. (2010), "European regional Structural Funds: how large is the influence of politics on the allocation process?", *Journal of Common Market Studies*, 48(3), 501–28.

Buzogány, Á. and Korkut, U. (2013), "Administrative reform and regional development discourses in Hungary: Europeanisation going NUTS?", *Europe-Asia Studies*, 65(8), 1555–77.

Cadot, O., Röller, L.-H. and Stephan, A. (2006), "Contribution to productivity or pork barrel? The two faces of infrastructure investment", *Journal of Public Economics*, 90(6–7), 1133–53.

Castells, A. and Solé-Ollé, A. (2005), "The regional allocation of infrastructure investment: the role of equity, efficiency and political factors", *European Economic Review*, 49(5), 1165–205.

Charron, N., Dijkstra, L. and Lapuente, V. (2014), "Regional governance matters: quality of government within European Union member states", *Regional Studies*, 48(1), 68–90.

Csengődi, S., Csite, A., Felföldi, Z. and Juhász, M. (2006), "Az I. nemzeti fejlesztési terv forráselosztási mechanizmusai: hét kistérség fejlesztési tapasztalatai" ["The resource allocation mechanism of the first national development plan: experiences of seven microregions"], *Európai Tükör*, 11(9), 74–92.

Dąbrowski, M. (2012), "Shallow or deep Europeanisation? The uneven impact of EU Cohesion Policy on the regional and local authorities in Poland", *Environment and Planning C: Government and Policy*, 30(4), 730–45.

Dąbrowski, M. (2014), "Towards place-based regional and local development strategies in Central and Eastern Europe? EU Cohesion Policy and strategic planning capacity at the sub-national level", *Local Economy*, 29(4-5), 378–93.

Dellmuth, L. M. (2011), "The cash divide: the allocation of European Union regional grants", *Journal of European Public Policy*, 18(7), 1016–33.

Dellmuth, L. M. and Stoffel, M. F. (2012), "Distributive politics and intergovernmental transfers: the local allocation of European Union Structural Funds", *European Union Politics*, 13(3), 413–33.

Ederveen, S., de Groot, H. L. F. and Nahuis, R. (2006), "Fertile soil for Structural Funds? A panel data analysis of the conditional effectiveness of European Cohesion Policy", *Kyklos*, 59(1), 17–42.

Ferry, M. and McMaster, I. (2013), "Cohesion Policy and the evolution of regional policy in Central and Eastern Europe", *Europe-Asia Studies*, 65(8), 1502–28.

Grabbe, H. (2001), "How does Europeanization affect CEE governance? Conditionality, diffusion and diversity", *Journal of European Public Policy*, 8(6), 1013–31.

Heitshusen, V., Young, G. and Wood, D. M. (2005), "Electoral context and MP constituency focus in Australia, Canada, Ireland, New Zealand, and the United Kingdom", *American Journal of Political Science*, 49(1), 32–45.

Hox, J. (2010), *Multilevel Analysis: Techniques and Applications*, second edition, New York: Routledge.

Ion, E. (2014), "Public funding and urban governance in contemporary Romania: the resurgence of state-led urban development in an era of crisis", *Cambridge Journal of Regions, Economy and Society*, 7(1), 171–87.

Kálmán, J. (2011), *Derangement or Development? Political Economy of EU Structural Funds Allocation in New Member States: Insights from the Hungarian Case*, Budapest, Hungary: Center for Policy Studies, Central European University, available at: https://cps.ceu.hu/sites/default/files/publications/cps-working-paper-eu-structural-funds-hungary-2011.pdf (accessed 22 February 2016).

Kemmerling, A. and Stephan, A. (2002), "The politico-economic determinants and productivity effects of regional transport investment in Europe", *European Investment Bank Papers*, 13(2), 36–60.

Kemmerling, A. and Bodenstein, T. (2006), "Partisan politics in regional redistribution do parties affect the distribution of EU Structural Funds across regions?", *European Union Politics*, 7(3), 373–92.

Kule, L., Krisjane, Z. and Berzins, M. (2011), "The rhetoric and reality of pursuing territorial cohesion in Latvia", in N. Adams, G. Cotella and R. Nunes (eds), *Territorial Developmemt, Cohesion and Spatial Planning, Regions and Cities*, London and New York: Routledge, pp. 291–319.

Le Gallo, J., Dall'Erba, S. and Guillain, R. (2011), "The local versus global dilemma of the effects of Structural Funds", *Growth and Change*, 42(4), 466–90.

Milio, S. (2007), "Can administrative capacity explain differences in regional performances? Evidence from Structural Funds implementation in Southern Italy", *Regional Studies*, 41(4), 429–42.

Milligan, K. and Smart, M. (2005), "Regional grants as pork barrel politics", *CESifo Working Papers* (1453), available at: www.econstor.eu/dspace/bitstream/10419/18817/1/cesifo1_wp1453.pdf (accessed 22 February 2016).

Pálné Kovács, I., Paraskevopoulos, C. J. and Horváth, G. (2004), "Institutional 'legacies' and the shaping of regional governance in Hungary", *Regional and Federal Studies*, 14(3), 430–60.

Papp, Z. (2013), *Legislators' Constituency Orientation under Party-Centred Electoral Rules: Evidence from Hungary*, Budapest, Hungary: Institute of Political Science, Corvinus University of Budapest.

Pilet, J.-B., Freire, A. and Costa, O. (2012), "Ballot structure, district magnitude and constituency-orientation of MPs in proportional representation and majority electoral systems", *Representation*, 48(4), 359–72.

Tobin, J. (1958), "Estimation of relationships for limited dependent variables", *Econometrica*, 26(1), 24–36.

Weingast, B. R., Shepsle, K. A. and Johnsen, C. (1981), "The political economy of benefits and costs: a neoclassical approach to distributive politics", *Journal of Political Economy*, 89(4), 642–64.

Wooldridge, J. (2012), *Introductory Econometrics: A Modern Approach*, Mason, OH: South Western College, Cengage Learning.

Zarycki, T. (2000), "Politics in the periphery: political cleavages in Poland interpreted in their historical and international context", *Europe-Asia Studies*, 52(5), 851–73.

16 The administrative capacity of the sub-national level in implementing Cohesion Policy in Romania
Lessons learnt and future recommendations

Septimiu-Rares Szabo

Introduction

The administrative capacity of the institutions involved in the management of EU Funds is directly correlated with the performance of Cohesion Policy. Consequently, for the 2014–20 period, the Commission made funding conditional on enhanced good governance. While the situation is often assessed at the central government level, the sub-national level also needs particular attention. Ever since the 1988 Cohesion Policy reform and the Treaty of Maastricht, the regional dimension of governance has been steadily increasing in significance in many parts of the EU as the sub-national authorities acquire more autonomy and more responsibilities. This increasing significance can be seen in the fact that around 55 per cent of total public investment in the EU28 in 2013 was carried out by sub-national authorities (European Commission, 2014), although the proportions vary considerably between countries. Nonetheless, responsibility for undertaking these investments does not automatically mean the devolution of decision-making powers. This is particularly true in Central and Eastern Europe, which does not have a tradition of empowering sub-national authorities. However, Cohesion Policy specifically requires central governments to devolve some responsibilities. Still, apart from Poland, the management systems in Central and Eastern Europe remain highly centralised. Romania is no exception. Systems in both the 2007–13 and 2014–20 periods were designed without decentralising much authority from Bucharest. Nonetheless, the creation of Regional Development Agencies (RDAs) as Intermediate Bodies (IBs) for the Regional Operational Programme (ROP) can be seen as good practice in the application of the partnership principle. Created at the request of the EU, these entities, located outside the public apparatus, managed to contribute decisively to the perceived success of the ROP. The current chapter looks into their capacity as compared to that of the other regional actors and, based on those observations, proposes some ways in which the partnership principle could be further developed in the next financial periods so that the impact of Cohesion Policy in Romania can be maximised.

Cohesion Policy in Romania

Romania has consistently been the EU member state with the lowest absorption rate. After eight years of implementation, the rate has only marginally passed 50 per cent, around 20 per cent below the EU average. While in the past years the situation has significantly improved,[1] Romania still lags behind its neighbours. Consequently, the European Commission (2014) estimated that the increase in GDP by 2022 as a result of Cohesion Policy will amount to only 2.4 per cent, much lower than the 4.1 per cent increase estimated for Poland.

As confirmed in the recent Country Specific Recommendations (Council of the European Union, 2014), the administrative capacity of the Romanian institutions has been a major factor in the low absorption rate. Many institutions faced a shortage and high turnover of staff, low salaries and limited technical expertise (Ecorys Lideea, 2013). This led to delays in contracting, evaluations and payments, a lack of strategic planning and mostly public procurement irregularities. In some serious cases, the European Commission decided to apply significant financial corrections and pre-suspensions or temporary suspensions of payments. Excessive bureaucracy, long and cumbersome public procurement procedures and a lack of national coordination were also significant factors. The structure of Cohesion Policy in Romania in the 2007–13 period was designed in a highly centralised way with all Managing Authorities (MAs) and almost all IBs located within the central government structures. Three types of regional IBs were created in 2007: RDAs for the ROP, regional directorates under the MA for the Environment/Major Infrastructure programme and regional bodies subordinated to the Ministry of Labour for the HR Development/Human Capital (HRD) programme. All these bodies will continue to act as IBs in the 2014–20 period.

Regional development and Cohesion Policy

The only legal levels recognised in the constitution are the county level, created in 1968, and the city/commune level. Nonetheless, in 1999, when negotiating the accession terms, the Romanian government agreed to create an additional regional layer with eight NUTS2 development regions established as voluntary associations without administrative status, legal personality or allocated funding, and therefore with no decision-making powers. In the 2000s, subsequent governments slowly entrusted the local and county levels with growing responsibilities, and currently there is a political desire to legalise the regional layer of government and, among other things, entrust it with the management of EU Funds.

Eight years after accession, there are still significant economic discrepancies between the eight regions. While Bucharest-Ilfov has reached 122 per cent of the EU average in terms of GDP per capita, the North-East region remains below 30 per cent and all of the others oscillate between 37 and 54 per cent (Eurostat, 2014). Thus, the government decided to mandate the Ministry of Regional Development, the Regional Development Councils (RDCs)[2] and the eight RDAs to reduce the disparities via several instruments, including the 2000–6 PHARE ESC programme and

Implementing Cohesion Policy in Romania 243

the ROP. However, as concluded in the *Competitive Cities* report (Ionescu-Heroiu et al., 2013), the eight regions have very different needs in terms of investments. While richer regions need to improve the quality of life and connectivity to surrounding areas, lagging regions still need significant investments in basic institutions and infrastructure. Nonetheless, although less developed regions were favoured, both the PHARE ESC programme and the ROP promoted equal and homogeneous funding opportunities.

Being outside the administrative apparatus and thereby beyond the reach of political interests, the RDAs were able to initiate longer-term strategic plans, including their own policies regarding recruitment and payrolls (Halkier, 2006). Nonetheless, due to their unique non-governmental status, the cooperation with the MA for the ROP, which had a tendency to micro-manage and duplicate the work of the RDAs, did not start particularly well (Harding, 2006). Still, despite some financial and staff turnover issues,[3] the RDAs managed to steadily increase their capacity for managing funds in the pre-accession period. After 2007, these bodies were also given a role in the cross-border cooperation programmes and the competitiveness programme.

The capacity of the other regional IBs varies. While the HRD programme IBs were used to implement PHARE ESC projects, the environmental IBs were created only when the new period started. Unlike RDAs, all of these IBs are public institutions employing mostly civil servants, who are difficult to recruit and more difficult to lay off. Thus, in 2007, most of them were lacking personnel. Even in 2014, the IBs under the HRD programme employed fewer than 50 people, while those under the environment programme employed between 10 and 20. Staff turnover, however, tends to remain low. In the evaluation report of the HRD programme (KPMG Romania, 2011), it was hinted that the division of tasks is not always respected as the ministry tends to micro-manage the IBs. Thus, these regional IBs also tend to be less known and less visible to potential beneficiaries. The environment IBs faced was high staff turnover in the early years due to low salaries and difficulties in recruiting qualified personnel. The evaluations of the programme (East West Consulting, 2013) suggest that the cooperation between the MA and the IBs is rather bureaucratic and that IBs have barely any role in the decision-making process. Nonetheless, the evaluation reports suggest that most IBs work efficiently within their given mandate.

The perceived success of the Romanian Regional Operational Programme

The ROP has been perceived as the most successful programme in Romania despite its complex and diverse portfolio of projects. The ROP has an allocation of €3.7 billion, making it the third largest programme after transport and environment. Its performance is explained by the fact that it is the most decentralised programme while also benefiting from experienced people in the MA and the RDAs. By the end of 2014, the ROP reached a commitment rate[4] of 117.7 per cent.

244 *Septimiu-Rares Szabo*

Nonetheless, at a rate of 57.14 per cent, the absorption rate still lags behind those of other ROPs in Central and Eastern Europe.

The MA maintains overall responsibility for management and implementation, but has delegated specific tasks to the eight RDAs and a centrally-run IB, Tourism. The IBs support potential beneficiaries with their applications, launch calls for proposals, assess the eligibility of applications, conclude project contracts, assess payment claims, monitor projects and contribute to the communication plan. While the ROP was not drafted in a truly top-down fashion and took into account the specificities of each region, it nonetheless favoured standardisation. The MA–IB relationship has been positive and collaborative, although the MA has been the dominant actor. The RDAs, while being service providers to the MA, which monitors and pays them based on their performance, have significant independence. They have been a tough partner for the MA as they did not respond directly to political pressures and most of the time were treated as equal partners in implementation. Overall, the division of tasks was effective, with the MA in charge of the strategic planning and coordination and the RDAs focused on the region-specific developments. However, there were times when the MA became overburdened with verifications and approvals designed to validate decisions at the RDA level, distracting it from the coordination tasks. Thus, a better definition of the RDAs' mandate in terms of the tasks they could reasonably accomplish with the available instruments would have probably led to even better results (Burduja et al., 2013a).

Due to their proximity, RDAs can respond quicker and better to emerging beneficiary needs. Even without significant decision-making powers, the RDAs created close working relations with many beneficiaries in their respective regions, earning their trust and respect, particularly when compared to other regional IBs. An RDA general director suggested that beneficiaries trust them because of their impartiality and that the ROP coordination model proved its viability. Thus, only 31.7 per cent of the 470 beneficiaries interviewed believed that RDAs have a low capacity, and only 8 per cent suggested that RDAs provided them with unsatisfactory assistance. As a result, only 4 per cent would not be interested in applying again for funding. It has to be mentioned, though, that the situation is far from perfect, and the capacity of several RDAs needs to be further improved. Some beneficiaries complained about the support received from RDAs in developing project applications and about the way the open calls were drafted. Furthermore, the less efficient coordination process undertaken by the MA generated some negative effects at the RDA level, creating delays in evaluations and payments (KPMG Romania, 2014). Nonetheless, all pitfalls aside, the RDAs are perceived as the main driving force behind localised regional development.

RDAs are also seen by their staff as autonomous, dynamic, fast-paced environments with significant promotion opportunities and decent wages, especially when compared with the other regional IBs. The fact that RDAs do not have to abide by all public-sector rules and procedures has led to a more efficient implementation when compared, for example, with the other IB under ROP, the Tourism IB, which struggled with resources. On the other hand, the fact that RDAs are monitored and paid based on performance indicators has significantly contributed to the internal effectiveness of all employees. Still, capacity and mechanisms for implementation vary across regions and there is little sharing of best practices or cooperation in general across the eight RDAs (Burduja et al., 2013a).

System architecture in future periods

In relation to the recent discussions about regionalisation and the responsibilities of future regions, in the past few years the government commissioned a couple of studies in order to investigate what future management systems might look like. In general, responsibilities could be retained at the national level, devolved to fully regionalised programmes or combined in mixed systems.[5] While it cannot be concluded which system is more efficient, Bähr (2008), after investigating the management structures in 13 EU countries between 1975 and 1995, suggested that Cohesion Policy is more effective in decentralised management systems. In the past few decades, the member states have started to empower sub-national authorities, although in many cases, particularly in Central and Eastern Europe, the role of the central government remains dominant.

Cohesion Policy regulations allow national governments to interpret the rules and adjust them as they see fit. Consequently, there are different set-ups in each member state. The Marshal's Offices set up in the 16 voivodeships in Poland were given the MA role for the 16 ROPs developed by the country for the 2007–13 period after having only a secondary role in the 2004–6 integrated centrally-run ROP. An additional programme focused on developing Eastern Poland was managed centrally. As these ROPs achieved better results than the national ones (Michie and Granqvist, 2013), for the 2014–20 period Poland decided to increase the allocation for the 16 multi-fund ROPs from 25 to 60 per cent. Initially, the system in the Czech Republic followed the same developments as in Poland, with centralisation in the 2004-2006 period followed by decentralisation in the 2007–13 period with eight ROPs and a centrally-run integrated programme. Nonetheless, the eight regional councils acting as MAs took different approaches in implementation and some have struggled with an unstable administrative capacity and staff turnover (Lanttanzio E Associati SpA, 2011). Thus, the Czech government decided to recentralise the system for the 2014–20 period by replacing seven ROPs with one integrated ROP managed centrally while continuing with a multi-fund ROP for Prague, managed by the City of Prague. Hungary also started with a centralised system in the 2004–6 period and then in the 2007–13 period switched to a system with seven centrally-run ROPs with RDAs as IBs. These were first put under the RDCs' control but were later moved under the central government's authority. For the 2014–20 period, Hungary proposed one ROP for the richer Central Hungary region and another integrated ROP for all of the other six regions, both managed centrally with the RDAs as IBs. Slovakia did not design any ROP in the 2004–6 period, but introduced two in the 2007–14 period: one for Bratislava and another one for the other three regions, both managed centrally with limited involvement of the sub-national level. For the 2014–20 period, Slovakia proposed only one centrally-run integrated ROP. Bulgaria proposed for both the 2007–13 and the 2014–20 periods only one integrated ROP, managed centrally with regional departments of the ministry as IBs.

As regards Romania, in a study commissioned by the ROP MA, Lanttanzio E Associati SpA (2011) proposed nine possible systems for redesigning future ROPs, divided into three main categories – centralised, mixed and decentralised – further divided into three systems – with only one integrated ROP, with two ROPs (one for Bucharest and one for the other seven regions) or with eight ROPs (one for each region of Romania). Among the strengths of the centralised system, the authors note unitary programming, the preservation of capacity in the same institutions, the fact that the co-financing is ensured from the state budget, a top-down approach as regards reducing the disparities between regions, and only minor amendments of the management and control system. On the negative side, the study suggests that the programming cannot fully integrate the regional specificities and that the central concentration weakens the link between the MA and the beneficiaries. While the system with eight ROPs handled by the ministry is still centrally driven, it seems to better take into account the particular regional necessities, as each programme is fully focused on a specific region and can include some bottom-up aspects. The mixed system is not very different from the centralised approach, since it foresees decentralisation only for the capital region, as seen in Hungary, the Czech Republic and Slovakia. Since Bucharest-Ilfov has quite different development needs compared to the other seven regions, the programme could be managed regionally. In the decentralised system, decisions could be taken more quickly and the strategic planning could be developed together with the beneficiaries. On the other hand, since the top-down approach would be almost entirely abandoned, the disparities between regions might actually increase. In addition, since the regionalisation process is not yet started, ensuring the programme's national co-financing would be difficult. Finally, the report suggests that without the central government's intervention, local governments would probably start competing with each other for higher allocations during the programme preparation phase. The decentralised system would need a radical modification of the current management system and, since Romania does not have yet a regional layer of administration with a legal identity, only an RDA or a similar body could realistically take over the role of MA in the region. The only exception would be in Bucharest-Ilfov where a potential metropolitan authority[6] could also be entrusted with the task.

Most beneficiaries would approve RDA-led ROPs as, in their view, the MA in Bucharest has been remote from the local problems. These ROPs could fund small and medium-sized regional- and local-level projects, while the ministry could continue with an integrated programme focused on strategic regional development. Based on further assessments and developments in the regionalisation process, the system could be further adjusted in order to reach an optimal set-up. However, RDAs should probably retain their current NGO status.[7] Most of them resist the idea of becoming public institutions, as this would lead to reduced independence from political pressures and constrain them to public-sector rules and procedures as regards recruitment and career developments (Burduja et al., 2013b).

On the other hand, both beneficiaries and RDAs could agree to continue with the current system as long as more tasks are devolved at the regional level. It can be argued that RDAs are not yet prepared to take over the task, since the MA role involves significant decision-making responsibilities that the RDAs could not acquire in only one financial period. To work efficiently, an MA needs strategic vision and coordination skills that are outside the RDA's responsibilities (Burduja et al., 2013a). In this regard, RDAs could encounter difficulties in achieving some of the strategic objectives within their regions (Bachtler and McMaster, 2007). In addition, barely any RDAs have been involved in negotiations at the international level. It should also be mentioned that national programmes have a somewhat lower workload and lower administrative costs compared to ROPs (Sweco International, 2010). Nonetheless, even if an integrated ROP is to be continued in the next period, the programme should fund more strategic and complex projects, across multiple priority axes and even across multiple OPs. In this regard, the programme should promote the competitive selection methods rather than the first-in-first-out procedure (Ionescu-Heroiu et al., 2014).

As the 2014–20 architecture is more or less decided (Government of Romania, 2014), practitioners should now focus on the 2021–7 period and maybe also on the 2028–34 period. With a consolidated administrative capacity after 21 years of managing EU Funds and 14 of managing post-accession funds, RDAs could probably receive more responsibilities. Nonetheless, since in the 2014–20 period they will probably continue with similar responsibilities as in the 2007–13 period, most of the RDAs will still not be prepared in 2021 to take over the role of MA from the ministry. If the regionalisation process is not completed by then, RDAs will probably have problems in providing the national co-financing and in redistributing public funds to beneficiaries. On the other hand, the centrally located MA should probably move to a framework with eight multi-fund (ERDF and ESF) ROPs, one for each region, rather than continuing with the integrated programme. In this regard, the regional IBs for the ESF programme could be integrated within the RDAs, which could then act as IBs for both programmes. Depending on future developments in the Bucharest-Ilfov region and future regulations, the MA could be either kept within the ministry or decentralised to the RDA or a potential metropolitan authority.

During the implementation of the aforementioned eight 2021–7 ROPs, the government should probably look into the possibility of devolving the role of MA for the 2028–34 period. It can be assumed that by the mid-2020s, Romania will have a revised constitution in which the regional layer is empowered with legal personality. Consequently, the ROPs proposed for the 2021–7 could be continued into the 2028–34 period with sub-national MAs. In one scenario, the non-governmental RDAs could be appointed in this role under the supervision of the regional governments/councils, which would provide the national co-financing for the ROPs. In another scenario, Romania could follow the Polish model and entrust the MA role directly to the regional governments/councils. In this case, the RDAs, with extensive responsibilities handed over, could continue acting as IBs. The central government could also propose some centrally-run integrated national programmes for reducing disparities between regions or some targeted programmes for the less developed areas of the country, similar to the Development of Eastern Poland programme. The government must also supervise carefully the handover process, as changes in implementation structures between programme periods may lead to difficult transition arrangements. As regards the environment IBs, these entities could be transformed into regional IBs for all of the national infrastructure sectoral programmes. While still under the supervision of the national government, these bodies should integrate some of the best practices seen in the RDAs.

Conclusions

Studies show that countries and regions with a weak administrative capacity do not make an effective use of Cohesion Policy, even though they need it the most (Begg, 2008). This is particularly true in the case of Romania. More than half a decade after accession, the GDP per capita in six regions out of eight remains below 50 per cent when compared with the EU27 average. On the other hand, one year before the final date of eligibility, half of the allocation made available by the EU has still not been absorbed. Consequently, the impact of Cohesion Policy in Romania remains limited.

In 2007, the lack of capacity and experience at the sub-national level was one of the reasons why the Commission did not really contest the adoption of a centralised implementation model. Nonetheless, it has continually urged the central authorities to implement the partnership principle and empower the sub-national authorities, especially in the area of regional development. While the government's reactions to this request were rather defensive, some of the sub-national actors became reliable partners for the implementation of Cohesion Policy. This applies particularly to the RDAs, which contributed decisively to the success of the ROP. Due to their unique non-governmental status, the RDAs proposed a different organisational culture focused on results-based management. As a result, these bodies earned the trust and respect of both the beneficiaries and the ministry. As they have slowly become the main driving force behind regional-level planning, it would be difficult at this point to imagine an ROP implemented without their involvement.

An increasing number of beneficiaries would welcome a redesign of the single integrated programme into eight ROPs, with the RDAs given an enhanced role. The fact that the ministry is inevitably removed from the problems encountered on the ground would justify this decision, because the RDAs have been there since the early 2000s responding quicker and better to emerging beneficiary needs. On the other hand, any radical change might undermine the accumulated institutional knowledge. Thus, the devolution of power should be made in small incremental steps. After assessing the situation in some other member states and the possible scenarios identified in a couple of reports commissioned by the Romanian authorities, this chapter proposes introducing in the 2021–7 period eight multi-fund ROPs managed centrally, or possibly regionally in the case of Bucharest-Ilfov. While still some way off in the future, the chapter also tries to make some proposals for the 2028–34 period. Starting from the assumption that by the mid-2020s the regionalisation process will be complete, the chapter proposes the introduction in 2028 of the first ROPs managed sub-nationally, with either the RDAs or future regional governments acting as MAs. Nonetheless, apart from thinking about how future programmes could be designed, Romania needs to look into the lessons learnt in the 2007–13 period and enhance its capacity for implementing Cohesion Policy at both central and sub-national levels.

Notes

1 The absorption rate was below 15 per cent at the end of 2012.
2 RDCs are territorial structures without juridical personality responsible for the regional development strategies and programmes and are formed from representatives of the local and county governments. RDCs oversee the activity of the RDAs and approve their budgets.
3 From a couple of employees in the early 2000s, staffing at each RDA reached 50 people in 2007 and 100 in 2013, while staff turnover stayed at low levels.
4 The commitment rate is calculated as the amount of contracted funds in all of the selected projects within one programme divided by the amount of commitments (legal pledges to provide finance, provided that certain conditions are fulfilled). Certain states contract more than the total amount of the commitments in order to obtain a higher absorption rate (since most projects will not absorb all the allocated funds).
5 In a report commissioned by DG REGIO (Sweco International, 2010) Denmark, Lithuania, Estonia, Latvia, Slovenia, Slovakia, Hungary, Greece, Sweden, Romania, Bulgaria, Cyprus, Malta and Luxembourg are considered centralised systems, Germany, Italy, the Netherlands, Austria and Belgium are considered regionalised systems and Poland, France, Finland, the Czech Republic, Spain, the UK, Ireland and Portugal are seen as mixed systems.
6 A proposal in this regard has been advanced several times but no real developments have actually been seen.
7 According to the new ESIF Regulations, member states can designate either a national, regional or local public authority or body or a private body as managing authority.

References

Bachtler, J. F. and McMaster, I. (2007), 'EU Cohesion Policy and the role of the regions: investigating the influence of Structural Funds in the new member states', *Environment and Planning C: Government and Policy*, 26(2), 398–427.

Bähr, C. (2008), 'How does sub-national autonomy affect the effectiveness of Structural Funds?', *Kyklos*, 61(1), 3–18.

Begg, I. (2008), 'Subsidiarity in regional policy', in G. Gelauf, I. Grilo and A. Lejour (eds), *Subsidiarity and Economic Reform in Europe*, Berlin and Heidelberg: Springer.

Burduja, S., Ionescu-Heroiu, M., Gaman, F., Radoi, V., Nesa, A., Ciobanu, C., Magheru, M., Ohranovic, N., McLean, K., Pauna, C. and Rodriguez, P. (2013a), *Assessment of the Communication and Collaboration between the Managing Authority and Intermediate*

Bodies of the Regional Operational Programme and Facilitation of Proactive and Direct Support for Beneficiaries: Final Report, Component I, Washington, DC: World Bank Group.

Burduja, S., Ionescu-Heroiu, M., Gaman, F., Radoi, V., Nesa, A., Ciobanu, C., Magheru, M., Ohranovic, N., McLean, K., Pauna, C. and Rodriguez, P. (2013b), *Assessment of the Communication and Collaboration between the Managing Authority and Intermediate Bodies of the Regional Operational Programme and Facilitation of Proactive and Direct Support for Beneficiaries: Final Report, Component II*, Washington, DC: World Bank Group.

Council of the European Union (2014), 'Council recommendation of 8 July 2014 on the National Reform Programme 2014 of Romania and delivering a Council opinion on the Convergence Programme of Romania, 2014', available at: http://ec.europa.eu/europe2020/pdf/csr2014/csr2014_council_romania_en.pdf (accessed 11 January 2015).

East West Consulting (2013), *Evaluarea POS Mediu*, evaluation commissioned by the Ministry of Environment and Climate Change, Bucharest: Government of Romania, available at: www.evaluare-structurale.ro/images/Y_upload_rapoarte/06_POS_MED/01.intermediara/Evaluare_POS_Mediu.pdf (accessed 11 January 2015).

Ecorys Lideea (2013), *Evaluation Report on the Administrative Capacity of the Beneficiaries and Authorities of CSF Funds*, study commissioned by the Ministry of European Funds, Bucharest: Government of Romania.

European Commission (2014), *Investment for Jobs and Growth: Promoting Development and Good Governance in EU Regions and Cities – Sixth Report on Economic, Social and Territorial Cohesion*, Brussels: European Commission, available at: http://ec.europa.eu/regional_policy/sources/docoffic/official/reports/cohesion6/6cr_en.pdf (accessed 11 January 2015).

Eurostat (2014), 'GDP per capita in the EU in 2011: seven capital regions among the ten most prosperous', available at: http://europa.eu/rapid/press-release_STAT-14-29_en.pdf (accessed 11 January 2015).

Halkier, H. (2006), 'Regional Development Agencies and multilevel governance: European perspectives', *Bölgesel Kalkınma ve Yönetişim Sempozyumu*, 3–17, available at: www.tepav.org.tr/upload/files/1321362529-2.Bolgesel_Kalkinma_ve_Yonetisim_Sempozyumu_Bildiri_Kitabi.pdf (accessed 11 January 2015).

Harding, R. (2006), 'Regional Development Agency experiences in England and Romania', *Bölgesel Kalkınma ve Yönetişim Sempozyumu*, 111–135, available at: www.tepav.org.tr/upload/files/1321362529-2.Bolgesel_Kalkinma_ve_Yonetisim_Sempozyumu_Bildiri_Kitabi.pdf (accessed 11 January 2015).

Ionescu-Heroiu, M., Burduja, S., Sandu, D., Cojocaru, S., Blankespoor, B., Iorga, E., Moretti, E., Moldovan, C., Man, T., Rus, R. and van der Weide, R. (2013), *Competitive Cities: Reshaping the Economic Geography of Romania*, Washington, DC: World Bank Group, available at: www-wds.worldbank.org/external/default/WDSContentServer/WDSP/IB/2014/02/20/000456286_20140220151016/Rendered/PDF/843240v10Full00s0Box382123B00OUO070.pdf (accessed 11 January 2015).

Ionescu-Heroiu, M., Burduja, S., Vu, H., Glenday, G., Giosan, V., Mot, M., Sandu, D., Iorga, E., Taralunga, N., Vintan, A., Huddleston, N., Tufis, P. and Gaman, F. (2014), *Identification of Project Selection Models for the Regional Operational Program 2014–2020 (Vol. 2): Summary Report*, available at: www-wds.worldbank.org/external/default/WDSContentServer/WDSP/IB/2014/02/26/000333037_201402261 21507/Rendered/PDF/850090WP0v20P10ls0Summary0Report0EN.pdf (accessed 11 January 2015).

KPMG Romania (2011), *First Interim Evaluation of SOP HRD*, Bucharest: KPMG Romania, available at: www.evaluare-structurale.ro/images/Y_upload_rapoarte/05_ POSDRU/01_POSDRU_Eval_Interim/Raport_Integral/M05_R01_EN.pdf (accessed 11 January 2015).

KPMG Romania (2014), *Actualizarea Evaluării Intermediare a Programului Operaţional Regional 2007–2013*, Bucharest: KPMG Romania, available at: www.inforegio.ro/ images/Evaluare/Raport_evaluare_POR_versiune%20finala.pdf (accessed 11 January 2015).

Lanttanzio E Associati SpA (2011), *Evaluarea Capacităţii Administrative a Regiunilor în Domeniul Dezvoltării Regionale*, Milan: Lanttanzio E Associati SpA, available at: www.fonduri-ue.ro/res/filepicker_users/cd25a597fd-62/Documente_Suport/ Evaluari/1_EVALUARI_POR/2_Eval_Cap_Adm_Regiuni.pdf (accessed 11 January 2015).

Michie, R. and Granqvist, K. (2013), 'Managing the 2007–13 Programmes towards full absorption and closure: review of programme implementation, Winter 2012–Spring 2013', IQ-Net Review Paper 32(1), available at: www.eprc.strath.ac.uk/iqnet/down loads/IQ-Net_Reports%28Public%29/Review%20Paper_32%281%29.pdf (accessed 11 January 2015).

Sweco International (2010), *Regional Governance in the Context of Globalisation: Reviewing Governance Mechanisms and Administrative Costs – Administrative Workload and Costs for Member State Public Authorities of the Implementation of ERDF and Cohesion Fund*, Stockholm: Sweco International, available at: http:// ec.europa.eu/regional_policy/sources/docgener/studies/pdf/2010_governance.pdf (accessed 11 January 2015).

Part IV
Institutions, territory and place-based policies

17 Territorial capital and EU Cohesion Policy

Ugo Fratesi and Giovanni Perucca

Introduction

The regions of the European Union (EU) are all eligible for Cohesion Policy support, although within different objectives and with different levels of support, mostly dependent on their development level and especially their GDP per capita, which in purchasing power standard is the main variable differentiating between convergence and competitiveness regions (in the 2007–13 programming period) and less developed, transition and more developed regions (in the 2014–20 programming period).

However, beyond GDP per capita, the regions of the EU are also extremely different in structural terms, and in particular they are characterized by very different systems of territorial assets of an economic, cultural, social and environmental nature. These elements, included under the comprehensive concept of *territorial capital*, represent the development potential of regions. In the words of the European Commission itself, the regional endowments of territorial capital have relevant policy implications, as:

> [e]ach region has a specific "territorial capital" that is distinct from that of other areas and generates a higher return for specific kinds of investments than for others, since these are better suited to the area and use its assets and potential more effectively.
>
> (European Commission, 2005: 1)

This chapter analyses the relationship between territorial capital and Cohesion Policy in a multi-dimensional way. Territorial capital, in fact, has many facets, which are sometimes related to each other, so that regions that are more endowed with some of them tend to also be more endowed with others. At the same time, Cohesion Policy is also multi-faceted, investing in a large number of different axes, which are not always related to each other or always directly targeted at stimulating economic growth.

Using statistical data on territorial capital endowment at the NUTS3 territorial level and detailed Cohesion Policy expenditure on 19 axes over the 2000–06 programming period, the chapter will identify what type of territorial capital is present in the EU regions and which Cohesion Policy mixes have been implemented in them.

The chapter is organized as follows. In the first section, we will review the literature on the importance of territorial capital for regional growth. The next section will discuss the relationship between Cohesion Policy and territorial capital. Then we will present a taxonomy of EU regions based on territorial capital, while the following section will show that regions differently endowed with territorial capital tend to adopt different policy mixes. Finally, we will conclude with the main policy implications of the chapter.

Territorial capital and regional growth

A very large number of factors influencing regional growth have been identified in the literature, some of them exogenous and others endogenous. From the 1980s onwards, special emphasis has been placed on the latter, which are widely considered more important for a modern regional economy than exogenous factors, such as external assistance or the cycles of demand. In particular, most endogenous factors of regional growth are indeed regional assets, which are present in the regions only after having been accumulated over the long term.

These factors include, for example, human capital, the accumulation of which is slow and the mobility of which is limited. The accumulation requires time and strong primary and higher educational systems, coupled with a productive environment in which workers can learn by doing and interacting. Unfortunately for lagging regions, the process of "brain drain" can hamper the accumulation of human capital in regions in which the educational system is strong but the private sector is unable to hire educated workers in jobs where their abilities are put to best use (Dotti et al., 2013; Fratesi and Percoco, 2014).

Other soft growth factors are perhaps even slower to develop, one clear example being the quality of formal and informal institutions. Institutional quality, for instance, is very different among the regions of Europe (Charron et al., 2014), and this pattern has most likely remained quite stable in the long term. The creation of relational capital – both bonding and bridging – also needs significant time, since relations cannot be formed without trust, and building trust needs repeated positive interactions.

Harder factors are also important in influencing regional growth, and in many cases these too need to develop over long periods of time and require continuous investment to be maintained. One classic example is infrastructure, which needs large investments and many years to be built, so that lagging regions tend to have poor infrastructures or be infrastructurally imbalanced (for example, having high-speed train connections, but lacking efficient road connections around the station).

Private capital, additionally, is less spatially mobile than commonly thought; financial capital can be moved everywhere in the blink of an eye, but once invested in firms and plants, private capital can no longer be moved. At the same time, purely financial movements are also slowed down and made more difficult by missing information, exchange-rate risk, uncertainty, different institutional settings in different places, administrative costs and so on.

These factors are only a few of the regional assets that constitute capital, the more traditional ones, but many others do exist. For this reason, Camagni (2008) has produced a taxonomy of territorial capital (a term that was first introduced by the OECD in 2001) based on the two dimensions of rivalry and materiality. In this taxonomy, represented in Table 17.1, the traditional factors, including those mentioned above, are classified as either private or public, and either tangible or intangible. However, other factors are intermediate in the classification: being common resources or impure public goods, and having an intermediate level of materiality. These factors include proprietary networks, landscape, cultural heritage, cooperation networks, governance of land and cultural resources, agglomeration and district economies, agencies for R&D transcoding and receptivity-enhancing tools.

Table 17.1 Territorial capital: a taxonomy.

Rivalry				
(high)	*Private goods*	**C** Private fixed capital stock Pecuniary externalities Toll goods	**I** Relational private services operating on: • external linkages for firms • transfer of R&D results	**F** Human capital Pecuniary externalities
	Club goods, impure public goods	**B** Proprietary networks Collective goods: • landscape • cultural heritage	**H** Cooperation networks Governance of land and cultural resources	**E** Relational capital
(low)	*Public goods*	**A** Resources: • natural • cultural (punctual) • Social overhead capital: • infrastructure	**G** Agglomeration and district economies Agencies for R&D transcoding Receptivity-enhancing tools Connectivity	**D** Social capital: • institutions • behavioural modes, values, trust, reputation
		Tangible goods (hard)	*Mixed goods (hard + soft)*	*Intangible goods (soft)*
		Materiality (high) ························→························ (low)		

Source: Camagni (2008).

EU Cohesion Policy and territorial capital

Having discussed the significant extent to which regional growth is linked to territorial capital, and hence to the structure of regions, we should now note that no other type of regional policy is expected to be as closely related to the concept of territorial capital as EU Cohesion Policy. In fact, since their very inception, Structural Funds have been devoted to enhancing cohesion in the EU by reducing regional disparities and increasing the long-term growth rates of lagging regions. This is consistent with the treaties of the EU, since the principle that it "shall promote economic, social and territorial cohesion, and solidarity among Member States" (European Union, 2010: article 3) is applied by stating that "the Union shall aim at reducing disparities between the levels of development of the various regions and the backwardness of the least favoured regions" (European Union, 2010: article 174). In particular:

> [t]he European Regional Development Fund is intended to help to redress the main regional imbalances in the Union through participation in the development and *structural adjustment* of regions whose development is lagging behind and in the conversion of declining industrial regions.
>
> (European Union, 2010: article 176, emphasis added)

Throughout the various programming periods during which Cohesion Policy has been organized, the focus on structure and long-term growth has been persistent. In the 2000–06 period, in particular, the regulations involved three objectives (lagging regions, economic and social conversion, and adaptation and modernization of policies and systems of education, training and employment) and stated that:

> [t]he Community shall contribute to the harmonious, balanced and sustainable development of economic activities, the development of employment and human resources, the protection and improvement of the environment, and the elimination of inequalities, and the promotion of equality between men and women.
>
> (European Union, 1999: L 161/7)

Despite the change in the objectives (which became speeding up the convergence of the least-developed member states and regions, strengthening regions' competitiveness and attractiveness as well as employment, and strengthening cross-border cooperation), the basic purpose of Cohesion Policy has been maintained for the 2007–13 programming period, during which the actions of the EU "shall be designed to strengthen the economic and social cohesion of the enlarged European Union in order to promote the harmonious, balanced and sustainable development of the Community" (European Union, 2006: L 210/36).

For the current 2014–20 programming period, the criteria have been officially adopted with a regulation by the Parliament in addition to the Council and, though the objectives have again been amended, with the addition of new thematic objectives and a new typology of regions (less developed, transition and more developed regions), the main target remains long-term growth, which is now also explicitly smart: "The ESI Funds shall provide support, through multi-annual programmes, which complements national, regional and local intervention, to deliver the Union strategy for smart, sustainable and inclusive growth" (European Union, 2013: L 347/341)

Based on the above discussion, we can assume a strong relationship between territorial capital and Cohesion Policies. This relationship may take two forms. First, regions characterized by different endowments of territorial capital are likely to adopt different growth strategies, investing the Structural Funds in those territorial elements whose lack inhibits the local growth potential. Second, territorial capital can enhance the impact of Cohesion Policy, since the local conditions of each region represent the soil in which public investments are expected to generate benefits in the medium and long term (Ederveen et al., 2006).

Despite the existence of a very extensive body of literature on the impact of Structural Funds on regional growth, the issue of the relationship between territorial capital and Cohesion Policy has received scant attention in the literature (Fratesi, forthcoming). As far as the influence of territorial capital on the impact of EU Structural Funds is concerned, there is a paper by the present authors (Fratesi and Perucca, 2014), which, in an analysis of Eastern European countries, found that some specific aspects of territorial capital are significantly affecting the impact of specific expenditure axes in the new member states. In a different context, but on similar lines, Dall'Erba and Llamosas-Rosas (2013) found an important influence of conditioning factors on the impact of policies on regional growth.

The present chapter is aimed at investigating the former mechanism through which territorial capital affects Cohesion Policy – namely, the relationship between the endowment of specific territorial assets and the allocation of the EU funds chosen by different typologies of regions. To do this, the next section provides an empirical analysis of the endowment of territorial capital in EU15 regions. Based on these findings, pointing out the existence of groups of regions characterized by similar combinations of territorial assets, the subsequent section will discuss the expected association between territorial capital and the investment strategies adopted.

Territorial capital: a taxonomy of EU regions

The first step in the study of the relationship between local assets and Cohesion Policy consists of an empirical analysis of the endowment of territorial capital in EU regions. Therefore, the aim of this section is to identify clusters of regions characterized by similar territorial conditions. Based on the taxonomy reported in Table 17.1, we collected data on EU NUTS3 regions,[1] as summarized in Table 17.2. All of the indicators refer to 2006, the last year of the programming period.

260 *Ugo Fratesi and Giovanni Perucca*

Table 17.2 Territorial capital in EU regions: data and sources.

Territorial capital indicator	Typology of territorial capital	Description	Source	Sectors of Figure 17.1
Accessibility	High materiality/ low rivalry	Population potential within 50 km air-line distance	ESPON	A
Bed places in tourist accommodation	High materiality/ intermediate rivalry	Per capita bed places in registered tourist accommodations	Eurostat	B
IP addresses	High materiality/ high rivalry	Number of registered IP addresses	ESPON	C
Female/male unemployment	Low materiality/ low rivalry	Ratio of female to male unemployment rates (aged over 15)	Eurostat	D
Human capital	Low materiality/ high rivalry	Highly educated residents (ISCED 5 and 6) as a proportion of the total number of residents	Eurostat	F
ISCO functions	Intermediate materiality/ high rivalry	Professionals and managers as a proportion of the total number of employed people	Eurostat	I

Clustering techniques are employed to investigate the spatial distribution of territorial capital. Model selection, based on the maximization of the Bayesian Information criterion,[2] identifies five diagonal clusters with varying volume and shape. The results are mapped in Figure 17.1, while Table 17.3 reports the mean values of the standardized indicators of territorial capital for each cluster.

The 37 regions included in the first category (Cluster A) are marked by the highest degree of physical accessibility. Their industrial specialization in the service sector and advanced manufacturing is reflected by the proportion of the total number of employed people who are managers or professionals. The concentration of economic activities (IP addresses) is well above that observed for the other clusters, and the same holds for the endowment of human capital. Based on this evidence, we label this cluster *core metropolitan areas*, comprising most of the EU countries' capitals.

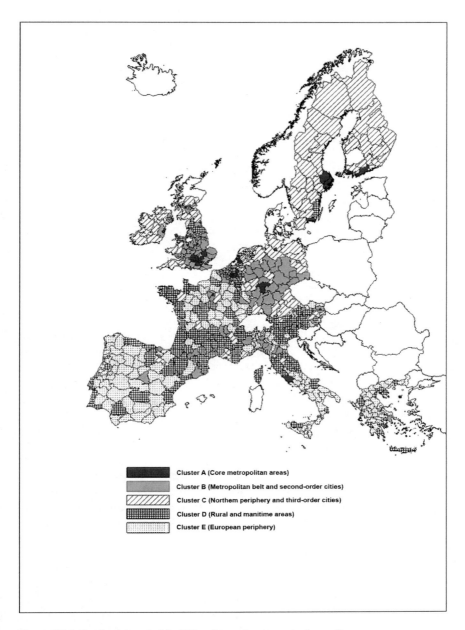

Figure 17.1 Territorial capital in EU regions: cluster analysis results.

Table 17.3 Territorial capital across clusters of EU regions: mean values of the standardized indicators.

Territorial capital indicators	Cluster A	Cluster B	Cluster C	Cluster D	Cluster E
Accessibility	**1.019**	**0.805**	−0.057	−0.285	−0.700
Bed places in tourist accommodations	−0.415	−0.570	−0.080	**1.142**	−0.408
IP addresses	**2.286**	−0.041	0.032	−0.132	−0.347
Female/male unemployment	−0.470	−0.546	**−0.609**	0.442	0.615
Human capital	**1.739**	0.419	**0.777**	−0.455	−0.864
ISCO functions	**1.966**	**0.559**	−0.019	−0.388	−0.586
Number of regions	*37*	*169*	*114*	*167*	*171*
Per capita GDP 2006 (thousands €)	*45.602*	*28.297*	*28.052*	*24.055*	*19.694*
GDP growth 2006–11	*0.032*	*0.004*	*0.017*	*−0.015*	*−0.039*
Funds as a share of GDP	*5.631*	*8.282*	*16.184*	*40.434*	*79.515*

Note: Mean values of the territorial elements characterizing each cluster in bold.

In the second group (Cluster B), we find regions characterized by a strong specialization in high-value-added functions, jointly with a significant endowment of both human and social capital. Most of these regions are home to some second-rank cities (such as Milan, Turin and Naples in Italy, Liverpool and Leeds in the UK, Madrid and Barcelona in Spain, and Leipzig, Berlin and Cologne in Germany) or, in some cases, are close to the major EU metropolitan areas (London, Paris, Dublin, Brussels). Therefore, the label identifying this cluster is *metropolitan belt* and *second-order cities*.

Cluster C comprises areas with, on average, low gender inequalities in the labour market[3] and high levels of human capital, while the poor physical accessibility is due by their peripheral geographical location. In fact, the majority of the regions included in this cluster are in Northern Europe, with the exclusion of the major urban centres and their surroundings. The rest of the areas in the cluster are intermediate urban areas mainly in France, the UK, Ireland and Germany. The group is named *northern periphery and third-order cities*.

With respect to Cluster A, both Cluster B and Cluster C are characterized, on average, by lower endowments of territorial capital. Comparing Cluster B with Cluster C, however, it is worth noting that they cannot be unequivocally ranked based on their local assets. Instead, the difference between the two clusters relates to the different combination of territorial capital components. The latter allowed these regions to reach a comparable stage of development, as shown by the average GDP per capita reported in Table 17.3.

Regions included in Cluster D, on the other hand, are marked by lower endowments of territorial capital when compared to the previous clusters. Most of the regions included in Cluster D are rural areas. This cluster mainly includes maritime areas on the Atlantic and Mediterranean coasts and the entire Alpine arc. Data reported in Table 17.3 indicate their specialization in the tourism sector. This cluster is labelled *rural and maritime areas*.

Finally, the most populated cluster is Cluster E, comprising 171 rural regions in Southern Europe (Spain, Italy and Greece) and France. On average, regions included in this cluster are characterized by the lowest endowments of territorial capital for all of the indicators included in the analysis. For this reason, we name this cluster *European periphery*.

The last two rows of Table 17.3 provide some evidence of the link between the endowment of territorial capital, the stage of development of the regions and their economic growth. The most deprived regions (those included in Cluster E) are those with the lowest levels of GDP per capita, and they experienced the worst economic slowdown between 2006 and 2011. The opposite holds for the core metropolitan areas (Cluster A) and, more generally, the ordering of the clusters based on their territorial assets is perfectly matched by their average levels of both wealth and economic growth. This finding supports the literature that suggests a positive relationship between territorial capital and growth (Perucca, 2014).

The research question addressed by the present chapter is whether the different clusters of regions identified by the empirical analysis are adopting different strategies in the investment of the EU funds they receive. The next section is devoted to this issue. The first part discusses the reason why we expect different types of regions to behave differently, while the second part presents some empirical evidence supporting this conjecture.

Territorial capital and the development policies of EU regions

The evidence provided in Table 17.3 indicates how EU regions are characterized by a variety of territorial assets, which have affected their socioeconomic development in the past and are likely to drive their future growth patterns. In light of this evidence, the purpose of the present chapter is to understand whether the strategy adopted by each region is dependent on its endowment of territorial capital. Our assumption is that different types of regions are likely to implement different kinds of policies, based on their level of development, as shown in Figure 17.2.

The priority of lagging regions is to create the physical preconditions for the attraction and generation of new economic activities. Therefore, we would expect them to focus mainly on infrastructural investments. Those areas that have already reached an intermediate stage of development, on the other hand, will probably allocate more funds to the assistance of the productive environment, supporting firms facing international competition and providing them with incentives to

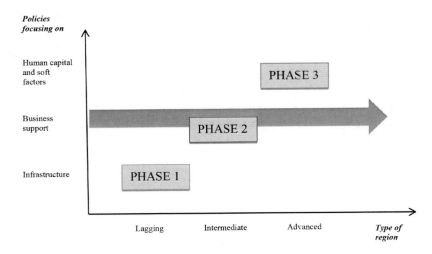

Figure 17.2 Expected allocation of Structural Funds in different types of regions.

promote R&D and innovation. Finally, the most advanced regions are those that will probably invest more resources in social policies, so as to enrich their endowment of human capital and other soft factors. Obviously this assumption does not imply that different types of regions will devote their entire budget to one or a few specific expenditure axes. Rather, we expect regions at different stages of economic development to allocate more or fewer resources than the others to each type of action, according to the mechanism outlined in Figure 17.2.

This hypothesis finds some empirical verification in the evidence from EU NUTS3 regions. Luckily, data for the 2000–06 programming period are not only available, but available with an axis articulation, which allows us to investigate the impacts of different types of policies. Table 17.4 shows, for each of the five clusters identified in the previous section, the average share of funds spent on each axis, jointly with the results of an analysis of variance.[4] The results highlight how, apart from the expenditures on agriculture and forestry, the differences among clusters are always statistically significant. For instance, core metropolitan areas (Cluster A) allocate, on average, 26.899 per cent of their funds to the support of SMEs and the craft sector. The regions characterized by the lowest endowments of territorial capital (Clusters D and E, where GDP per capita is also lower) are also those that devote more resources to investments in basic infrastructure such as transport, energy and environmental infrastructure. Policies in support of the productive environment (large business organizations, and SMEs and the craft sector) receive the largest share of funds for the regions at an intermediate stage of development (Clusters B and C). Finally, leading regions (Cluster A) invest more funds (in relative terms) in actions on human resources, from the labour market to social inclusion.[5]

Table 17.4 Proportion of funds per expenditure axis: analysis of variance among clusters.

Share of funds per axis of expenditure (clusters' means)
Percentage of total Structural Funds allocated to each axis

	Expenditure axes	Cluster A	Cluster B	Cluster C	Cluster D	Cluster E	F	Prob > F
11	Agriculture	0.005	0.307	0.236	0.060	0.038	1.11	0.351
12	Forestry	0.066	0.201	0.116	0.109	0.013	1.01	0.399
13	Promoting the adaptation and the development of rural areas	1.985	3.337	4.933	2.014	1.400	6.20	0.000
14	Fisheries	0.035	0.019	0.102	0.222	0.137	3.86	0.004
15	Assisting large business organizations	1.584	**2.231**	**2.552**	3.638	5.191	6.63	0.000
16	Assisting SMEs and the craft sector	26.899	**40.126**	**31.830**	21.229	16.977	33.55	0.000
17	Tourism	9.294	**7.646**	**11.871**	14.174	7.889	10.25	0.000
18	Research, technological development and innovation (RTDI)	4.606	**7.126**	**8.504**	5.310	4.323	7.50	0.000
21	Labour market policy	**0.756**	0.634	0.636	0.186	0.073	7.00	0.000
22	Social inclusion	**2.415**	2.765	1.359	0.293	0.171	13.69	0.000
23	Educational and vocational training not linked to a specific sector	**3.302**	1.496	2.780	1.224	1.318	4.20	0.002
24	Workforce flexibility, entrepreneurship, innovation, information and communication	**2.372**	0.660	1.275	0.266	0.087	5.67	0.000
25	Positive labour market actions for women	**0.480**	0.212	0.221	0.106	0.027	5.62	0.000

Productive environment: 11–18
Human resources: 21–25

(continued)

Table 17.4 (continued)

	Expenditure axes	Cluster A	Cluster B	Cluster C	Cluster D	Cluster E	F	Prob > F
31	Transport infrastructure	14.370	6.785	10.842	13.812	**22.350**	22.73	0.000
32	Telecommunications infrastructure and information society	4.802	3.097	4.794	**3.683**	3.815	2.56	0.037
33	Energy infrastructure (production, delivery)	0.380	0.518	0.847	**1.791**	1.112	6.93	0.000
34	Environmental infrastructure (including water)	3.723	3.084	5.360	**10.030**	12.037	19.94	0.000
35	Planning and rehabilitation	16.954	15.162	6.763	15.516	**16.372**	12.93	0.000
36	Social and public health infrastructure	2.033	1.658	1.404	3.204	**4.086**	9.86	0.000

Basic infrastructure

Share of funds per axis of expenditure (clusters' means)
Percentage of total Structural Funds allocated to each axis

Note: Mean values of the territorial elements characterizing each cluster in bold.

Empirically, EU regions appear to mostly follow the patterns of Figure 17.2, with less developed regions investing more of their funds in basic infrastructural assets, and the richest ones paying more attention to social and economic issues. Even if this is the common practice, it is not a given that each type of region invests in the type of funds that gives more returns in terms of GDP growth.

It has to be recognized that the impact of policies does not simply depend on the policy itself, but also strongly depends on the context in which policy is applied. The hypotheses that we tested empirically in two related papers, one for Western European countries (Fratesi and Perucca, 2015) and one for Eastern European countries (Fratesi and Perucca, 2014), are therefore the following. The first concerns the relationship between territorial capital and economic growth: regions characterized by higher endowments of territorial assets are expected to perform, in terms of GDP growth, better than the others. The second research question refers to the extent to which territorial capital acts as a filter for the economic growth impact of regional policies. As discussed above, this mechanism is assumed to vary across different types of regions, defined based on the territorial capital endowment.

As far as Eastern European countries are concerned (Fratesi and Perucca, 2014), Cohesion Policy appeared to be effective (in terms of GDP growth) only in regions characterized by specific territorial conditions, such as the presence of high value-functions in the case of labour market policies and human capital in the case of innovation, information and telecommunication policies.

Similar results apply to the EU15 regions. Adopting a classification of regions based on their endowment of territorial capital, research by the same authors (Fratesi and Perucca, 2015) found a significant relationship between Cohesion Policy investments and GDP growth once interactions with different endowments of territorial capital are taken into account.

Conclusions

This chapter has provided an analysis of the interrelation between territorial capital and Cohesion Policy. On the one hand, territorial capital can act as a facilitator or an inhibitor to the impact on growth of policies whose main target is economic. On the other, those policies whose direct targets are more social and political can contribute to the creation or re-creation of territorial capital, in its softer aspects, so that in the very long term this also contributes to growth.

First, regions more endowed with territorial capital appear to outperform others in terms of GDP growth. This could make a positive message emerge for the impact of Structural Funds policies on economic growth: it appears that investments made with Structural Funds, which mostly target the enhancement of territorial capital, are useful insofar as they provide the pre-requisites of long-term growth.

Moreover, there appears to be a clear relationship between the endowment of territorial capital and the policy choices made by the regions of the EU. The poorest regions, which are also those receiving the most funds, tend to be lagging in all categories of territorial capital and mostly target investments in basic infrastructure, whose impact on growth is normally not immediate but which provide the necessary preconditions for future growth. Intermediate regions, whose endowment of territorial capital is higher and which already possess basic infrastructure, generally invest in policies whose impact on growth is expected to be more direct, such as those in support of large and small firms, of innovation and of tourism.

At the same time, richer regions receive fewer funds but can afford to use these funds in axes whose direct relation with growth is weaker, in order to achieve social and political goals. However, even in this case, there is the possibility of positive impact on growth in the long term; these policies contribute to the improvement of soft aspects of territorial capital and this is expected to pay off in the very long term, since those regions more endowed with territorial capital are also those whose growth rates are higher.

Investing in the structural assets of the regions, therefore, is overall a useful policy, and this policy appears to be superior in the medium and long term to the simple provision of assistance to lagging regions and their people.

Appendix

Among the broad variety of approaches available (Everitt and Hothorn, 2011), we chose to adopt model-clustering methods. In the model-based approach, data are assumed to originate from a mixture of probability distribution (Fraley and Raftery, 2002):

$$f(x) = \sum_{k=1}^{G} \tau_k f_k(x) \qquad (17.1)$$

where x indicates the set of observations, f_k is the probability density function of the observation in group k and τ_k is the probability that an observation comes from the kth mixture component $\sum_{k=1}^{G} \tau_k = 1$.

Each cluster can be formally represented by a parametric distribution, like a Gaussian (with mean μ_k and covariance matrix Σ_k) in the continuous case. The maximization of the likelihood function of the mixture density with respect to the observed data (Heath et al., 2007) allows the estimation of the parameters of the cluster distributions (τ_k, μ_k and Σ_k). Several parameterizations of Σ_k can be assumed, starting from the most common one, $\Sigma_k = \lambda I$, leading to spherical clusters of the same size. The latter parametrization corresponds to the K-means approach, which is the most popular in empirical analyses but which, however, is not able to identify non-spherical clusters with different volume and shape.

In the present chapter, the R (R Development Core Team, 2008) package mclust (Fraley and Raftery, 1999) is employed, so as to test several parameterizations with a variety of distributions (spherical, diagonal and ellipsoidal) and variable shape and volume.

Notes

1 In the case of Germany, due to the nonavailability of data at NUTS3 level, NUTS2 regions are used. This is also justified by the fact that German NUTS3 regions are much smaller than in other countries, while the German NUTS2 regions tend to be a similar size to NUTS3 regions in other countries. The practice of keeping Germany at a higher scale is not uncommon in the literature; for example, it was already argued and implemented almost 20 years ago by Paci (1997).
2 See the Appendix for details of the clustering technique used.
3 The ratio of female to male unemployment rates has to be interpreted in the opposite direction compared with the other indicators; positive values of the ratio suggest gender imbalances disadvantaging women in the labour market.
4 Axes 11–14 are not discussed since the allocation of funds to these categories of expenditure mainly depends on the morphological regional characteristics. Only maritime regions, for instance, are expected to devote funds to fisheries.
5 These regions also devote quite a large proportion of funds to transport and telecommunication technologies, which may sound counterintuitive based on what is discussed in Figure 17.2. However, the reason for this choice lies, in our opinion, not in the lack of these territorial elements (as showed in the previous section) but, instead, in the occurrence of congestion effects typical of metropolitan areas.

References

Camagni, R. (2008), "Regional competitiveness: towards a concept of territorial capital", in R. Capello, R. Camagni, B. Chizzolini and U. Fratesi (eds), *Modelling Regional Scenarios for the Enlarged Europe: European Competitiveness and Global Strategies*, Berlin: Springer Verlag, pp. 33–48.

Charron, N., Dijkstra, L. and, Lapuente, V. (2014), "Regional governance matters: quality of government within European Union member states", *Regional Studies*, 48(1), 68–90.

Dall'Erba, S. and Llamosas-Rosas, I. (2013), "Does federal expenditure promote growth in the recipient countries?", paper presented to the NARSC Conference, Atlanta, GA, 13–16 November.

Dotti, N. F, Fratesi, U., Lenzi, C. and Percoco, M. (2013), "Local labour markets and the interregional mobility of Italian university students", *Spatial Economic Analysis*, 8(4), 443–68.

Ederveen, S., Henri, L. F. and Nahuis, R. (2006), "Fertile soil for Structural Funds? A panel data analysis of the conditional effectiveness of European Cohesion Policy", *Kyklos*, 59(1), 17–42.

European Commission (2005), "Territorial state and perspectives of the European Union", scoping document and summary of political messages, Brussels: European Commission, May.

European Union (1999), "Council Regulation (EC) No 1260/1999 of 21 June 1999 laying down general provisions on the Structural Funds", Brussels: European Union.

European Union (2006), "Council Regulation (EC) No 1083/2006 of 11 July 2006 laying down general provisions on the European Regional Development Fund, the European Social Fund and the Cohesion Fund and repealing Regulation (EC) No 1260/1999", Brussels: European Union.

European Union (2010), *Consolidated Version of the Treaty on the Functioning of the European Union*, Brussels: European Union.

European Union (2013), "Regulation (EU) No 1303/2013 of the European Parliament and of the Council of 17 December 2013 laying down common provisions on the European Regional Development Fund, the European Social Fund, the Cohesion Fund, the European Agricultural Fund for Rural Development and the European Maritime and Fisheries Fund and laying down general provisions on the European Regional Development Fund, the European Social Fund, the Cohesion Fund and the European Maritime and Fisheries Fund and repealing Council Regulation (EC) No 1083/2006", Brussels: European Union.

Everitt, B. and Hothorn, T. (2011), *An Introduction to Applied Multivariate Analysis with R*, New York: Springer.

Fraley, G. and Raftery, A. E. (1999), "mclust: software for model-based cluster analysis", *Journal of Classification*, 16(2), 296–306.

Fraley, G. and Raftery, A. E. (2002), "Model-based clustering, discriminant analysis, and density estimation", *Journal of the Statistical Association*, 97(458), 611–31.

Fratesi, U. (forthcoming), "Impact assessment of European Cohesion Policy: theoretical and empirical issues", in S. Piattoni and L. Polverari (eds), *Handbook on Cohesion Policy in the EU*, Cheltenham, UK: Edward Elgar.

Fratesi, U. and Percoco, M. (2014), "Selective migration, regional growth and convergence: evidence from Italy", *Regional Studies*, 48(10), 1650–68.

Fratesi, U. and Perucca, G. (2014), "Territorial capital and the effectiveness of Cohesion Policies: an assessment for CEE regions", *Investigaciones Regionales*, 29, 165–91.

Fratesi, U. and Perucca, G. (2015), "Territorial capital and the impact of Cohesion Policy". *mimeo*, Politecnico di Milano, Milan, Italy.

Heath, J. W., Fu, M. C. and Jank, W. (2007), "Global convergence of Model Reference Adaptive Search for Gaussian mixtures", working paper, Smith School of Business, University of Maryland.

OECD (2001), *OECD Territorial Outlook*, Paris: OECD.

Paci, R. (1997), "More similar and less equal: economic growth in the European regions", *Weltwirtschaftliches Archiv*, 133(4), 609–34.

Perucca, G. (2014), "The role of territorial capital in local economic growth: evidence from Italy", *European Planning Studies*, 22(3), 537–62.

R Development Core Team (2008), *R: A Language and Environment for Statistical Computing*, Vienna: R Foundation for Statistical Computing, available at: www.r-project.org/ (accessed 25 February 2016).

18 What institutional arrangements exist to ensure coherent EU Cohesion Policy planning and implementation?

Liga Baltiņa and Tatjana Muravska

Introduction

The persistent regional disparities in the European Union (EU) have led to a questioning of the effectiveness of the EU Cohesion Policy. Achieving Cohesion Policy goals is a challenge for each member state and its national institutional framework, considering that it is multi-dimensional in nature. The debate about the efficiency of Cohesion Policy measures was intensified by the decrease of the available financial resources due to the global financial crisis and the preparations for the 2014–20 EU funding period. Public administration reforms, as one of the responses to the changes in the financial situation, are often based on the need to improve the operational efficiency of public administration. In the context of Cohesion Policy, such reforms include improving the effectiveness of regional and local administrative structures and emphasizing the role of coordination and cooperation, as well as the development of new governance implementation tools for achieving regional development goals and growth, which are based not only on natural resources, territorial accessibility and changes in the external environment but also on knowledge and the skills to make use of them.

A number of researchers recognize that there is a correlation between the effectiveness of the institutional structure and growth. This chapter highlights the effectiveness of the institutional framework as one of the most important elements in achieving Cohesion Policy goals. The rapidly changing external environment emphasizes that the most important elements of institutional structures are those that provide the capacity to adapt to different conditions and situations.

Given the fact that the place-based approach is also described as a method for implementing public administration functions used to facilitate efficiency and results to be achieved within a given geographic area (Arefi, 2008), the authors analyse the place-based approach in the context of Cohesion Policy planning and in close conjunction with the nature of public administration.

A place-based approach is put forward as a solution to promote Cohesion Policy and is a topical EU discussion point (ESPON, 2014). The authors emphasize the need to further discuss the opportunities to apply a place-based approach in Cohesion Policy planning, since planning is the key element among functions of public administration. Planning involves the determination of goals for a given period in the future, as well as the necessary resources and actions for achieving those goals (Fox *et al.*, 2004). Policy planning requires specific information to be collected, analysed and transformed into sufficient evidence that can be used for decision-making and for ensuring planning capacity. Planning capacity is closely linked to setting up an appropriate institutional framework and a need for cooperation between different sectors. A different set of available territorial resources and changes in the external environment mean that the same approach to Cohesion Policy cannot be applied in all EU member states.

Although one of the objectives of Latvian accession to the EU was the steady development of the country, after ten years of membership there are still significant disparities between the regions. Latvia is among those EU member states that have the largest regional disparities. Most of the socio-economic indicators of the regions in Latvia are still below the EU average, which raises the question of the efficiency of territorial governance in the country and calls for more focused action to accelerate the equalization of socio-economic indicators of the territories. In this chapter, the authors provide an insight into the institutional framework that has been implemented in Latvia and discuss the main elements of the place-based approach. On the basis of the survey carried out in Latvian municipalities, the main factors influencing Cohesion Policy planning in Latvia and what may affect the application of the place-based approach have been analysed (Baltiņa, 2014).

Regional disparities and the quality of government

It has been discussed that the use of a place-based approach in regional development policy planning and implementation is in line with development trends in public administration (Baltiņa, 2014). This approach outlines policy integration and the cooperation of institutions that promote the creation of more open public administration (Sládeček, 2012), and highlights a focus on results and the need for the implementation of continuous improvements in the processes of governance (Smith, 2002). The authors remark that the place-based approach contributes to the development of results-oriented public administration and emphasizes the importance of qualitative information and knowledge about territorial resources and the development potential necessary for decision-making.

The interrelation between the role of territorial resources, the exploitation of their development potential and the institutional framework has been stressed by several authors (for example, Stimson *et al.*, 2011). Figure 18.1 shows a direct relationship between territorial resources, institutional framework and regional development as the result to be achieved (solid arrow), and it also demonstrates the indirect relationship between territorial resources and regional development (dashed arrow).

A number of scholars recognize that there is a correlation between the effectiveness of the institutional structure and growth (Chavance, 2008; Menard and Shirley, 2008). Several authors indicate the need for place-based innovation in public administration that would facilitate the development of an appropriate and

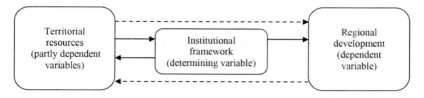

Figure 18.1 Interrelation between territorial resources, institutional framework and regional development.

flexible institutional framework (Adams *et al.*, 2010). In addition, there is also a correlation between the existing regional disparities and the effectiveness of public administration (World Bank, 2008) – the greater the regional disparities, the lower the indicator of efficiency of public administration.

To further discuss the above-mentioned statements, the authors studied various sets of indicators over the 2007–13 period and looked at the three most evident correlations: GDP per capita and quality of government, innovation and quality of government, and GDP per capita and innovation. The first two correlations imply that better institutions would promote growth and investment. Therefore, a higher quality of governance should be associated with greater GDP per capita (see Figure 18.2) with a strong correlation over the 2007–13 period. This correlation declines slightly in 2010 (below 0.85); however, this is most likely due to lagged effects from the 2008 financial crisis and austerity packages subsequently enacted, as after 2010 this correlation increases again as some parts of the EU's economy began to recover.

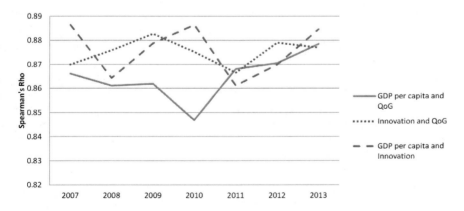

Figure 18.2 Spearman's Rho correlations of GDP per capita, quality of government index and innovation, 2007–13.

Source: Authors' calculations based on Eurostat data, European Quality of Government Index and Innovation Index.

Better-quality institutions should allow for a more stable and healthier business climate, thus allowing private-sector firms to make long-term investments in new and innovative technologies. The authors observe a strong correlation between innovation and the quality of government, as illustrated in Figure 18.2.

The role of regions and an exploration of the Latvian context

Previous applications of the place-based approach in the EU show an increased role of the regions in achieving Cohesion Policy objectives, which gradually prompted a discussion of the role of regions in regional development planning and in the creation of a better territorial governance model, and clearly showed the need to strengthen the role of the regions. Institutional theory emphasizes that the territorial governance model should be flexible enough to be able to react to changes in the economic and social environment by implementing the appropriate actions. This also applies to the question of the regions not just as administrative units, but as active participants in regional development planning.

To illustrate the links between the efficiency of the institutional framework and regional disparities, the authors have explored the Latvian context. The analysis of the institutional framework with a specific focus on the role of the planning regions provides useful information about governance related to the process of administrative territorial reform and discussions about the role of the planning regions since the mid 2000s. The increasing regional disparities in Latvia continue to represent the main challenge for the National Development Plan. Several factors influence the achievement of Cohesion Policy objectives, but proper governance seems to be a crucial precondition for the success of Cohesion Policy at the national, regional and local levels.

One of the main implemented measures directly relating to regional development planning is the administrative territorial reform that was completed in June 2009. It resulted in a reduction in the number of local municipalities from 524 to 119. However, the authors' analysis shows that even though the administrative territorial reform led to a reduced number of municipalities, it did not bring about any other changes in the governance model or in organizational structure. Also taking into account the existing differences in the municipalities in terms of the size of the population and geographical area, the reform did not result in municipalities that were equal in terms of administrative and financial capacity (VRAA, 2012). The authors, based on their research, conclude that changes in regional development in Latvia are highly driven by changes in the external environment. This was observed in 2008–9 when the rapid economic downturn made cuts to government spending a necessity.

The analysis of the developments of the institutional framework in Latvia show that the EU policy initiatives, such as multi-level management, the implementation of the Partnership Principle and the requirements for setting the EU funds implementation system, are important factors affecting the development of public administration; for example, due to the availability of EU funds, public administration in Latvia has expanded. However, this has not had an impact on deciding on the role of planning regions in achieving regional development goals and a common point of view has not yet been reached. There is no definition of the term "region" in the legislative documents in Latvia. Only the Law on Regional Development states that since 2006 the planning regions in Latvia are derived public entities and are under the supervision of the Ministry of Environmental Protection and Regional Development.

In prior studies commissioned by the State Regional Development Agency and Central Statistical Bureau, the regions are discussed as a potential governance level that could ensure a link between the national and local levels, meaning cooperation between local governments and state institutions, but none of these research projects has viewed regions as significant bodies that could be involved in regional development planning with a clear set of objectives and responsibility within this process. According to the authors, uncertainty over or the absence of a regional level of governance identified in policy statements and regional development studies is one of the most important problems of Latvian regional development planning; this was corroborated by the results of the survey of local governments (Baltiņa, 2014).

No clear decisions have yet been made on the status of the regions and their role in achieving Cohesion Policy goals at the national and regional levels. This shows the need for appropriate changes in the institutional framework that should be closely linked to the process of Cohesion Policy planning and implementation. Therefore, the authors pay special attention to the question of the status of the planning regions and their role in regional development planning in Latvia.

Within the study, the authors conclude that the development of territorial resources is an important factor in implementing the place-based approach and requires an efficient governance model, but it does not necessarily imply a need for regional-level authorities (Blöchliger and Charbit, 2010). The authors consider that in Latvia the biggest cities can fulfill the role of the regional governance level in finding solutions to the problems that are common for several municipalities. In this case, the formation of voluntary city-regions can take place, the boundaries of which are determined by the participants, as only a common agreement on cooperation can contribute to the creation of stronger authority. Accordingly, this type of functional city-region is one of the solutions for promoting the cooperation of local authorities in developing common transport and economic infrastructure and in building another type of cooperation. According to Bite (2012), the national, regional and local development centres defined in Latvia are mainly established for the needs of EU funds distribution and are not considered as functional regions, and the cooperation between local municipalities is weak.

The establishment of functional regions must be a voluntary choice made by municipalities and it should not be decided by the government. It should be mentioned that the attempt by the Ministry of Environmental Protection and Regional Development to outline the functional regions in separate planning documents is not based on existing collaborative actions among local authorities, but mainly on unifying geographical features, such as the coastline or the border area. This can be characterized as a "top-down" approach, which does not correspond to the place-based approach. It should be noted that the establishment of functional regions is by no means a substitute for defined administrative areas, but is a parallel initiative to existing structures, as their roles and responsibilities are different. The functional regions can foster integrated planning and hence build capacity in specific areas. For example, they might contribute to the monitoring of regional development and might increase public participation in regional development. The current regional development trends show that the establishment of city-regions and cross-border regions as voluntary associations of local governments, without strictly defined borders and without an elected council, is one of the options to promote regional development in Latvia. With regard to the establishment of functional regions, it is important to develop a mechanism under which the development plan of the functional region, as well as new activities and initiatives, can obtain the approval of national and local institutions. The authors consider that such an approach would contribute to the modernization of the current governance model and would promote its flexibility as well as facilitate the use of the place-based approach in regional development in Latvia without requiring additional funding.

The benefit of using a place-based approach is that it does not require strict administrative boundaries, but rather highlights the role of the territory where the integration of different policies may be effective and allows the pursuit of small-scale initiatives in a smaller area, without the need to cover the entire region. According to Blöchliger and Charbit (2010), this approach allows action to be taken appropriate to the territory's particular resources and development potential, ranging from strategic spatial planning to creative local cultural initiatives.

The present authors point out that the use of the place-based approach in regional development emphasizes effective utilization of existing territorial resources and that it should also emphasize the improvement of the quality of work and services of the existing institutions and the organizations. The establishment of new bodies promotes greater resource disintegration rather than improving the cooperation between existing structures.

Cooperation versus coordination

Public administration reforms are often based on the need to improve operational efficiency and to create more accessible public administration. However, in the context of regional development, such reforms include changes in regional and local administrative structures and measures to be taken to improve their effectiveness. These changes emphasize the role of coordination, cooperation and development of new governance implementation tools for achieving regional development goals.

Based on the analysis of practices in EU member states, one of the most commonly identified problems concerned with public administration is an inefficient or non-existent cooperation mechanism between the national and regional or local governments, which results in insufficient cooperation between different levels of public administration. To date, EU member states have not generally seen the need to change their institutional systems significantly in order to promote regional development (Charbit, 2011); however, their intention is to improve the coordination of sectoral policies, and this is constantly emphasized. There are several options available to achieve this improvement, according to their scope and the instruments used. Improvements in coordination can be carried out at the national, regional and local levels, for example, through cooperation agreements and agreements between institutions at regional and national levels.

The analysis shows that there are different approaches and different instruments for enhancing coordination, determined by characteristics such as the size of the country, population, government structure, cooperative practice between the national, regional and local levels, and other state-specific features. The unclear role of regions in Latvia and the inexistent mechanism for sectoral cooperation has contributed to a need for the establishment of new structures for solving existing problems (for example, the establishment of a cross-sectoral coordination centre in Latvia). However, the authors note that, in fact, coordination is often associated with additional reporting and greater bureaucratic burden. It is therefore necessary to develop a form of collaboration that includes the delegation of functions, clear principles of cooperation, the development of common goals and joint actions to achieve these objectives.

With regard to the 2014–20 planning period, in order to implement a more integrated approach, EU member states are emphasizing the need to ensure better inter-institutional coordination and to respond to territorial challenges. In response to the need to implement a more integrated approach, a variety of implementation arrangements are adopted; some EU member states move towards a more centralized implementation of EU funds (for example, one programmer per fund or a single programmer for all three funds), while some continue to implement both national and regional operational programmes.

Within the place-based approach, it is important to balance compliance with the hierarchical structure with the possibilities of implementing various cooperation initiatives at the regional and local levels. Therefore, the reform of public administration is not the determining factor if the current system is dynamic enough to take flexible decisions and ensure effective cooperation between all levels of government. Collaboration in administration of the territory can be successfully implemented both by identifying administrative boundaries and by using less formal instruments of cooperation. For example, in France there are urban communities, such as the Lille metropolitan area (the city of Lille and its surrounding municipalities), which has its own administration that includes the leaders of all of the local governments within the territory, and together they plan and implement measures related to such essential functions for territorial development as spatial planning, transport and housing. Large cities in Germany are implementing a less formal form of cooperation, whose main objective is the promotion of economic development in large cities and their nearest local governments to enhance the regions' competitiveness at the European level, by pooling resources to ensure more integrated development and together find solutions to issues such as demographic and climate changes.

The authors agree with scholars who emphasize that the most important elements of institutional structures are those that provide the capacity to adapt to different conditions and situations (Karlsson *et al.*, 2012). Territorial resources in regional development, in turn, should be seen as the provision of an environment suitable for the transfer of knowledge and the development of new models of cooperation that facilitate the economic development of regions and innovation (Camagni, 2002). The authors see the cooperation between government institutions and organizations at the national, regional and local levels as one of the most important prerequisites of the place-based approach. Several researchers have recognized the importance of promoting the involvement of regional and local governments and the non-governmental sector in decision-making (Porter and Wallis, 2002; Panara and De Becker, 2011).

The survey of local municipalities of Latvia reveals several problems regarding inter-institutional cooperation in Latvia and helps to elaborate possible solutions (see Table 18.1).

The authors see a need for an in-depth investigation into the increasing role of intangible factors in the promotion of regional development, such as participation in cooperation networks and the development of social capital. It has been observed that regions that are actively involved in various cooperation networks are better able to see the opportunities and to mobilize their resources to promote regional development, as well as consider these networks as an essential social capital (Karlsson *et al.*, 2012). It is assumed that the institutions and organizations that are active in the creation of new knowledge engage in various cooperation networks to spread their knowledge and best practices (Capello and Dentinho, 2012). The authors observe that by combining these aspects, public administration as it develops is gradually moving away from the hierarchy and towards cooperation and networking.

In applying the place-based approach in regional development planning, one of the most important steps is the availability of functional regional development assessment tools. The regional development challenges arising from the impact of globalization and changes in the external environment facilitate the need to conduct a regular assessment of the changes in territorial resources and development potential; it is necessary to provide a regular review of territorial resources according to changes in the external environment in regional development strategies, to preserve and promote the competitiveness of the regions. Resource dynamics are important in long-term development planning, as they are associated with a region's ability to support an interaction between the available resources in a changing external environment, and covers innovation, learning, collaboration, management and forecasting ability (Eisenhardt and Martin, 2000; Cooke *et al.*, 2012).

Main factors affecting the use of the place-based approach

A survey of representatives of 119 local governments in Latvia was carried out (Baltiņa, 2014).[1] The survey shows that in achieving EU Cohesion Policy goals

Table 18.1 Factors affecting the use of the place-based approach in regional development planning in Latvia at national, regional and local levels (in percentages).

Factor	Proposed solution
Ineffective exchange of information between various government levels	• Unified, location-based access to the summarization, storage and use of sectoral data • Website for all regional development documents and implementation procedures • Unified and multi-functional system for assessing changes in territories' development
Inefficient administrative capacity at the local and regional levels	• Improvement of strategic planning skills • Improvement of territorial information analysis skills
Uncertainties about the competencies of sectoral ministries, lack of coordinated actions	• Clear objectives for Latvian regional development at the EU, national, regional and local levels • Unified methodological framework for the use of the place-based approach in the planning and implementation of sectoral policies
Discrepancy between the administrative and functional territory	• Methodological framework for the establishment of functional territories • Capacity assessment of local governments • Methodology for the creation of an 'effective' territorial unit • Cooperation of local governments in the planning of development and the implementation of joint projects
Discrepancies in the established policy objectives	• Agreement on the main objectives and interests at the EU, national, regional and local levels
Lack of compliance with the principle of transparency	• Methodological framework for the assessment of institutional quality at the national, regional and local levels • New mechanisms to improve society's engagement

and positive changes in the development of the territory of the municipality, greater importance is given to the availability of EU funds than to the implemented regional development policy measures. However, more than a third of respondents believed that the implemented regional development policy measures in the 2004–11 period had no real impact on territorial development at the local level. These results show that regional development policy measures implemented thus far are not considered to have contributed significantly to real improvements at the local level.

Regarding the territorial development goals in Latvia, respondents most frequently assigned the highest priority to the need to increase the welfare of the population in Latvia, and the second most important objective was named as the need to promote the development of human resources. The answers to this question on the objectives for the next planning period indicate the need to emphasize and promote the welfare of the population.

With regard to the most important changes to be made to the current governance model, most respondents (64.3 per cent) stated that a clear division of roles and responsibilities between the national, regional and local levels should be designated. As the most significant measure to promote regional development, almost all respondents (98.5 per cent) pointed to the promotion of economic activity. Almost all respondents (92.8 per cent) also indicated the need for clear national objectives at the EU level. This shows that the majority of respondents associated the implementation of a place-based approach with the need to establish clear objectives for regional development.

The survey shows that to increase the role of local governments in regional development planning and implementation, there is a need for better coordination between local, regional and national planning authorities, as well as organizations representing various interest groups. Respondents highlighted the need to improve the understanding of regional development issues, including the EU's regional development trends and regional development instruments.

The survey highlighted the issue of improving infrastructure as the most important territorial development problem to be addressed at the national, regional and local levels. Respondents' answers to questions about the territorial development issues mark the need for the equal involvement of all levels of government in regional development planning and implementation. Respondents' answers identify the issues of regional development for which the greatest cooperation between all levels of government must be ensured: strategic planning, improvements in infrastructure, and social and educational issues (see Figure 18.3).

In the promotion of business development, the national level has the most important role (with regard to common development priorities and local authorities) due to managing territorial resources and their potential.

The results of the survey form the basis for the following conclusions and recommendations for changes in institutional arrangements in Latvia to ensure coherent EU Cohesion Policy planning and implementation.

Conclusions and recommendations

A well-established legal and institutional framework is the foundation for ensuring regional development, and therefore the improvement of policy documents and their mutual coherence is one of the starting points. Given that the use of the place-based approach also includes the improvement of regional development documents, there is a strong need to clarify the terms used in these documents and to agree on key regional development principles.

The study confirms that in Latvia there is no single access point to all regional development policy planning and implementation documents in an aggregated form. The aggregation of documents concerning regional development policy, planning and implementation in one site would facilitate the work of local governments, planning regions, sectoral ministries and other stakeholders, as well as promoting compliance with these documents when drafting other regional development planning and implementation documents.

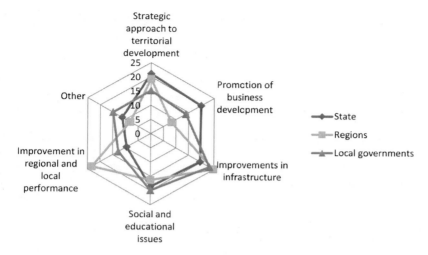

Figure 18.3 Most important regional development issues to be addressed at the national, regional and local levels in the 2014–20 planning period.

Note: Total number of respondents = 265.

The study shows that there is a strong need for high-quality and timely statistical data at the regional and county levels. Most often, the EU-level statistics and research do not represent the actual situation in Latvia at the regional level. With regard to the implementation of regional development assessments, the regional development planning and forecasting system in Latvia is still non-functional.

Institutions responsible for Cohesion Policy planning and implementation in Latvia have to be encouraged to show the link between the use of national and EU funding and achieving Cohesion Policy goals, and to find tools for collecting information and evidence so as to be able to assess the impact of policies on territorial development.

It should be noted that administrative territorial reform, in an attempt to create stronger local governments, the developed national strategy for sustainable development and the accumulated experience of the EU funds management could contribute to the application of the place-based approach in regional development in Latvia; however, the main bottlenecks are associated with the low capacity of the planning regions and the lack of a common position among sectoral policies about the use of the place-based approach in regional development planning. The study shows that administrative capacity at the national, regional and local levels is an important prerequisite for the use of the place-based approach in regional development planning, as it is linked to the ability to develop an up-to-date business environment and to provide citizens with the necessary services. The importance of the place-based approach in Cohesion Policy planning has not yet been adequately recognized in the practice of public administration in Latvia.

Note

1 Heads of development and planning departments, and local government specialists working in these departments, participated in the survey as respondents.

References

Adams, N., Cotella, G. and Nunes, R. (eds) (2010), *Territorial Development, Cohesion and Spatial Planning: Knowledge and Policy Development in an Enlarged EU*, New York: Routledge.
Arefi, M. (2008), *Asset-Based Approaches to Community Development*, Nairobi: UN-HABITAT.
Baltiņa, L. (2014), "A place-based approach in EU regional development and its application in Latvia", *Baltic Journal of European Studies*, 4(1), 34–53.
Bite, D. (2012), "Pašvaldību sadarbība Latvijā" doctoral thesis Riga, Latvia: University of Latvia.
Blöchliger, H. and Charbit, C. (2010), "Subcentral governments and the economic crisis: impact and policy responses", Working Paper No. 752, Paris: OECD.
Camagni, R. (2002), "On the concept of territorial competitiveness: sound or misleading?", *Urban Studies Journal*, 39, 2395–411.
Capello, R. and Dentinho, T. P. (eds) (2012), *Networks, Space and Competitiveness: Evolving Challenges for Sustainable Growth*, Cheltenham, UK: Edward Elgar.
Charbit, C. (2011), "Governance of public policies in decentralised contexts: the multi-level approach", OECD Regional Development Working Papers No. 4. Paris: OECD.
Chavance, B. (2008), *Institutional Economics*, London: Routledge.
Cooke, P. N., Parrilli, M. D. and Curbelo, J. L. (eds) (2012), *Innovation, Global Change and Territorial Resilience*, Cheltenham, UK: Edward Elgar.
Eisenhardt, K. and Martin, J. (2000), "Dynamic capabilities: what are they?", *Strategic Management Journal*, 21(10–11), 1105–21.
ESPON (2014) *Towards Better Territorial Governance in Europe: A Guide for Practitioners, Policy and Decision Makers Based on Contributions from the ESPON TANGO Project*, Luxembourg: ESPON & Politecnico di Torino, available at: www.espon.eu/export/sites/default/Documents/Publications/Guidance/Governance/ESPON_Governance_Handbook.pdf (accessed 12 April 2016).
Fox, W., Schwella, E. and Wissink, H. (2004), *Public Management*, Stellenbosch: Sun Press.
Karlsson, C., Johansson, B. and Stough, R. R. (eds) (2012), *Entrepreneurship, Social Capital and Governance: Directions for the Sustainable Development and Competitiveness of Regions*, Cheltenham: Edward Elgar.
Menard, C. and Shirley, M. (2008), *Handbook of New Institutional Economics*, Berlin: Springer.
Panara, C. and De Becker, A. (2011), *The Role of the Regions in the EU Governance*, Berlin: Springer.
Porter, D. R. and Wallis, A. D. (2002), *Exploring Ad Hoc Regionalism*, Cambridge, MA: Lincoln Institute of Land Policy
Sládeček, V. (ed.) (2012), *Current Development Tendencies in Public Administration*, Special Edition of *Contemporary Administrative Law Studies*.
Smith, G. A. (2002), "Going local", *Educational Leadership*, 60(1), 30–3.

Stimson, R. J., Stough, R. R. and Nijkamp, R. (eds) (2011), *Endogenous Regional Development: Perspectives, Measurement and Empirical Investigation*, Cheltenham, UK: Edward Elgar.

VRAA (Valsts reģionālās attīstības aģentūra) (2012), *Pārskats "Reģionu attīstība Latvijā 2011"*, Riga: VRAA.

World Bank (2008), *World Development Report 2009: Reshaping Economic Geography*, Washington, DC: World Bank.

19 Integrated territorial investment
A missed opportunity?

Iván Tosics

Emerging interest in urban areas: the development process of the new Cohesion Policy

The emerging interest in urban areas in general and in integrated urban development in particular is the result of a long policy development process. Not going back too far in history, the major steps of this process are summarized in Table 19.1, starting from the 2008 economic and financial crisis. The crisis helped us to understand that the multitude of challenges in Europe (such as climate change, energy, ageing, social polarization and mobility) and their complex interactions can only be handled by an integrated approach.

This short overview, covering only the last few years, illustrates well the ups and downs in EU urban policy development. Following earlier setbacks (for example, around the time of the 2004 enlargement), the end of the last decade brought about some real progress, such as the acceptance of the concept of integrated development with integrated territorial investment (ITI) and community-led local development (CLLD) as tools to achieve it. The original ideas of the European Commission (EC), however, have been substantially "watered down" by the resistant member states, and the resulting regulation compromise has proved to be too weak to achieve the original aim (to provide with a global grant instrument wide-ranging decision-making autonomy for the cities).

Lessons learnt during the development process of the new Cohesion Policy

The coverage of Cohesion Policy

As it became clear that the post-2013 Cohesion Policy would get less financial resources than it had before, the idea emerged to allocate all of the resources to the poorer regions. The option to exclude the richer countries from Cohesion Policy was most heavily criticized by Danuta Hübner, who argued that this would change Cohesion Policy into Charity Policy, with all of its problems. The final outcome of the negotiations meant that all EU countries were still included, but that resources were heavily concentrated on the poorest countries. This solution was a compromise, however, with serious effects on the regulation itself.

Table 19.1 Major steps since 2008 to develop the new Cohesion Policy approach to urban areas.

Date	Event/milestone	Remarks
2009	Barca report	The influential Barca report paved the way for the return of the EU framework for multi-level governance based on area-based interventions towards horizontal integration of different sectoral policies.
2010	Toledo Declaration	'It must be a political priority to empower European cities to tackle future challenges . . . a stronger emphasis on the integrated approach and sustainable urban development, a stronger focus on territorial and social cohesion'. (European Union, 2010).
early 2011	Polish Ministry paper	This paper proposed the introduction of a global grant instrument for cities with the prerequisite for cities to prepare an integrated urban development programme, based on integrated urban development strategy (Swianiewicz et al., 2011).
2011	Speech of Danuta Hübner at the 5th Cohesion Forum	Hübner argued for true simplification: to have one territorial strategy for an area to which all funds contribute. However, he admitted that this was only a dream as all ministers/funds want their own programmes.
2012	Speech of Johannes Hahn at the EU Urban Forum	Hahn argued for the importance of ITIs: money from different priorities or funds can be put together into one customized 'bundle', allowing the use of a wide range of different projects to address the particular needs with coordinated policies. The instrument should be as flexible as possible.
2013	Council of the EU	The Council adopted the Cohesion Policy package for the 2014–20 period.
2014	Open Days	The EC made repeated 'victory statements', emphasizing how many countries and cities have already signed up for the new Article 7 tools, especially ITIs. These statements were in sharp contrast to the complaints of many of the cities themselves.

Conditionality and a common European Urban Policy framework

During the discussions, many experts argued for a stronger, more binding regulation: it was suggested that firm conditions (compulsory elements) for the use of Cohesion Policy resources should be introduced. The idea of a common European model of urban development as a policy framework was also raised.

Neither of these ideas has been realized. Firm conditions were rejected by many countries, who opposed forceful steps towards integrated solutions. One of the arguments was the lack of experience and weak administrative "culture" of those poorer countries that get the large majority of the money. The richer countries also opposed firmer regulation because this would have caused them more trouble than the very limited financial rewards would have been worth. As regards the need for a common European framework for urban development, there was general support but the idea of giving more authority to the EC with regard to urban policy was rejected.

The new Article 7 tools

Under the new regulation, the compulsory urban dimension (Article 7) was ideally meant to be a multi-level governance structure in which a national/regional-level policy framework would stimulate and regulate integrated interventions in selected cities. Thus the intention was broader than it was in the case of the URBAN Community Initiative; the integrated interventions had to be part of city-wide (or even city-region-wide) development strategies, but they were not required to focus on deprived areas.

The essence of the new tools can be summarized as follows:

- Article 7 of the ERDF regulation:

  At least 5% of the ERDF resources allocated at national level under the Investment for growth and jobs goal shall be allocated to integrated actions for sustainable urban development where cities, sub-regional or local bodies responsible for implementing sustainable urban strategies ("urban authorities") shall be responsible for tasks relating, at least, to the selection of operations.

  (European Union, 2013: 296)

This should be undertaken through ITI, or through a specific operational programme or priority axis.

- The extension of CLLD to urban areas, ensuring that neither public nor private actors can dominate decision-making. This helps to involve the population in the planning and implementation of area-based interventions in deprived neighbourhoods and in the control of people-based (i.e. sectoral, not area-based) policies.

The new regulation and the new tools raised the hopes for more integrated urban development policies. ITI was considered to have the potential to handle territorial mismatch (the discrepancy between administrative and functional urban areas) and make planning more strategic, while CLLD was considered to have the potential to make planning more democratic.

Let us examine whether these expectations (especially that of ITI, which is the focus of this chapter) proved to be realistic.

Article 7 tools: the state of affairs

The estimated magnitude of Article 7 programmes in the different EU countries

By the end of 2014, the EU member states had signed their Partnership Agreements with the EC. These documents include the national approach to the implementation of Article 7 of ERDF regulation: how much money will be spent on sustainable urban development and how the cities/urban areas in which the ringfenced money will be spent will be selected. This amount is estimated to be around €14.5 billion (almost 8 per cent of the ERDF allocation) for the 28 countries across the whole programming period.

It is not easy to get an overarching picture of how and where the money for Article 7 will be spent. In some countries, the allocation of the resources will be competitive; in other words, the selected cities will only be known later, as a result of a bidding procedure. In view of the lack of precise information, only a rough estimate can be prepared about the allocation of money for Article 7.

To get a meaningful indicator of the financial significance of the Article 7 regulation, it is important to relate the allocated amount of Article 7 money to the size of the relevant population on which the money will be spent. As the latter is as yet unknown in many countries, it can be replaced with the size of the urban population, simulated by the new OECD indicator showing the population living in the functional urban areas of a given country (OECD, 2012).

On the basis of the calculations, the following three groups of countries can be identified as being in very different situations as regards Article 7 funding:

1. *high Article 7 resources (per capita) compared to the size of the urban population*: Slovakia 185, Estonia 126, Czech Republic 126, Hungary 108, Poland 96, Portugal 94, Slovenia 88, Greece 73 (Bulgaria, Croatia, Latvia, Lithuania and Romania also belong to this group);
2. *medium Article 7 resources (per capita) compared to the size of the urban population*: Italy 34, Spain 34;
3. *low Article 7 resources (per capita) compared to the size of the urban population*: Finland 15, France 11, Germany 10, Sweden 10, Ireland 9, Belgium 8, the UK 7, Austria 6, Denmark 4, the Netherlands 2, Luxembourg 0.

As shown above, Article 7 funding is most significant for the peripheral EU countries (the east and central European and the poorer south European countries), whereas it is almost insignificant in the richer north-western countries. The differences are shocking; cities in the peripheral countries might receive 10–20 times more Article 7 resources per capita than cities in the richer countries.

The appropriate spending of Article 7 resources requires complex knowledge and experience as all aspects of integrated urban development have to be considered: horizontal integration between policy areas (policy management), vertical integration between different levels of government (multi-level governance) and territorial integration between neighbouring municipalities (cooperation in functional urban areas). The cities that will receive the highest amount of Article 7 money relatively are those whose authorities are least experienced in the complex planning, governance and implementation mechanisms needed for the required integrated use of these resources.

Country and city case studies

Experience gathered in international meetings shows that there are large differences in the national perceptions of the Article 7 regulation; some countries pay substantial attention to the issue, whereas others do not consider it as a topic worthy of spending too much time and effort on. Some of the latter countries are explicitly annoyed by the complexity of the Article 7 regulation and look for an easy way to handle it (for example, to give all of the Article 7 money to only one city, as in Austria).

The outcome of the above simulation of the relative financial significance of the Article 7 regulation shows huge differences in the amount of money allocated, which largely explains the differences in the reactions of countries. As further illustration, more qualitative information is summarized below about the differences between countries/cities belonging to the three different categories according to the financial background for Article 7. The cases are "reconstructed" from different sources: presentations at seminars (for example, the URBACT seminar on the integrated approach and the UDN-URBACT workshop held in Brussels on 9 October 2014), Czischke and Pascariu (2015) and also some information from the CEMR (2014) study.

Example of a high Article 7 resource country: Poland

In Poland, ministers decided quite early in favour of ITI as the tool to implement Article 7. Over 5 per cent of ERDF and ESF resources are transferred to the Regional Operational Programme (ROP) from which the ITIs will be financed. The target cities are the capitals of the 16 regions and the Regional Development Ministry made the Functional Urban Area (FUA) approach compulsory – namely, that ITIs have to be created at the level of metropolitan areas, not just the city itself. In each case, an ITI association has to be established, led by the core city. As regards the composition of this association, the ministry prepares a list of municipalities as potential members and the core city has to ensure that at least half of these municipalities voluntarily join the ITI association.

The ITI association has to develop and approve the ITI strategy. On that basis, agreement has to be reached between the Managing Authority (MA) (which is at the regional level) and the city authority. The smallest responsibility that could possibly be delegated to the association is project selection, which has to be based on project ranking (each project has to affect at least two municipalities and has to have soft and hard aspects). Surprisingly, some regional seat city authorities do not want to become Intermediate Bodies (IBs) as they consider project selection for their FUA a very large and difficult task (in terms of ranking projects and working towards the agreement of everybody).

The ITI money is transferred to the association through the ROP, and the regional MA decides how much money is devoted to the ITI (Warsaw gets the smallest amount, €165 million).

Example of a medium Article 7 resource country: Italy

Italy has a separate chapter in the Partnership Agreement for Article 7. Dedicated urban axis is the main form of organizing Article 7; only one region will use ITI. A national programme will be prepared for the 14 largest cities, which were recently merged with their surrounding provinces, thereby creating the Metropolitan Cities. These city authorities will become the IBs within the dedicated urban axis. The institutional reform changes the city borders and makes the approach unified across the country, creating metropolitan authorities through direct elections. It is still a matter of debate how much power and autonomy the new level will get as regards integrated urban development.

Example of a low Article 7 resource country: France

In France, the new Contract de Ville policy includes the integrated urban approach. Municipalities have to define their deprived areas on the basis of nationwide indicators. According to the Partnership Agreement, 10 per cent of ERDF resources (and 1.8 per cent of ESF resources) will be dedicated to Article 7. Regional authorities will become the MAs; in the case of France, this is a step towards decentralization. As a further step towards decentralization, inter-municipal associations will also get a larger role. Regional authorities can decide whether to use ITI or urban axis. By contrast to this flexibility, there is a national decision to reject multi-fund financing; ESF is instead regulated at the national level.

The implementation of integrated urban development using Article 7 resources: variations and issues

Financial matters and integration

Table 19.2 includes a few cases of ITIs in which the financial circumstances are more or less known.

The very different levels of funding create very different circumstances for integrated development. As a general rule, if funding is reduced, then either only a few specific projects can be implemented rather than overarching programmes, or smaller target areas have to be selected to allow the concentration of the resources. Examples of both approaches can be found among the city case studies:

290 Iván Tosics

Table 19.2 Preliminary estimates of ITI funding in selected urban areas.

Urban area (core city)	Approx. money for ITI (millions €)	Approx. size of population (millions)	Estimated financing (€ per capita)
Wroclaw	300	0.90	333
Warsaw	165	2.65	62
Finland	80	2.20	36
Lille	34	1.20	28
Randstad	50	2.50	20

Source: Author's own calculation based on case studies presented in various seminars and publications.

- In absolute terms, Warsaw receives a relatively substantial sum; however, this has to be spent on joint projects with the neighbouring municipalities. As €165 million is not sufficient to finance an overall strategy of metropolitan development, only a few concrete projects could be selected: bicycle lanes, parking lots for park-and-ride services, an integrated electronic ticketing system for public transport, the economic promotion of the metropolitan area.
- In French cities, the ITI resources have to be spent on the most deprived neighbourhoods ("sensitive urban areas"), selected on the basis of nationwide indicators.

Compared to these two types of approaches, some medium-sized (mainly Polish) cities get much higher amounts of money for their ITIs. At present it is an open question how these city authorities will be able to organize integration at the FUA level. Lessons from the Urban II (2000–6) programme showed that it is much easier to organize integration on a small scale, in neighbourhoods, with interventions around the magnitude of €10 million. This argument has been made by Paul Jeffrey in a debate at the *Social and Economic Conflicts of Transition Towards Democracy and Market Economy. Central and Eastern Europe 25 Years After* conference, organized by the Metropolitan Research Institute in Budapest in November 2014.

The challenge of how to use ITI (if substantially funded) to organize integrated urban development at the FUA level needs further consideration. Programmes that reach beyond the administrative boundaries of the core city are less likely to concentrate on deprived areas; however, if they do, they might be more efficient in handling externalities (NODUS, 2010).

Critical issues in the implementation of integrated urban development using Article 7 resources

On the basis of the briefly described examples, a number of critical issues can be identified which endanger the fulfilment of the original aims of Article 7 – namely, to foster urban development in an integrated way.

Thematic concentration and result orientation

Thematic concentration and result orientation are essential aims of the new approach of Cohesion Policy, linked to the Europe 2020 strategy. Not to criticize the importance of these aims in themselves, it is nevertheless clear that both are very much against locally determined (participatory, bottom-up) integrated thinking.

Thematic concentration in particular can be considered as an obstacle from the perspective of the integrated approach, as the designated priority objectives might be very different from the needs and ideas of the local actors.

Result orientation – the strictly required use of ex-ante indicators and rigorous monitoring methods to check whether the original objectives have been achieved – eliminates most opportunities for flexibility. City authorities implementing ITIs have to report back to all funding bodies; the tool moves further and further away from the original intention of a global grant (which would allow city/urban authorities to develop their own integrated strategy, to collect money from different funds and sources for that purpose and to use this money without having to consider conditions imposed by those from whom it came).

Multi-fund financing

One of the basic requirements for integrated development is a mixture of different types of interventions, including (among others) physical and social. This leads to the perennial topic of separation and the fragmentation of the ERDF and ESF funds at the level of the EC. As Jan Olbrycht, head of the Urban Intergroup in the European Parliament, said at the UDN-URBACT conference in Brussels in October 2014: "ITI is aiming for multi-fund financing in a situation when the Commission itself could not achieve cooperation between ERDF and ESF".

Even if there have been some attempts to define joint rules for the five European funds, the reality is that ERDF and ESF are very different as regards institutions, definitions and strategies. Some of the member states further aggravate the problem with national ESF regulation, excluding any opportunity for ESF resources to be used at a regional or local level as part of integrated interventions.

Similar problems are present in the relationship between the urban and rural funds. In reality, it is more and more difficult to distinguish urban areas from rural areas. However, as regards EU funding, this is required as the first step of programming. It is hard to imagine integrated development in functional territories until it holds that rural development cannot be included in urban programmes and vice versa. Many analysts think that the new issue of urban–rural cooperation is only hiding this basic conflict and cannot bridge the gap caused by the separation of rural and urban development.

"Delephobia"

This new expression (born in 2014) describes the hesitation of MAs to share management and implementation functions with local authorities. To delegate some functions (power) to the local level is an important aspect of integrated development; in order to genuinely involve all actors, some role or responsibility should be given to them. However, many MAs consider local authorities as inexperienced in Cohesion Policy matters and thus as having the potential to endanger the financial accountability of the programmes.

From the perspective of the MAs, which have final responsibility, it is understandable that delegation only happens if trust develops towards the IBs, which are the city authorities (or FUA-level associations of local governments). However, in countries in which urban authorities have a long history and experienced staff, delephobia is difficult to understand. Germany is one of the countries in which MAs reject the devolution of power and responsibilities to city authorities (Tödtling-Schönhofer and Hamza, 2014).

From the perspective of the city authorities, at least three different strategies can be observed:

1. Many city authorities are self-conscious and fight against the MAs in order to get more delegated power from them (for example, Italian Metropolitan Cities).
2. Another group of city authorities would in principle be able to take over more power but refrain from doing so due to fiscal austerity (for example, English city authorities that have lost a very substantial proportion – over 40 per cent – of their staff).
3. There are some city authorities that do not want to become IBs, not even for the minimal task of project selection, as they do not have the knowledge and capacity for that.

Training for city authorities

According to the Cohesion Policy regulation, project selection is the very least that should be delegated to the local level. Although this task seems to be a small part of integrated development, it is important to explore whether the projects have strategic fit and relevance, and correspond to local needs. Exploring projects, ranking them and working towards the agreement of everybody can be a huge task in FUAs.

In the case of city authorities or newly formed metropolitan partnerships that are unwilling to take over even this minimal task, the training of existing personnel is of crucial importance. Such training can be done using Technical Assistance (TA) resources for areas that have some formal delegation.

In some countries, many efforts are made to train city authorities to become better prepared for their tasks under Cohesion Policy. In France, for example, substantial training activity is included in the TA budget to allow city authorities to prepare. In Italy, the maximum possible resources are given to TA, including a national committee to support the 14 new IBs (which are the Metropolitan Cities). A network between the Metropolitan Cities is also being established.

However, the lack of knowledge is not solely the failure of the city authorities. As Mendez et al. (2012) emphasize, while the CLLD instruments are based on the existing LEADER approach, ITIs are new and there is a lack of detail on how they can be used most effectively in practice. This refers to the overdue and slow development of guidance by the EC.

Conclusion

Integrated urban development is not only one of the territorial aims of Cohesion Policy; neither does it refer only to the "urban" areas as opposed to "rural" and "remote" areas. It is much more: a framework and method for better and more inclusive planning and development at the local level. For this reason, the partial failure of the efforts of the EC to introduce a compulsory common framework for integrated urban development has potentially serious consequences for the performance of the whole Europe 2020 agenda.

In the old EU member states, the integrated approach to urban development has some history and is relatively well known (though is still not applied everywhere). Despite this, the richest countries of the EU were unwilling to fully support the new approach of the EC towards integrated development, and successfully prevented key elements of it from becoming compulsory for all countries.

In the new EU member states and peripheral southern European countries, the integrated approach is relatively new. The promise of a high level of EU funding, if coupled with innovative national regulations, has already led in some countries (for example, Poland and the Czech Republic) to positive changes in metropolitan cooperation and strategic thinking. In other countries, however, changes are not so positive; the national and regional authorities want to retain their exclusive powers while there are serious capacity problems at the local level, and many of the city authorities are not happy to be delegated further powers and responsibilities.

The analysis has shown that the EC created a potentially very good tool; ITIs led at the local level might awaken the interest of city authorities in territorial and vertical cooperation. However, the substantially weakened form of the Article 7 regulation allowed national and regional authorities to easily avoid the implementation of cooperative forms of integrated urban development.

What went wrong? Why is there a danger that the new tools for integrated urban development will achieve less integration than was the case with the URBAN Community Initative (which received substantially less funding)? Paradoxically, one of the reasons might actually be the difference in funding. The success of URBAN was partly due to its well-defined model and limited scale (around €10 million of EU funding for the integrated development of clearly designated local neighbourhoods), which allowed for flexibility from the EU's perspective. To have much larger amounts of money in the form of ITIs (up to €300 million) means that the task of integrated urban development becomes much more complex, less transparent and less influenced by the local communities, and that there is a much higher risk of corruption. These dangers logically give rise to the need for much tighter control from the EC's perspective, which, however, kills the flexibility of the tool.

Another reason might be the weakness of explanations of and guidance about ITI. If there is no clear view of what an ITI might be, and if its magnitude might vary between €3 million and €300 million (!), then it is hard to give a clear and concise description. By the time the Partnership Agreements had to be negotiated with the EC, the member states could still not access sufficiently detailed guidance about ITIs,[1] which would have allowed informed decisions, and only the first out of four ITI Scenarios was ready.[2] No wonder that many countries decided against using ITI, or decided to only use it very cautiously, on an experimental basis. The brevity of the ITI factsheet was called "flexibility" by the EC; however, it was understood by the member states to be a weakness of regulation, with the danger that any national regulation of ITIs could later be questioned by the EC and, even worse, by the auditors.

Taken into account the high potential of the ITI tool, its programming by the member states, as shown in the Partnership Agreements, cannot be considered a success (as claimed by the EC). On the contrary, this story marks a lost opportunity.

What can be done? This short analysis shows that there is a big need for capacity-building in those countries that will receive the most Article 7 resources relative to the size of the urban population. The capacity-building efforts should take place not only at the city level but also at the regional and national level, both in the public administration and in the EU-related institutions.

In the course of the capacity-building efforts, an important role should be given to those city, regional and national authorities that are the most experienced in integrated urban development. It is important to note that these cities will not necessarily become Article 7 cities in the new programming period due to the low amount of such resources in their countries.

Needless to say, this capacity-building has to be undertaken in a relatively intensive way, owing to the tight time schedules set for the Article 7 cities (ITI strategies have to be developed quickly, preferably by the end of 2015, to allow enough time for the implementation).

The ITI circumstances are very different from country to country, depending on the one hand on the national framework for ITI in the given country, and on the other on its history and "culture" of integrated urban development. Thus the needs have to be explored at a national level, and country-specific work seems to be the most helpful.

Even if Article 7 (and ITI in particular) can be considered as a lost opportunity from the perspective of integrated urban development, the EC can still do a lot to improve the situation. The emphasis has to be on better communication and guidance and more help to develop the best possible programmes under the given national regulations. In this regard, the European knowledge exchange programmes (for example, URBACT) could and should play an important role.

Notes

1 All EU regulations and guidance can be found approached on the Special EU Programmes Body website (SEUPB, n.d.). While the CLLD factsheet is dated May 2014 and includes 53 pages of text and seven pages of appendices, the ITI factsheet is dated January 2014 and includes ten pages of text and three pages of appendices. This is despite the fact that much more EU money will be spent on ITI than on CLLD.
2 To highlight what an integrated territorial approach could look like when implementing the Europe 2020 strategy, the Commission developed four "Scenarios", each describing how ITI can be used in practice. Three of the four scenarios, however, were published only in early 2015.

References

Barca, F. (2009), *An Agenda for a Reformed Cohesion Policy: A Place-Based Approach to Meeting European Union Challenges and Expectations*, independent report, Brussels: European Commission, available at: http://ec.europa.eu/regional_policy/archive/policy/future/pdf/report_barca_v0306.pdf (accessed 22 March 2016).

CEMR (2014), *Cohesion Policy: The Use of Integrated Territorial Investments (ITI) by Member States*, CEMR overview, Brussels: CEMR, June, available at: www.ccre.org/img/uploads/piecesjointe/filename/CEMR_survey_on_Integrated_Territorial_Investments_2014_EN.pdf (accessed 2 March 2016).

Czischke, D. and Pascariu, S. (2015), "The integrated approach to sustainable urban development in 2014–2020: implementing Article 7", Final Thematic Report, URBACT, available at: http://urbact.eu/sites/default/files/art_7_final_thematic_report.pdf (accessed 11 March 2016).

European Union (2010), *Toledo Declaration: Toledo Informal Ministerial Meeting on Urban Development, Toledo, 22 June 2010*, Brussels: European Union, available at: http://ec.europa.eu/regional_policy/archive/newsroom/pdf/201006_toledo_declaration_en.pdf (accessed 2 March 2016).

European Union (2013), "Regulation (EU) No. 1301/2013 of the European Parliament and of the Council of 17 December 2013 on the European Regional Development Fund and on specific provisions concerning the Investment for growth and jobs goal and repealing Regulation (EC) No. 1080/2006", *Official Journal of the European Union*, 20.12.2013, 289–302.

Mendez, C., Kah, S. and Bachtler, J. (2012), "The promise and perils of the performance turn in Cohesion Policy", IQ-Net Thematic Paper 31(2), Glasgow, UK: European Policies Research Centre, University of Strathclyde, available at: www.eprc.strath.ac.uk/iqnet/downloads/IQ-Net_Reports%28Public%29/Thematic%20Paper_31%282%29.pdf (accessed 2 March 2016).

NODUS (2010), "Linking urban renewal and regional spatial planning", URBACT Working Group, Lead Partner: Catalunya, Lead Expert: Ivan Tosics, available at: http://urbact.eu/sites/default/files/import/Projects/NODUS/outputs_media/NODUS_Final_Report_def_01.pdf (accessed 11 March 2016).

OECD (2012), *Redefining "Urban": A New Way to Measure Metropolitan Areas*, Paris: OECD, available at: www.oecd-ilibrary.org/urban-rural-and-regional-development/redefining-urban_9789264174108-en (accessed 28 February 2016).

SEUPB (n.d.), "EU Regulations and Guidance", available at: www.seupb.eu/2014-2020Consultations/backgroundinfo/euregulations.aspx (accessed 1 March 2016).

Swianiewicz, P., Atkinson, R. and Baucz, A. (2011), *Background Report on the Urban Dimension of the Cohesion Policy post 2013*, Warsaw: Polish Presidency, July, available at: www.esponontheroad.eu/dane/web_espon_library_files/708/background_report_urban_dimension_of_cp.pdf (accessed 2 March 2016).

Tödtling-Schönhofer, H. and Hamza, C. (2014), "The role of cities in Cohesion Policy 2014–2020", presentation for the European Parliament, Committee on Regional Development, Vienna, Austria: Metis GmbH, available at: http://raffaelefitto.it/wp-content/uploads/2014/09/REGI_2014.09.23_Study-on-Role-of-Cities-in-Cohesion-Policy-2014-2020.pdf (accessed 2 March 2016).

20 The place-based approach in development policy
A comparative analysis of Polish and EU[1] space

Jacek Zaucha and Tomasz Komornicki

Introduction

Poland recently become an EU leader in the promotion of a territorial approach within development policy (Cohesion Policy at the EU level) (Doucet *et al.*, 2014; Faludi, 2015). In Poland, the long-term national development strategy encompasses both the socio-economic and the territorial dimension. This type of approach to development – namely, one that is territorially sensitive and integrated – was then highlighted and promoted at the EU level by the Polish presidency of the EU Council at various events and in various documents both officially published (Böhme *et al.*, 2011; MRR, 2011a, 2011c) and prepared as background papers (MRR, 2011b). In this chapter, we investigate the progress of the implementation of this approach in Poland at the regional level and compare this with the situation in selected other EU countries. We focus on a place-based approach formally invented by Barca (2009) and sometimes described in the literature as the "cream of the crop" as regards institutional approaches to policy territorialisation (Zaucha *et al.*, 2014: 251).

In the chapter, we compare the findings of two surveys related to the implementation of the place-based approach conducted jointly by the Institute of Geography and Spatial Organization of the Polish Academy of Sciences and the Institute of Development of Sopot. The first survey was conducted on behalf of the Network of Territorial Cohesion Contact Points (NTCCP) in 2012 and covered 25 EU countries plus Norway and Switzerland (Zaucha *et al.*, 2013). The second survey covered 16 Polish NUTS2 regions (voivodeships) and was executed in 2014 as a part of the research project "Concept of territorial cohesion in Cohesion Policy: Implications for economic growth" (no. 2012/05/B/HS4/04212) financed by the Polish National Science Centre.

Development policy in Poland

In Poland, development policy is defined in a parliamentary bill, the Polish Act of 6 December 2006 on the principles of development policy. It is considered to be a set of interrelated activities undertaken and implemented in order to ensure the sustainable development of the country, to provide socio-economic, regional and spatial cohesion, and to increase the competitiveness of the economy and the creation of new jobs at national, regional and local levels. This policy is jointly implemented by the Council of Ministers (the national government of Poland) and local and regional governments in accordance with their competences.

In Poland, as already stated, the socio-economic and territorial dimensions of development were merged into one strategic document that gives foundations for other key policies in the long run. For the medium-term perspective, the National Spatial Development Concept 2030 is a part of the system of national strategic documents that ensures the implementation of the developmental goals at every level of government and underpins the territorial approach in all other documents (Korcelli et al., 2010). At the regional level, directly elected regional assemblies or regional parliaments (legislative power) and Marshals of voivodeships (executive bodies) are entrusted with the responsibility of managing intraregional development policy. At this level, two basic regional strategic documents are created: the Regional Development Strategy and the Regional Spatial Development Plan. They serve as a basis for funds allocation. EU-funded Regional Operational Programmes (ROPs) managed by regional authorities in two programming periods (2007–13 and 2014–20) are based on them (Woźniak, 2010). Comparing Polish regions with those of other countries, the former enjoy a very strong formal development mandate (for example, an independence vis-à-vis the central government that is enshrined in law), coupled with the necessary financial resources (ROPs). Moreover, Polish regions are large (around two million inhabitants), which gives additional weight to the intraregional development policy, and, in many cases, they have accumulated the relevant policy experience due to, for example, active participation in EU policies and initiatives. Polish regional governments sign regional contracts with the central government to ensure vertical coordination and compatibility between policies. The contract also makes it possible for them to influence both the government's policy and investments on their territory.

The local level in Poland also has its own development policy. However, Polish municipalities are generally small (there are 2,479 altogether), with the exception of some large cities. Unfortunately, the work on establishing metropolitan areas as a policy entity has only recently begun in Poland. Thus the local level is disregarded in the surveys presented below.

As indicated by the Ministry of Regional Development (MRR, 2010: 16), territorially oriented policy is "(1) focused on the use of endogenous potential, territorial resources, and knowledge, and (2) allows for the implementation of interventions directed at developmental challenges, and precisely tailored to local conditions". Other authors (Zaucha et al., 2013: 8–9) emphasise instead the institutional aspect – in other words, the necessity of dialogue between the institutions administering the given territory and those representing the interests of the territory as a whole.

The essence of the place-based approach

"Place-based" is a very popular term among researchers, but is used in various different ways and contexts. However, such confusion over terminology is an

Place-based approach in development policy 299

inevitable part of research dealing with territorial issues (Dühr *et al.*, 2010: 30). The notion of "place-based" has usually been associated in the literature with local issues, processes or phenomena attached to a given place. For instance, Neumark and Simpson (2015) consider enterprise zones, EU Structural Funds and industrial cluster policies targeting underperforming areas as place-based policies. A very similar understanding of the term can be found in Olfert *et al.* (2014). Kwan (2009) associates "place-based" with conventional and static areal units used for studying the contextual determinants of health. Phadke *et al.* (2015) use the notion of "place-based scenarios" without defining the term; however, it can be understood that those scenarios are place-specific.

But all of these examples are some distance from the place-based concept developed by Barca (2009). In the Science Direct repository, 5,418 records can be found when searching for "place-based" but only 18 when the search is narrowed to Barca's particular concept, and most of those 18 only refer to the place-based approach in passing. Thus we can conclude that place-based policy-making, as proposed by Barca, is not a popular research subject. Recently, only a few publications have concentrated on the topic (Zaucha *et al.*, 2013; Doucet *et al.*, 2014; Faludi, 2015).

These publications adequately encapsulate the essence of the place-based approach in line with Barca's intentions. Thus here it is sufficient to summarise only key elements of this approach, drawing on what is available in the literature (Figure 20.1). However, even this simple illustration clearly shows that the definition of the place-based approach should not be narrowed into taking into account merely the local context, as stressed by some researchers (Jucevičius and Galbuogienė, 2014). It is more a way of bringing together different developmental scales and contexts in order to make development happen. Compared to a multi-level governance concept, the place-based paradigm attaches more attention to the developmental context conditioning policy interventions, with less attention given to the formal mandates of the various developmental actors.

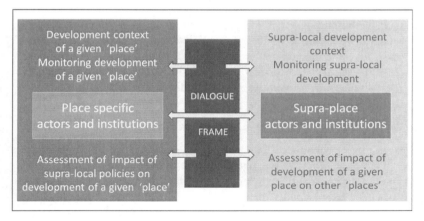

Figure 20.1 Key elements of the place-based approach.
Source: Szlachta and Zaucha (2012).

The place-based approach as developed by Barca can be considered as being composed of the following ingredients (Doucet et al., 2014: 6):

1. developmental actors/agents capable of harmonising/coordinating the development of different "places" together;
2. developmental actors/agents capable of guiding, influencing and fostering the development of a given "place";
3. knowledge of the overall developmental context (in other words, the developmental goals and priorities important at the supra-place scale and the best means for pursuing them and monitoring progress to that end);
4. recognition of territorial diversity in pursuing overall developmental goals (in other words, acknowledgement that there are different ways of addressing developmental goals and priorities for different parts of the territory under the influence of institutions mentioned under Point 1);
5. knowledge of developmental specificity in a given place (such as territorial capital and other types of local/regional potential);
6. knowledge of the impact of supra-local policies on local development and of local policies on supra-local development;
7. an institutional framework for multi-level governance dialogue;
8. dialogue between different developmental agents described under Points 1 and 2, with an essential part of this dialogue captured by the notions of vertical and horizontal integration.

Barca considers underdevelopment to be the result of the failure of different levels of governance to deliver necessary institutions and/or investments for a given place in order to ensure growth. If we take only two levels of governance, place-specific and supra-place, they are hampered by different deficiencies. The former is prone to rent-seeking and local egoism, while the latter might be tempted into a "one-size-fits-all" approach to policy-making, resulting in local resistance and a waste of resources. To avoid all of these deficiencies, the developmental actors should work within a dialogic framework based on sharing knowledge and evidence. It is also important to underline here, after Faludi (2015: 8), that "places are not the same as jurisdictions, so they cannot be managed by governments alone". Thus the place-based concept should not be associated with formally created territorial units such as counties, municipalities or regions.

The consequences of the place-based approach

The consequence of acknowledging the relevance of the place-based approach is the diversification of policy in line with the needs of the existing contexts. This is called "territorialisation" and has been described in detail by, for example, Zaucha et al. (2014). In practice, this means different objectives and/or measures of supra-local policies for different places as well as the existence of place-specific policies, all performed in some kind of concertation. The practical meaning of such an approach with regard to national development policies has been explained by Böhme *et al.* (2011: 87–128) using two territorial characteristics that vary from place to place: accessibility and intensity of networking between city regions. The ultimate result should be a different policy focus (concentration), different conditions and different financial solutions to be implemented in different places. For example, in Polish regions with high European and national accessibility, the development policy should concentrate on public transport linking city centres with their hinterlands; the condition of undertaking public interventions should be the existence of road pricing and the integration of transport systems within metropolitan areas; and preference should be given to solutions that combine grants and loans (Böhme *et al.*, 2011: 105). In this context, it should be acknowledged that, if introduced by the European Commission in the current programming period, thematic concentration might be counterproductive in diminishing the efficiency of Cohesion Policy if not coupled with issue-based concentration, which means the necessary flexibility under the place-based approach to allow for policies to be fine-tuned in relation to the interplay between developmental scales.

The measurement of progress in implementing the place-based approach

When the various developmental actors are asked whether their policies/interventions/actions are tailored to the socio-economic and territorial context (varying according to the place), usually the answer is affirmative. Indeed, the awareness of such a necessity seems high. However, spatially blind policies and strategic documents still prevail. An example might be our flagship strategy, Europe 2020. However, fortunately even here the need for territorialisation has recently become the subject of serious discussion, involving not only the academic sphere but also institutional proponents of the strategy (see, for example, Haase, 2015: 27–32). For those reasons, instead of assessing the extent of policy territorialisation (which might be difficult and prone to subjective bias), we decided to examine the existence of the necessary pre-conditions for the introduction of the place-based approach: knowledge of the developmental context at various geographical scales, the existence of a place-based dialogue and procedures for assessing the impact of policies across scales. The responses were given by members of the NTCCP for EU countries and by competent representatives of Polish regional governments (usually directors of the departments responsible for spatial and regional development or of the specialised agencies subordinate to them).

Unfortunately, we had to limit the scope of our research to the existing administrative units (countries and regions), although we did try to examine the diversity of actors taking part in place-based policy-making. Thus we only partially managed to fulfil Faludi's (2015) call for an analysis of the actors without formal jurisdiction (in other words, a no-man's-land concept). In line with the key elements of the place-based approach, we evaluated knowledge of the developmental context, the capacity to assess the impact of policies across geographic scales and the existence of a place-based dialogue. We also assumed that comparison between answers given by respondents representing national (EU) and regional

(Poland) tiers of government is justifiable due to a good knowledge of regional issues among NTCCP members. Surveys were conducted in 2012 and 2014; the time difference is acceptable as the introduction of a place-based paradigm belongs to the class of long-term processes that evolve rather slowly.

Knowledge of the developmental context

In both surveys we asked for details of the different methods of collecting knowledge used by regional (in the EU cases, also local) authorities necessary for their active engagement in a place-based dialogue with other developmental actors. We received answers from 26 countries and 16 Polish regions. The findings are presented in Figure 20.2.

Comparing the findings in Figure 20.2, it can be easily noticed that regions put a lot of emphasis on the collection of relevant knowledge. Polish regions rely much more on existing statistical information and regular monitoring systems than their EU counterparts. This is partially thanks to the establishment, on the initiative of the national government, of the network of central and regional territorial observatories (RTOs). Appreciation of this process is quite high among regional authorities. However, the very frequent use of available statistical data (some regional authorities even have agreements with regional Bureaus of Census with regard to data processing and the preparation of specific reports for them) should be regarded as less positive. On the one hand, it makes regional development policies more evidence-based, but on the other, such data

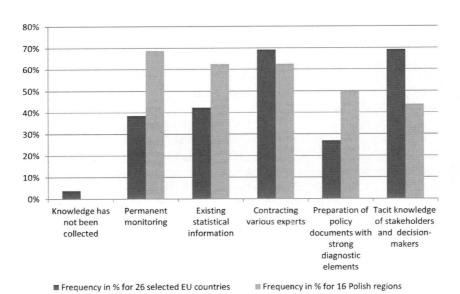

Figure 20.2 Frequency of usage of different methods of collecting knowledge necessary for the place-based approach by regional (and local) authorities.

are usually only available after a significant time delay, and this diminishes their usefulness in supporting many future-oriented decisions. In Poland, the process of gathering new knowledge is very intense during the preparation of regional strategic documents, which possess a strong diagnostic element. Thus in only a few cases has permanent monitoring been used on a regular basis so far, and knowledge collection has been subject to specific volatility, driven by EU programming periodicity. A very important drawback to the knowledge collection of Polish regions is their continued limited capacity to elicit the tacit knowledge of stakeholders and decision-makers. This is a very important skill which makes policies better tailored to the changing circumstances. However, the proper elicitation of such knowledge requires specific experience and immunisation against the rent-seeking behaviour of stakeholders and the domination of vested interests. Moreover, giving more emphasis to tacit knowledge creates the opportunity, at least in Poland, to incorporate the stakeholders without jurisdiction into the development process (as postulated by Faludi (2015)). Tacit knowledge is in many cases of an aspatial character, whereas the regularly collected data are usually based on existing statistical units and thus poorly fitted to the no-man's-land idea.

Summing up this part of the analysis, we can say that the knowledge necessary for the active engagement of regional authorities in a place-based dialogue has been collected in Poland, and so this should not be regarded as a barrier to the implementation of a place-based approach. In fact, Polish regions are slightly ahead of their EU counterparts. They are in a phase in which the ways of gaining knowledge about regional processes are changing. Increasing emphasis is placed on the creation of consistent systems. However, the most striking observation revealed by the Polish survey is that knowledge is accumulated, but information management is often random and non-systematic (see Zaucha *et al*., 2015). The process of sharing knowledge currently constitutes a weakness in the implementation of the place-based approach. Polish regions must learn how to influence the decisions of other actors by sharing accurate information. Currently, passive methods of doing so dominate: printed and electronic materials. This is perhaps also a challenge for other regions in the EU, and the issue requires more intensive regional research.

Influencing the policies of other actors across geographic scales

All of the Polish regions declared that they have conducted some kind of assessment of national EU policies concerning the socio-economic development and spatial structures of their regions. However, 7 of the 16 regions chose the option "Partly", which may indicate that these activities have been in some manner limited. The assessments are mostly carried out during the preparation of strategic documents for a given region and from the perspective of their compliance with supra-regional policies. Other opportunities to conduct such analysis are given by the announcement of key EU documents (for example, Trans-European Transport Networks or cross-border areas) or the renewal of national policies (for example, the transport policy). Those assessments are therefore one-off activities of a passive character. As one respondent indicated, in spite of the fact that those kinds of evaluations are conducted, "what fails to be analysed is [the policies'] influence on the development of, for instance, GDP". Thus, it seems that this might be a weakness in implementing the place-based approach in Poland.

This was confirmed by other findings obtained. We also asked, for example, about the methods used by regional authorities for assessing the impact of development policies managed at the national (in the Polish case, also EU) level of governance on the socio-economic and territorial development of their regions. The findings are presented in Figure 20.3.

The findings in Figure 20.3 are in line with the earlier observations about the existence of severe problems in conducting assessment of the supra-regional policies by Polish regional authorities. In this respect, Polish regions are lagging behind their EU counterparts. Instruments of assessment are absent and interactions with stakeholders rarely take place. The most frequently used methods, consultation with national ministries (mentioned by 6 of the 16 regions) and preparation of joint documents by all regions within the framework of co-operation of regional Marshals (mentioned by 5 regions), are not even listed in Figure 20.3 as they are very specific to Poland. Even external expertise is used much less frequently by Polish regions than by their EU counterparts. All of this weakens the position of Polish regions in a place-based framework.

Moreover, as already stated, the capacity of Polish regions to influence the behaviour of other developmental actors by sharing knowledge is limited. In both surveys we investigated how frequently the explicit expectations towards other levels of governance in the official programming documents are revealed. It seems that in the EU cases, 73 per cent of countries (19 of 26) confirmed that such expectations are contained in the regional and/or local socio-economic or territorial strategic documents. In the Polish case, this was acknowledged by

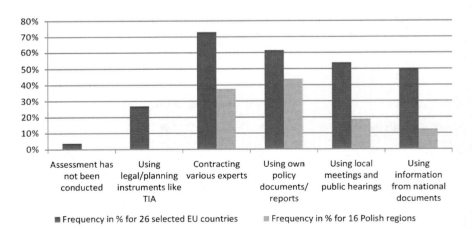

Figure 20.3 Local[2] and/or regional authorities' and stakeholders' assessments of the impact of development policies managed at the national and EU[3] level of governance on the socio-economic and territorial development of their territories.

56 per cent of regions (9 of 16). This finding confirms the observation that there is considerable room for improvement in the usage of knowledge as a vehicle for improving the implementation of a place-based approach.

To conclude this part of the discussion, we should add that the assessment of the impact of regional policies suffers from similar shortcomings as the assessment of the impact of national policies (Figure 20.4). Local governments in Poland carry out analyses of the development policies of the region in connection with the process of elaboration of the regional or local documents. The national level usually limits itself to checking the formal compliance of regional documents with national strategic ones. Regions are engaged in analysing the policies of other regions even less frequently and usually only do so if they have an interest in elements of strategy that affect their territory (for example, common problems, an infrastructural or ecological corridor, or tourism). The search for conflicts prevails over the search for synergy. Analysis of the development of foreign regions sometimes seems more important than analysis of the development of neighbouring regions within Poland. However, the preparation of macro-regional strategies (covering two or more regions in Poland) has slightly changed this pattern recently.

Place-based dialogue

In Poland, the place-based dialogue between national and regional governments is based on legal provision – namely, so-called territorial contracts. As pointed

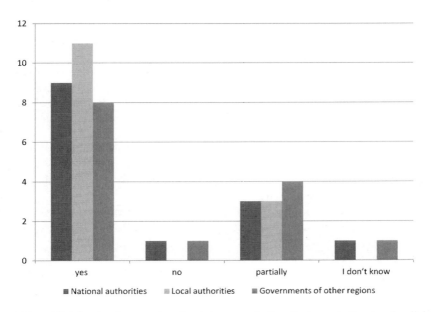

Figure 20.4 Regional respondents' opinions on whether the impact of regional policies is analysed by other authorities.[4]

out by Woźniak (2013), the contract is an agreement concluded between the regional and central governments in which the latter commits to supporting the most important projects in the given region, agreed during bilateral negotiations, following on from the government's policy towards that region and the regional development strategy:

> According to the National Regional Development Strategy, the contract is to be the most important planning instrument, ensuring the implementation of public policies with territorial impact in Poland, including operational programming. It specifies the objectives and tasks of individual signatories and instruments for their achievement.
>
> (Woźniak, 2013: 5)

In 2012, a place-based dialogue anchored in legal provisions existed in 14 of the 26 selected EU countries. It can be assumed that Poland is among the leaders in pursuing a place-based dialogue since it puts emphasis on contractual agreements as a framework for such a dialogue,[5] whereas in the EU cases the dominant instruments are a hierarchy of planning (policy) documents, strategic environmental assessments and environmental impact assessments (Zaucha et al., 2013: 18). Another striking difference was satisfaction with such a dialogue, where 48 per cent of EU respondents were of the opinion that the dialogue does not work and is not sufficient. In Poland, the reverse was true; of the 15 Polish regions that answered this question, all of them rated their satisfaction with the dialogue between regional and national tiers as above average and five (33 per cent) assigned it the highest grade. Only one region rated their satisfaction with the dialogue with national authorities as around average, whereas other "types" of dialogue were assessed much more highly.

However, in spite of high levels of satisfaction, Polish respondents also enumerated several barriers hampering the place-based dialogue. This might indicate that in at least a few Polish regions the expectations with regard to the quality of the dialogue are quite limited. The four most important types of barrier are as follows:

1   barriers associated with the egoism and rent-seeking behaviour of local authorities;
2   barriers associated with legal stipulations, bureaucracy and the setting of competences at the central and regional levels;
3   barriers associated with the unwillingness of developmental actors to share information and the superficial character of consultations (an inadequate culture of dialogue);
4   barriers associated with the deficit of social capital, of which a misunderstanding of the concept of integration and a lack of transparency were two examples given.

When comparing these barriers with those identified by the EU survey (Figure 20.5), it is clear that the key obstacles are similar in Poland and in the EU: rent-seeking

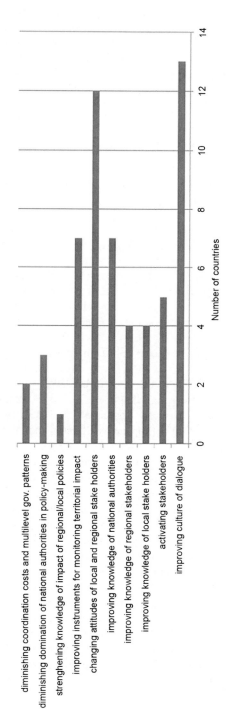

Figure 20.5 EU respondents' opinions on what changes would help to remove barriers to a place-based dialogue.
Source: Zaucha *et al.* (2013: 41).

behaviour and an inadequate culture of dialogue. In the Polish case, barriers related to the dominance of the national government are slightly more important and a deficit of knowledge is less important, which confirms the previous observations. Bearing in mind that both key barriers are of a soft nature, a plea should be made for a strong educational/behavioural component necessary for the proper implementation of a place-based approach both in Poland and in the EU.

Discussion and conclusions

The intraregional policies of Polish regions seem to fulfil the criterion of being territorially sensitive. In all of the Polish regions, policy goals and measures are territorially diversified. Knowledge of the territorial developmental context has been greatly improved. RTOs have been established. Territorial contracts have been signed between national and regional governments and also between local and regional governments. Place-based dialogue is enshrined in law. However, some important mental barriers still exist that hamper the introduction of a place-based approach. The most important of these relate to co-operation (knowledge sharing, influencing the impact of other actors, culture of dialogue, rent-seeking behaviour). Moreover, it seems that Polish regional authorities have some problems in understanding the benefits of a place-based approach.

Bearing in mind that the place-based approach is part of a broader concept of territorial cohesion (Zaucha et al., 2015), we asked respondents to describe the meaning of this concept. The findings confirmed that their comprehension of the concept is usually narrower than that presented in the theoretical studies. Territorial cohesion is usually correctly associated by Polish regional authorities with the implementation of an appropriately directed spatial policy and with the use of the endogenous potential (greater policy efficiency, greater regional resilience, increased well-being). However, they also frequently understood territorial cohesion as socio-economic cohesion, but in a spatial context. Thus the reasons for a place-based approach might sometimes be narrowed to a discussion of redistribution issues and thereby neglect important features of investments and institutions that should ensure the prosperity of a given place in line with its specific endowments and circumstances, as proposed by Barca (2009). This is in opposition to Barca's original concept, which counterpointed the traditional policy focus on the compensation for regional differences in unit capital costs (due to productivity gaps) and on the rebalancing of labour and capital flows. All of this calls for a two-pronged strategy in the introduction of a place-based approach at least in Poland. Legal measures (for example, integrated strategic documents, the introduction of territorial contracts or RTOs) should be coupled with a properly targeted information campaign and networking to deepen understanding of the essence and benefits of a place-based approach among regional decision-makers and civil servants. Poland is leading the way in terms of legal arrangements, but is lagging behind in the behavioural domain.

Notes

1 The analysis also includes other countries of the so-called ESPON space (Norway, Liechtenstein, Switzerland and Iceland).
2 Only EU cases.
3 Only the Polish case.
4 Only 14 regions answered this question.
5 Also frequently mentioned were cross-border networks (agreements), the work of the assembly of regional Marshals and integrated territorial investments (also based on contractual arrangements), an instrument that had only recently been introduced by the EU.

References

Barca, F. (2009), *An Agenda for a Reformed Cohesion Policy: A Place-Based Approach to Meeting European Union Challenges and Expectations*, independent report prepared at the request of Danuta Hübner, Commissioner for Regional Policy, Brussels: European Commission, available at: http://ec.europa.eu/regional_policy/archive/policy/future/pdf/report_barca_v0306.pdf (accessed 1 June 2015).

Böhme, K., Doucet, P., Komornicki, T., Zaucha, J. and Świątek, D. (2011), *How to Strengthen the Territorial Dimension of "Europe 2020" and EU Cohesion Policy*, Warsaw: Ministry of Regional Development.

Doucet P., Böhme K. and Zaucha J. (2014), "EU territory and policy-making: from words to deeds to promote policy integration (debate article)", *European Journal of Spatial Development*, available at: www.nordregio.se/Global/EJSD/Debate/EJSD%20debate%20Doucet%20et%20al.pdf (1 December 2014).

Dühr, S., Colomb, C. and Nadin, F. (2010), *European Spatial Planning and Territorial Cooperation*, London and New York: Routledge.

Faludi, A. (2015), "Place is no man's land", *Geographia Polonica*, 88(1), 5–20.

Haase, D. (2015), *The Cohesion Policy Dimension of the Implementation of the Europe 2020 Strategy*, Brussels: European Parliament.

Jucevičius, R. and Galbuogienė, A. (2014), "Smart specialisation: towards the potential application of the concept for the local development", *Procedia: Social and Behavioral Sciences*, 156, 141–5.

Korcelli, P., Degórski, M., Drzazga, D., Komornicki, T., Markowski, T., Szlachta, J., Węcławowicz, G., Zaleski, J. and Zaucha, J. (2010), "Eksperski projekt koncepcji przestrzennego zagospodarowania kraju do roku 2033", *Studia KPZK*, 128.

Kwan, M.-P. (2009), "From place-based to people-based exposure measures", *Social Science & Medicine*, 69(9), 1311–13.

MRR (2010), *Krajowa Strategia Rozwoju Regionalnego 2010–2020: Regiony, Miasta, Obszary Wiejskie*, July, Warsaw: Ministry of Regional Development.

MRR (2011a), "Territorial dimension of EU policies: strategic programming, coordination and institutions territorially sensitive for an efficient delivery of the new growth agenda – 'who does what and where?'", issue paper, October, Warsaw: Ministry of Regional Development.

MRR (2011b), "Territorial dimension of development policies", post-seminar publication, July, Ostróda, Poland: Ministry of Regional Development.

MRR (2011c), "Effective instruments supporting territorial development: strengthening urban dimension and local development within Cohesion Policy", issue paper, September, Warsaw: Ministry of Regional Development.

Neumark, D. and Simpson, H. (2015), "Place-based policies", in G. Duranton, V. Henderson and W. Strange (eds), *Handbook of Regional and Urban Economics*, vol. 5, Amsterdam: Elsevier, pp. 1197–287.

Olfert, M. R., Partridge, M., Berdegué, J., Escobal, J., Jara, B. and Modrego, F. (2014), "Places for place-based policy", *Development Policy Review*, 32(1), 5–32.

Phadke, R., Manning, C. and Burlager, S. (2015), "Making it personal: diversity and deliberation in climate adaptation planning", *Climate Risk Management*, 9, 62–76, available at: www.sciencedirect.com/science/article/pii/S2212096315000236 (accessed 3 March 2016).

Szlachta, J. and Zaucha, J. (2012), "For an enhanced territorial dimension of the Cohesion Policy in Poland in the 2014–2020 period", Institute for Development Working Paper 002/2012/(06), available at: www.instytut-rozwoju.org/WP/IR_WP_7.pdf (accessed 3 March 2016).

Woźniak, J. (2010), "Legal system of Polish regions: implications for the regional policy", in P. Churski and W. Ratajczak (eds), *Regional Development and Regional Policy in Poland: First Experiences and New Challenges of the European Union Membership*, Warsaw: Studia Regionalia KPZK PAN [Committee for Spatial Economy and Regional Planning, Polish Academy of Sciences], pp. 194–202.

Woźniak, J. (2013), *Study on European Union's New Multiannual Financial Framework 2014–2020 from the Polish Perspective*, Warsaw: Senat RP, available at: www.senat.gov.pl/gfx/senat/userfiles/_public/k8/ue/wyszehrad/temat_1_ekspertyza_2_en.pdf (accessed 25 June 2015).

Zaucha, J., Świątek, D. and Stańczuk-Olejnik, K. (2013), *Place-Based Territorially Sensitive and Integrated Approach*, Warsaw: Ministry of Infrastructure and Development.

Zaucha, J., Komornicki, T., Böhme, K., Świątek, D. and Żuber, P. (2014), "Territorial keys for bringing closer the territorial agenda of the EU and Europe 2020", *European Planning Studies*, 22(2), 246–67.

Zaucha, J., Brodzicki, T., Ciołek, D., Komornicki, T., Mogiła, Z., Szlachta, J. and Zaleski, J. (2015), *Terytorialny Wymiar Wzrostu i Rozwoju: Spójność, Potencjały i Użyteczność*, Warsaw: Difin.

Index

Entries for EU countries have their codes shown in brackets. This is how the country is represented in some of the figures.

Index entries for contributors do not include page references for their biographical information or their contributing chapters.

Page numbers followed by an italicised n: t or f refer to notes, tables or figures respectively.

absolute convergence hypothesis 55
absorptive capacity: demand and supply-side effects 37, 38f; and good governance 171, 173; less-developed regions 76, 222; national variation (CEECs) 173–4; regional variation in policy outcomes 25, 28; Romania 242, 244; and youth unemployment 5, 151–2, 155–66
accessibility 81, 271, 301; see also motorways and expressways (Poland)
accountability 178, 181, 187, 191, 206, 292; see also transparency
Acemoglu, D. 35, 116
additionality principle 22
administrative capacity: accession of CEEC countries 209, 242; administrative and political embeddedness 6, 172, 174–80, 181–2; as a bottleneck in management of EU funds 6, 182, 281; Cohesion Policy effectiveness (1989–2012) 20; cooperation versus coordination 272, 276–8, 300; detrimental effect of aid 187; link with governance 171, 172–4; methodological choices 22; and the Partnership Principle 6, 206, 207; place-based institutional framework 7, 272–4; planning regions (Latvia) 272, 274–6, 277, 278–81; Public administration reforms 271; Romania's sub-national level 7, 242–9; see also corruption

administrative embeddedness 172, 174–7, 180, 181
Algarve 13t, 14, 17f
Alliance of Free Democrats (SZDSZ) 224, 229t, 237t
Amsterdam, Treaty of 140
Andalucía 13t, 14, 16, 17f
Anselin, L. 102, 105, 107, 108
Aquitaine 13t, 14, 16, 17f
Arellano, M. 158
Article 7 tools: country and city case studies 288–9; EC 'victory statements' 285t; evaluation 293–4; implementation variations and issues 289–93; intentions of regarding urban development 286; national-level financial significance of 287–8; statement on gender equality 146
Asheim, B. 115
Austria (AT): Article 7 funding 287; Burgenland 13t, 14, 16, 17f; corruption risk analysis 199f, 201t; funds by area of intervention 71f; GDP growth per capita and GVA per worker (2000–2006) 73f; youth unemployment 128, 153, 154f

Bähr, C. 25, 245
Barca Report (2009) 173, 285t, 297, 299–300, 308
Barrios, S. 59t, 64t
Barro, R. J. 55, 59t, 74, 76

312   *Index*

Basile, R. 74
Basilicata 13*t*, 14, 17*f*
Becker, S. O. 21, 28, 56, 57*t*, 58*t*, 60, 61, 62, 63*t*
Belgium (BE) 71*f*, 73*f*, 199*f*, 201*t*, 287
benefit dependence 37
bias: methodological 24, 29, 60, 61, 66; *see also* territorial distribution bias
Big Lottery Fund's Talent Match 5, 127, 130, 132–3, 134–6, 137
Bite, D. 275
Blöchliger, H. 276
Bloom, S. 222
Blundell, R. 27, 158
Bodenstein, T. 26, 221, 233
Böhme, K. 297, 301
Boldrin, M. 24, 36, 56, 59*t*, 64*t*
Bond, S. 158
Boschma, R. 117, 119
Bouvet, F. 22, 221, 233
Braithwaite, M. 141
Brandt, M. 129, 136
Bucharest-Ilfov 242, 246, 247, 249
Bulgaria (BG): administrative and political embeddedness 172, 175, 176, 178, 180, 182; Article 7 funding 287; corruption risk analysis 199*f*, 200*f*, 201*t*; fund allocation (2007–2013) 34*t*; municipal level wealth bias 222
bureaucrats: capacity of 117, 187, 206, 207, 300; partnership interpretation 6, 207–8, 210–17; Partnership Principle failures 206, 207; veto player 178, 209–10
Burgenland 13*t*, 14, 16, 17*f*
business cycles 61, 152, 157, 158, 160*t*
Bussoletti, S. 24, 25, 58*t*, 61, 64*t*, 74

Camagni, R. 257, 278
Campania 13*t*, 14, 17*f*
Canova, F. 24, 36, 56, 59*t*, 64*t*
CEECS (Central and Eastern European Countries): absorption data 157, 244; Article 7 funding 287; corruption risk analysis 199*f*, 200*f*, 201*t*; EU admission 33, 208–9; investment strategies 49–51; macroproportions 33–4; Partnership Principle 206, 207–8, 210–17; political factors of fund distribution 222–3, 241, 245–6; regional variation in fund absorption 173–4; RIS3 policy 118, 119*t*, 120, 121*t*, 122, 123; territorial capital and economic growth 259, 267; *see also* Bulgaria; Czech Republic; Hungary; Latvia; Poland; Romania; Slovakia; Slovenia
centralization: as an institutional factor 25, 26; "*Delephobia*" 7, 241, 292; future system architecture (CEEC) 245–8; for inter-institutional coordination 277; and Partnership Principle 207, 241, 248; pre-accession requirements 209, 242; Regional Development Agencies (Romania) 241, 242, 243–9; RIS3 implementation 122; territorial distribution bias 220, 221, 222, 223, 235
Charbit, C. 276, 277
Chardas, A. 174
Charron, N. 171, 173, 189, 193, 256
Choudhry, M. T. 152, 155
Cinalli, M. 129
cities *see* metropolitan areas; urban policy development
Civic Party (PO, Poland) 223, 224, 226, 227*t*, 236*t*
civil society: Big Lottery Fund's Talent Match 127, 130, 132; discouraged by foreign aid 187, 188; and distribution bias 226, 228; partnership in centralised CEEC states 207, 212, 217
CLLD *see* community-led local development
Common Agricultural Policy (CAP) funds 26, 27, 38, 39–40, 42*t*, 45, 48, 49, 51
community-led local development (CLLD) 284, 286, 293
competitiveness: administrative cooperation (Germany) 277; and business cycle variance 61; challenges following Great Recession 144; expenditure by area of intervention 78, 81, 243, 263–4; and inclusive employment 141; in neoclassical growth theory 55; Poland 47–8, 297; procurement process competition 190, 192, 199; strategic focus on 1, 12, 69, 70, 119*t*, 258; and sustainable development 33, 36, 297
conditionalities: Cohesion Policy reform (2013) 1, 2, 50, 285–6; and gender mainstreaming 147, 148; for place-based development 301; smart and specialisation 4, 116
conditioning factors: contextualization-identifiction synergy agenda 3,

29; literature review 3, 21, 23–8; methodological challenges 21, 22–3
contextualization approaches to Cohesion Policy analysis 21, 23–7, 29
convergence clubs 56, 65
Cooke, P. 115, 278
cooperation: central and regional administration (Romania) 243; and corruption 188; cross-border 51, 243, 245; integrated urban development 287, 291, 293; public administration reform 271; regional planning capacity (Latvia) 272, 275, 276–8, 279t, 280; territorial capital, taxonomy 257t
core metropolitan areas (Cluster A) 260, 261f, 262, 263, 264, 265t, 266t
corruption: conclusions 200–1; data and variables 6, 188–95; integrated territorial investment 294; results 6, 195–200; theory of 187–8
corruption risk index (CRI) 190, 192, 193, 194, 195–6, 197t, 198, 199, 200
counterfactual methods 3, 12, 21, 23, 27–8, 29
Crescenzi, R. 21, 24, 26, 27, 28, 57t, 61, 63t
CRI *see* corruption risk index
Croatia (HR) 199f, 201t, 287
Cyprus (CY): corruption risk analysis 199f, 201t
Czech Republic (CZ) 34t, 199f, 200f, 201t, 245, 287

Dall'Erba, S. 22, 25, 58t, 64t, 221, 233, 259
decentralization: Article 7 resources (France) 289; for Cohesion Policy effectiveness 245; "*Delephobia*" 7, 241, 292; for inter-institutional coordination 277; Poland 220, 222, 223, 241, 245; pre-accession requirements 209, 242; Regional Development Agencies (Romania) 241, 242, 243–9
De Dominicis, L. 57t, 63t
"*Delephobia*" 7, 241, 292
Dellmuth, L. M. 221
demand-side effects, of inflow of external funds 37–8, 40, 49
demographic implications of funding initiatives (Latvia): data 102–7; findings and conclusions 5, 101, 109–11, 112t; measurement of 107–8
Denmark (DK) 71f, 73f, 199f, 201t, 287
differentiation 51, 65

distribution bias *see* territorial distribution bias
divergence 36, 56, 101
Dotti, N. F. 173, 256
Dühr, S. 26, 299
Dytiki Ellada 13t, 14, 16, 17f

East Central Europe (ECE) 221–2; *see also* Czech Republic; Hungary; Poland; Slovakia
Eastern European Countries *see* CEECS (Central and Eastern European Countries)
East Germany (German Democratic Republic, GDR) 36, 37
ECE *see* East Central Europe
econometric studies: absorption capacity and youth unemployment 152, 157–60; data quality 4, 57t, 58t, 59t, 61–2, 65; on demographic impact of Cohesion Policy (Latvia, 2007–13) 102, 105, 107–11, 112t; future work, suggestions 65–6; methodological challenges 4, 56–61, 65; relevance of results 62–5, 66; spatial autocorrelation 24–5, 60, 105, 107; Structural Fund impact (Pontarollo's semi-parametric model) 70, 72–80
Ederveen, S. 24, 25, 35, 59t, 64t, 222, 259
education: coherent planning and implementation 280, 281t; econometric data 57t, 58t; endogenous factor of growth 256; fund allocation 43, 265t; Ministry of (Romania) 176–7; and youth unemployment 127, 128, 129, 133, 136, 154, 155
embeddedness: administrative 172, 174–7, 180, 181; defined 174; political 172, 174, 177–80, 181
employment: as an econometric study variable 57t; demographic changes (Latvia) 103, 109, 110, 111, 112t; equal opportunities policy 141; in EU agenda 1, 5; gender mainstreaming 140–9, 262, 265t; impact of Great recession (2008) 128, 144; job creation (1989–2012) 17, 19; role of ESF and ERDF 5; unemployment rates as source of demographic data 103; *see also* labour markets; youth (un)employment
endogeneity: external aid and divergence 36, 37, 56; methodological allowance for 24, 28, 60, 61, 158; territorial

314 Index

capital 256, 298; and territorial cohesion 298, 308
endogenous growth theory 56
entrepreneurship 6, 14, 18, 74, 117, 151, 156, 265*t*
environmental policy 13, 18, 147
equal opportunities *see* gender mainstreaming
ERDF *see* European Regional Development Fund
ESF *see* European Social Fund
ESIF *see* European Structural and Investment Funds
Esposti, R. 24, 25, 26, 58*t*, 61, 64*t*, 74
Estonia (EE) 34*t*, 199*f*, 201*t*, 287
Europe 2020 (strategy for smart, sustainable and inclusive growth): competitiveness 12; fund alignment 1, 2, 4, 5, 50; gender mainstreaming 141, 147–8, 149; integrated territorial investment 291, 293, 295*n*2
European periphery (Cluster E) 261*f*, 262*t*, 263, 265*t*, 266*t*
European Regional Development Fund (ERDF): data for econometric studies 57*t*, 58*t*, 59*t*, 62, 65; gender mainstreaming 142, 143, 145, 147; objectives of 151, 155–6, 258; theory-based evaluation of 3, 11, 12–20; utility (1989–2012) 18–19; youth (un)employment 5, 151, 155–6, 157, 158, 159, 160*t*, 163–4*t*; *see also* Article 7 tools
European Social Fund (ESF): Article 7 multi-fund financing 291; gender mainstreaming 6, 142, 145, 147; youth (un)employment 5, 127, 137, 151, 155, 157, 158, 159, 160*t*, 161–3*t*
European Structural and Investment Funds (ESIF) 1, 2, 5, 5–6, 127, 128, 146–9, 258–9
European Union 2010 258, 285*t*
expertise: administrative capacity (Romania) 242; bottom-up RIS3 processes 119; environmental policy 18, 147; and the interpretation of partnership 211–12, 214, 216, 217; political and administrative embeddedness 175, 176, 177, 180; regions (Poland) 304

Faludi, A. 297, 299, 300, 301, 303
Ferry, M. 37, 101, 171, 172, 222, 223
Fésüs, G. 101

Fidesz (conservative) government 223, 224, 225, 226, 228, 231*t*, 233–4, 235, 237*t*
financial capital 256–7
Finland (FI) 71*f*, 72, 73*f*, 199*f*, 200*f*, 201*t*, 287, 290*t*; *see also* Itä-Suomi
Fischer, M. 58*t*, 60, 64*t*
Fixed Effect (FE) methodology 24
Foray, D. 115, 116
Fotopoulos, G. 74
France (FR): Article 7 funding 287, 289, 290; city authorities 292; corruption risk analysis 199*f*, 200*f*, 201*t*; funds by area of intervention 71, 71*f*; GDP growth per capita and GVA per worker (2000–2006) 73*f*; Lille metropolitan administration 277; Objective 1 regions 13*t*, 14, 16, 17*f*; youth unemployment 128
Fratesi, U. 24, 36, 57*t*, 59*t*, 61, 62, 63*t*, 64*t*, 72–3, 159, 256, 259, 267
Freitag, M. 154–5
functional regions 23, 275–6, 278, 279*t*, 286, 288, 290

Galicia 13*t*, 14, 16, 17*f*
GAM *see* General Additive model
Garcia-Milà, T. 26
Garcilazo, E. 57*t*, 63*t*, 69
GDP *see* Gross Domestic Product/income
GDR *see* German Democratic Republic
gender mainstreaming: economic rationale 141; ESIF role 5, 146–9; expenditure by region type 262, 265*t*; gender awareness 5–6, 140, 142–3, 145, 148; programming period (2014–20) 5, 144, 145, 146–9; Scottish case study 5, 142–6
General Additive model (GAM) 74
Generalised Linear Models (GLMs) 74
German Democratic Republic (GDR) 36, 37
Germany (DE): Article 7 funding 287; convergence 25; corruption risk analysis 199*f*, 200*f*, 201*t*; counterfactual analyses 28; ERDF effectiveness study 13*t*, 14, 16, 17*f*; funds by area of intervention 71, 71*f*; GDP growth per capita and GVA per worker (2000–2006) 73*f*; metropolitan and urban administration 277–8, 292; political bias in fund distribution 221; youth unemployment 128, 153, 154*f*
Giua, M. 21, 24, 26, 27, 28, 57*t*, 61, 63*t*

Giugni, M. 128, 129
Gleditsch, K. S. 105, 108
GLMs *see* Generalised Linear Models
governance: and absorption capacity 171, 173; administrative embeddedness 172, 174–7, 180, 181; Article 7 tools 286, 288; Barca report 173, 285*t*, 299, 300; EU-national comparison (Poland) 304; as a funding condition 241; and GDP 273; Political clienteles 173, 182; political embeddedness 172, 174, 177–80, 181; and regional disparities (Latvia) 271, 272, 274–6, 280; and RIS3 policy agenda 4, 115, 116, 117, 119*t*, 120, 122, 123; theoretical link with EU funding 186, 187–8; *see also* administrative capacity; corruption
Great Recession: and the efficiency debate 271; gender mainstreaming 142, 144, 146; resilience (Poland) 33; and youth unemployment 5, 128, 151, 152, 153
Greece (GR or EL): Article 7 funding 287; convergence 25; corruption risk analysis 199*f*, 200*f*, 201*t*; ERDF funds in Dytiki Ellada 13*t*, 14, 16, 17*f*; female employment rate 147; funds by area of intervention 70, 71*f*, 81; GDP growth per capita and GVA per worker (2000–2006) 72, 73*f*; youth unemployment 128, 153, 154*f*
Gress, B. 74
GRINCOH project 49
Gross Domestic Product/income (GDP): defining RIS3 priorities 119*t*; econometric methodology 56, 57*t*, 58*t*, 59*t*, 61, 63*t*, 64*t*, 66, 73; economic development (Poland) 39–44, 52*n*3, 304; fund distribution (Hungary) 229*t*, 230*t*, 231*t*, 232*t*, 233, 237*t*, 238*n*7, 238*n*10; fund distribution (Poland) 227*t*, 228, 236*t*, 238*n*6, 238*n*10; and governance quality 273; growth by funding area (2000–2006) 69, 71–2, 73, 75*t*, 77*f*, 78, 80–1; regional disparity (Romania) 242, 248; and territorial assets 255, 262, 263, 264, 267; and youth unemployment 155, 157, 160*t*, 161*t*, 162*t*, 163*t*, 164*t*, 165*t*, 166*t*
GVA (Gross Value Added per worker) 69, 71, 73, 75*t*, 76, 78, 80, 81

Haase, D. 301
Hagen, T. 21, 25, 28, 58*t*, 60, 62, 64*t*, 156, 160

Hahn, Johannes 285*t*
Hank, K. 129, 136
high article 7 resources 287, 288–9
Hübner, Danuta 284, 285*t*
human capital development: by territorial characteristics 7, 70, 71, 264, 265; econometric study review 63*t*, 64*t*, 65; economic growth and productivity (GDP and GVA) 4, 69, 73, 75*t*, 76, 78*t*, 79*t*, 267; management of (Romania) 176, 242; Poland 39*t*, 40, 42, 46; regional classification 257*t*, 260, 262, 264, 265, 267
Hungarian Socialist Party (MSZP) 224, 229*t*, 233, 234, 235
Hungary (HU): Article 7 funding 287; centralized system of 220, 223, 245; corruption risk analysis 199*f*, 200*f*, 201*t*; distribution bias 6–7, 220, 223–6, 228–34, 235; fund allocation (2007–2013) 34*t*; Partnership Principle 6, 208, 210, 212–13, 214, 215, 216

Iacobucci, D. 116–17, 118, 119
identification approach to Cohesion Policy analysis 3, 21, 23, 27–8, 29
infrastructure development: demographic situation (Latvia) 109, 110; ERDF achievements (1989–2012) 13, 14, 16, 17, 18, 19; ERDF funding and gender awareness 143; international comparison 70, 71; and local construction industry stimulation 36, 39; multi-level governance for 280; Poland's subnational levels 39, 40, 42–3, 48, 49, 51; political bias 221; pre-conditions for under TEN-T 26; productivity and GDP per capita growth 4, 69, 73, 74, 75*t*, 76, 78, 80, 81; regional administration (Romania) 243, 245; and territorial capital 256, 257*t*, 263, 264, 266*t*, 267, 268; transport 26, 36, 43, 81, 177, 266*t*, 269*n*5, 275; *see also* motorways and expressways (Poland)
innovation: Cohesion Policy effectiveness 13, 18, 19, 25, 116; investment following Great Recession 144; and quality of governance 273, 274; recommendations for 2014–2020 planning period (CEECs) 50, 51; strategic focus on 1, 116; and sustainable growth 33; and territorial capital 264, 265*t*, 267, 278; *see also* RIS3 policy

innovation economic theory 56
institutionalised grand corruption:
  conclusions 200–1; defined 188;
  procurement data and variables
  188–95, 201*t*; results 195–200
institutions: absorption capacity 171,
  173, 222, 242; administrative capacity
  (Romania) 7, 242–9; administrative
  and political embeddedness 6, 171, 172,
  174–80, 181; analytical approaches to
  Cohesion Policy 25, 26; and corruption
  186, 187, 188, 192, 196, 197; in
  econometric studies 55, 57*t*, 60,
  63*t*, 64*t*; as a growth factor 24, 55,
  69, 81, 241, 256, 271; Partnership
  Principle 208, 209, 213, 214, 216,
  217; place-based administrative
  capacity 7, 272–4, 280; planning
  capacity 271–2; planning regions
  (Latvia) 272, 274–6, 277, 278–81;
  regional governance and RIS3 policy
  4, 115, 116, 117, 120, 122, 123;
  territorial capital taxonomy 257*t*
integrated territorial investment (ITI):
  Article 7 aims 286; country and city
  case studies 288–9; evaluation of 7,
  293–4; implementation variations and
  issues 289–93; weak compromise of
  284, 293
Ireland (IE): Article 7 funding 287;
  corruption risk analysis 199*f*, 201*t*;
  ERDF effectiveness study 13*t*, 14, 16,
  17*f*; funds by area of intervention 70,
  71*f*, 81; GDP growth per capita and
  GVA per worker (2000–2006) 72,
  73*f*; RIS3 survey response 118
Italy (IT): Article 7 funding 287,
  289; city authorities 292, 293;
  corruption risk analysis 199*f*, 200*f*,
  201*t*; funds by area of intervention
  70–1, 71*f*, 81; GDP growth per
  capita and GVA per worker
  (2000–2006) 72, 73*f*; Objective 1
  regions 13*t*, 14, 17*f*, 28; youth
  unemployment 128, 153, 154*f*
Itä-Suomi 13*t*, 14, 16, 17*f*
ITI *see* integrated territorial investment
Jacquot, S. 141
Jeffrey, P. 290

Kemmerling, A. 26, 221, 222, 233
Kirchner, A. 154–5
Knill, C. 174, 206
Komornicki, T. 36

labour markets: ERDF achievement
  study 13, 17*f*, 18; EU fund impact in
  Poland 37, 41, 44, 46, 47–8; female
  participation 140–9, 262, 265*t*; free
  access across Europe 49; skills deficits
  14, 25, 147; and youth unemployment
  128–9, 136, 137, 154, 155, 157–8, 159*t*;
  see also employment
Landes, D. S. 35
Latvia (LV): Article 7 funding 287;
  corruption risk analysis 199*f*, 201*t*;
  demographic changes 5, 101, 102–11,
  112*t*; distribution bias 222; fund
  allocation (2007–2013) 34*t*; institutional
  framework 272, 274–6, 277, 278–81
Le Gallo, J. 56, 58*t*, 61, 63*t*, 64*t*, 222
legitimacy 129, 137, 210, 211, 213, 216
LeSage, J. P. 58*t*, 60, 64*t*
line ministries 209, 214
Lisbon Agenda 12, 69, 70, 71, 80, 81, 141
Lithuania (LT) 34*t*, 199*f*, 201*t*, 287
Llamosas-Rosas, I. 259
local-level administration: Germany
  277–8, 292; political and wealth bias
  220, 222, 224, 225–6, 228, 229*t*, 231*t*,
  233–4, 235; *see also* municipalities;
  urban policy development
low article 7 resources 287, 289
low carbon economy 1, 4
Luxembourg (LU) 71*f*, 72, 73*f*, 153*f*,
  199*f*, 201*t*, 249*n*5, 287

McGuire, T. 26
Malta 153*t*, 186, 195*f*, 199*f*, 203*n*1,
  249*n*5
Mankiw, N. G. 76
Matthews, S. A. 108
Maynou, L. 57*t*, 63*t*, 69
MDP *see* Missing Declared Population
medium article 7 resources 287, 289
Mendez, C. 151, 156, 293
methodology: absorption capacity and
  youth unemployment study 152,
  157–60; bias 24, 29, 60, 61, 66;
  challenges to Cohesion Policy study
  21, 22–3; cluster analysis 260, 261*f*,
  268; contextualization-identification
  synergy agenda 3, 29; corruption in
  EU funds study 186–7, 188–200;
  distribution bias study 224–6; literature
  review of 3, 21, 23–8; place-based
  policy implementation (Poland)
  297; political embeddedness and
  administrative capacity study 172;

potential accessibility 87, 88–9; RIS3 success study 117–18; Scottish gender mainstreaming study 142; *see also* econometric studies
metropolitan areas 260, 261*f*, 262, 264, 277; Article 7 tools 288, 289, 290, 292, 293; core metropolitan areas (Cluster A) 260, 261*f*, 262, 263, 264, 265*t*, 266*t*; integrated territorial investment 288, 289; metropolitan belt and second-order cities (Cluster B) 262, 265*t*, 266*t*
Midelfart-Knarvik, K. H. 25, 36, 56, 59*t*, 64*t*
migration, demographic change (Latvia) 101, 102, 103, 109, 110, 111, 112*t*
Milio, S. 159, 171, 173, 174, 206, 222
Misiag, J. 41, 42
Missing Declared Population (MDP, Latvia) 103, 109, 110, 111, 112*t*
Mohl, P. 21, 25, 28, 58*t*, 60, 61, 64*t*, 156, 160
Moran's I test 107, 109, 110
Moretti, E. 37
motorways and expressways (Poland): construction programme 89, 90*f*; internal/intranational accessibility 5, 87, 90–1, 92*f*, 94, 95, 96, 97*f*; international connectivity 5, 92–3, 94, 95, 96, 98*f*; programming period (2014–20) 5, 96–9; for territorial cohesion 4–5, 87, 88, 93–5
MSZP *see* Hungarian Socialist Party
municipalities: administrative and political embeddedness 180; Bulgaria 180, 222; France 277, 289; ITI strategy (Poland) 288; Latvia 103, 105, 106*f*, 107, 110, 111, 222, 272, 274–81; place-based strategic documentation (Poland) 298; road potential of (Poland) 87, 88, 90–9; territorial Cohesion Policy impact (Poland) 3, 37, 40, 41, 44, 47–9; wealth distribution bias 220, 222

National Development Agency (Hungary) 212, 223
National Development Plan (Latvia, 2007–2013) 102, 279
neoclassical growth model 24, 55, 56, 57*t*, 58*t*, 59*t*, 60, 61
Netherlands (NL): Article 7 funding 287, 290*t*; corruption risk analysis 199*f*, 201*t*; funds by area of intervention 71, 71*f*; GDP growth per capita and GVA per worker (2000–2006) 73*f*; youth unemployment 128, 153, 154*f*

Neumark, D. 299
non-governmental sector *see* civil society
Nord-Pas-de-Calais 13*t*, 14, 17*f*
Nordrhein-Westfalen 13*t*, 14, 17*f*
Norte 13*t*, 14, 17*f*
North-East England 13*t*, 14, 17*f*
Northern Europe 118, 123, 262
northern periphery and third-order cities (Cluster C) 262, 265*t*, 266*t*
Novak, K. 57*t*, 63*t*, 69
NUTS2 regions: corruption indicators 193*t*; Germany 269*n*1; Hungary 224; Poland 223, 224, 225, 297, 301–8; Romania 242; youth unemployment 128, 153–4
NUTS3 regions: Hungary 224, 225; LAUs (Latvia) 102–3; Poland 42–4; territorial capital and fund allocation 7, 255–6, 259, 264
NUTS4 units: Poland 44–6

Objective 1/Convergence regions: econometric studies 56, 57*t*, 58*t*, 61, 62, 63*t*, 64*t*, 65; economic growth 28, 61, 63*t*, 64*t*; ERDF achievements (1989–2012) 13, 14, 15, 16, 17*f*; as main EU beneficiary 70, 238*n*2; political distribution bias 221; spillover 23, 25
Olbrycht, J. 291
Olfert, M. R. 299
omitted variable bias 24, 29, 60, 61, 66
Overman, H. G. 25, 36, 56, 59*t*, 60, 64*t*

PAD index *see* Potential Accessibility Dispersion (PAD) index
panel data approaches to Cohesion Policy analysis 24, 25, 29
Parker, D. M. 108
Partnership Principle: actor-centred explanation of 207; as an example of 'bureaucratic menace' 206; background 208–10; Europeanization explanations of 207; interpretations of 6, 207–8, 210–17; Romania, programming period (2014–20) 241
pay gap (gender) 140, 148
Pellegrini, G. 28, 57*t*, 61, 63*t*
Perucca, G. 57*t*, 62, 63*t*, 259, 263, 267
Petrova, V. 222
Pinho, C. 69
place-based dialogue 301, 302, 303, 305–8
place-based policymaking: defined 271, 298–300; importance of institutional framework and administrative capacity

7, 272–4; planning regions (Latvia) 272, 274–6, 277, 278–81; policy/documentation vs. implementation (Poland) 7–8, 297–8, 301–8; and smart specialisation 1, 115–16; strengthened in the regulatory overhaul (2013) 1, 271; terminology 298–300; territorialisation 300–1; *see also* territorial capital; urban policy development
planning capacity: cooperation versus coordination 276–8; defined 271–2; Germany 277; Lille 277; regional institutional framework (Latvia) 272, 274–6, 277, 278–81
Poland (PL): Article 7 funding 287, 288–9, 290; corruption risk analysis 199*f*, 200*f*, 201*t*; decentralized system of 220, 223, 241, 245; distribution bias 6–7, 220–1, 224–8, 235; Partnership Principle 6, 208, 211, 213, 214, 215, 216; place-based policy/documentation vs. implementation 7–8, 297–8, 301–8; regional funding-economic growth correlation 3, 36–7, 39, 41–9; sixteenth and seventeenth century economic stagnation 35; territorial data deficiencies 40–1; transport systems 301; *see also* motorways and expressways (Poland)
Polish People's Party (PSL) 223, 224, 226, 227*t*, 236*t*
political bias in fund distribution 7, 221, 222, 224–6, 227*t*, 228–34, 235
political embeddedness 172, 174, 177–80, 181
pork barrel politics *see* political bias in fund distribution
Porter, M. E. 69
Portugal (PT): Article 7 funding 287; corruption risk analysis 199*f*, 200*f*, 201*t*; ERDF effectiveness study 13*t*, 14, 17*f*; funds by area of intervention 70, 71*f*, 81; GDP growth per capita and GVA per worker (2000–2006) 73*f*
potential accessibility *see* motorways and expressways (Poland)
Potential Accessibility Dispersion (PAD) index 5, 88, 93–4, 95
pre-accession process 209
procurement and corruption risk: conclusions 200–1; data and variables 188–95, 201*t*; results 195–200
productive environment: expenditure by region type 70, 263, 264, 265*t*; expenditure (Poland, 2007–2013) 39–40; funding and economic growth 4, 69, 73, 75*t*, 76, 77*f*, 81; and human capital accumulation 256; national spending levels 70–1
productivity: Cohesion Policy impact 14, 28, 36, 58*t*, 64*t*; econometric study of 4, 69–70, 72–81; Lisbon Agenda 12, 69, 70, 81; national gross domestic product-gross value added comparison 70–2; and sustainable growth 33
Pronk, J. P. 34, 35
Propensity Score Matching (PSM) 27, 28
PSL *see* Polish People's Party
PSM *see* Propensity Score Matching
public consciousness 49
Puigcerver-Peñalver, M. 58*t*, 64*t*

quality of life 17, 18, 47, 49, 243

Ramajo, J. 25, 58*t*, 64*t*
randomized experiments 24, 27–8, 130
RDD (Regression Discontinuity Design) 27, 28, 57*t*, 58*t*, 61
Rees, T. 141
relational capital 256, 257*t*
resilience 5, 127, 129, 133–6, 137
reverse causality bias 24, 60
RIS3 policy: ex ante condition for funding 116; need for national co-ordination 51; policy failures 116–17; policy outcomes 119–20; priorities and focus 117, 118, 119*t*, 122; and regional variation 4, 117, 120–3
Robinson, J. A. 35, 116
Rodríguez-Pose, A. 24, 26, 36, 57*t*, 59*t*, 61, 62, 63*t*, 64*t*, 69, 72–3, 116, 159, 173
Romania (RO): absorption rate 242; administrative capacity 7, 172, 175–7, 178–80, 182, 242–9; Article 7 funding 287; centralized system of 241, 242, 246; corruption risk analysis 199*f*, 200*f*, 201*t*; distribution bias 223; fund allocation (2007–2013) 34*t*
Rosik, P. 88, 92
rural and maritime areas (Cluster D) 261*f*, 262*t*, 263, 265*t*, 266*t*
Russia 35, 37, 96

Sachsen-Anhalt 13*t*, 14, 16, 17
Sala-i-Martin, X. 76
Scotland 5, 142–6
SDM *see* Spatial Durbin models
self-efficacy 129
SEM *see* Spatial Error Models

Simmons, R. 128
Simpson, D. 299
skills deficits 14, 25, 147
SLM *see* Spatial Lag Models
Slovakia (SK) 6, 34*t*, 199*f*, 200*f*, 201*t*, 208, 211, 245–6, 287
Slovenia (SI) 6, 34*t*, 199*f*, 201*t*, 208, 211, 215, 287
smart specialisation 1, 4, 51, 115–16; *see also* RIS3 policy
social capital 155, 257*t*, 262, 278, 306
social cohesion: ERDF achievements (1989–2012) 13, 18; infrastructure investment 51; strategic focus 1, 4, 70, 146, 151, 154, 155, 258, 285*t*
soft capital: accumulation of territorial capital 256, 257*t*, 264, 267, 268; fund allocation 7, 69–70, 71, 80, 264, 268; policy impacts 18, 25; youth unemployment 129; *see also* human capital
Southern Europe: RIS3 policy 118, 119*t*, 120, 121, 122–3; youth unemployment 128
Spain (ES): Article 7 funding 287; convergence 25; corruption risk analysis 199*f*, 200*f*, 201*t*; ERDF effectiveness study 13*t*, 14, 16, 17*f*; funds by area of intervention 70, 71*f*, 81; GDP growth per capita and GVA per worker (2000–2006) 72, 73*f*; infrastructure fund allocation 26; RDD studies 28; sixteenth and seventeenth century failures 35; youth unemployment 128, 153, 154*f*
spatial autocorrelation/connectivity 24–5, 29, 60, 105, 107
Spatial Durbin models (SDM) 57*t*, 58*t*, 60, 74, 108, 110, 111, 112*t*
Spatial Error Models (SEM) 108, 110, 111, 112*t*
Spatial Lag Models (SLM) 60, 107, 108, 110, 112*t*
spillover 23, 25, 60, 102, 105, 107, 108, 110, 111
Stephan, A. 222
Stoffel, M. F. 221
Strobl, E. 59*t*, 64*t*
structural adjustment 13, 16, 18, 258
supply-side effects, of inflow of external funds 37–8, 40, 49
sustainable growth: administrative capacity 6, 171, 281; disjuncture with fast productivity growth 33, 71–2, 80; strategic focus 1, 4, 70, 258, 259; urban development 285*t*, 286, 287; *see also* innovation

Sweden (SE) 71*f*, 73*f*, 147, 199*f*, 200*f*, 201*t*, 287
SZDSZ *see* Alliance of Free Democrats

Talent Match 5, 127, 130, 132–3, 134–6, 137
Technical Assistance 175 39*t*, 181
territorial capital: in Barca's place-based approach 300; and Cohesion Policy reform 271; and GDP growth 262*t*, 267; and institutional framework in place-based planning 272, 273*f*, 275, 276; in literature overviews 57*t*, 63*t*; and regional growth factors 255, 256–7; and SF fund allocation 7, 259, 263–7; taxonomy of EU regions 259–63
territorial cohesion: Cohesion Policy's interaction with other EU policies 26; ERDF achievements (1989–2012) 13, 18; Poland 4–5, 87, 88, 93–5, 297, 308; strategic focus 21, 258
territorial distribution bias: centralization 220, 221, 222; data and methodology 224–6; literature review 221–3; Operational Programmes (Poland and Hungary) 223–4; political 7, 221, 222, 224–6, 227*t*, 228–34, 235; political background (Poland and Hungary) 223; wealth 220–1, 222, 224, 226, 227*t*, 228–33, 234, 235
thematic concentration/objectives 1, 4, 122, 147, 148, 259, 291, 301
theory-based evaluation: ERDF achievements (1989–2012) 3, 11, 13–20
Thompson, R. 128
Tobit model 6, 226, 229*t*, 231*t*
Toledo declaration 285*t*
Tomova, M. 57*t*, 63*t*
tourism 18
transparency: countering politicization of EU fund use 182; and ITI size 294; municipalities (Latvia) 279*t*; and partnership 206, 213–14, 216, 217; policy reforms (2013) 2; procurement processes 190, 192
transport infrastructure 26, 36, 43, 81, 177, 266*t*, 269*n*5, 275; *see also* motorways and expressways (Poland)

unemployment *see* employment
United Kingdom (UK): Article 7 funding 287; corruption risk analysis 199*f*, 200*f*, 201*t*; English city authorities 292; ERDF impact (North-East England) 13*t*, 14, 17*f*; funds by area of intervention

71*f*; GDP growth per capita and GVA per worker (2000–2006) 73*f*; gender mainstreaming (Scotland) 5, 142–6; RDD studies 28; RIS3 survey response 118; youth (un)employment and Talent Match 5, 127, 128, 129, 130, 132–7

urban policy development: evolution of 284, 285*t*; functional city-regions (Latvia) 275; *see also* Article 7 tools

veto player 178, 209–10
Vironen, H. 101

Ward, M. D. 105, 108
wealth bias in fund distribution 7, 220–1, 222, 224, 226, 227t, 228–33, 234, 235

women *see* gender mainstreaming
Woźniak 298, 306

YEI (Youth Employment Initiative) 127, 128, 151

youth (un)employment: and absorptive capacity 5, 151–2, 155–66; labour market structure 128–9, 136; levels of 128, 152–4; personal resilience development 5, 127, 129, 133–6, 137; risk factors 129, 154–5; Structural Fund initiatives 5, 127, 128, 155; youth participation in programme design and delivery 5, 127, 129, 130, 131–3, 136

Zaucha 297, 298, 299, 300, 303, 306, 308